LINGUISTICS AND SECOND LANGUAGE ACQUISITION

MODERN LINGUISTICS SERIES

Series Editors

Professor Noël Burton-Roberts
University of Newcastle upon Tyne

Dr Andrew Spencer
University of Essex

Each textbook in the **Modern Linguistics** series is designed to provide a carefully graded introduction to a topic in contemporary linguistics and allied disciplines, presented in a manner that is accessible and attractive to readers with no previous experience of the topic, but leading them to some understanding of current issues. The texts are designed to engage the active participation of the reader, favouring a problem-solving approach and including liberal and varied exercise material.

Noël Burton-Roberts founded the **Modern Linguistics** series and acted as Series Editor for the first three volumes in the series. Andrew Spencer has since joined Noël Burton-Roberts as joint Series Editor.

Titles published in the series

Phonology   Philip Carr
Linguistics and Second Language Acquisition   Vivian Cook
Morphology   Francis Katamba

Further titles in preparation

Linguistics and Second Language Acquisition

Vivian Cook

150th YEAR

M

MACMILLAN

First published 1993 by
THE MACMILLAN PRESS LTD
Houndmills, Basingstoke, Hampshire RG21 2XS
and London
Companies and representatives
throughout the world

ISBN 0–333–55533–3 hardcover
ISBN 0–333–55534–1 paperback

A catalogue record for this book is available
from the British Library

Printed and bound in Great Britain by
Biddles Ltd, Guildford and King's Lynn

The Scrabble tiles on the cover design are reproduced by
kind permission of J.W. Spear and Son PLC, Enfield
EN3 7TB, England.

Contents

Preface

This book arose out of the problems of teaching second language acquisition in a linguistics department, when existing books were not written from a linguistics perspective. I am grateful to the annual generations of students who have lived with the evolving ideas and organisation of this material. I am also indebted to the following people who provided vital reactions to the various stages of its development: Noël Burton-Roberts, Rod Ellis, Hans Dechert, Roger Hawkins, Eric Kellerman, Patsy Lightbown, Nanda Poulisse, Clive Matthews, Mike Sharwood-Smith, Vera Regan, and Lydia White; needless to say, few of them would agree with everything here, particularly the interpretation of their own work. The book would never have been finished without the constant inspiration of David Murray, Charlie Parker and, as always, Sidney Bechet.

VIVIAN COOK

Acknowledgements

The author and publishers wish to thank the following for permission to use copyright material.

Ablex Publishing Corporation, for the extract from H. Dechert (1987), 'Understanding Producing', in *Psycholinguistic Models of Production*, eds H. Dechert and M. Raupach;

Gunter Narr Verlag, for the extract from H. Wode (1981), *Learning a Second Language*;

Hodder & Stoughton, for the extract from R. W. Bley-Vroman, S. Felix and G. L. Ioup (1988), 'The Accessibility of Universal Grammar in Adult Language Learning', *Second Language Research*, **4**(1);

Mouton de Gruyter, a division of Walter de Gruyter & Co., for the extract from N. Poulisse (1989/1990), *The Use of Compensatory Strategies by Dutch Learners of English*.

Every effort has been made to trace all the copyright-holders, but if any have been inadvertently overlooked the publishers will be pleased to make the necessary arrangements at the first opportunity.

List of Abbreviations

ACT	Adaptive Control of Thought
AGR	Agreement
AH	Accessibility Hierarchy
AP	Adjective phrase (A″)
BSM	Bilingual Syntax Measure
CA	Contrastive Analysis
COALA	Computer Aided Linguistic Analysis
CP	Complement phrase (C″)
CS	Communicative strategies
ECP	Empty Category Principle
EFL	English as a Foreign Language
E-language	External language
ESL	English as a Second Language
GB	Government/Binding (theory)
IL	Interlanguage
I-language	Internal language
INFL(I)	Inflection
IP	Inflection phrase (I″)
L1	First language
L2	Second language
L3	Language other than L1 or L2
LAD	Language Acquisition Device
LARSP	Language Assessment Remediation and Screening Procedure
LFG	Lexical-Functional Grammar
LV	Local Variable
MAL	Micro-Artificial Language
N	Noun
Neg	Negation
NL	Native Language
NP	Noun phrase (N″)
P	Preposition
PBD	Principal Branching Direction
PP	Prepositional phrase (P″)
RRC	Restrictive relative clause
SLA	Second language acquisition
SLOPE	Second Language Oral Production English
SOV	Subject, Object, Verb (order)
SVO	Subject, Verb, Object (order)
TL	Target language
TNS	Tense

TPR	Total Physical Response (teaching method)
UG	Universal Grammar
V	Verb
VOS	Verb, Object, Subject (order)
VP	Verb phrase (V″)
ZISA	Zweisprachenerwerb italienischer und spanischer Arbeiter

1 The Background to Current Second Language Acquisition Research

1.1 THE GOALS OF SECOND LANGUAGE RESEARCH

Relating second language acquisition to linguistics means looking at the nature of both linguistics and second language research. Chomsky (1986a, p. 3) defined three basic questions for linguistics:

(i) What Constitutes Knowledge of Language?

The prime goal of linguistics is to describe the language contents of the human mind; its task is to represent what native speakers know about language – their linguistic competence. Achieving this goal means producing a fully explicit representation of the speaker's competence, that is to say, a generative grammar of a 'particular language'. From the outset, this question defines linguistics as based on the internal reality of language in the individual mind rather than on the external reality of language in society.

(ii) How is Knowledge of Language Acquired?

A second goal for linguistics is discovering how knowledge of language comes into being – how linguistic competence is acquired by the human mind. Chomsky proposes to achieve this goal by describing how innate principles of the child's mind create linguistic competence, that is to say how the child's mind turns the language input it encounters into a grammar by using its built-in capabilities. Phrased in another way, knowledge of language is not only created by the human mind but also constrained by its structure.

(iii) How is Knowledge of Language Put to Use?

Language knowledge can be used in many ways – for communicating, for planning, for worship, for declaring war, for saving the rain forest, or for achieving the myriad of goals human beings may have. Discovering how knowledge of language is used means, according to Chomsky, seeing how it relates to thinking, comprehension, and communication. This involves

1

both the psychological processes through which the mind understands and produces speech, and the processes through which speech is adapted to an actual moment of speaking in a particular context of situation. To some, this area of use is covered by the speakers' 'communicative competence' (Hymes, 1972) – their ability to adapt language to communicate with other people; to others, use is covered by 'pragmatic competence' – knowing how language relates to situation for any purpose the speakers intend (Chomsky, 1980).

For second language research these questions need to be rephrased to take in knowledge of more than one language, in other words as multilingual rather than monolingual goals.

(i) What Constitutes Knowledge of Languages?

A person who speaks two languages knows two grammars; two systems of language knowledge are present in the same mind. One goal of second language research is to describe grammars of more than one language simultaneously existing in the same person.

(ii) How is Knowledge of Languages Acquired?

A person who knows two languages has been through the acquisition process twice. Second Language research must explain the means by which the mind can acquire more than one grammar. It must decide whether the ways of acquiring a second language differ from those for acquiring a first, or whether they are aspects of the same acquisition process.

(iii) How is Knowledge of Languages Put to Use?

People who know two languages can decide how to use them according to where they are, what they are talking about, who they are talking to, and so on. Describing their language use means showing how knowledge of two or more languages is used by the same speaker psychologically and sociologically. As Labov (1970a, p. 21) points out, 'Research in stable bilingual communities indicates that one natural unit of study may be the linguistic repertoire of each speaker rather than individual languages'.

Linguistic approaches to second language (L2) research deal with minds that are acquiring, or have acquired, knowledge of more than one language. The three questions are central to the relationship between linguistics and second language research. Second language research answers the knowledge question (1) by describing the grammars of the second language speaker, their differences and similarities from that of a monolingual speaker, and how they interact with each other. The importance of second language research lies not in its account of the knowledge and acquisition of the L2 in isolation, but its account of the second language present and acquired in a mind that already knows a first – the state of knowledge of two languages I have called 'multi-competence' (Cook, 1991b). Second language research answers the acquisition question (2) by seeing how this complex state of knowledge of two languages originates. It answers the use question (3) by examining how knowledge of both languages is put to use. The present book covers approaches to second language research that are in some way related to this agenda for linguistics. The three questions will be referred to throughout as the knowledge question, the acquisition question, and the use question.

The main foundations of this book are then the Chomskyan goals for linguistics, in which knowledge of language is the central issue. This emphasis distinguishes it from, for example functionalist theories of linguistics that combine language as a system of meaning with language as an aspect of social reality (Halliday and Hasan, 1985). One reason for concentrating on the Chomskyan view is its central position as the most comprehensive theory in current linguistics, encompassing both description and acquisition within the same framework, and as the central linguistic theory against which other theories measure themselves. Another reason is that linguistic theories such as functionalism have sadly not been applied to L2 learning on a comparable scale; systemic grammar for example (Halliday, 1975; 1985a), though sporadically mentioned at a general level, has hardly figured in actual L2 research. Tomlin (1990) provides an overview of functionalist work on Second Language learning, within a broader sense of functionalism.

The assumption implicit in the very title of this book is that linguistics is indeed relevant to second language acquisition research. Second language learning takes many forms and occurs in many situations; in particular second languages are not only picked up by learners in natural circumstances similar to first language acquisition but are also taught in classrooms. Hence there is often a tension between approaches to second language research that see ideas about language and about language acquisition as directly relevant and approaches that see the ways in which the mind acquires other types of knowledge as more fruitful than the questions of linguistics. Given the diversity of L2 learners and L2 learning, obviously neither position is completely true, as we shall see throughout. This book takes the 'modular' view that the knowledge of a second language is an aspect of language knowledge rather than of some other type of knowledge.

Chomsky divides linguistics into *E-language* (External language) and *I-language* (Internal language) approaches. The E-language tradition in linguistics is concerned with behaviour and with social convention, in short with language as an external social reality; hence its methodology is based on collecting large samples of spoken language data. The grammar of the language is derived by working out the 'structures' or patterns in these data; 'a grammar is a collection of descriptive statements concerning the E-language' (Chomsky, 1986a, p. 20). The I-language tradition in linguistics on the other hand is concerned with mental reality and with knowledge, in short with representing the internal aspects of the mind: it is based on linguistic competence. Observable behaviour is only one way of getting into these non-observable aspects. I-language research may use any type of data that is available to it – 'perceptual experiments, the study of acquisition and deficit or of partially invented languages such as Creoles, or of literary usage or language change, neurology, biochemistry and so on' (Chomsky, 1986a, pp. 36–7). In practice its easiest source of data is enquiring whether single sentences conform to the speaker's knowledge of language – is "John is eager to please" a sentence of English, say? The I-language approach to linguistics is inherent in the goals specified above; 'linguistics is the study of I-languages, knowledge of I-languages, and the basis for attaining this knowledge' (Chomsky, 1987). This book accepts linguistics as the study of I-language; this serves on the one hand to provide its perspective on the issues of second language acquisition, on the other to delimit the bounds of what it is *not* concerned with.

A related distinction that underlies much linguistics is that between 'competence' and 'performance' (Chomsky, 1965b). In an I-language theory the speaker's knowledge of language is called 'linguistic competence'; the speaker's use of this knowledge is 'performance' – 'the actual use of language in concrete situations' (Chomsky, 1965b, p. 4). Competence is a state of the speaker's mind – what he or she knows – separate from performance – what he or she does while producing or comprehending language. The knowledge that constitutes linguistic competence is only available to the speaker through processes of one type or another; competence is put to use through performance. An analogy can be made to the Highway Code regulations for driving in the UK. The driver probably knows the Code and has indeed been tested on it to obtain a driving licence; in actual driving, however, the driver has to relate the Code to a continuous flow of changing circumstances, and may even break it from time to time. Knowing the Highway Code is not the same as driving along a street; the relationship between the Code the person knows and actual driving is complex and indirect. So phrasing the first question for linguistics in terms of knowledge rather than use is a commitment to a competence model based on knowledge rather than to a performance model based on process. The other two questions of acquisition and use presuppose an answer to the competence question. For second language research the first question is then what it means to know a second language – what is the knowledge of language of a person who knows English and

Japanese, or French and Arabic, or any other combination involving more than one language in the same mind?

The competence/performance distinction has fundamental methodological implications for research. Competence as knowledge in the mind cannot be tapped directly but only through various forms of performance. Often these may distort our view of competence; the inefficiencies of memory, the complex psychological processes of production, even the physical limitations of breathing, all affect performance but are irrelevant to the underlying knowledge of language. Studying examples of the speaker's actual performance is not a good guide to competence; as with driving, any actual speech is bound up with the complexities of the situation and of mental processing. As a native speaker, I know English but it would be hard to establish my knowledge solely from the limited examples of what I actually say. The methodological difficulty for research is how to deduce knowledge of language from examples of performance of different kinds, tricky enough in the first language, but still more difficult for second language research, as we shall repeatedly find.

Before proceeding further, it is necessary to establish some of the terms to be used. The term 'second language' (L2) is used to mean a language acquired by a person in addition to the first language (L1); in other words no distinction is made here between 'second' and 'foreign' language learning. The learner's second language will sometimes be referred to as the target language (TL), that is, the language that the learner is heading towards. Second language *acquisition* (SLA) is not distinguished from second language *learning* (L2 learning), as is done, for example, in Krashen's theory to be described later. The general area of linguistics concerned with all three multilingual goals is 'second language research'; the specific area concerned with acquisition is 'second language acquisition (SLA) research'. When it is necessary to give examples of sentences that would be ungrammatical if uttered by natives, these are marked with an asterisk. Phonetic script is avoided, except for incidental examples when a point depends on it.

1.2 THE SCOPE OF THIS BOOK

The book attempts to present some major aspects of SLA research in relationship to linguistics for those concerned with the discipline of SLA research. While it assumes that the reader has an interest in linguistics and is generally familiar with the ideas presented in an introductory course or textbook, it does not assume a knowledge of the diverse background concepts used in SLA research; explanations of these are normally interwoven here with the discussion of SLA. The empirical basis of research is emphasised by presenting the actual methodology and results rather than just the conclusions or interpretations, enabling readers to judge for themselves the validity of the conclusions that are reached. In one dimension, the progression is, broadly speaking, historical, starting in this chapter with the earlier work, ending in the last two chapters with contrasting theories around which work is currently taking place. In another dimension, it surveys a range of SLA research methods and techniques, moving for instance from observational data in Chapter 2 to experiments in Chapter 7 to grammaticality judgements in Chapter 9. In a third dimension, it considers the crucial problems involved in relating SLA to linguistics, looking for example at the problem of syntactic models in Chapter 2, the relationship to neighbouring disciplines in Chapter 4, and the issues involved in using the Universal Grammar (UG) theory in Chapter 9. Finally, Chapter 10 presents an account of the main psychological alternatives to the linguistics approach.

The book is thus selective within SLA research, describing the work that can be related to I-language linguistics rather than the vast array of approaches that are currently being adopted in this field. Chapter 2 deals with the first major studies of SLA based on data from the speech of L2 learners, selecting the areas of grammatical morphemes and negation. Chapters 2 to 5 look at general explanations of second language acquisition based to a greater or lesser extent on this type of data. Chapter 3 deals with the Input Hypothesis of Stephen Krashen. Chapter 4 concerns the creole-based studies conducted by Roger Andersen and John Schumann and with theories concerned with variation. Chapter 5 looks at the stages approach put forward by Manfred Pienemann as the Multidimensional Model and the Teachability Hypothesis and at their links to psychological processing. Chapter 6 turns to alternative approaches that investigate the learner's internal strategies for learning and communication, particularly the learning strategies of J. Michael O'Malley and Ann Chamot and the compensatory strategies of Eric Kellerman and Nanda Poulisse. Chapter 7 starts looking at data from other areas of syntax, particularly relative clauses. Chapter 8 goes on to the acquisition of syntax in the principles and parameters model of syntax, concentrating on the pro-drop parameter, binding, and the head direction parameter. Chapter 9 looks at explanations of this in terms of the UG theory of language acquisition, particularly subjacency and word order. Chapter 10 contrasts the linguistic approaches of other chapters with those based on speech processes and the psychological theories of John Anderson and Brian MacWhinney.

By and large the treatment does not aim at completeness of coverage but concentrates on representative areas and pieces of research. Each chapter aims to present the area covered as fairly as possibly through detailed description of key pieces of research, to provide a criticism of it in terms of

SLA research in general, and to consider its relationship to the general aims of SL research. The results have sometimes to be simplified, adapted, or recalculated to get a reasonably uniform presentation. Boxes summarising key pieces of research are provided. The research that is cited has normally appeared in journals, books, and PhDs in the field, rather than in unpublished documents or MA dissertations, so that the reader may in principle have access to the references and can be certain that they have had proper scrutiny by the academic community. Occasional exceptions are made, usually for work that forms an integral part of an argument that is being cited or that is in the process of publication. While any selection and presentation of research reflects a personal view of what is important to the field, my own more idiosyncratic terms and opinions are signalled as such in the text to distinguish them from more consensus views.

A set of activities is provided at the end of the book. These are intended to bring the reader closer to the research described in a particular chapter, usually by presenting some data and seeing how it fits the research paradigm concerned. These activities can be done individually, in pairs, or in small groups.

It is also necessary to describe what is not in this book. The area of SLA research is now so large that the approach had to be highly selective, even within the linguistically relevant material. Types of areas that have been excluded are:

- those that have stronger links to non-linguistic disciplines, for example research into codeswitching, vocabulary, or individual variation conducted from a psychological perspective;
- those that have proper linguistic connections, but required too extensive a presentation to fit within the scope of this book, for instance phonology, or have not appeared in accessible publications to date, for example the European Science Foundation project;
- those that have a basis in linguistics very different from the I-language orientation presented above, such as work into speech functions or vocabulary, again requiring too great a level of background presentation for inclusion in a book of this type;
- those that are primarily concerned with the application of SLA research to language teaching, a large and contentious subject that needs separate treatment to cover adequately, since it also requires the discussion of a range of teaching methods and approaches.

To give some alternative sources for these absent areas, recent work in L2 phonology can be found in Leather and James (1990) and Wieden and Nemser (1991). Pujol and Véronique (1991) provide a complementary account of some of the less accessible European-based and European Science Foundation work, which is not generally included here.

Conference proceedings such as those of the European Second Language Association (EUROSLA) can give an idea of the breadth and depth of contemporary work in second language research, for example Ketteman and Wieden (1993) and Sajavaara (forthcoming). Cook (1991a) provides a broad introductory account of the application of second language research ideas to language teaching.

1.3 EARLY SECOND LANGUAGE ACQUISITION RESEARCH

SLA research began to be recognised as a discipline in its own right during the 1970s, the point at which the outline in Chapter 2 starts. Yet there had already been approaches to L2 learning that made use of ideas from linguistics, either directly, or indirectly via first language acquisition research. Let us look briefly at some of the ideas that laid the foundations for later work.

(1) Weinreich and Language Contact

In his important book *Languages in Contact*, Uriel Weinreich (1953) discussed how two language systems relate to each other in the mind of the same individual. The key concept was *interference*, defined as 'those instances of deviation from the norms of either language which occur in the speech of bilinguals as a result of their familiarity with more than one language' (Weinreich, 1953, p. 1). Interference can happen in all the systems of language knowledge. Speakers may carry over the L1 phonological system by ignoring distinctions made in the L2 but not in the L1; for example some French learners fail to distinguish between the two English phonemes /i:/ and /i/ as in "keen" /ki:n/ and "kin" /kin/ because they are not distinct in their L1. Or, at the grammatical level, speakers impose inappropriate L1 word orders on the L2; German learners of English produce "Yesterday came he" modelled on the equivalent German sentence "Gestern kam er". Interference covers not only the effects of the L1 on the L2 but also the effects of the L2 on the L1, as in the gradual loss of the L1 by some bilinguals (Seliger and Vago, 1991). Interference, according to Weinreich, happens on two dimensions – the actual speech of the bilingual and the bilingual's knowledge of language: 'In speech, interference is like sand carried by a stream; in language, it is the sedimented sand deposited on the bottom of a lake' (Weinreich, 1953, p. 11). Though Weinreich's book deals mostly with the bilingual knowledge of language rather than with its development, that is to say with the knowledge question rather than with the acquisition question, the notion of interference represents a constant theme in SLA research. A recent discussion of Weinreich's work can be found in Selinker (1992).

A second aspect of Weinreich's work that proved influential for the emerging study of second languages, along with the work of others, was the relationship of the two languages in the individual mind. Weinreich's example is the concept/word (signified/signifier) relationship between the English word "book" and the equivalent Russian word "kniga". One possibility is that bilingual speakers have two separate concepts in the mind corresponding to the two separate words; they know what English "book" means and they know what Russian "kniga" means but there is no direct link between the two languages in their minds: the two language systems coexist side by side, at least so far as their lexicons are concerned. Weinreich used the term 'coordinative bilingualism' for this state; it came to be known as 'coordinate' bilingualism by later writers, for example Ervin & Osgood (1954). A second possibility is that bilinguals have a single concept of a '*book*' which is related to the two different words /kniga/ and /buk/ in the two languages: the two languages are related via a single concept. This is 'compound' bilingualism where the two languages are linked in the mind at the level of concepts. A third possibility is that the concept leads, not to the L2 word directly, but to the L2 word via the L1 word; an English speaker of Russian might connect the Russian word /kniga/ directly to the English word /buk/ rather than to the concept '*book*': the second language is derived from the first rather than having a separate existence. This type, called 'subordinative' bilingualism by Weinreich, has been amalgamated with coordinate bilingualism by later writers.

These three types of bilingualism are contrasted in the following diagram, adapted from Weinreich:

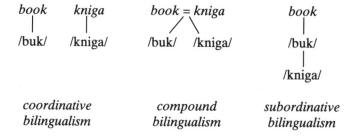

coordinative   compound   subordinative
bilingualism   bilingualism   bilingualism

Some experiments seemed to show the validity of the distinction between compound and coordinate bilingualism. For instance, continuous repetition of a word in *one* language caused the loss of its connotative (emotional) meaning in both languages for compound bilinguals, in only *one* for coordinate bilinguals (Jakobovits and Lambert, 1961). Other experiments showed that the distinction did not always apply. In one, bilingual subjects were given words in English and French, some of which were accompanied by electric shocks which could be avoided by pressing a button (Olton, 1960, cited in Grosjean, 1982); later they were tested on translation equivalents for the same words in the other language. Compound bilinguals should react faster than coordinate bilinguals as they have a single system; however the reaction times for compound and coordinate bilinguals were no different. In addition, rather than using the distinction in Weinreich's way to refer to a state of knowledge, much of the discussion applied it to the different situations that cause people to be either compound or coordinate (Ervin and Osgood, 1954).

The distinction between coordinate and compound bilingualism has been subject to much later criticism and has indeed been dismissed by many critics; McLaughlin (1978, p. 8) for example maintains that 'the distinction has not been validated experimentally and is difficult to maintain in practice'. Nevertheless it provided a focus for research for many years; reviews can be found in Grosjean (1982) and Romaine (1989). From a linguistics perspective, the main faults of the SLA research seem to lie in restricting the scope to vocabulary rather than looking at the diverse aspects of language knowledge used by Weinreich, and using connotative meaning for testing vocabulary rather than the referential meaning with which Weinreich was concerned. It should also be noted that the connection between concept and word is now seen as vastly more complex than the linear relationship in Weinreich's diagrams, as described for example in Garman (1990).

Weinreich defines bilingualism as 'the practice of alternately using two languages' (Weinreich, 1953, p. 1), a straightforward and practical definition in terms of use. The term 'bilingual' has, however, been defined in many ways. At one extreme is the maximal definition of the balanced bilingual 'with native-like control of two languages' (Bloomfield, 1933), perhaps better expressed as the 'ambilingual' (Halliday, MacIntosh and Strevens, 1964): only native-like use counts. At the other pole is the minimal definition of 'the point where a speaker can first produce complete meaningful utterances in the other language' (Haugen, 1953, p. 7): any use of an L2 counts. A discussion of the ramifications of the term can be found in Hoffman (1991). Because of this wide variation in usage, the terms 'bilingual' and 'bilingualism' are mostly avoided in this book, the more neutral terms 'L2 user' or 'L2 learner' or my own term 'multi-competence' being used instead.

(2) Lado and Contrastive Analysis

Robert Lado's influential book *Linguistics Across Cultures* (Lado, 1957) in some ways complements Weinreich. Lado has the overall objective of helping language teaching. He describes a system of *Contrastive Analysis* (CA) which lays down how to carry out a rigorous step-by-step comparison of the L1 and the L2 in terms of their phonology, grammar, writing systems, and culture. The 'fundamental assumption' is *transfer*; 'individuals tend to transfer the forms and meanings, and the distribution of forms and meanings of their native language and culture to the foreign language and culture' (Lado, 1957, p. 2). Thus he describes how Spanish learners add an "e" before English consonant clusters starting with /s/ so that "school" /sku:l/ becomes /esku:l/ in order to conform to the syllable structure of Spanish; how a Chinese learner of English finds "the man with a toothache" difficult because modifying phrases such as "with a toothache" come before the noun in Chinese; and so on. The most difficult areas of the L2 are those that differ most from the L1; 'Those elements that are similar to his native language will be simple for him, and those elements that are different will be difficult' (Lado, 1957, p. 2). Consequently language teaching should concentrate on the points of difference: 'The problems often require conscious understanding and massive practice, while the structurally analogous units between languages need not be taught' (Lado, 1964, p. 52). In this view L2 learning consists largely of the projection of the system of the L1 on to the L2. This will be successful when the two languages are the same – called 'positive' transfer by some; it will be unsuccessful whenever the L2 fails to correspond to the L1 – 'negative' transfer. While Weinreich was interested in interference between two language systems, Lado saw benefits as well as disadvantages coming from the first language system; he spent most time on the problems caused by differences between the two languages, because the similarities could take care of themselves.

Extensive research fleshed out Contrastive Analysis with detailed comparisons of English and other languages, as witness the books in the Contrastive Linguistics series, for example, Stockwell, Bowen and Martin (1965). Research started, not from the L2 learners themselves, but from the linguistic description of the two languages; the learners' behaviour was to be predicted from the linguistic comparison, within limits. Lado's procedure was to take the best available structural descriptions of the two languages and compare them 'pattern by pattern' (Lado, 1957, p. 69). Much other work in L2 learning has followed the concept of Contrastive Analysis, if not the actual procedures laid down by Lado, thoughtfully reviewed in Odlin (1989). The conventional criticisms are that many of the differences predicted by Contrastive Analysis do not in fact turn out to be problems for the learners and, vice versa, many of the learners' actual problems are not predicted. Even Lado considered that the analysis 'must be considered a list of hypothetical problems until final validation is achieved by checking it against the actual speech of students' (Lado, 1964, p. 72).

A long European tradition in Contrastive Analysis predates the work of Lado. Major projects have been carried out in the comparison of German/

English at Kiel, known as the PAKS project, Polish/English at Posnan, and Finnish/English at Jyvaskyla; these have expanded the type of syntactic analysis and have widened the areas of comparison between the languages: Sajavaara (1981) provides a sympathetic account. The concept of transfer has indeed been another refrain in second language research, vehemently rejected by some, defended by others, rechristened or reinterpreted by others, as we shall see throughout this book.

Weinreich and Lado share not just an overall belief in the importance of the L1/L2 relationship but also the concept of language structure through which this relationship takes place. Both see phonology primarily as a list of phonemes (minimal contrastive sounds such as /p/ and /b/ in "pane" /pein/ versus "bane" /bein/) and allophones (variations in the pronunciation of phonemes related to phonetic environment or style, for example, initial aspirated "p" /pit/ versus final unaspirated "p" /tip/). Weinreich compares two languages, Romansh and Swiss German, by displaying the phonemes of both and giving notes on allophones; Lado represents the phonemes of the two languages on charts, say English /d/ and Spanish /d/, and goes on to compare allophones, say the two Spanish allophones for /d/. Weinreich treats grammatical interference as having two types: morphological interference, such as plural endings, which he claims occurs rarely; and interference in grammatical relations, such as word order, which 'is extremely common in the speech of bilinguals' (Weinreich, 1953, p.37); Lado sees grammar as 'structures', such as the word order of questions, the use of intonation and pauses for grammatical effect, and morphology such as English third person "'s". Both go on to relate the two languages at levels of vocabulary and culture.

Their ideas therefore fall within the broad American structuralist tradition of phrase structure, going back at least to Bloomfield (1933). In phrase structure syntax or 'immediate constituent analysis', the sentence is split into smaller and smaller segments till it can be split no more (Bloomfield, 1933). The sentence "Robert likes Indian food" is split in two: a Noun Phrase (NP) consisting of the Noun "Robert" and a Verb Phrase (VP) consisting of "likes Indian food". The Verb Phrase (VP) is split into the Verb "likes" and the NP "Indian food". In turn the Verb is split into the Adjective "like" and the third person "s"; the NP into the Adjective "Indian" and the Noun "food". This can be represented as the familiar tree structure:

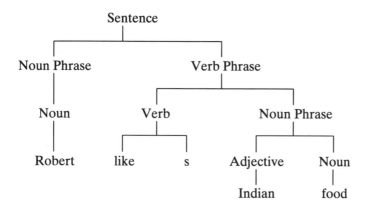

While this type of analysis was appropriate to its own historical context, later chapters will show the limitations this tradition imposed on SLA research.

A further strand in Lado's thinking is the model of language learning he assumes. Lado talks of grammatical structure as 'a system of habits' (Lado, 1957, p.57); speakers control habits which they use to produce speech automatically and without thinking. Such habits are acquired through exposure and practice; they are based on 'laws of language learning' such as 'exercise', 'familiarity of response', and so on (Lado, 1964, p.45). This reflects the mainstream behaviourist view of language learning prominent in linguistics from Bloomfield (1933) onwards, reaching its climax in the psychological work of Skinner (1957), and its downfall in the attack by Chomsky (1959). Bloomfield described L1 children as starting with a repertoire of sounds they already make spontaneously, say "da". These sounds become associated with things or actions; children form habits of associating "da" with the doll that is frequently given to them when they say it. Then the children's speech is shaped by interaction with others – they know when to say "da" because of the way in which adults react when they say it. Such Stimulus–Response views of learning were advanced in much writing for language teachers in the 1960s as well as Lado, for instance Moulton (1966) and Brooks (1960). It is this view of language acquisition against which much SLA research revolted.

(3) 1960s Views of First Language Acquisition; the Independent Grammars Assumption and the Language Acquisition Device

The approaches represented by Weinreich and Lado posed questions about the relationship of the L1 to the L2 and about the nature of language learning that have continued to concern SLA research in one form or another ever since. A major additional source of ideas for the emerging

discipline was the development of a new concept of first language acquisition in the 1960s.

The structuralist account of language learning typified by Bloomfield
(1933) had been seriously undermined by the syntactic arguments in
Chomsky (1957) and the acquisition arguments in Chomsky's review of B.
F. Skinner's *Verbal Behaviour* (Chomsky, 1959). Chomsky insisted that
behaviourist accounts of language learning ignored the nature of language
itself. A human language enables one to say and understand sentences one
has never heard before; the unforgettable sentence "My guineapig died
with his legs crossed" cited by Dakin (1973) is perfectly easy for the child to
produce and for the listeners to comprehend even though they have never
heard it before and are never likely to hear it again. Chomsky (1959) saw
this *'creative aspect of language use'* as the core of human language. The
fact that humans can cope with new sentences distinguishes them from
animals using either animal or human languages: animals can say only a
fixed number of things rather than the infinite number that can be said in a
human language. This ability to create and understand novel sentences
cannot be acquired by any form of Stimulus–Response learning, *inter alia*
because it is not controlled by past experiences.

A major concept that developed out of these ideas of Chomsky's during
the 1960s can be termed the *independent grammars assumption*. This refers
to the belief that the child should be treated as a speaker of a language of
his or her own rather than as a defective speaker of adult language who has
inefficiently mastered the rules (McNeill, 1966). Suppose a child learning
English says "Him go shop". This could be taken as equivalent to the fully
grammatical adult sentence "He is going to the shop", in other words what
the child might say if he or she were an adult. So what the child is 'really'
trying to produce is a present continuous tense "am going", a third person
subject "he", and an adverbial phrase "to the shop", ending up with the
adult version "He is going to the shop". But, if the child is treated as a
speaker of another language, the system of this distinct language has to be
discovered from the child's speech rather than assumed to be a defective
grammar of English. Consider again the child who says "Him go shop".
Without seeing more of the child's sentences, "him" suggests that in the
child's grammar, though not in English, there is no distinction between the
pronouns "him" and "he"; "go" that there are no grammatical endings
such as "-ing"; "shop" that an adverbial phrase does not need a preposition
nor a noun phrase an article; and so on. These apparent 'mistakes' conform
to regular rules in the child's own knowledge of language; they are only
wrong when measured against adult speech.

In methodological terms, treating L1 children as speakers of unknown
languages led to writing grammars for their speech, as was done by Braine
(1963), Klima and Bellugi (1966), Brown (1973), and many others. The
independent grammars assumption influenced much of the SLA work to be

described later. Calling it an 'assumption' acknowledges the fact that it is a methodological premise rather than a discovery. To demonstrate its correctness requires, not so much showing that learners' languages may be analysed as systems in their own right – anything can be analysed as a system in some sense – but showing by some objective means that this is preferable to analysing them as defective variants of the target. The opposite was in fact argued by Smith (1973), namely that the phonology of children acquiring the first language could be described more effectively in terms of adult language than as a system of its own, contrary to the independent grammars assumption.

The assumption had both theoretical and practical sides. In terms of theory, learners had to be recognised as having their own language systems; research therefore had to look at the children in their own right – as children rather than as defective adults. The standard behaviourist assumption that children acquire the bits of the adult grammar one at a time was now untenable; children had complete systems which developed as systems rather than by adding pieces of the adult grammar incrementally. In terms of research practice, data from children's speech were now the best evidence of their grammars, obliging researchers to look closely at their actual speech.

The major change in first language acquisition in the 1960s was the growing importance of the mind compared to that of the environment. While the answer to Chomsky's first question 'What constitutes knowledge of language?' was still uncertain, the presuppositions of the question had been accepted: the subject matter of linguistics was the contents of the human mind – knowledge of language – rather than the description of behavior. The problem of how people learn language, whether first or second, is the problem of how the mind acquires knowledge of a particular kind – linguistic competence.

Chomsky (1964) put the mentalist account of language acquisition in a dramatic form by outlining two 'devices' on paper, one for using language, one for learning language:

(a) utterance $\longrightarrow$ $\boxed{\text{A}}$ $\longrightarrow$ structural description

(b) primary $\longrightarrow$ $\boxed{\text{B}}$ $\longrightarrow$ generative grammar
linguistic data

Model (a) represents a device that assigns structure to utterances it receives. Answering the use question (iii) about how knowledge is put to use means finding out the properties of the 'black box' device labelled 'A' that are used in listening. Model (b) represents a device that constructs a 'generative grammar' of linguistic competence out of the samples of language it encounters (the 'primary linguistic data'): it is a *Language Acquisition Device* (LAD) that shows how people learn language. Answering the acquisition question (ii) on how knowledge of language is acquired involves finding out the properties of the black box labelled 'B'; 'We can think of general linguistic theory as an attempt to specify the character of the device B' (Chomsky, 1964, p. 26). This device in the mind is specific to language; it works quite differently from other forms of learning, and leads to knowledge that is distinctively linguistic rather than sharing properties with other aspects of knowledge.

This paradigm shift in thinking defined the problem of language acquisition as how children construct grammars in their mind from the actual language they hear. To establish the contents of the mind involves conceptualising model (b) as a black box whose operations can be investigated: into one end of the black box go the raw materials, out the other comes the shiny product. The box cannot be opened to see what is going on inside. But inferences about what happens in the middle can nonetheless be made by comparing what comes out with what goes in. So a comparison of the speech children hear with the grammars they develop in their minds reveals the ways in which they are acquiring language. Children are active participants in acquisition rather than passive sponges; children's minds create a grammar from the meagre materials they are given. Language acquisition is a process in which a highly complex state of knowledge is created out of the utterances that are heard.

How do children change their grammars into adult linguistic competence over time? They act, as it were, like scientists testing out a theory; 'To acquire language, a child must devise a hypothesis compatible with presented data – he must select from the store of potential grammars a specific one that is appropriate to the data available to him' (Chomsky, 1965a, p.36). An important component in LAD is an 'evaluation measure' – a means by which one possible grammar can be evaluated as better than another. Most L1 acquisition researchers, however, did not utilise the concept of an evaluation measure so much as that of 'hypothesis-testing' in which the child first gets a hypothesis, then tests it out, and finally reformulates it in the light of the results. For example children hypothesising that English negation occurs at the beginning of the sentence might say "No singing song"; they then assess how successful they have been by getting feedback from their parents or by comparing their own sentence with more sentences they hear. According to their success or failure, they will go on to revise their hypothesis into a form that is closer to the negation rules for English. 'Each successive hypothesis is an interim grammar accounting more successfully for the data he is exposed to. The last hypothesis is the final adult grammar of competence in the language' (Cook, 1969, p. 208). This can be called the *hypothesis-testing* model.

Few of these 1960s interpretations of Chomskyan views are held by linguists nowadays in quite the form they are presented here. To take two examples, the LAD has now become incorporated in the wider Universal Grammar theory, in the process changing in several ways; hypothesis-testing is now scorned as an explanation for language acquisition in the sense used here in which the children try out guesses and get feedback on their success (essentially because it is argued that appropriate feedback has not been found to occur in actual transcripts of conversations with children). Their modern developments will be presented in Chapter 9. Nevertheless, the independent grammars assumption and the hypothesis-testing model, presented here in the context of first language acquisition, are crucial to the development of SLA research to this day and to many of the claims it is still making.

(4) Approximative Systems and Interlanguage

What started SLA research going as a discipline in its own right was the realisation that people such as Lado and Weinreich had been over-simplistic in seeing L2 learning only as a relationship between the L1 and the L2. A learner at a particular point in time is in fact using a language system which is neither the L1 nor the L2. Describing it in terms of the L1 and the L2 misses the distinctive features of L2 learning: a *third* language system is involved – that of the L2 learner – which also needs to be described. In other words, the independent grammars assumption applies to L2 learning as well as to first language acquisition, in this case involving independence from both L1 and L2. Nemser (1971) captured this insight through the term '*approximative system*': 'Learner speech at a given time is the patterned product of a linguistic system, L_a [approximative language], distinct from L_s [source language] and L_t [target language] and internally structured'. An approximative system has some properties present in neither the L1 nor the L2; Nemser cites Serbo-Croat learners of English producing "What does Pat doing now?" though this construction is part of neither English nor their first language. This approximative system gradually approaches the target language, although it seldom merges with it totally; sometimes it reaches a stable plateau, such as the persistent pronunciation of English /sw/ as /sv/ by 'veteran' German learners who pronounce "sweet" as /svi:t/ rather than /swi:t/ (Nemser, 1971). The Contrastive Analysis approach of comparing two whole languages to predict interference or transfer yields only a partial picture of L2 learning; the focus should be on the learner's own system as it develops closer towards the L2: 'only by treating language learners' language as a phenomenon to be studied in its own right can we hope to develop an understanding of the processes of second language acquisition' (Corder, 1978, p.71). As we shall see, in fact SLA research often falls back on to the easier option of comparing the learner's language with the native's rather than adhering fully to the independent grammars assumption.

'Interlanguage', often abbreviated to IL, was the term introduced by Larry Selinker (1972) that became widely accepted for the L2 learner's independent language system. Indeed at one stage 'interlanguage' was effectively the name for the whole field of L2 research, as witness the 1970s journal *Interlanguage Studies Bulletin* that became *Second Language Research* in the 1980s. Selinker emphasised not just the existence of interlanguage but also where it came from. He looked for its origin in the processes through which the mind acquires a second language. L2 learning differs from first language acquisition in that it is seldom completely successful; 5 per cent of L2 learners have 'absolute success' in his view. The L2 'fossilises' at some point short of the knowledge of the native speaker, for example 'German Time–Place order after the verb in the English IL of German speakers'. Selinker (1972) proposed that the lucky 5 per cent of successful L2 learners take advantage of a 'latent language structure' in the mind like that used in first language acquisition, that is to say the LAD. The 95 per cent of learners who are less successful rely on a 'psychological structure' also 'latent in the brain' and 'activated when one attempts to learn a second language', but distinct from the latent language structure. Interlanguage therefore attempts to explain the fossilisation in the L2 learner's system noted by both Nemser and Selinker. Both interlanguage and approximative system lay stress on the change in the learner's language system over time, as will be developed in the next chapter. According to Selinker (1992), the difference between interlanguage and Nemser's approximative system is that interlanguage does not necessarily converge on the target language.

Selinker (1972) claims that interlanguage depends on five central processes that are part of the 'latent psychological structure':

- *language transfer*, in which the learner projects features of the L1 on to the L2, as in the Weinreich/Lado picture, an example being 'American retroflex /r/ in their French IL'.
- *overgeneralisation of L2 rules*, in which the learner tries to use L2 rules in ways which it does not permit, as in the example "What does Pat doing now?" used above.
- *transfer of training*, when teaching creates language rules that are not part of the L2, as when a teacher's over-use of "he" discourages the students from using "she".
- *strategies of L2 learning*, such as simplification, for example when the learner 'simplifies' English so that all verbs may occur in the present continuous, yielding sentences such as "I'm hearing him".
- *communication strategies*, such as when the learner omits communi-

catively redundant grammatical items and produces "It was nice, nice trailer, big one", leaving out "a".

The crucial insight contributed by Selinker is not the actual processes that he puts forward – many variants of these will be seen in Chapter 6 – but his insistence that an explanation is called for in terms of the processes and properties of the mind. He postulates not only an independent grammar but also a psychological mechanism for creating and using it. Transfer is only one of at least five processes involved in interlanguage in the individual mind. In the version stated here, one difficulty is that the term 'interlanguage' is often used to refer both to the learner's knowledge of the second language and to the actual speech of L2 learners – an E-language sense of interlanguage as a collection of sentences as well as an I-language sense of knowledge of language. Selinker (1972) is also ambiguous about whether the five processes are for the creation of interlanguage or for its use, witness remarks such as 'I would like to hypothesise that these five processes are processes which are central to second language learning, and that each process forces fossilisable material upon surface IL utterances.' Communication strategies seem a process for managing spur-of-the-moment speech, that is to say to do with the use question; transfer of training on the other hand, seems a process for acquiring interlanguage knowledge, that is, an answer to the acquisition question.

The interlanguage concept provided SLA research with an identifiable field of study that belonged to no one else; 'what gave SLA its excitement was the concept of interlanguage' (Davies, Criper, and Howatt, 1984, p. xii). The concept itself has been developed in various ways by later researchers, as we shall see; a review can be found in Selinker (1992).

(5) Error Analysis

Basing L2 learning research on learners' interlanguages changes not only the relationships between the L1 and the L2 but also the type of evidence studied by second language research. Linguists answer the knowledge question by seeing whether a particular sentence fits the grammar of the native speaker; does *"Is the man is who here tall?" conform to the speaker's knowledge of English? This will be called '*single sentence evidence*' in this book. The I-language linguist needs no wider body of data than such evidence. Even if Weinreich (1953, p. 3) recommends using 'the recorded speech of bilinguals in guided conversation', he and Lado typically discuss single sentence examples of interference and transfer taken away from the learning context and from actual learners.

L1 acquisition research has problems with such single-sentence evidence since it is difficult to ask L1 children directly whether "Is the man who is here tall?" is a proper sentence. Children are by and large incapable of saying whether a particular sentence is generated by their grammar, even if occasional researchers argue that there are ways round this (McDaniel and Cairns, 1990). Hence first language acquisition research has mostly resorted to other means than single sentences; it has to infer the child's knowledge of language in other ways, usually by analysing the child's performance – making large-scale transcripts of children's speech, testing their comprehension, devising cunning production tasks, and so on.

One of Selinker's concerns in 1972 was to establish the study of interlanguage on a proper basis. He considers the appropriate evidence for L2 learning to be 'attempted meaningful performance' in an L2; that is to say, he excludes language elicited in drills or experiments. The only data he regards as relevant are 'the utterances which are produced when the learner attempts to say sentences of a TL [target language]'. These are to be compared with sentences spoken by native speakers of the L1 and the L2. The five processes he mentions should in principle have discernible effects on the learners' actual speech.

Selinker's research methodology is concerned with the description of learners' speech. It forms part of a tradition associated with the work of Pit Corder (Corder, 1967; 1971; 1981). Corder (1967) suggests that both L1 and L2 learning consist of the learners applying strategies to the language input that they have heard to get an internal grammar. If a child says "This mummy chair", it would be meaningless to claim that the child was making a mistake; instead we interpret this as 'evidence that he is in the process of acquiring language'. Similarly a sentence such as "You didn't can throw it" should not be considered a mistake so much as a sign of the L2 learner's own interlanguage. Indeed the word 'mistake' is, strictly speaking, a misnomer; the L2 learner's sentence is correct in terms of the learner's own interlanguage grammar, incorrect only if the L2 learner is assumed to be a defective native speaker of the L2. Sentences produced by L2 learners are signs of their underlying interlanguage, not of their deficient control of the L2.

This view led to the complex methodology for studying second language acquisition known as *Error Analysis*, which approaches L2 learning through a detailed analysis of the learners' own speech. Corder (1971) proposes three stages in Error Analysis:

(a) *Recognition of idiosyncrasy*. The researcher looks at the learner's sentence to see if it conforms to the L2 grammar, either overtly or covertly in terms of its use or meaning. Such analysis involves reconstructing what the learner was attempting to say by asking him or her what was intended (an 'authoritative reconstruction'), or by inferring the learner's intentions from our interpretation of the whole context of situation (a 'plausible interpretation') (Corder, 1973, p. 274). This stage should yield a grammar of the learner's own interlanguage.

(b) *Accounting for the learner's idiosyncratic dialect.* The researcher sees how the learner's interlanguage sentences can be described; 'the methodology of description is, needless to say, fundamentally that of a bilingual comparison' (Corder, 1971). In other words, even if the theory of Contrastive Analysis is avoided, there is still a need for the researcher to know the L1 of the learner to be able to account for the errors.

(c) *Explanation.* The researcher tries to explain why the deviations from the grammar of the second language have arisen. The main explanation put forward by Corder (1971; 1973) is interference from L1 'habits', on the lines of Lado, and learning by 'hypothesis-testing'.

Corder (1973) gives the example of a learner sentence "I am told: there is bus stop". This is reconstructed as "I am told: there is the bus stop". The error would be classified as an omission in grammatical terms, and so the learner's grammar of articles is seen to differ from that of English. This invites an interference explanation, checked by looking at the learner's L1 to see if it lacks articles, and an hypothesis-testing explanation, checked by seeing if the learner is systematically using a 'simplification' process unrelated to English or to the L1.

Two main methodological difficulties with this are recognised by Corder. One harks back to the distinction between competence and performance: Corder (1971) refers 'to errors of performance as *mistakes*, reserving the term *error* to refer to the systematic errors of the learner', that is, errors of competence. Finding out the learner's interlanguage means disentangling errors that result from competence from mistakes that come from performance, just as in the study of native speakers. Indeed the term 'error' may be misleading when applied to L2 learning; the concern is with the actual sentences produced by L2 learners rather than with their deviation from the target language: 'If we call his sentences deviant or erroneous, we have implied an explanation before we have ever made a description' (Corder, 1971).

The second difficulty is the nature of error: how do we know when the learner has made an error and how do we know what it consists of? Some errors may be concealed; Corder (1973) cites "I want to know the English" as making superficial sense but concealing the error of incorrect insertion of "the". The researcher has to discover what the learner really had in mind in order to reconstruct what an appropriate English sentence would have been – "I want to know the English (people)" or "I want to know (the) English (language)". As Corder (1974, p. 127) puts it, 'The problem is: how do we arrive at a knowledge of what the learner intended to say?' The recognition of error and its reconstruction are subjective processes; the error is not a clearcut objective 'fact' but is established by a process of analysis and deduction.

Corder's views of learning are within the hypothesis-testing paradigm of 1960s first language acquisition work. Applied to L2 learning, this suggests that L2 learners 'progress by forming a series of increasingly complete hypotheses about the language' (Cook, 1969, p. 216). Errors are 'a way the learner has of testing his hypotheses about the nature of the language he is learning' (Corder, 1967), and therefore vital to the L2 learning process. The concept of hypothesis-testing became an integral component in much SLA research. Ellis (1982, p. 207) claimed that 'The principal tenet of IL theory, that the learner constructs for himself a series of hypotheses about the grammar of the target language and consciously or unconsciously tests these out in formal or informal language contexts, has withstood the test of both speculation and considerable empirical research.' Hypothesis-testing also played a role in the development of the communicative approach to language teaching, which devised pair-work and group-work activities so that the students could test out their hypotheses in the classroom.

The Error Analysis methodology, as systematised over the years, became a fruitful source of research ideas and the key element in many PhD dissertations. Representative work can be seen in Svartvik (1973), Arabski (1979), and Danchev (1988); clear-headed discussions of Error Analysis can be found in van Els *et al.* (1984) and Long and Sato (1984). In itself Error Analysis was a methodology for dealing with data, rather than a theory of acquisition. The facts to be explained are found in the learner's speech; the proper description of these suggests explanations in terms of the processes of L2 learning and of their sources in the L1 or L2.

Such an approach represents a view of scientific method that tries to find regularities in a collection of facts; the corpus of language you record will yield all the rules, provided you analyse it sufficiently. So far as first language acquisition is concerned, this methodology was attacked generally by Chomsky (1965b) as 'a general tendency . . . to assume that the determination of competence can be derived from description of a corpus by some sort of sufficiently developed data-processing technique'. Speech performance is one type of evidence among many, limited in what it can reveal about competence and constrained by the skill of the analyst in going beyond simple patterns, as will be seen in the next chapter. There is a paradox in Selinker and Corder suggesting that, on the one hand the object of description is the learner's knowledge of language; on the other, that the preferred research method should be the analysis of learners' performance. The learners' speech is only one form of performance data, linked to competence in complex ways; certain aspects of linguistic competence cannot be established through this means or may be distorted in various ways. This paradoxical relationship between knowledge and evidence will indeed form one theme of this book.

A number of issues were raised by the early researchers concerning the relationship of the L1 to the L2 (interference, compound and coordinate bilingualism, transfer), the nature of the L2 learner's grammar (interlanguage, phrase structure), the type of learning theory relevant to L2 learning (habit-formation, hypothesis-testing), and the methodology of research (Contrastive Analysis, Error Analysis). Many of these ideas and much of the research methodology came out of contemporary first language acquisition research; indeed a popular research question was whether these two processes of L1 and L2 learning were in fact the same (Cook, 1969; Ervin-Tripp, 1972). Yet they began to take on a momentum of their own. To some people, these were influences that shaped the questions they posed and the methodology they adopted; to others they were dogma to be revolted against.

SLA research grew out of many language-related disciplines. Linguistics was influential through linguists who were concerned with society and bilingualism, such as Weinreich. First language acquisition came in through the adaptation of the 1960s techniques and ideas originally devised to confirm or disconfirm Chomsky's ideas. Language teaching was brought in by applied linguists trying to develop language teaching through a better understanding of language learning, such as Lado and Corder. There was no uniform background for researchers in either their goals, their views of language, or their methodology; people were not trained in SLA research *per se* but came to it from other academic disciplines, not necessarily linguistics.

So far, the multilingual goals for SLA research have been presented as an extension of Chomsky's monolingual goals to cover the restricted situation in which people know more than one language. In my own view, this does not go far enough. Many people in England may well find it remarkable that someone can use more than one language in their everyday life. However in the Cameroon a person might use four or five languages in the course of a day, chosen from the two official languages, the four lingua francas, and the 285 native languages (Koenig, Chia, & Povey, 1983). There may be more people in the world like the Cameroonian than like the Englishman. Knowing a second language alongside the first is a normal part of human existence for most human beings, even if few know the L2 to the same extent as the L1. In officially monolingual countries, many of the inhabitants know more than one language: for example the population of the United States in 1976 included nearly 28 million people whose mother tongue was not English (Wardhaugh, 1987). Even England may harbour fewer monolinguals than one might suspect: 30.1 per cent of children in the London Borough of Haringey spoke languages other than English at home (Linguistic Minorities Project, 1983). The proper questions for linguistics itself to answer may be the multilingual rather than the monolingual versions; multi-competence should be treated as the norm rather than monolingual linguistic competence. All human beings are capable of acquiring and knowing more than one language, at least to some extent. The starting point for linguistics could be argued to be the mind with two languages, not the mind with one. As Jakobson (1953) put it, 'Bilingualism is for me the fundamental problem of linguistics.'

2 Sequences in Second Language Acquisition

This chapter develops the ideas and methodology described in the first chapter by concentrating on the two areas of grammatical morphemes and negation, which were most prominent in the late 1970s and early 1980s. Both typically rely on earlier models of syntax derived from structuralist linguistics. Both use data gathered from observations of learners' speech to discover the sequence of L2 acquisition.

2.1 GRAMMATICAL MORPHEMES

A morpheme can be defined as the smallest unit of language that conveys a meaning or that has a role in grammatical structure; "clarinet" is a single morpheme as it cannot be split into meaningful smaller units; "supermarkets" is three morphemes as it can be split into "super + market + s", each element of which has some independent meaning of its own. A morpheme may be 'free', that is, a word in itself such as "book", or it may be 'bound', that is, attached to other items, such as "-s" in "books". Bound morphemes are 'inflectional' if they add inflections to a word; in "cats" the plural morpheme "-s" is added as an inflection to "cat". They are 'derivational' if they derive one word from another; "unkind" ("un + kind") is a different word from "kind" rather than an inflected form of the same word. A further division, used in one guise or another in language teaching for many years, is between lexical morphemes, sometimes known as 'content words', for example "table", "whisper", and "red", and grammatical morphemes, sometimes known as 'function words', such as "the", "of", and "only". The proportion of lexical to grammatical morphemes varies in language use; Halliday (1985b, p. 80) calculates 1.2 to 2 lexical items per clause in spoken English, and 3 to 6 in written English.

The first language acquisition research of the 1970s used the concept of grammatical morpheme to refer to morphemes that have a grammatical rather than a lexical function in the sentence, including not only free morphemes, such as "the" and "is", but also bound morphemes, such as the "-ing" that signals progressive ("is doing"), and the "-s" that signals plural number in noun phrases ("books"). Roger Brown (1973) observed that children in the early stages of first language acquisition appear to leave out grammatical morphemes rather than lexical morphemes, producing sentences such as "Here bed" or "Not dada"; grammatical morphemes

25

gradually appear in their sentences over a period of years. He accordingly investigated the emergence of 14 grammatical morphemes in three selected children up to the age of four. Two hours of their speech were recorded every month and were analysed to see how many times per recording each morpheme occurred in 'obligatory contexts' – occasions on which a native speaker is obliged to use particular morphemes in the sentence. Brown recognised four types of obligatory context: linguistic, nonlinguistic, linguistic prior context, and linguistic subsequent context. The child was regarded as having acquired a morpheme when it was supplied in over 90 per cent of obligatory contexts for three consecutive recordings; the separate points at which each morpheme was acquired were put in sequence to get an order of acquisition. The orders for each of the three children were then averaged to get a common sequence for first language acquisition. This methodology reflects the independent grammars assumption to the extent that it seeks to describe the child's actual speech; the concept of obligatory context nevertheless effectively ties the description in to a comparison with the adult target speech.

Dulay and Burt (1973) adapted Brown's approach to SLA research in order to answer the question 'Is there a common sequence with which children acquiring English as a second language learn certain structures?' (Dulay and Burt, 1973, p. 252). Their subjects were 151 Spanish-speaking children aged 6–8 learning English as a Second Language in the USA in three locations: 95 in Sacramento, 30 in East Harlem, and 26 in San Ysidro. They collected samples of speech through the BSM (Bilingual Syntax Measure); this test elicits a range of grammatical structures by asking the learners 33 questions about a series of seven cartoon pictures. They used a set of eight grammatical morphemes, or 'functors' as they called them, namely:

- the *plural morpheme* attached to nouns and usually written as "-s" ("the books");
- the *progressive morpheme* attached to lexical verbs and written as "-ing" ("He's looking");
- the *copula forms of "be"*, that is to say, some form of "be" used on its own as a main verb ("This is London", "He was there");
- the *auxiliary forms of "be"*, that is to say, "be" occurring as an auxiliary with a lexical verb ("She is going");
- the *articles "the" and "a"* occurring with nouns ("a dog", "the cat");
- the *irregular past tenses*, that is to say, verbs with past tenses that do not conform to the usual "-ed" form of the past tense morpheme in English ("came", "ate", etc.);
- the *present singular morpheme "-s"* that signals the third person of the present tense ("He waits")

- the *possessive morpheme "-s"* attached to nouns and noun phrases ("John's book", "the King of England's daughter").

Each obligatory context for a grammatical morpheme was scored on a three point scale: a missing grammatical morpheme counted as 0 ("She's dance"); a misformed grammatical morpheme counted as 0.5 ("She's dances"); and a correct grammatical morpheme counted as 1.0 ("She's dancing"). These scores were averaged to get a proportion out of 1.00 for each morpheme. Then the scores were put in order to yield a sequence going from the morphemes that were supplied most often to those that were supplied least often. Taking the scores from the Sacramento group, the sequence from (1) most frequent to (8) least frequent was as follows:

1	2	3	4	5	6	7	8
plural	*-ing*	cop.	aux.	*the/a*	irreg.	3rd-person	possessive
-s		be	be		past	*-s*	*-s*

Sequence of grammatical morphemes for the Sacramento group of 95 children learning English (adapted from a graph in Dulay and Burt, 1973, p. 255)

There were clear differences in the success with which different morphemes were supplied; the Sacramento children, for example, scored 1.0 for plural "-s", 0.6 for irregular past forms, 0.5 for the third person "-s", and 0.15 for the possessive "-s". In other words 'there does seem to be a common order of acquisition for certain structures in L2 acquisition' (Dulay and Burt, 1973, p. 256). The technique of grammatical morphemes research was then found to work for L2 acquisition.

This result was important for the emerging discipline of SLA research in the early 1970s. Demonstrating the existence of an L2 sequence of acquisition proved there was a point to developing SLA research separately from the study of the L1 and the L2 and from L1 acquisition; in short, L2 learners had interlanguages of their own that were valid objects of study. So Dulay and Burt (1980) went on to claim, based chiefly on grammatical morpheme research, that the discovery of a common acquisition sequence for L2 learners is 'surely one of the most exciting and significant outcomes of the last decade of second language research'.

Dulay and Burt soon went beyond a sequence of particular items to group the morphemes into 'hierarchies' of those that tend to go together in the sequence (Dulay and Burt, 1974a). Let us take the hierarchy given in Krashen (1977) as it uses the same morphemes with the addition of regular past tense forms, that is, "-ed" endings:

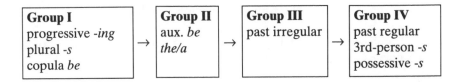

Group I includes "-ing", plural "-s" and copula "be"; it precedes Group II auxiliary "be" and the articles, which in turn come before the past irregular Group III which comes before the Group IV past regular, third-person "-s" and possessive "-s". Krashen argued that it was more meaningful to discuss acquisition in terms of a hierarchy of morphemes than morpheme by morpheme.

Research summary: H.C. Dulay and M.K. Burt (1973), 'Should We Teach Children Syntax?', *Language Learning*, 23(2), pp. 245–58

Aim: 'Is there a common sequence with which children acquiring English as a second language learn certain structures?' (Dulay and Burt, 1973, p. 252)

Aspect of language: eight grammatical morphemes: plural "-s", progressive "-ing", copula "be", auxiliary "be", articles "the/a", irregular past, third-person "-s", possessive "-s"

Data type: sentences elicited via the BSM (Bilingual Syntax Measure) – cartoon description

L2 learners: 151 Spanish-speaking children aged 6–8 learning English in the USA

Method of analysis:

(i) scoring 8 grammatical morphemes supplied in obligatory contexts

(ii) ordering these from most often supplied to least often supplied

Results: 'there does seem to be a common order of acquisition for certain structures in L2 acquisition' (Dulay and Burt, 1973, p. 256).

Extensions to the Grammatical Morphemes Research

The paper by Dulay and Burt (1973) was massively influential in content and methodology. Some accidental feature of the actual experiments by Dulay and Burt might, however, be responsible for the sequence rather than L2 learning itself, say the type of test used (the BSM), or the age of the learners (6–8), or their first language (Spanish), or their situation (whether or not they were in a classroom). Many other experiments replicated the basic design of this research while varying the conditions and changing the actual morphemes studied. It might, for example, be a matter of transfer from the L1. Dulay and Burt (1974a) compared 60 Spanish and 55 Chinese children learning English: the learner's L1 did not seem to affect the sequence to a great extent; 'the sequences of acquisition of 11 functors obtained for Spanish and Chinese children are virtually the same' (Dulay and Burt, 1974a, p. 49). Hakuta (1974; 1976), however, studied one Japanese five-year-old child called Uguisu whose sequence over 60 weeks was very distinctive; for example plural "-s" came last in the sequence rather than first (Dulay and Burt, 1973) or fifth (Dulay and Burt, 1974a).

Other studies varied further dimensions of the research:

(a) *Krashen, Sferlazza, Feldman, and Fathman (1976)* tested 66 adults from mixed L1s rather than children, and used a picture questioning task called SLOPE (Second Language Oral Production English), rather than the BSM. Choosing the five morphemes that overlap with the nine here, the sequence they found from (1) most frequent to (5) least frequent was:

1	2	3	4	5
plural	*-ing*	*the/a*	poss.	3rd person
-s			*-s*	*-s*

Sequence of grammatical morphemes for 66 mixed adult learners (from Krashen *et al.*, 1976, p. 148)

This differed from the Dulay and Burt (1973) sequence only in that the 3rd person "-s" and possessive "-s" changed places at the end of the sequence. Thus the basic sequence appeared impervious to the age of the learner or to the form of test; 'child and adult ESL learners do not differ significantly with respect to which aspects of English grammar they find hard and which aspects they find easy' (Krashen *et al.*, 1976, p. 149). While this research also suggested that the type of elicitation task made little difference, Larsen-Freeman (1975) nevertheless found that tasks such as interview, imitation, and writing produced different sequences.

(b) *Makino (1980)* examined whether the sequence might be peculiar to L2 learners in an environment where the L2 is actually spoken, that is, the USA, rather than in their home country where it is not spoken. He used a fill-in-the-blanks task with 777 high school students of English studying in their own country, Japan. The scores were calculated in three different ways, which produced only slight variation. Taking the method in which only completely correct answers counted (I), the following sequence occurred:

1	2	3	4	5	6	7	8	9
-ing	*the/a*	plural	cop.	poss.	aux.	reg.	3rd person	irreg.
		-s	*be*	*-s*	*be*	past	*-s*	past

Sequence of grammatical morphemes for 777 Japanese children (from Makino, 1980, p. 126)

This sequence correlated statistically with the sequences of Dulay and Burt, and of Krashen. The conclusion is that the sequence is broadly true of L2 learners in classrooms in their own country as well as those in a foreign country.

(c) *Lightbown (1987)* investigated 175 French-speaking children aged 11–17 learning English in Canadian classrooms through recordings and data elicited from oral picture description over several months. For the six morphemes that were used, she found an overall sequence:

1	2	3	4	5	6
cop.	aux.	plural	*-ing*	3rd-person	possessive
be	*be*	*-s*		*-s*	*-s*

Sequence of grammatical morphemes for 175 French-speaking children (Lightbown, 1987, p. 174)

The most important difference from Dulay and Burt (1973) and Krashen (1977) is that the auxiliary "be" has gone ahead of plural "-s" and "-ing", both in Krashen's first group. Over time the children stayed at a high level for copula "be" and for auxiliary "be"; plural "-s" started low and gradually improved; "-ing" started at 69 per cent, fell to 39 per cent, and rose to 60 per cent only with the oldest children. Children in classrooms were indeed following a similar sequence to those outside. Similarly Perkins and Larsen-Freeman (1975) found little change over a month for the sequence of grammatical morphemes for Spanish-speaking adults in both taught and untaught groups, with the exception of an improvement in possessive "-s": 'instruction does not radically alter order of acquisition' (Perkins and Larsen-Freeman, 1975, p. 241).

The research outlined here is a selection from the large number of papers using variations of the same research techniques; amplifications can be found in Dulay, *et al.* (1982) or Larsen-Freeman and Long (1991). Whatever the explanation and whatever the minor discrepancies, the research has uncovered something new and strange: there are sequences for grammatical morphemes common to virtually all L2 learners that are not explicable solely in terms of their L1s or their learning situations.

Problems with Morpheme Research

This line of research, however, came increasingly under fire. One obvious point is that the findings are specific to English and have not been replicated with other L2s, apart from Spanish in VanPatten (1984). They can be generalised to languages that also have both bound and free grammatical morphemes, if equivalents could be found to "-ing", plural "-s", and so on. The findings cannot, however, be applied to languages such as Chinese that have no morphological component to the grammar. Work with first language acquisition of languages with 'rich' morphology, that is, those that use inflectional morphemes far more than English, shows 'fairly rapid and error free mastery of inflection' (Goodluck, 1991, p. 58): one Icelandic two-year-old used 40 inflectional endings within a 30-minute conversation. Grammatical morphemes may be a problem in the acquisition of English rather than a general learning sequence, however interesting in their own right.

The main linguistics issue is the heterogeneity of the morphemes involved; as Maratsos (1983) puts it for first language acquisition, 'the morphemes do not belong to any coherent structural group'. On the one hand, the studies usually mix bound and unbound morphemes as if they were the same, despite the correlation found by Krashen *et al.* (1978) between L1 and L2 learners for bound rather than free morphemes. On the other hand, they bring together disparate aspects of grammar. The usual set of nine morphemes includes the morphology of the main verb ("-ing", regular and irregular past tense, third person "-s"), the morphology and syntax of the noun phrase (possessive "-s", plural "-s", "the/a"), and auxiliary and copula forms of "be"; thus these items blur the conventional linguistic distinction between morphology (grammar below the word) and syntax (grammar above the word) as well as crossing different phrase types. While these aspects of grammar are related at some highly abstract level, such as the Inflectional Phrase to be described in Chapter 8, this is hardly discussed in the research, VanPatten (1984) being one exception. In other words the grammatical morphemes are an arbitrary and linguistically unjustified collection. In a sense the research ignores their *grammatical* nature; grammar is a system in which everything plays its part in conjunction with the rest, not a list of distinct items like a dictionary; grammatical morphemes are being treated here as discrete lexical items to be acquired one after the other, rather than as part of grammatical structures and systems.

A morpheme has allomorphs that are realised in several different ways according to phonological or grammatical environment – "a" becomes "an" before vowels for example. In the traditional analysis the morpheme for plural "-s" may be pronounced as /s/ ("books"), /z/ ("days"), or /iz/ ("wishes"); the past tense "-ed" morpheme is regularly pronounced /t/, /d/

or /id/; in both cases the choice depends on the final phoneme of the word. Most of the nine morphemes in the list have variant allomorphs of this kind, even "-ing", as we see in Chapter 4. The grammatical morpheme studies, however, pay little heed to allomorphic variation: provided the morpheme occurs, its form does not matter. Yet children acquire allomorphs of a morpheme in a definite sequence in the first language; for example the classic "wugs" experiment used nonsense words to show that L1 children learn the /s/ and /z/ allomorphs of plural ("cats", "dogs") before the /iz/ allomorph ("fishes") (Berko, 1958). Indeed this is corroborated for L2 learning by Wode (1980; 1981), who found a sequence of acquisition for the plural allomorphs going from /s/ to /z/ to /iz/ for four German children learning English. The L2 research is blurring important aspects of the sequence by not taking allomorphs into account.

But the L2 research is not consistent in using morphemes rather than allomorphs. Two of the categories in the list are regular and irregular past forms; these are not different morphemes but different allomorphs of the same morpheme. Further examples, present in some of the research, are the difference between regular and irregular third person "-s", and the difference between 'short' "-s" and 'long' "-es" plural for nouns, in both cases allomorphs of one morpheme. While it may well be interesting to know how L2 learners tackle these regular and irregular forms, this is a different issue from the acquisition of the grammatical morphemes themselves or from looking consistently at all their allomorphs.

Nor has the main research taken into account the extent to which the presence or absence of bound morphemes is linked to the actual lexical item involved. Abraham (1984) showed that L2 success with third person "-s" depends on the word used; "look" is an 'easy' verb with 17 per cent errors; "eat" is 'difficult' with 49 per cent, and "take" is 'medium difficult' with 30 per cent. Ellis (1988) compared the accuracy of production of third person "-s" and copula "-s" in different contexts; he found 'systematic variability according to context' in the speech of one L2 child, who supplied "-s" more often with pronoun subjects than with noun subjects, a similar finding to Lightbown (1987). Pica (1984) argued that sequences are affected by how often a particular lexical item is used: two L2 learners who are describing their visit to the USA might use the word "visit" frequently; the fact that one expresses the past tense through "visit", the other through "visited" might mean one getting a good score, the other a poor score, even if they were both completely correct with other verbs. The absence of a bound morpheme is related to vocabulary choice as well as to syntax.

Moreover, morphemes are discussed in terms of physical presence in the sentence; the experimenter looks for the occurrence of the morpheme in the obligatory context. This says nothing about meaning. Does an L2 speaker using the progressive "John is going" mean the same as a native or something different? For instance, the boy studied by Wagner-Gough

(1978) used "Sitting down like that" as an imperative rather than a progressive. The many uses of the progressive ("be" + "-ing"), or of the articles "the/a", or of the copula "be" are not tested: all that matters is whether or not the learner supplies the actual item. The correct use of the English zero article in "Pigeons are birds", for instance, is unassessable by a method that only counts presence of visible items.

So, all in all, the sequence consists of disparate items that are not operating at the same level in the grammar. There are still no studies of the acquisition of morphology in an L2 that take account of the basic concepts of morphology in linguistics described, say, in Bauer (1988); nor is heed paid either to the detailed analyses of English inflectional morphology, such as Zwicky (1975), or to the sophisticated level of morphology used in first language acquisition, reported in Goodluck (1991) and Bates *et al.* (1988). It will also be interesting when L2 research catches up with the production and comprehension techniques used with inflectional morphology in recent studies of dysphasics (Gopnik and Crago, 1991).

What was more problematic for grammatical morpheme research than these linguistic design faults was the recognition that the concept of sequence was more complex than had been realised. To arrive at the L1 sequence of acquisition, Brown (1973) ordered the morphemes according to the acquisition points at which children achieved 90 per cent success *over time*; to get an L2 sequence, Dulay and Burt (1973) put morphemes in order based on their scores *at a single moment of time*. So sequence is conceived in two divergent ways: the L1 order is an *order of acquisition* based on the chronological points when the forms attain a certain level of accuracy in children's speech; the L2 order is an *order of difficulty* of production based on the scores of learners on a single testing occasion. But something which is easy to start with does not necessarily get easier with time, and vice versa; some errors are persistent. Lee (1981), for example, found differences between three different levels of Korean students; the auxiliary forms were easiest of all for the lowest and highest groups, but eighth out of ten for the middle group; position in the sequence of difficulty varied dramatically. Lightbown (1987) too found that the course of acquisition of "-ing" over time was far from smooth.

Both senses of order are interesting and useful; de Villiers and de Villiers (1973) showed that the L1 accuracy order was similar to Brown's L1 acquisition order, with some exceptions: for example, third-person "-s" appeared earlier than expected, "-ing" later. Porter (1977) nevertheless showed discrepancies between the two in the L1: 'The strong evidence shown for an invariant order of morpheme acquisition for L1 learners learning English . . . did not correlate with the order of functor acquisition in L1 learners as determined by the BSM' (Porter, 1977, p. 59). Order of acquisition and order of difficulty pose separate research issues, one answering the acquisition question, the other the use question. Krashen

(1977) nevertheless interprets most L2 studies as showing similarities between the two processes of acquisition and processing, once methodological issues such as low numbers of examples are discounted.

Sometimes this distinction is phrased in terms of a methodological difference between *longitudinal* and *cross-sectional* research. Longitudinal research follows the same learner or learners over a period of time; minimally they are observed at time 1 and time 2 and then comparisons are made between their state of knowledge at these two times. Thus Hakuta (1974) uses a longitudinal design as it follows the same learner, Uguisu, over 60 weeks; it establishes a series of states of language knowledge that can be related developmentally. A cross-sectional study, on the other hand, looks at different learners at different moments in time and establishes development by comparing these successive states in different people (Ingram, 1989, p. 13); this is called "pseudo-longitudinal" in Adams (1978). That is to say, rather than following 20 beginning L2 learners for a year, the researcher takes 20 beginners and compares them with 20 learners who have been learning for a year, as if they were the same people; Lightbown (1987) is then a combination of a cross-sectional and a longitudinal study. Cross-sectional studies can still provide information about acquisition by comparing the successive knowledge states as if they existed in the same person; learners at stage I know X, learners at stage II know Y; therefore learners progress from X to Y.

The mainline grammatical morpheme studies are often called cross-sectional in the L2 literature as they test learners at a single moment in time for each learner, for example as in Dulay and Burt (1973). In my view, this is a misleading use of the term 'cross-sectional' as these studies do not compare groups of learners at different cross-sectional levels to establish a series of developmental language states, but either lump all the learners together into one group (Dulay and Burt, 1973), or separate them by first language (Dulay and Burt, 1974a) or criteria other than chronological development. They do not provide cross-sections of acquisition so much as orders of difficulty pooled across learners at different stages. A further term, *single-moment* studies, needs to be coined to distinguish this approach from the true cross-sectional design. Different types of conclusion may be derived from research with single-moment, cross-sectional, and longitudinal designs.

One of the side issues considered in this research was whether L2 learning is the same as L1 acquisition. The sequences can be put side by side as follows, taking Dulay and Burt (1974a) as representative of L2 and Brown (1973) of L1, and using the seven morphemes they have in common (copula "be" and auxiliary "be" cannot be compared as Brown distinguishes contractible and uncontractible forms of each):

1	2	3	4	5	6	7	
the/a	*-ing*	plural	reg.	irreg.	poss.	3rd person	[*in Dulay and*
		-*s*	past	past	*s*	-*s*	*Burt, 1974a*]

1	2	3	4	5	6	7	
-ing	plural	irreg.	poss.	*the/a*	reg.	3rd person	[*in Brown,*
	-*s*	past	-*s*		past	-*s*	*1973*]

Comparison of L1 and L2 sequences for seven grammatical morphemes

There are broad similarities between the two sequences; all the morphemes occur within a range of two positions, apart from the articles "the/a" (1 versus 5). Making the same comparison with a fuller range of morphemes, Dulay, Burt, and Krashen (1982, p. 211) conclude 'the irregular past tense, the article, the copula and the auxiliary show the greatest amount of difference'. VanPatten (1984), however, separates the morphemes into NP, V, and AUX groups and finds that, within each group, there is no difference between L1 and L2. The main similarity between L1 and L2 is not so much the details of the sequence as the fact that both L1 and L2 acquisition *have* sequences at all.

The similarities in the sequence of grammatical morphemes are explained by Dulay and Burt as caused by 'creative construction' – 'the subconscious process by which language learners gradually organise the language they hear, according to rules they construct to generate sentences' (Dulay *et al.* 1982, p. 11). This view of language learning attributes the learner's grammar to internal processes of learning rather than to the properties of the L1 invoked by Contrastive Analysis. Dulay and Burt (1974b) categorised errors from 179 Spanish-speaking children either as developmental (that is, attributable to 'natural' creative construction) or as L1 interference from Spanish. Out of a total of 513 errors, 447 (87.1 per cent) were developmental, 24 (4.7 per cent) were interference. On their calculations, the L1 contribution is extremely small. The concept of creative construction relies on the independent-grammars assumption discussed in the last chapter: L2 learners are seen as having regular grammars of their own, which can be established from samples of their speech. It differs from Selinker's interlanguage proposal in emphasising the built-in mental structure rather than the processes through which interlanguages come into being. It does not, however, specify what this innate structure might be, simply adopting a version of hypothesis-testing: 'Learners reconstruct rules for the speech they hear, guided by innate mechanisms which cause them to formulate certain types of hypotheses about the language system being acquired until the mismatch between what they are exposed to and what they produce is resolved' (Dulay and Burt, 1978, p. 67). It leads in due course to the Input Hypothesis model to be discussed in the next chapter.

2.2   NEGATION AND THE LEARNER'S LANGUAGE SYSTEM

The study of negation again starts from the independent grammars assumption. Milon (1974) looked at the development of Ken, a seven-year-old Japanese-speaking boy learning English in Hawaii, over a period of six months, and wrote rules to capture the child's grammar at each stage. Klima and Bellugi (1966) had written independent grammars for the development of negation in the first language, using rules of the form:

$$A \rightarrow B\ C$$

that is, phrase A 'consists of' ($\rightarrow$) elements B and C; these are based on the rewriting formalism introduced into linguistics by Chomsky (1957).

Milon therefore wrote a grammar for Ken at stage 1 to account for such sentences as "No my turn" and "No more sister". The grammar requires a single rule that a sentence (S) consists of a Nucleus and a possible negative element "not", "no", or "no more", that is to say:

$$S \rightarrow \left\{ \begin{array}{l} \textit{not} \\ \textit{no} \\ \textit{no more} \end{array} \right\} \text{Nucleus}$$

Stage 1 of negation in a Japanese boy learning English (based on Milon, 1974)

At stage 2 the child produced sentences such as "I no look" and "You no can go"; the rule is that negative elements are placed inside the sentence and consist of a negative element or negative auxiliary (Aux^{neg}) occurring between the subject Nominal and the Predicate. The negative auxiliary may be *neg* ("not" or "no") or a negative Verb (V^{neg}) such as "don't". At this stage negation still consists of the insertion of negative elements into the sentence rather than their attachment to auxiliaries; "don't", "can't", and "no can" are equivalent to "not" and "no" rather than consisting of "can" + "not" or "do" + "not"; to the child "don't" and "can't" each consist of one morpheme rather than two ("do" + "n't" and "can" +

"n't"). This can be expressed in the following rewriting rules; again each symbol on the left consists of the symbols on the right.

$$S \rightarrow \left\{ \begin{array}{l} \text{Nominal} \\ \text{Neg} \end{array} \right\} (\text{Aux}^{\text{neg}})\ \text{Pred}$$

$$\text{Aux}^{\text{neg}} \rightarrow V^{\text{neg}}$$

$$\text{Neg} \rightarrow \left\{ \begin{array}{l} \textit{no} \\ \textit{not} \end{array} \right.$$

$$V^{\text{neg}} \rightarrow \left\{ \begin{array}{l} \textit{can't} \\ \textit{don't} \\ \textit{no can} \end{array} \right.$$

Stage 2 of negation in a Japanese boy learning English (based on Milon, 1974)

Milon goes on to discuss parallels between Ken's stage 3 and Klima and Bellugi's stage III but does not provide rules, as these would require looking in detail at negation in Hawaiian Creole, the variety that Ken was learning, rather than the standard English implied by Klima and Bellugi. Milon's work showed the feasibility of writing L2 grammars for stages of an L2 learner's development. There was indeed a strong similarity between the L2 stages and the first two L1 stages found by Klima and Bellugi (1966). One difference is Ken's use of the additional negative elements "no more" and "no can". Yet both of these sound perfectly plausible as L1 utterances; Bloom (1970) reports finding "no more" frequently in the speech of one L1 child. Another difference is Ken's use of auxiliaries in questions and declaratives in stage 2, not found by Klima and Bellugi (1966).

A more complex approach to the acquisition of negation is exemplified in the work of Henning Wode. His overall purpose was 'to characterize the nature of naturalistic L2 acquisition within an integrated theory of language acquisition' (Wode, 1981, p. 91). He followed the daily progress of his own four German-speaking children aged 3:11 to 8:11 while they were in the USA for six months. He made transcripts of the learners' speech, virtually every day, supplemented by occasional comprehension tests. The account reported here is based on Wode's 1981 book; less detailed versions occur in Wode (1977; 1984). The children were compared not only with themselves learning German as an L1 but also with four children learning English as an L1, and with 34 German-speaking children learning English in a classroom. From this, he aimed to derive a sequence of acquisition for negation that would be universal for L1 learning, for L2 learning, and for different languages. He established the following sequence:

Stage I: Anaphoric negation. In the children's earliest sentences, such as "Kenny no" and "No my is the better one", "no" 'stands for' a whole sentence and so is called 'anaphoric' negation. It also occurs outside the structure of the sentence, and so is called 'external' negation. Most studies find that the external anaphoric form, such as English "no" or German "nein" or Arabic "la", is learnt before other forms.

Stage II: Non-anaphoric external negation. At the next stage the children produced sentences such as "No finish" and "No sleep"; in these the negative element is still external but is part of the structure of the sentence in meaning rather than substituting for a whole sentence; that is, it is non-anaphoric. This is equivalent to Milon's first stage, in which a negative occurs before or after a Nucleus, except that the Nucleus is defined more closely. The stage occurs in both L1 and L2 learning. Wode found two sub-stages: **IIA "no"** + **Adjective/Verb/Noun**, as in "No bread" and "No fair"; and **IIB "no"** + **Verb Phrase**, as in "No drink some milk".

Stage III: Internal "be" negation. Next, the children produced sentences such as "That's no good" and "Lunch is no ready", that is to say X *"be" "no"/"not"* Y. "No" and "not" are now internal to the sentence, and are found chiefly with forms of the copula "be", as in "That's no good" and "It's not German. It's England."

Stage IV: Internal full verb negation, and "don't" imperative. At the next stage, the children said "You have a not fish", or "Don't say something"; they placed the negative elements "no" and "not" before or after full verbs, as in "I'm not missed it" or "You can't have that"; they also produced imperatives starting with "don't", such as "Don't throw the rocks on Kitty". The main structures are then *Subject Verb negation X* as in "Birgit catch no fish" and *Subject negation Verb Phrase* as in "I not get away from Larsie". The auxiliary "don't" is restricted to imperatives rather than occurring in other contexts. During this complex stage L2 learning starts to diverge from L1 acquisition under the influence of the form of negation in the L1; for example the use of *Verb + negation*, as in "Birgit catch no fish", seems peculiar to German learners of English and may reflect post-verbal negation in German.

Stage V: Suppletive non-imperative "do". Finally, the children started saying sentences such as "I didn't have a snag", and "I don't saw the water". The full range of forms for "do" support (that is, supplying "do" for negation when no auxiliary is present to attach the negation to) is found in sentences such as "You didn't can throw it" and "They don't last any game".

These five stages cover the children's progress over six months; still to come is the link between "any" and negation seen in target sentences such as "I don't have any money". The stages can be shown as follows:

I	II	III	IV	V
anaphoric external	non-anaphoric external	internal "be"	internal full verb & "don't" imperative	suppletive "do" non-imperative
	IIA *no*+A/V/N			
	IIB *no*+VP			
Kenny no	*No finish*	*That's no good*	*You have a not fish*	*You didn't can throw it*

Stages in the acquisition of negation by four German children (Wode, 1981)

Wode's main conclusions from this research are not just the actual sequence of acquisition for negation but also the uniqueness of the structures *Neg + X* and *Subject Neg VP* found at stages II and III, which he claims are due to universal strategies active in both L1 and L2: 'these and other strategies are part of man's basic devices to acquire language' (Wode, 1980, p. 294). He sees these as the 'biological endowment' underlying Dulay and Burt's creative construction process. Wode's work on negation then provides a further illustration of the concept of stages of development and of the nature of the learner's developing interlanguage system.

Research summary: H. Wode (1981), *Learning a Second Language* (Tubingen: Narr).
Aim: to describe the stages in acquisition of negation
Learners: four German-speaking children aged 3:11 to 8:11 learning English in the USA
Aspect of language: negative elements
Data type: naturally occurring sentences recorded in a diary, supplemented with some tests
Method of analysis: use of transcripts
Results: a clear sequence of acquisition for negation with features unique to L2 acquisition

---

Further Work with Negation

Negation has also been studied by several other researchers, extending the discussion of English to other L1s and varying the research techniques.

(a) *Cancino, Rosansky and Schumann (1978)* looked at six Spanish speakers learning English – two children aged 5, two teenagers, and two adults – who were visited every fortnight for ten months. This was one aspect of a major 1970s study which was reported in several publications, and will be referred to repeatedly in later chapters. Rather than writing grammars, Cancino et al (1978) tried to 'catalogue the various negating devices ("no", "don't", "can't", "isn't", etc.), and to determine the proportion of each negating device in each sample to the total number of negatives'; they excluded anaphoric negation and the formulaic expressions "I don't know" and "I don't think so". A graph for each learner showed the percentage of each negative element on each successive occasion. This established a common developmental sequence of frequency for four stages:

Stage I: at the first stage the most frequent negative form was *"no"* + *Verb* as in "I no understand";
Stage II: was dominated by *"don't"* + *Verb* as in "I don't look the clock at this time";
Stage III: was marked by the use of negative auxiliaries such as "can't" as in "You can't tell her";
Stage IV: the last stage saw the appearance of "do" in a range of forms ("does", "didn't", and so on), indicating that it is now an auxiliary for the learner separate from the negative element, as in "One night I didn't have the light."

I	II	III	IV
"no"+Verb	"don't"+Verb	negative aux	"do" forms
I no understand	*I don't look the clock at this time*	*You can't tell her*	*One night I didn't have the light*

Stages in the acquisition of negation for six Spanish learners (adapted from Cancino *et al.*, 1978)

The first three stages seem to be subdivisions of Wode's complex stage IV, using the full Verb and negative auxiliary; stage IV equates with Wode's stage V in that both incorporate the full use of "do" support.

(b) *Eubank (1987)* studied the acquisition of German negation by six classroom learners over nine months. German differs from English because negation with full verbs follows object NPs and some adverbs in the sentence. He found the following sequence in their development.

I	II	III
Neg X	S Neg	Internal Neg
nein hier	*ihr harr ist* *schwartz nicht*	*die ah Mann hat keine* *Heft*

Stages in classroom L2 learning of German negation by six learners (from Eubank, 1987)

Stages I and III are familiar, except in so far as they depend on German negation rules. But Stage II is peculiar. The learners have decided incorrectly to put a negative at the end of the sentence, that is, *Sentence + Negation*, getting such ungrammatical sentences as "Das ist gut Kaffee nicht" (that is good coffee not) and "Der Mann hat Mund nicht" (the man has mouth no). Eubank argues that this is a product of the classroom situation, due in part to the pressure on students to talk in 'complete' sentences, and in part to the effectiveness of sentence-final negation as a communication strategy.

(c) *Hyltenstam (1977)* used a different approach from those seen so far, which is taken up in work seen in later chapters. In Swedish the negative element "inte" comes *after* the finite verb in main clauses, but *before* the finite verb in subordinate clauses; modern analyses of Swedish in fact derive the order of the main clause from that in the subordinate clause (Rizzi, 1990), on the lines to be discussed in Chapter 9. A group comprising 160 adults who had been studying Swedish for three weeks had to insert the negative element into sentences either before the verb or after it; 12 sentences had test items in the main clause, 12 in the subordinate, and equal numbers of sentences had finite verb or finite auxiliary. They were tested twice, five weeks apart. The overall scores for main clauses showed better performance at inserting negation with the auxiliaries than with the verbs; for the subordinate clauses the reverse was true. Scoring of the individual sentences showed that the sentences formed a continuum of difficulty for the learners. A simplified version of the results for four English-speaking learners at time 2 is as follows:

No subordinate/main clause distinction:

Subject no.	Aux + Neg	V + Neg
50	75	25
37	100	100

Subordinate/main clause distinction:

Subject no.	Main clause		Subordinate clause	
	Aux + Neg	V + Neg	Aux + Neg	V + Neg
86	100	100	83	33
215	100	100	100	100

Four adult English learners of Swedish negation (adapted from Hyltenstam, 1977, p. 397)

Subjects 50 and 37 had not mastered the difference between main and subordinate clauses; Subject 50 was better at auxiliaries than at verbs, while Subject 37 was the same on both. Subjects 86 and 215 knew the difference between main and subordinate clauses but Subject 86 was still better at Auxiliaries, while 215 knew both. The learner at the top is worst; the learner at the bottom is best; in between come the other subjects. Such a pattern is called an implicational scale. It is not a simple sequence of acquisition in which one thing follows another in a linear fashion as in the morpheme studies; it is a two dimensional array in which success goes from left to right along the rows and from top to bottom down the columns. This is true not just of the 4 English-speaking learners but also of the other 156 learners; 'it is possible to construct one scale for all learners irrespective of their native language' (Hyltenstam, 1977, p. 401). All learners score better from left to right; as they develop, they move down and along the scale. Each step implies the ones that precede it. Those that 'backslid' during the experiment moved backwards up the scale, progressively losing the forms. The sequence of negation put in linear form is then:

Stage I	Stage II	Stage III	Stage IV	Stage V
Neg + Verb	Aux + Neg	Verb + Neg	Neg + Aux	Neg + Verb
(main)	(main)	(main)	(subordinate)	(subordinate)

Stages of acquisition for Swedish negation (after Hyltenstam, 1977, p. 404)

Like the other sequences described by Cancino *et al.* (1978) and Wode (1981), progress through the stages is gradual, each new rule being used more frequently over time and in a greater number of contexts. The concept of implicational scale will be returned to in the discussion of variation in Chapters 4 and 5; negation also figures in Chapter 4 which looks in more detail at some of the work by Cancino *et al.* (1978).

Overall these negation studies demonstrate clear orders of acquisition over time; they are genuinely longitudinal. Some studies find more detail, others collapse stages into one; none find forms that are dramatically out of step, say *"don't"* + *Verb* occurring early, or anaphoric "no" occurring late. Is this order influenced by L1 transfer? Cancino *et al.* (1978, p. 210) found that their first stage *"no"* + *Verb* was not only similar to L1 acquisition but also 'to the way the negative is formed in Spanish, for instance "(yo) no tengo agua" '. Wode (1981) attributes the *"be"* + *"not"* stage III and the imperative and post-Verbal negation of Stage IV to the German L1 of his L2 learners. Ravem (1968), however, found his Norwegian-speaking child producing *"not"* + *Verb Phrase* rather than *Verb* + *"not"*, as happens in Norwegian. Hyltenstam (1977) found his 160 learners of Swedish could be fitted into the same scale despite their 35 L1s. Stauble (1984) found overall similarities between Japanese and Spanish learners; the main difference was the use of both "no" and "not" by early Japanese learners compared to "no" for Spanish. The effects of the L1 seem to be minimal.

There is, then, a common sequence of L2 acquisition, at least for the three languages reported. According to Wode (1981), this sequence includes the specific developmental structures *Neg + X*, as in "No the sun shining", and *Subject Neg Verb Phrase*, as in "I no want envelope", which universally occur in studies of L1 acquisition across languages as diverse as Latvian and Hungarian, and in studies of L2 acquisition of English and German as well as in pidgin and creole languages. As Felix (1984, pp. 135–6) puts it, 'Why is it that children use sentence-external negation, even though there are no such constructions in the speech they hear? What motivates the child to create sentences such as "Tommy no like milk" in the absence of any input forcing such a construction?' There is evidence for a common grammar at particular stages of language development, more or less regardless of L1 or L2.

2.3 EXPLANATIONS FOR STAGES OF SECOND LANGUAGE ACQUISITION

This chapter has used the areas of grammatical morphemes and negation to support the claim of SLA research that there is a sequence of syntactic development for L2 learners. While we have chosen in this chapter the two areas of syntax that have perhaps been most explored, research with a variety of constructions came to similar conclusions; some will be seen in later chapters; others can be found in standard broad introductions such as Larsen-Freeman and Long (1991) or Ellis (1985a).

The answer to the acquisition question must concern the means by which the learner acquires a second language rather than simply stating the stages through which the learner develops. However useful a description of the learner's stages may be, it is only one of many types of evidence that could be used. This is not the view in much SLA research, where sequence is often taken as having a value in its own right. To take a representative quotation, 'Researchers have finally discovered the major reason behind such apparently intractable errors: the third person "-s" and *has* appear relatively late in the order in which learners naturally acquire linguistic structures' (Dulay *et al.*, 1982, pp. 200–1). But the order of acquisition is not the reason behind errors; it is a generalisation about errors which still lacks a reason. To me, such remarks are more like Newton announcing that apples fall to the ground than the discovery of the theory of gravity – describing one limited instance rather than explaining it. The discovery of an order of acquisition is finding some data; the researcher's job is to explain the cause of this order – to postulate a theory of gravity rather than a theory of apples falling. The existence of L2 sequences is no more than an interesting fact, a complex fact it is true, but nevertheless crying out for an explanation.

Some possible explanations can be illustrated from Ellis (1985a), who uses the example of the developmental structure *"no" + Verb Phrase*, as in "No finish book", to show how the same fact might be explained by:

- a *transfer strategy* from languages such as Spanish which have pre-verbal negation and null subject sentences;
- a *production strategy* of dropping subjects but having auxiliaryless negation before the verb;
- an *acquisition strategy* that reflects a universal part of the human mind;
- an *interactional strategy* in which the learner repeats part of the preceding sentence with "no" in front of it.

Other types of strategy will be discussed in Chapter 6.

Felix (1987) is an advocate for explaining the negative sequence through the idea of acquisition strategy; 'the basic developmental pattern . . . is seen as something that specific properties of human mental organisation impose upon the acquisition process'. At one level this is a truism; if the sequence is not caused by the environment (and clearly the negative forms such as *Neg X* that are peculiar to L2 learners are not heard by them in native speech), what else could it be but the product of the human mind? At another level this explanation is imprecise; the bases for production, transfer, and interaction are indeed all somewhere in the mind; but attributing the sequence to the human mind is only the first step towards finding an explanation, as it fails to specify which part of the mind is involved and how. Cognitive explanations in terms of aspects of the mind need to be made precise; the mind is unlikely to directly store the information that "no" should precede "be" when learning a second language; such syntactic details presumably derive from general properties that affect other aspects of the grammar. An explanation for order of development in psychological terms will be discussed in Chapter 4.

To return to grammatical morphemes, a further possibility put forward by Hakuta (1974) follows up the explanation in terms of semantic complexity suggested by Brown (1973) by bringing in ideas that the learner already knows in the L1: 'a morpheme containing a new semantic notion (i.e. number, definite/nondefinite) will be acquired later than a morpheme expressing an already-existent notion' (Hakuta, 1974). Frequency has also been suggested as an explanation for the sequence of grammatical morphemes by Larsen-Freeman (1976), who found a link between the sequence and the frequency with which the morphemes occurred in the speech of the parents of the L1 children that Brown studied. While the sequence may reflect properties of the language input the learner encounters, as we saw with Perkins and Larsen-Freeman (1975), learning inside or outside a classroom seems to make surprisingly little difference despite the different types of input. Pica (1985) nevertheless found that a taught group were better at plural "-s" and third person "-s" than an untaught group, but worse at "-ing". Lightbown (1987) showed that the surprisingly high scores of the early learners on "-ing" and auxiliary "-s" with pronouns reflected the prominence given to "-ing" and pronoun + third person "-s" in the first stages of teaching. Explanations based on the frequency in the input need more precise information about the statistical properties of speech addressed to L2 learners in various situations. However, even conceding that frequency is a crucial factor, there is still the need to provide an explanation *why* frequency is important to learning. VanPatten (1984) suggests that some morphemes are more redundant communicatively than others and so the learners start with the morphemes which are most essential to communication.

2.4   THE CONCEPT OF STAGE

A problem that is little discussed in the L2 research is the concept of stage. From similarities such as those for negation, Felix (1984, p. 135) concludes 'language acquisition proceeds in developmental stages' and 'the sequence of stages is ordered'. But what *is* a stage? Ingram (1989) finds six meanings of "stage" in L1 acquisition research, ranging from *continuous stage* in which a measure such as age is used to compare learners, to *plateau stage* where a characteristic behaviour remains constant, to *co-occurrence stage* where two or more arbitrary behaviours overlap, to *succession stage* in which one group of behaviours is succeeded by another group, to *principle* and *implicational stages* when several different behaviours are related by one principle or when one aspect of behaviour necessarily implies another. The stages used in SLA research are essentially *post hoc*; the researcher works them out from the data rather than searching the data for forms that support a prior hypothesis. The L2 grammatical morphemes research started with 'continuous' stages and used the acquisitional hierarchy to group behaviours together into 'co-occurrence' stages where several grammatical features were employed; these were not, however, related to a 'principle' stage. Milon's work with negation could indeed be seen in terms of 'co-occurrence' stages in that he attempts complete grammars for the L2 learner for a moment in time. The remaining research uses either 'succession' stages in describing how one type of behaviour succeeds another, whether completely replacing it or gradually increasing in frequency, or *post hoc* 'co-occurrence' stages. Proper explanations of the stages of L2 development would seem to invite principle-based stages if they are to provide us with more interesting insights. SLA research needs to consider why the sequence of stages is so important to L2 acquisition, particularly when the unique feature of second language acquisition is that there is no common final stage at which all L2 learners have the same knowledge.

2.5   SYNTACTIC ASPECTS OF GRAMMATICAL MORPHEME AND NEGATION RESEARCH

The types of syntax involved in negation research and grammatical morphemes research are in some ways complementary. Morphemes are seen as physical forms realised in speech at certain points in the sentence. Negation is mostly seen as short formulas specifying the nature and sequence of the items that can be used, whether morphemes, words or phrases or the insertion of a negative element into particular positions in the sentence. *"Don't" + Verb* is a formula stating that negation consists of the item "don't" followed by any main Verb. *Subject + Neg + Verb Phrase* is a formula that negation consists of an NP followed by any negative element followed by any Verb Phrase. Both areas of research tend to treat language as formulas or 'structures' specifying the sequence and variation of elements, based on the phrase structure model mentioned in the last chapter. Though still a commonplace in language teaching, such formulas are intrinsically limited as a theory of syntax. On the one hand, they do not make large enough generalisations, a description of a language ending up as a vast list of structures, say the 50,000 'structural features' suggested by Belasco (1971), something that would be virtually impossible for any learner to master.

   On the other hand they are too superficial, being concerned with the surface order of elements rather than the deeper forms of syntax to be seen in later chapters. In much of this research, syntax is not seen as an abstract system of rules in an I-language sense; negation only means the physical presence of negative elements in a sample of language. The research does not deal for the most part with concepts of negation that can be related to current linguistics but with the notion of structures or patterns in the structuralist tradition. Exceptions are the work by Milon (1974) and Hyltenstam (1977). Clahsen (1988) provides an alternative explanation for more or less the same negation facts within the UG model to be described in Chapter 9.

2.6 OBSERVATIONAL DATA IN SECOND LANGUAGE ACQUISITION RESEARCH

In methodological terms, much of the negation research has relied on transcripts of learners' speech elicited in one way or another, which we shall call *observational data*; exceptions are the negative insertion test in Hyltenstam (1977) and the informal tests in Wode (1981). Grammatical morpheme research similarly relied chiefly on observations of learners' sentences, albeit elicited by testing instruments; one exception is the battery of tasks in Larsen-Freeman (1976). The advantage of such observational data is that at best they provide clear and unchallengeable evidence of natural unadulterated speech or writing; no one can dispute what Wode's children or Dulay and Burt's subjects actually said, however much they may want to challenge the researchers' interpretation of this. The disadvantages, however, are many. One is that such data only reveal the learner's ability to produce speech or writing, not whether he or she can understand or read it. It may be dangerous to take what the learner says as a sign of what the learner understands. What can we safely assume from the learners who said "I'm not missed it" about the ways that they understood a sentence such as "I haven't seen him yet"? Comprehension may indeed precede production, as argued in first language acquisition by Fraser, Bellugi and Brown (1963); but they might also form distinct processes, as suggested by Clark and Hecht (1983).

A further difficulty is the representativeness of the sample. Caution must be maintained over the actual elicitation techniques. It is one thing to observe children in their natural situation, as in Wode's research; it is another to look at samples of speech elicited through techniques such as the BSM as these alter the context of speech in several ways. Even the standard recorded interview technique provides a slanted view of language because an interview, like any register of language, has particular rules of its own, such as the right of interviewers to guide the conversation through leading questions while refusing to reveal their own opinions.

It is comparatively easy to test frequent forms through natural data as large numbers will appear in any sample: the grammatical morphemes research was useful as it is virtually impossible to construct an English sentence without using several of them. It is more difficult to search observational data for less frequent forms, say negative passive questions, which might well be vital to a complete understanding of the learner's competence. Hence observational data work reasonably when they are used to investigate simple, frequent constructions; they fall down when the researcher wants to know about less common forms.

A distortion may also be imposed on the data by the concept of 'obligatory context'. Spotting an obligatory context is subjective; to know which morpheme is missing, the researcher has to guess what meaning the learner has in mind, sometimes far from easy. Deciding "that book" 'means' "that is a book" rather than "I want that book" or "those are books" means knowing or deducing the whole context of situation in which the sentence is embedded, a difficult enough task with native adults let alone with language learners. In effect most L2 researchers appear to have restricted Brown's (1973) fourfold definition of obligatory context to linguistic context rather than looking at the discourse in which the sentence is found.

Learners might also get things half right or might oversupply particular items. Pica (1984) compares scoring by obligatory context with scoring by 'target-like use', which adds to the scores for obligatory context results from suppliance in non-obligatory contexts; she arrives at rather different scores for the same people, e.g. a person who supplies a 'misformed' past irregular three times would score 50 per cent on an obligatory context scale, 0 per cent on a target-like use scale. Both such possibilities ignore the independent grammars assumption in that they deny the learner's grammar is an independent system; they measure it by native standards of obligatory context rather than its own. Error Analysis often fell back on contrasting L2 learners with natives rather than looking at them in their own right. The grammatical morphemes research indeed tried various ways of scoring the presence of grammatical morphemes so that the score is not sheer occurrence, as suggested above, but a score that is weighted in various ways. The different scoring schemes have not been described here as they are a topic of immense complexity, but of largely historical interest; discussions can be found in Dulay, Burt, & Krashen (1983) and Hatch (1978).

The concept of avoidance is also a problem. Learners' avoidance of particular forms was first spotted by Schachter (1974) in connection with Error Analysis: L2 learners are probably aware which aspects of the L2 they find difficult and therefore try to avoid them. Schachter found that Japanese learners of English make few mistakes with English relative clauses even though Japanese is very different from English in this respect; the reason is that they *avoid* using relative clauses in English. Any natural L2 data may under-represent the learner's problems and hence distort the description of competence. This is partly prevented by putting the learners in situations where they cannot avoid particular forms – the aim of tests like the Bilingual Syntax Measure; their speech is no longer natural communication but artificial to some extent.

Above all, the learners' speech is an example of 'performance', that is, a sample of 'the actual use of language in concrete situations', rather than of their underlying 'competence', their knowledge of the language (Chomsky, 1965b, p. 4); it is a sample of the processes of speech not a direct reflection of their state of knowledge. This line of L2 research is indeed for this reason sometimes called 'performance analysis'. It is clear that many other factors than linguistic competence are relevant to performance; the speakers' memory processes, their interpretation of the sociological situation, their physiological limitations, and so on, all influence their speech, and all these may be affected differently in an L2. The occurrence of a particular form in data collected from actual speech does not necessarily prove the existence of a particular grammatical rule in the learner's mind. It might, for example, be a phrase that the learner has memorised by heart purely as a sequence of sounds; or it might be a sentence that is accidentally right because the learner was really trying to say something else. A learner's sentence such as "No my turn" may mirror interlanguage grammar rather poorly. Disentangling the part played by linguistic competence in an actual example of speech from all the performance processes is a hard, though necessary, process. There is a danger of attributing something to language knowledge, or to lack of language knowledge, which is in fact due to some other factor. L2 performance should at least be compared with L1 performance rather than with L1 competence. Whatever the linguist may assume about the knowledge of native speakers, it is still necessary to know how natives employ a form in speech to be able to compare like with like. Logically, information is needed, for example, whether native speakers themselves ever leave out grammatical morphemes or produce malformed negatives in discourse, rather than assuming their performance totally reflects their competence; British undergraduates, for instance, are prone to leave out bound grammatical morphemes in examination essays!

It is irrelevant to the knowledge question whether a linguist's single sentence example such as "John is eager to please" has ever actually been said: what counts is whether the sentence can be described by the rules of a native speaker's grammar. The context for the sentence is virtually irrelevant; the important question is whether the grammar generates the sentence. This poses a severe problem for the use of observational data, particularly when they are not the product of finished speakers of the language but of learners; the object of study is not the actual sentences that the learner produces but the underlying knowledge system to which these have a complex relationship. Further discussion of observational data can be found in Cook (1986; 1990a). Observational data nevertheless remain perhaps the best evidence for acquisition studies, provided that the chain of interpretation between performance and competence is remembered. Transcripts of large amounts of L2 learners' language are now available from sources such as the CHILDES project (MacWhinney, 1991), or the Longman Corpus of Learner English (available from Longman, Harlow, Essex).

This chapter has shown how SLA research developed the ideas and methodology it had largely taken from 1960s linguistics. Its prime concern was to establish sequences of acquisition, usually independent of those in the L1. While these were held to reflect processes going on in the minds of the learners, more attention was in fact paid to the sequences themselves than to their explanation, leaving the way open for the broader L2 models to be described in the next two chapters. Its extreme dismissal of the role of the L1 was in part a reaction to the notion of transfer as incorporated in Contrastive Analysis and habit-formation theory. At its best, this research laid a solid foundation of observations of learners' speech on which other research would rely; it established sequences of acquisition that appeared to be grounded on specifically linguistic facts. At its worst, it limited the scope of SLA research to the study of certain types of learner performance rather than the investigation of their linguistic competence, and it chose to follow a limited concept of syntactic structure unrelated to contemporary linguistics.

3 The Input Hypothesis Model

The next three chapters look at the ways in which more general theories of second language acquisition have drawn on the type of syntactic evidence and the view of sequence of acquisition discussed in the previous chapter. This chapter is concerned with the Input Hypothesis proposed by Stephen Krashen. During the late 1970s Krashen put forward an account of SLA first known as the Monitor Model after its main claim about the role of monitoring in language learning (Krashen, 1979). In the early 1980s this was expanded into a broader-based model, described in Krashen (1981; 1982). The aspect of the model that became most developed was termed the *Input Hypothesis*, the title of Krashen's last major theoretical book (Krashen, 1985a) and the name by which the model will be known here. From the beginning, Krashen's ideas have been the subject of controversy. The discussion here does not follow all their ramifications but concentrates on the Input Hypothesis as put forward in Krashen (1985a), working back where necessary to earlier formulations. Initially the model will be presented as far as possible through the evidence and claims that he makes himself.

3.1 THE FIVE HYPOTHESES

The theory consists of five linked 'hypotheses': input, acquisition/learning, monitor, natural order, and affective filter; these are summarised on p.55 below. The Input Hypothesis is simply stated: 'humans acquire language in only one way – by understanding messages or by receiving "comprehensible input" ' (Krashen, 1985a, p. 2). That is to say, language acquisition depends upon trying to comprehend what other people are saying. Provided that the learner hears meaningful speech and endeavours to understand it, acquisition will occur. L2 acquisition fails to occur when the learner is deprived of meaningful language, say by classroom activities that concentrate on the forms of language rather than on meaning, or by a psychological block that prevents otherwise useful language from gaining access to the learner's mind.

Listening is the crucial activity. L2 learners acquire a new language by hearing it in contexts where the meaning of sentences is made plain to them. Speaking is either unnecessary or is positively harmful; active knowledge of how to use an L2 never comes from production; its only positive virtue may be that it provokes other people into speaking themselves, thus providing more listening material for the learner to work on. 'Speaking is a

result of acquisition and not its cause' (Krashen, 1985a, p. 2). This emphasis on listening at the expense of production distinguishes Krashen's theory
from most others, for instance from 'communicative' teaching theories,
which stress the importance of the learner speaking.

Various qualifications have to be made to this broad claim. Krashen
distinguishes knowledge that is acquired from knowledge that is learnt –
'the *Acquisition/Learning Hypothesis*'. The process of L2 'acquisition' uses
the language faculty in essentially the same unconscious way as first
language acquisition; it leads to the ability to actually use the L2. In the
process of language 'learning', however, knowledge is gained through
conscious understanding of the rules of language. Hence 'learning' occurs
in the second language, but is extremely rare in the first; it is furthermore
only available to L2 learners who are capable of understanding rules, say
those above a certain age. Krashen accepts that other things than comprehensible input can lead to language knowledge of a kind; but he denies that
the form such knowledge takes is capable of being the basis for normal use
of language. If you learn the set of English pronouns by heart or you
consciously understand the various meanings of English tenses, you indeed
know something about English. But this 'learnt' knowledge cannot be used
to express something that you actually want to say.

'Learnt' knowledge comes into play through the 'Monitoring' of speech;
Monitoring provides a conscious check on what the speaker is saying.
Anything the learner wants to say comes from acquired knowledge; learnt
knowledge can Monitor this speech production before or after actual
output. Learners who use their acquired knowledge to say "He is going"
can check against their learnt knowledge whether "he" is the appropriate
pronoun, whether the present continuous is the appropriate tense, whether
"is" should agree with "he", and so on. Monitoring uses learnt knowledge
as a quality check on speech originating from acquired knowledge. It takes
place 'before we speak or write or after [self-correction]' (Krashen, 1982,
p. 15). The '*Monitor Hypothesis*' claims that consciously 'learnt' knowledge is only available for Monitoring rather than usable in other ways. The
following diagram encapsulates the crucial relationships:

The Monitor Model of L2 production (adapted from Krashen, 1981, p. 7)

The extent to which a given learner uses Monitoring depends on several factors: tasks that focus on 'form' rather than meaning, such as 'fill-in-the-blank' tasks, will encourage Monitoring; the personality of learners varies between those who under-use Monitoring, over-use Monitoring, or use Monitoring optimally. Note that 'Monitoring' with a capital letter is distinct from 'monitoring' with a small 'm' found in first language use, because it employs consciously known and verbalisable rules rather than 'feel' for language. It is important to realise Krashen's firm belief that 'learnt' knowledge can never be converted into 'acquired' knowledge; learning a rule for the past tense consciously never allows one to develop an unconscious ability to use the past tense in speech; Krashen's theory 'is a "no interface" position with respect to the relationship between acquisition and learning' (Krashen, 1985a, p. 38).

To be useful to the learner, the input must be neither too difficult to understand nor too easy. This is conceptualised by Krashen in terms of the learner's current level, called i, and the level that the learner will get to next, called $i + 1$. For the learner to progress rather than remain static, the input has always to be slightly beyond the level at which he or she is completely at home; the gap between the learner's i and the $i + 1$ that he or she needs is bridged by information drawn from the situation and from the learner's previous experience. 'We also use context, our knowledge of the world, our extra-linguistic competence to help us understand' (Krashen, 1982, p. 21). Comprehensible input relies on the actual language forms being incomprehensible, not the total message. This concept has indeed been called 'incomprehensible input' because the learners always have to struggle to derive meaning for the parts they do *not* understand rather than understanding the sentence completely (White, 1987). The learners progress continually from stage i to stage $i + 1$ along a pre-set series of stages. So the model requires a precise developmental scale on which i and $i + 1$ can be located. This scale invokes the natural order hypothesis: 'we acquire the rules of language in a predictable order, some rules tending to come early and some late' (Krashen, 1985a, p. 1). The developmental scale is made up of 'rules' treated as discrete items learnt in sequence. It is largely based on the sequences of acquisition which were discussed in the previous chapter.

But it is still necessary to explain why acquisition is not equally successful for all L2 learners, even when they receive apparently identical comprehensible input; 'comprehension is a *necessary* condition for language acquisition but it is not sufficient' (Krashen, 1982, p. 66): something more than comprehensible input is needed. For acquisition to take place, the learner has to be able to absorb the appropriate parts of the input. There can be 'a mental block that prevents acquirers from fully utilizing the comprehensible input they receive for language acquisition' (Krashen, 1985, p. 3). This block, called 'the affective filter', might be because 'the acquirer is unmotivated, lacking in self-confidence, or anxious' (Krashen, 1985a, p. 3). The *Affective Filter Hypothesis* ascribes variation between learners to their psychological states. If the filter is 'up', comprehensible input cannot get through; if it is 'down', they can make effective use of it. In particular the reason why younger learners are better at L2 acquisition over the long term is that 'the affective filter gains dramatically in strength at around puberty' (Krashen, 1985a, p. 13). Older learners are cut off from proper access to comprehensible input by the increased strength of the filter.

The following diagram captures these relationships. It is adapted from Gregg (1984), who combines Krashen's diagrams of production and acquisition into one:

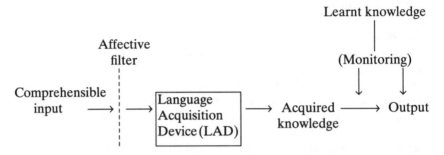

The Input Hypothesis Model of L2 learning and production (adapted from Krashen, 1982, pp. 16 and 32; and Gregg, 1984)

In Krashen's words, 'comprehensible input and the strength of the filter are the true causes of second language acquisition' (Krashen, 1982, p. 33), one positively, one negatively.

The Language Acquisition Device (LAD) seen in Chapter 1 features prominently in the model, though it is seldom discussed in detail. To Krashen, the LAD is made up of the natural language learning abilities of the human mind, totally available in L1 acquisition, available in L2 acquisition according to the level of the filter; this construct is called the 'organiser' in Dulay *et al.* (1982). Language input comes into the mind; LAD processes it and produces an internal grammar of the language. This seems equivalent to the black-box LAD from Chomsky (1964), as Krashen (1981, p. 110) suggests, though without the evaluation measure. Krashen (1985a, p. 25) updates this to the later Chomskyan image of 'the mental organ devoted to language'. During 'acquisition' the innate mental structures of LAD treat the input in various predetermined ways to derive knowledge of language. The process of 'learning', unlike the process of 'acquisition', uses 'faculties of mind outside the LAD' (Krashen, 1985b, p. 30).

On the other hand the first language does not bulk large in the model, either in production or learning. Krashen allocates to the L1 the fall-back role suggested by Newmark and Reibel (1968). Transfer from L1 to L2 is due to ignorance rather than to the inevitable transfer of habits: L2 learners often want to say more in the L2 than they can express, because of their low knowledge of the L2. The gap between their intentions and their speech is filled by rules borrowed from the L1; 'the L1 may "substitute" for the acquired L2 as an utterance initiator when the performer has to produce in the target language but has not acquired enough of the L2 to do this' (Krashen, 1981, p. 67). The causes of such transfer are that the learner has been forced to speak too soon, contrary to the initial need for the learner to be silent, or has been asked to perform an inappropriate task such as translation (Dulay *et al.*, 1982, p. 119).

The **Input Hypothesis**: 'humans acquire language in only one way – by understanding messages or by receiving "comprehensible input" ' (Krashen, 1985a, p. 2)

The **Acquisition/Learning Hypothesis**: 'adults have two distinctive ways of developing competences in second languages . . . *acquisition*, that is, by using language for real communication . . . *learning* . . . "knowing about" language' (Krashen and Terrell, 1983, p. 26)

The **Monitor Hypothesis**: 'conscious learning . . . can only be used as a *Monitor*, or an editor' (Krashen and Terrell, 1983, p. 30)

The **Natural Order Hypothesis**: 'we acquire the rules of language in a predictable order' (Krashen, 1985a, p. 1)

The **Affective Filter Hypothesis**: 'a mental block, caused by affective factors . . . that prevents input from reaching the language acquisition device' (Krashen, 1985a, p. 100)

Krashen's Five Hypotheses

3.2 KRASHEN'S EVIDENCE FOR THE INPUT HYPOTHESIS

Let us look at the evidence in favour of the Input Hypothesis cited by Krashen (1985a), supplemented when necessary from other sources.

(a) People speak to children acquiring their first language in special ways
Krashen (1985a) reviews some 1970s work on 'motherese' or 'caretaker talk', that is to say, speech addressed to children acquiring their first language. Motherese concentrates on the 'here and now' rather than on the

abstract and remote; this, coupled with its syntactic simplicity (Cross, 1977), gives it the qualities of comprehensible input. Motherese is not 'finely-tuned' to an exact $i + 1$ level one step ahead of the child, but 'roughly tuned' to the children's level, termed by Krashen elsewhere the 'net' – 'the speaker "casts a net" of structure around your current level, your i' (Krashen and Terrell, 1983, p. 33).

(b) People speak to L2 learners in special ways
Some L2 learners encounter special language through the 'teacher talk' addressed to students in the classroom. Krashen (1981) claims that this is slower, is well-formed, has shorter sentences (Henzl, 1973), and has simpler syntax (Gaies, 1977). The special variety of 'foreigner-talk' spoken by natives to foreigners outside the classroom has similar characteristics; foreigner-talk is simplified syntactically (Freed, 1980), and shows signs of adaptation to the foreigner's level (Krashen, 1981, p. 131). These characteristics, while not the direct cause of acquisition, greatly improve the comprehensibility of the input; 'the teacher, the more advanced second language performer, and the native speaker in casual conversation, in attempting to communicate with the second language acquirer, may unconsciously make the "100 or maybe 1000 alterations in his speech" that provide the acquirer with optimal input for language acquisition' (Krashen, 1981, p. 132).

(c) L2 learners often go through an initial Silent Period
Krashen (1982) reviews case histories that show that children often stay silent in the L2 at first and start to talk at a later stage. Ervin-Tripp (1972), for example, found that English-speaking children did not volunteer speech in French-speaking schools for a prolonged period; according to Dulay, *et al.* (1982, p. 23), Hakuta (1974) 'was unable to begin his study of a Japanese child Uguisu until some five months after the subject had been exposed to English because she produced almost no speech before that time'. New overseas students at Essex University where I teach start every academic year by complaining that their children will not speak English and end the year by complaining that their children speak English better than they do. During this Silent Period in the L2, 'the child is building up competence in the second language via listening, by understanding the language around him' (Krashen, 1982, p. 27).

(d) The comparative success of younger and older learners reflects provision of comprehensible input
Krashen *et al.* (1982) analyse a large number of studies to come up with the now widely held view that adults are better at short-term L2 learning, children at long-term L2 learning. The reason is that 'older acquirers progress more quickly in early stages because they obtain more compre-

hensible input, while younger acquirers do better in the long run because of their lower affective filters' (Krashen, 1985a, p. 12). This is claimed to be because older learners have greater experience of the world, can use the L1 to overcome communication problems in the L2 more easily, and are better at conversational management.

(e) The more comprehensible input the greater the L2 proficiency
Some research results show that a larger amount of exposure to the L2 leads to proficiency. Krashen (1982) points out that students' length of residence in the foreign country correlates with cloze test scores (Murakmi, 1980) and with dictation (Oller, Perkins and Murakmi, 1980); the length of 'time abroad' of the learners goes with the level of foreign language proficiency (Carroll, 1967). Krashen (1989) also claims that reading skills improve according to the amount of reading done, and that vocabulary acquisition in the L1 is helped by listening to stories. Sheer exposure without comprehension is often useless to acquisition; watching television in the L2 will only be useful if it is in some way comprehensible.

(f) Lack of comprehensible input delays language acquisition
Children of deaf or blind parents are sometimes delayed in language development (Long, 1983) because of the lack of appropriate comprehensible input.

(g) Teaching methods work according to the extent that they use comprehensible input
Teaching methods that are comprehension-based, such as Total Physical Response (TPR) (Asher, 1986) and the other listening-first methods presented in Winitz (1981), have, Krashen claims, been shown to have clear advantages over traditional audiolingual methods. This is because they make use of comprehensible input, not only in the spoken language but also in the written; 'an approach that provides substantial quantities of comprehensible input will do much better than any of the older approaches' (Krashen, 1982, p. 30).

(h) Immersion teaching is successful because it provides comprehensible input
Immersion language teaching uses a second language as the medium of instruction in the school, most famously in French immersion schools in English-speaking Canada; 'it is the comprehensible input factor that is responsible for the success of immersion' (Krashen, 1985a, p. 17). Krashen finds a similar effect in 'sheltered' classes where non-native university students are taught academic material in circumstances designed to make it comprehensible to them.

(i) Bilingual programmes succeed to the extent that they provide comprehensible input

Bilingual teaching maintains the use of the mother-tongue alongside the L2; one current example is the maintenance of the three languages of Singapore spoken by its inhabitants (Chinese, Tamil, Bahasa Malaysia) alongside English in the schools. The successful programmes are, according to Krashen, those that provide comprehensible input.

Linguistics and the Input Hypothesis Model

Krashen is proposing a general theory of second language acquisition that attempts to answer the three questions posed in Chapter 1. He suggests that knowledge of language in L2 users takes two forms: acquired and learnt knowledge. Such knowledge is created by two separate processes: 'acquisition' using the natural built-in processes of the mind, and 'learning' using conscious rational processes. The use of the L2 can involve a distinct process of Monitoring which brings the speaker's learnt knowledge to bear on the sentences produced by acquired knowledge.

In many ways Krashen's answers are within the general agenda set by linguistics. The division into acquired and learnt knowledge reflects the division of the mind into modular faculties; the language faculty is separate from other faculties, such as the number faculty or the faculty of mathematics (Chomsky, 1980a). Linguists often assume that language itself is learnt only through the language faculty, without utilising other faculties or general learning abilities. The rules of a second language might be apprehended as conscious information through other faculties of the mind than spontaneous language learning as well as through the usual language faculty route, for example by a linguist working with a language he or she does not speak. Krashen's distinction between acquired knowledge and learnt knowledge is thus a variant on a familiar linguistics theme. Similarly Krashen makes the Chomskyan Language Acquisition Device (LAD) a core element in his model. The fact that acquisition relies on built-in abilities of the mind reflects an assumption of the Chomskyan theory already seen in preceding chapters in Selinker's concept of 'latent language structure' or Wode's universal strategies of the human mind.

The function of LAD is indeed to turn language input into a grammar of the language. The Chomskyan LAD, however, works independently of the features of the input. The point of this conceptualisation is to discover the properties of LAD itself, not the properties of the input. But Krashen is concerned with the properties of the input, rather than the processes of the mind; he leaves the process of acquisition as mysterious as ever. To Krashen, L2 acquisition is driven by the language environment rather than by the mind and it is limited by the filter. The conditions for successful acquisition matter more to him than the processes of acquisition. The model does not interest itself in how comprehensible input is dealt with by the mind. At best, certain features of language, such as grammatical morphemes, seem to have a natural order of acquisition built-in to the mind, which is not so much explained by the Input Hypothesis as taken for granted.

Krashen claims that learners make sense of comprehensible input by extra-linguistic means. Gregg (1984) uses Chomsky's argument for the stimulus-free nature of language to show that there are no situational aids which would actually help in acquiring, say, the third person singular "-s". McLaughlin (1987) points out that use of feedback is incompatible with the claims for the Silent Period since those dealing with the learners would not know the language level of their silent listeners well enough to provide adequate feedback. White (1987) accepts that some non-linguistic information is needed but questions 'Krashen's implication that this is the *only* way we can make use of input which is beyond the current grammar'; she argues that the passive construction could be learnt by lexical generalisation independent of contextual clues and that the 'triggering' of grammatical change, discussed in Chapter 9, is not driven by meaning. In many ways Krashen is proposing a view of language acquisition similar to the interactionist L1 model of Bruner (1983), which sees parents as providing carefully controlled language for their offspring within the context of social interactions. Krashen's model differs in that the process relies on comprehension alone rather than on two-way conversations.

Krashen is also proposing something very different from the hypothesis-testing model put forward in the 1960s, which was often linked to LAD, as described in Chapter 1. In the Input Hypothesis model, the learner does not test hypotheses but progresses along a pre-ordained sequence. Hypothesis-testing necessitates trying out the rules and getting feedback; hence it was abandoned by linguists after it became obvious that such feedback rarely occurs in L1 acquisition (Brown and Hanlon, 1970). Comprehensible input, however, is effective regardless of whether the learner ever speaks or gets feedback. In a way, Krashen is closer to the more recent model of Universal Grammar (UG), to be described in Chapter 9, which also does not rely on feedback. But the Input Hypothesis nevertheless relies on specific properties of the input where UG theory uses characteristics to be found in any spoken language. Krashen makes no suggestions about the internal structure of the Language Acquisition Device: the black box is still as mysterious as ever. True as this may have been of the LAD of the 1960s, the Universal Grammar equivalent of the 1980s made very detailed claims about the nature of the acquisition device.

The linguistic content of Krashen's work is based almost entirely on the phrase structure analysis and grammatical morphemes discussed in Chapter 2. Hence it is open to the same objection of lack of coverage; it hardly begins to cover linguistic competence in terms of syntax, and seldom mentions phonology or vocabulary. The analysis is based on treating rules as items: you learn one rule after another, as you learn one vocabulary item after another. Rules do not form a total system – a grammar – but are separate items. All language learning, not just vocabulary, is then acquiring discrete items one at a time rather than acquiring an interlocking grammatical competence. This seems to ignore the very nature of syntax: whatever syntactic theory one adopts, the distinctive feature of syntax is that it forms an overall system rather than a list of items. This point will reoccur in the discussion of the Multidimensional Model in the next chapter. It is central to the independent-grammars assumption that rules of the target language are *not* learnt additively but that each stage of interlanguage has a system of its own.

The Evidence for the Input Hypothesis

Let us examine the support for the Input Hypothesis that 'comprehensible input (CI) is the essential environmental ingredient in language acquisition' (Krashen, 1989). In one sense comprehensible input is so blindingly obvious that it has to be true; except for occasional off-beat language teaching methods, it is unimaginable that the constant provision of incomprehensible speech actively promotes language learning. In this sense comprehensible input is simply an overall requirement within any theory of SLA. The chief difficulty, pointed out by McLaughlin (1987) for example, is the lack of definition of comprehensible input itself. In a way it is circular: anything that leads to acquisition must be comprehensible input, so comprehensible input is whatever leads to acquisition. The theory lacks an explicit independent specification of the linguistic forms used in comprehensible input and of the types of situational help that make them comprehensible – its most central aspect.

Another difficulty is the implied relationship between listening and speaking. In this model, acquisition depends on listening; it is not important whether the learner speaks or not. Gregg (1984) points to a lack of evidence for the claim that speaking does not help acquisition, compared to the oft-held belief that practice in speaking is indeed helpful to L2 acquisition; McLaughlin (1987) claims that access to one's own speech is an important source of information in a hypothesis-testing view of language. Swain (1985) argues that adequate progress in the L2 depends on interaction; listening is ineffective if it is not within a process of interactive negotiation. The actual relationship between speaking and listening is unknown. While speaking may be parasitic on listening, some theories have assumed the opposite, such as the articulatory loop theory of memory that relates internal processing to covert articulation (Baddely, 1986); Sinclair and Ellis (1992) indeed show within this framework that repeating Welsh words aloud helps their acquisition compared to silent acquisition.

Some L1 theorists insist on the initial separation of listening and speaking, and see the child's problem essentially as learning how to relate them (Clark and Hecht, 1983). Issidorides and Hulstijn (1992) show that, while L2 learners of Dutch had problems producing Dutch word order, they had little difficulty in comprehending them – the two aspects of language were distinct.

In Cook (1991a) a distinction was made between the process of *decoding* speech, in which the users utilise a code they already know to understand a message, and the process of *codebreaking* speech, in which they try to work out the code itself by understanding a message. Decoding speech has the aim of discovering the message by using processes that are already known. Codebreaking speech has the aim of discovering the processes themselves from a message. Krashen's theory conflates decoding and codebreaking; to Krashen decoding *is* codebreaking. The acquisition question and the use question are collapsed into one by equating using with acquiring.

Let us come back to the more specific evidence for the Input Hypothesis cited by Krashen. The evidence that there is special speech addressed to children in first language acquisition [claim (a)] and that lack of comprehensible input delays first language acquisition [claim (f)] is not directly relevant to SLA as it concerns L1 learning; it needs L2 evidence to be convincing.

Claim (b), that people speak to L2 learners in special ways, is probably true to some degree, even if the studies cited are not extensive. But the existence of a special variety of language addressed to learners does not show that it *helps* them to learn language; people have been speaking to dogs in special ways for thousands of years, without any of them learning to speak. There is no necessary cause-and-effect relationship between special speech and effective learning – no indication that special speech helps learners rather than being simply a conventional register. While Krashen does not claim explicitly that simplified speech causes acquisition, the weaker claim that caretaker speech helps by increasing comprehensibility is unclear without more precise details. Gregg (1984), taking account of work such as Newport (1976) with 'motherese', points out that it is not so much that speech to learners is syntactically simpler as that it is different from that addressed to native adults. White (1987) argues that simplified input may in fact deprive the learner of information vital to acquisition, an argument anticipated by language teachers who advocate the use of authentic speech in the classroom to fill gaps in the normal edited classroom language. Above all, it is never certain that it is the *comprehensibility* of the input that counts rather than its simplicity.

The initial Silent Period of L2 learners [claim (c)] is an intriguing observation about L2 learning; Gibbons (1985), however, not only found the evidence provided by Krashen unsatisfactory but also found an average Silent Period of only 15.2 days for a sample of 47 children ranging from 4:7

to 11:9 years learning English in Australia, with the Silent Period ranging in length from 0 to 56 days. A non-speaking initial period does not show the necessity of comprehensible input; it may, however, tell one a great deal about the young child's embarrassment, isolation and sheer difficulty in coping with a novel L2 environment. As Hakuta (1974) said of the Japanese child Uguisu, 'very possibly it was a matter of confidence rather than competence that she started talking'. Nor may this be unique to L2 learning situations; according to an experienced playgroup supervisor, if you take the same period of 15 days, at least one in four English-speaking children are silent in their L1 when they start attending playgroup at around two and a half years.

The differences between younger and older L2 learners [claim (d)] are plausible, if still controversial. But they are often attributed to differences in cognitive, social, or physical development; it is not clear that comprehensible input is the crucial factor. McLaughlin (1987) points out that the here-and-nowness of speech addressed to younger children should mean they actually get *more* comprehensible input than older learners, hence they should do better in the short term rather than worse.

Claim (e), that the quantity of comprehensible input matters, is difficult to sort out from claims about quantity of language exposure; no one denies that, within limits, it helps to hear more language rather than less. Claim (f) was covered with claim (a) above.

The evidence for the influence of comprehensible input on language teaching – claims (g), (h), (i) – largely consists of generalisations about complex teaching situations which involve so many factors relating to the student, the teacher, and the situation that it is impossible to separate out comprehensible input. The view that older methods ignored comprehensible input is surely incorrect; indeed, most methods of the past 30 years insisted on the importance of making the meaning of sentences clear to students, whether by the audiovisual method, the situational method, or the communicative method. Perhaps only doctrinaire audiolingualism de-emphasised comprehensible input in its structural drills, even if its advocates still asserted the priority of the passive oral skill of listening (Lado, 1964). Take the following description of the four elements in language teaching:

> First, there is a direct appeal to the ear, by which the language is acquired. Secondly this appeal is made in circumstances where there is a direct relation, ipso facto, established between the sound and the things signified . . . Thirdly the same living appeal to the ear is continuously and for a considerable length of time repeated. Fourthly the appeal is made under circumstances which cannot fail strongly to excite the attention, and to engage the sympathies of the hearer. In these four points, lies the whole plain mystery of Nature's method.

Apart from the style, little betrays that this account of the virtues of comprehensible input was not written by Krashen in 1985 but by J. S. Blackie in 1845 (cited in Howatt, 1984). Comprehensible input has been the core of many teaching methods, in spirit if not in name.

The advantages of immersion teaching [claim (i)] are currently seen as less compelling than Krashen makes out; in some cases immersion seems to lead to a fossilised classroom pidgin. Swain (1985) found many faults in immersion learners after seven years of French, despite the wealth of unarguably comprehensible input they had received. Evidence from immersion teaching is not clear-cut since the situation includes many factors of situation and of learner other than comprehensible input. The evidence for the superiority of listening-based methods [claim (h)] is striking, but does not depend directly on comprehensible input; nor have comparisons taken place between listening-based methods and so-called communicative methods, or indeed mainstream EFL methods (Cook, 1986).

3.3 EVIDENCE FOR THE OTHER HYPOTHESES

So far the Input Hypothesis has been treated separately from the other four hypotheses. Let us review the evidence for these briefly. Some such distinction as the acquisition/learning hypothesis has been held by many people. In the first half of this century, for instance Palmer (1926) proposed a distinction between the 'spontaneous' and 'studial' capacities for learning language. Undoubtedly this distinction conforms to the conscious ideas of many L2 teachers and students. Research evidence for the separation of acquisition from learning is hard to find. Krashen (1985a) and Dulay *et al.* (1982) cite none; Krashen (1982) and Krashen and Terrell (1983) cite the use of error correction in L2 teaching as relying on a separate process of 'learning'. The hypothesis is more an assumption than a discovery.

Evidence for the Monitor Hypothesis is also held to be evidence for acquisition/learning. Originally Krashen claimed Monitoring depended on availability of time, but this claim now seems to be abandoned (Krashen, 1985a, p. 22) in the face of research by Hulstjin and Hulstjin (1983) that, *inter alia*, showed that lack of time pressure was no more beneficial to learners who knew the rules explicitly than to those who did not, as described in Chapter 10. Krashen emphasises the limitations of Monitoring, and often claims that it only works for 'rules of thumb' that make sense for the learner (Krashen, 1981). Krashen (1982) discusses case histories which show Monitoring at work: a Chinese learner of English known as P, for instance, produced spontaneous mistakes in speech that she could correct according to conscious rules but made far fewer mistakes in writing. No one would deny that some learners find consciously learnt rules unhelpful, nor that real-time language use cannot depend purely on consciously learnt linguistic knowledge, as those of us who used to spend three hours on a paragraph of Latin composition will attest, nor that some consciously acquired rules cannot be converted into actual use – before typing "receive" I still have to recite "*i* before *e* except after *c* or before *g*". But such evidence does not prove that consciously learnt knowledge is useless, that all of it is available only via the Monitoring process, or that, at least for some learners, some of it does not convert into acquired knowledge. After all, many generations of students were taught English in Dutch and Scandinavian universities by studying the works of such grammarians as Jespersen, Zandvoort, and, more recently, Quirk. According to Krashen, their academic knowledge has had no effect on their ability to use English in real life situations. Yet many of these students are among the most fluent L2 speakers of English. At Essex University, all modern language undergraduates have to take a course in the linguistic description of the language, because, the teachers claim, it has an important effect on their language proficiency. The Monitor hypothesis and the claim for no-interface between acquired and learnt knowledge seem to have insufficient evidence of their own to outweigh the obvious counter-evidence.

But there are other hypotheses waiting in the wings. The Monitor Hypothesis is closely linked to the Natural Order hypothesis. As support for natural order, Krashen (1985a) cites the examples of grammatical morphemes and negation seen in the last chapter, and others such as "easy/eager to please" (Cook, 1973). Even if the sequences described in the last chapter were accepted as valid, this would still amount to some small proportion of what a full developmental scale would require, to be equivalent, say, to those described for first language acquisition in LARSP (Crystal *et al.* 1976) or in the Bristol project (Wells, 1985). Hence the actual sequence on which the *i* and *i* + *1* levels can be based is too crude to support the links between natural order and comprehensible input for more than a fraction of L2 learning at best. It is presumably true that acquiring certain aspects of language requires hearing examples of them in circumstances that help the learner to make sense of them; but there is as yet no clear L2 developmental scale that sets out the precise ladder on which *i* and *i* + *1* form rungs, as McLaughlin (1987), for example, points out.

Natural orders for grammatical morphemes are found in 'Monitor-free' conditions; unnatural orders are found when Monitoring is involved in 'pencil and paper "grammar"-type tests'. Monitoring causes an 'increase in relative rank of two morphemes, regular past and the third person singular marker' (Krashen, 1982, p. 101). Krashen does not explain *why* such a natural order occurs or why these morphemes are particularly susceptible to Monitoring; the hypothesis simply states it *does* occur. Whether or not the natural order is interfered with by Monitoring, whether or not this shows a distinction between 'acquisition' or 'learning', whether or not this requires the notion of comprehensible input, all depends on a chain of interlinked interpretations of research, never producing the bedrock on which the others can rest.

Finally the Affective Filter hypothesis takes care of any variation that has not been covered so far. The usual arguments presented by Krashen (for example, Krashen, 1981) for an Affective Filter are: aptitude goes with 'learning' and attitude goes with 'acquisition', based on Gardner and Lambert (1972); integrative motivation (the desire to take part in the target culture) goes with proficiency in situations with rich intake available (Gardner and Lambert, 1959); children have lower filters because of their difference in conceptual level (Elkind, 1970). All these claims reinterpret research carried out with other aims as evidence for a filter. For example, although Gardner and Lambert (1959) showed integrative motivation was important in high school learners in Montreal, it is Krashen's inference that this goes with an Affective Filter or with the type of language they were given in the classroom. It is possible to accept all these factors as having some effect on L2 learning without accepting the existence of a filter or a connection with comprehensible input. There is also a paradox in Krashen's reliance on the Affective Filter to explain success or failure in acquisition. The natural processes of LAD which are central to his model are independent of the filter in the first language: all children learn their first language. While it is possible to see attitudes as having a distinctive effect on the L2 process, it is hard to see why they should affect 'acquisition', which supposedly underlies 'natural' learning of both L1 and L2, rather than conscious 'learning'.

3.4 MODELS IN SECOND LANGUAGE ACQUISITION RESEARCH

As can be seen from the above, Krashen's ideas are both stimulating and frustrating. They raise expectations by suggesting simple, plausible explanations for phenomena that many L2 users recognise; they provide immediate connections with the classroom. A simple set of propositions, each of which makes sense about L2 learning and which cumulatively seem to fit together in a whole system, has great attractions. Part of the success of Krashen's model has been its sheer scope and inclusiveness. Yet the evidence for these ideas is elusive. Little direct evidence is provided for any of the five hypotheses separately; they are linked through a chain of inferences and through continual reinterpretation of pre-existing research in terms of the model rather than through research designed specifically to explore its claims. For this reason the model is like an axiom-based mathematical or theological system that makes sense in its own terms but is not verifiable in terms of the world outside, rather than a scientific theory that is testable.

Since it first appeared, Krashen's work has been the subject of impassioned attacks, perhaps because of the frustrations involved in tracking down the empirical basis for its claims. Intuitive as Krashen's theory may be, it nevertheless attracts many people dealing with L2 learning, particularly teachers. Ellis (1990a, p. 57) talks of 'the lucidity, simplicity, and explanatory power of Krashen's theory'. Lightbown (1984, p. 246) praises its combination of 'a linguistic theory (through its "natural order" hypothesis), social psychological theory (through its "affective filter" hypothesis), psychological learning theory (through its acquisition-learning hypothesis), discourse analysis and sociolinguistic theory (through both the comprehensible input hypothesis and the "monitor" hypothesis)'. Krashen at least attempted to make a large proposal which dealt with everything from learners' motivations to grammatical morphemes, from LAD to language teaching. Perhaps its very scope made it too easy to find fault with some aspect of it.

My own view is that Krashen's hypotheses do not, on closer inspection, conform to the three linguistic questions. The knowledge question is answered by postulating an opposition between acquired and learnt knowledge; but these are both knowledge of the L2 with no clear relationship to the co-existing L1 knowledge; L2 acquired knowledge is a paler version of L1 knowledge, weakened by the filter and its fall-back relationship to the L1. The L1 has a minor role in compensating for ignorance of the L2 rather than being a coexisting element in the mind and a continual presence in acquisition. The acquisition question is answered by describing the features of the environment and the individual's mind that help or hinder acquisition rather than the acquisition processes themselves; the relationship to the L1 system is not specified apart from the notion of fall-back. Having effectively cut the L1 off from the L2, Krashen also cuts off acquired from learnt knowledge, not allowing one to grow into the other during the process of acquisition. The use question is answered by postulating a single crucial process of production – Monitoring – rather than a full range. The overall problem is the failure to recognise that the L2 user has two languages in one mind. The Krashen theories treat L2 acquisition as an impoverished version of L1 acquisition rather than having the complexity and richness of multi-competence.

The Input Hypothesis is perhaps the most extensive and controversial model of second language acquisition. What is the status of such models in SLA research? Informally a model is an attempt to relate several aspects of some area in an overall framework; it ascends one level of explanation from a single topic of research. One type of model can be considered a metaphor; the Greeks used models of the mind based on marionettes; later models have been based on metaphors with hydraulics, mechanics, and computers. The importance of such metaphors for understanding the world is discussed by Lakoff and Johnson (1981). The black box LAD model with its input/output relationship is of this metaphorical type, as is the thought experiment of Schrodinger's Cat in physics. A metaphoric model is an aid to understanding and no more. The appeal of Krashen's model is this metaphorical mode; the arrows from acquired knowledge, the block imposed by the Affective Filter, the black box of LAD, all help us to understand L2 acquisition. A model in this sense eventually succeeds or fails according to the lively research ideas it stimulates. But, as we have seen, Krashen's ideas have led to bitter controversy rather than to the development of a research paradigm or new research.

A model can alternatively be understood as a construct in which each element is empirically verifiable; every box, every arrow, has to be supported by precise evidence. To count as a model in this sense, the Input Hypothesis would have to justify each of its elements in terms of hard evidence. But no exact definition of comprehensible input is provided, no clear way of separating acquisition from learning, no real evidence for the Monitor, no real explanation for the natural order, and so on. Though couched as scientific 'hypotheses' and seeming to draw on a mass of concrete research, the Input Hypothesis Model is too vague and too unsupported to count as an empirically verifiable model of SLA that is more than metaphoric. A contrast can be made with the Socio-educational model of Gardner (1985), which also lays out the relationship between different aspects of L2 acquisition in terms of motivation, aptitude, and the like. But each of Gardner's boxes is supported by tests specially designed to provide appropriate evidence and each of the connecting arrows has been tested mathematically for its strength. Gardner's model lies outside the scope of this book as it is psychologically rather than linguistically based; it is described briefly in Cook (1991a). But, whether one agrees with it or not, it sets a standard for model creation in that all its claims depend on actual evidence. The problem with the Input Hypothesis is how you could show it was wrong. In the comic science fiction novel *The Twilight of the Vilp* (Ableman, 1969), Professor Pidge claims that a cardboard box is a perfect model of the human mind with the origin of language being the words "Sundazil Polishing Powder" stencilled on the side. A model that has no way of being proved wrong is as scientific as Professor Pidge's.

The other general question about models in SLA research concerns their relationship with other disciplines. It is perfectly proper for SLA research to postulate theories of its own to explain its own area. It is also proper for it to offer its discoveries to other disciplines to help them solve *their* problems. So SLA research may produce information of interest to first language researchers, to cognitive psychologists, to theoretical linguists, or to language teachers. It is also appropriate for SLA research to take insights and methods from these disciplines when they are useful to it; much of the SLA research discussed so far has been indebted to the first language acquisition research of the 1960s in one way or another. But SLA research has to be cautious when it starts making claims that go outside its territory. Krashen's claims that there are two forms of language knowledge make assertions about areas that belong to the allied disciplines of philosophy, psychology and linguistics. The model assigns consciousness the particular role of Monitor; again the value of consciousness in human life is something which extends across philosophy to psychology and to linguistics. Acquiring a language and using a language are considered the same activity of utilising comprehensible input, a redraft of the core acquisition and use questions of linguistics. If an SLA model is to make claims outside its remit, they must at least be reconcilable with current models used in these areas. SLA research cannot redesign the whole of the human mind to fit its own convenience, ignoring all the disciplines that also deal with the mind.

The point of a model then is its help with understanding a complex area and with opening ways forward. In Gardner's words: 'A true test of any theoretical formulation is not only its ability to explain and account for phenomena which have been demonstrated but also its ability to provide suggestions for further investigations, to raise new questions, to promote further developments and open new horizons' (Gardner, 1985, p. 167). SLA models are useful in so far as they develop and increase our understanding of L2 learning; they hinder if they are not stated precisely enough to be be testable and if they are regarded as final solutions to be defended to the bitter end rather than as working hypotheses to be changed or dropped when necessary. The main thrust of this chapter has been that, while Krashen proposed a theory that was extremely stimulating and that provided the first attempt at wider explanation of second language acquisition, it did not have sufficient substance on which to build newer and better theories.

4 Pidgins, Creoles, and Variation

This chapter looks at models of second language acquisition in which the L2 learner is seen as functioning within society, represented here by two influential versions: models that exploit the resemblances between learner languages and pidgins and creoles; and models that emphasise the variation in the learners' use of language. The chapter then goes on to research that takes the use question as central to linguistics; how is knowledge of languages put to use? The approach mostly utilises data taken from L2 learners' speech, overlapping with that seen in Chapter 2.

4.1 PIDGINISATION AND ACCULTURATION

The preceding chapters have shown that the speech of L2 learners appears to be reduced in scope in diverse ways – they 'leave out' grammatical morphemes, they 'simplify' negation, and so on. From the late 1960s on, people began to notice similarities between the reduced language system of the L2 learner and other 'simplified' forms of language, in particular creoles and pidgins. Perhaps these resemblances are not fortuitous; pidgins are evolving language systems like interlanguages, changing from one time to another. The dynamics by which pidgins and creoles come into being and the development of the L2 learner's interlanguage might be governed by the same factors.

The overall characteristic of a pidgin is that it 'has been stripped of everything but the bare essentials necessary for communication' (Romaine, 1988, p. 24). Typically it is a contact language between two groups, neither of which speaks it as a first language, and one of which is socially dominant. Tok Pisin, for instance, evolved in New Guinea for communication between the indigenous inhabitants and the English-speaking colonials. According to Romaine (1988), pidgins rely on a constant relationship between form and meaning so that one form always carries one and the same meaning. Using her examples of Tok Pisin to illustrate pidgins in general, this leads to:

- invariable word order, with most pidgins having SVO order: "Mi tokim olsem" (I said this to them);
- a minimal pronoun system without gender or case: "Em i go long market" (he/she/it is going to market);

69

- absence of agreement markers for number or negation: "Sikspela/ wanpela man i kam" (six men/one man came);
- infrequent use of prepositions; a reduced lexicon: Tok Pisin "gras" covers English "grass", "moustache" (mausgras), "feather" (gras nilong opisin), and "eyebrow" (gras antap long ai);
- a lack of inflectional morphology: "haus bilong John" (John's house).

Pidginisation is the process through which native speakers of two L1s evolve a contact language so that they can both function within the same locality. Grammatical and other complexity is sacrificed for the sake of day-to-day communication; 'pidginisation thus constitutes restrictions in use accompanied by reduction in form' (Andersen, 1983, p. 4). Once a pidgin is formed, it may be 'depidginised' by gaining features of the socially dominant language at the expense of the pidgin forms. Thus pidginisation is the diachronic process through which a pidgin language is created, not the psychological process through which a particular individual attempts to communicate with someone else. A contemporary instance can be seen in the Italian evolved by Spanish immigrants in German-speaking Switzerland (Schmid, 1993).

Schumann and Alberto

The original study relating pidgins to second language acquisition research is reported most fully in Schumann (1978a). This focused on one of the group of six Spanish-speaking learners of English studied in Cancino *et al.* (1978) mentioned in Chapter 2, namely Alberto, a 33-year-old Costa Rican polisher who had lived in Massachusetts for four months. The speech data were collected at fortnightly intervals over ten months from spontaneous conversations, from speech elicited through techniques such as the Bilingual Syntax Measure, from preplanned excursions to restaurants, and from exercises in which he was asked to negate sentences.

The issue was whether Alberto's sentences resembled those of a pidgin language. It was not so much that the end point of Alberto's learning was a pidgin as that the process through which he was acquiring an L2 was similar to pidginisation – the creation of a lingua franca for social purposes. The research concentrated on syntactic structures related to the auxiliary, in particular negation, inversion, the possessive and plural "-s" forms, the past tense, and the progressive "-ing". Schumann did not score a particular moment at which a form was acquired, as in the Brown approach, but traced the percentage with which it was supplied in obligatory contexts longitudinally over the 20 sessions, as we saw in the related work by Cancino *et al.* (1978) described in Chapter 2.

In general, the six learners went through definite sequences for the constructions studied. The exception was Alberto, who stood out from the others by sheer lack of progress. Let us start with negation. Of the four rules Cancino *et al.* (1978) found in the other learners, which are described in Chapter 2, he used only the first two; the earliest "no + V" rule ("I no understand good") most often, followed by the "don't V" rule ("Don't know"). He never progressed to the "Aux–Neg" rule and to the range of "do" forms used by the other learners.

Alberto inverted subject and auxiliary in questions only 5 per cent of the time while the other learners did so between 19 per cent and 56 per cent; his inversion questions were also restricted to certain verbs – "say" and "like" as in "What did you say to me?". He did, however, sometimes move the whole verb, as in "What are doing these people?". Nor was he very good at supplying the other grammatical morphemes, apart from the 85 per cent he scored for plural "-s". Possessive "-s" occurred in only 9 per cent of obligatory contexts; the regular past tense in 7 per cent, irregular past in 65 per cent, and progressive "-ing" in 60 per cent.

	%
plural *-s*	85
irregular past	65
progressive *-ing*	58
possessive *-s*	9
regular past	7
inversion	5

Alberto's scores for certain structures in obligatory contexts (taken from various points in the text of Schumann, 1978a)

Schumann found Alberto's use of auxiliaries particularly noteworthy. He adapted the Brown criterion for acquisition of a form by accepting that it is acquired when it occurs in 80 per cent of obligatory contexts over three transcripts, at least twice in each transcript, and at least ten times overall. On this basis, the only auxiliaries Alberto possessed were "can" and some copula forms of "be". The other five learners acquired between four and 18 auxiliaries, with an average of 12, seen in the following figure comparing Alberto with another learner called Jorge, a 12-year-old Spanish-speaking near-beginner:

	1	2	3	4	5	6	7
Alberto	*is*	*am*	*can*	*are*	–	–	–
Jorge	*is*	*can*	*do*	*does*	*was*	*did*	*are*

Sequence of acquisition of auxiliaries for Alberto and Jorge (from Schumann, 1978a)

The overall figures for the occurrence of auxiliaries are also relevant. The following chart gives the auxiliary and copula forms, based chiefly on charts in Schumann (1978a, pp. 59 and 62) and Andersen (1981, p. 171); to make the differences clear it is divided here into three bands: over 80 per cent (Schumann's level for acquisition), 10–80 per cent, and under 10 per cent. Actual figures are given as well as percentages.

	Auxiliaries			**Forms of copula** *be*		
over 80%	*can*	85%	70/83	*are* (1pl)	100%	3/3
				were (2)	100%	2/2
				am	98%	63/64
				is	94%	969/1035
10%–80%:	*am*	75%	3/4	*was* (1sing)	67%	4/6
	is	71%	45/63	*are* (2pl)	52%	13/25
	will	38%	17/47	*were* (3pl)	33%	1/3
	do	35%	96/277	*are* (3pl)	29%	23/78
	are (3pl)	22%	5/27			
under 10%	*would*	8%	1/13	*was* (3sing)	6%	2/34
	does	1%	1/75			
	did	1%	1/90			
	was	0%	0/3			
	could	0%	0/3			
	have	0%	0/3			
	has	0%	0/3			

Occurrence of auxiliaries and copula "be" in Alberto's speech (adapted from Schumann, 1978a, pp. 59, 62)

None of the auxiliaries except "can" were mastered at the 80 per cent level; two singular forms of the copula "be" ("am" and "is") were mastered, but not the main plural or past forms ("are" and "were"). In addition "need", which is not regarded by Schumann as an auxiliary (Schumann, 1978a, p. 63), occurs 103 times, as in "You need go one more year?" To sum up, 'In general Alberto can be characterised as using a reduced and simplified form of English' (Schumann, 1978a, p. 65); in the main he uses pidginised speech with some depidginisation as he approaches English norms for plural "-s" and so on.

What could be the explanation for Alberto's lack of success? Schumann dismisses age and cognitive level, as a Piaget test showed him to be 'at the onset of formal operations' (though this is characteristically entered in the teens rather than the thirties). The important clues are the resemblances between Alberto's speech and pidgins. According to Schumann (1978a, p. 75), these were:

- use of "no", as in "I no see": a single pre-verbal negative form is typical of pidgins;
- lack of inversion, as in "Where the paper is?": this corresponds to the tendency for pidgins to have a single word order and to prefer stable relationships between form and meaning;
- lack of auxiliaries, as in "She crying": pidgins too lack auxiliaries;
- lack of possessive "-s", as in "The king food": this corresponds to the typical lack of inflectional morphology in pidgins;
- unmarked forms of the verb, as in "Yesterday I talk with one friend": lack of present "-s" and of past tense "-ed" and so forth is again similar to the lack of inflections in pidgins;
- lack of subject pronouns, as in "No have holidays": this is similar to the reduced pronoun systems of pidgins.

Some of the ways in which Alberto's speech fails to resemble pidgins are explained by Schumann as transfer from his L1 Spanish. Thus Alberto's comparative success with the copula forms ("is" 94 per cent, "am" 98 per cent), which are often missing in pidgins, 'is probably due to positive transfer from Spanish' (Schumann, 1978a, p. 75), as is his comparative success with plural "-s" (85 per cent), with "need", and with the auxiliary "can" (85 per cent). Andersen (1981) in addition explains Alberto's success with "-ing" (58 per cent) in terms of a Spanish equivalent "-ndo". The reverse argument is also true in that some of the forms noted by Schumann as pidgin-like are characteristic of Spanish, for example 'missing' subject pronouns, which will be discussed in Chapter 8.

Andersen (1981) makes a more detailed comparison of Alberto's L2 speech with the pidgin spoken by 24 speakers of Hawaiian Pidgin English described in Bickerton and Odo (1976). The similarities he finds are:

- pidgin speakers also have a "no V" rule for negation; 'Alberto as second language learner is a pidginised negator' (Schumann, 1978a, p. 182);
- Bickerton's data show pidgin speakers lack inversion of subject and verb in questions, as does Alberto;
- the more pidgin speakers 'that use each morpheme, the higher the percentage of correct use for Alberto' (Schumann, 1978a, p. 187): hence the success with "is" and with "-ing" is typical of both pidgin speakers and Spanish speakers;
- while Alberto, like pidgin speakers, expresses possession through word order rather than through "-s", he transfers the Spanish word order to English – "food king" rather than "the king's food".

Why should Alberto's speech be pidginised? Schumann looks for an explanation in social and psychological factors. Here we shall develop the factors in the social situation common both to pidgin users and to Alberto rather than the emotional factors that also affect L2 learners' development. Pidgin languages are used for communication rather than for functions of language such as the 'integrative' function that indicates membership of a social group and the 'expressive' function that allows one to become 'a valued member of a particular linguistic group' through effective public use of language (Schumann, 1978a, p. 76); the pidgin speaker carries out everything but communication through the first language. There is a lack of social and psychological solidarity between the participants in the pidgin situation, since they share nothing but essential communication. Pidginisation is then found where there is social distance between the speakers – the British Raj memsahib and the Indian cook conversed in 'kitchen Urdu'.

Schumann (1976) developed the concept of *social distance* in L2 learning in terms of several factors:

- dominance: a group of L2 users may either dominate a native group (French colonists in Tunisia), be dominated by another group (American Indians in the south-west USA), or be on an equal footing with them;
- integration: an L2 group may decide to assimilate and give up its own life-style, to acculturate and maintain its own culture at the same time, or to preserve its own culture and reject the other;
- enclosure: based on Schermerhorn (1970), an L2 group decides to have 'high' enclosure, in which it remains separate from the other, or to have 'low' enclosure, in which it mixes with the other group;
- other factors are: cohesiveness and size of the group; congruence or similarity between the two cultures, attitudes of the two groups to each other, and the intended length of residence of the learners in the country.

In addition to social distance, there is also *psychological distance* (Schumann, 1975), made up of affective factors such as:

- language shock, for example the 'dissatisfaction and even a certain sense of guilt' we feel when we cannot express ourselves in the L2;
- cultural shock, for instance feelings of rejection or homesickness;
- motivation, such as the integrative and instrumental motivations studied by Gardner and Lambert (1972).

These social and psychological factors create good or bad L2 learning situations. A good situation occurs when neither group is dominant, when both groups want assimilation, 'where the two cultures are congruent, where the L2 group is small and non-cohesive, where both groups have positive attitudes towards each other, and where the L2 group intends to remain in the target language area for a long time' (Schumann, 1976, p. 141). Schumann's example is American Jewish immigrants to Israel learning Hebrew. Any situation where the reverse obtains – one group is dominated by the other, wants to remain enclosed, and so on – will be a bad L2 learning situation. An example not given by Schumann might be Palestinians wishing to learn Hebrew in Israel.

This general account of success and failure in L2 learning is called the *Acculturation Model* after one of its key features – acculturation or 'the social and psychological integration of the learner with the target (TL) group' (Schumann, 1986, p. 379). The overall relationship between the two groups as perceived by their speakers forms the crucial factor in success, which therefore depends upon 'the degree to which a learner acculturates to the target language group' (Schumann, 1978b). SLA is in a sense a spin-off from the process of acculturation rather than an independent process. The Acculturation Model is intended 'to account for SLA under conditions of immigration where learning takes place without instruction' (Schumann, 1986, p. 385). The model does not apply readily to situations where there is no effective contact between the two groups, say, the learning of Italian in England, or where an international language is involved, such as English or Swahili, that is not firmly attached to a particular group of native speakers somewhere in the world.

Schumann hypothesises 'that pidginisation may characterize all early second language acquisition and that under conditions of social and psychological distance it persists' (Schumann, 1978a, p. 110). The early speech of all six learners showed signs of pidginisation. While the others depidginised towards English, Alberto remained essentially at this stage. The reason was that he had preserved his social distance from English. His answers to a questionnaire about his activities revealed that, while he appeared at first sight to have a good overall attitude, he 'made very little effort to get to know English-speaking people' (Schumann, 1978a, p. 267); he did not like television and listened mostly to Spanish music; he had a night job which prevented him going to day classes. Consequently his English stayed at a pidginised level.

Limitations of the Work with Alberto

Schumann's methodology is the detailed observation of one individual's speech. Hence its claims are limited to production, as in Chapter 2. It is impossible to tell what English Alberto understood from such data.

The data are presented chiefly as percentages rather than figures: for instance Alberto supplied 85 per cent of "can", 100 per cent of "are" (first-person plural). Schumann presents raw figures for some forms, so that 85 per cent for "can" can be seen to mean 70 out of 83, while 100 per cent of "are" (first-person plural) means 3 out of 3. Clearly percentages are not very meaningful in themselves without such information, which is not available for most of the items in the chart on p. 71. As we saw in Chapter 2, the use of obligatory contexts in fact measures the learner's speech against the target language rather than accepting the independent grammars assumption; Alberto's speech is viewed from the perspective of English rather than in its own right; whether it is pidginised or not seems to depend on how it treats the rules of English, not on its own internal systematicity.

Though Schumann has five subjects available, his main interest lies in explaining why Alberto is so bad. A single learner may be idiosyncratic in all sorts of ways. Alternative explanations such as age and cognitive level are scarcely meaningful with only one subject as there is no one to compare him with who differs only on the relevant dimension. The fact that only one L1 is involved is also a handicap, particularly when, as Gilbert (1981) points out, many of the apparently pidginised features of Alberto's speech, such as preverbal negation, could be attributed to Spanish. A single learner studied in detail can provide important insights, but, without a comparison to other learners, it is never possible to tell which features are peculiar to that learner and which can be generalised to other learners. The same criticism has often been levelled at the L1 discussions of their own children by Smith (1973) and Halliday (1975). However detailed the work with Alberto may be, it concerns *one* learner; the peculiarities of Alberto cannot be separated from the aspects he shares with other learners. A study of a single learner can provide brilliant insights into one person, as the work of Schumann (1978a) or Halliday (1975) proves; nevertheless it needs confirmation from many learners before what is idiosyncratic about the individual can be disentangled from what is typical of all learners. Moreover, while Smith (1973) and Halliday (1975) at least use successful children, Schumann deliberately chooses a learner who is unsuccessful. One bad L2 learner doesn't make a theory. Indeed, Schmidt (1983) studied a Japanese learner of English, called Wes, whose English was almost as bad as Alberto's; after three years he had achieved 100 per cent on "-ing" but only 43 per cent on plural "-s", 8 per cent on possessive "-s", and 0 per cent on irregular past tense. Yet Wes was an extrovert who was fully integrated into the English-speaking community of Hawaii and used English for 'something between 75 per cent and 90 per cent' of 'meaningful interactions' (Schmidt, 1983, p. 141). Schumann (1986) reviews other evidence for acculturation, largely MA theses, most of which do not confirm the model. The strongest evidence he cites comes from a PhD thesis by Maple (1982), which correlated English proficiency with acculturation in 190 Spanish-speaking students in the USA; however, as Schumann (1986, p. 388) points out, 'he got these results on a population for which the model was not intended', namely a group of overseas students rather than an immigrant community.

Research summary: J. Schumann (1978a), *The Pidginisation Process: A Model for Second Language Acquisition* (Rowley, Mass.: Newbury House).

Aim: to test whether L2 learning was similar to pidginisation

Learners: essentially Alberto, a 33-year-old Costa Rican polisher

Data type: observational data from spontaneous conversations and elicited material over a ten-month period

Aspects of language: syntactic structures related to the auxiliary, in particular negation, inversion, the possessive and plural "-s" forms, the past tense, and the progressive "-ing"

Method of analysis: scoring of percentage success for supplying forms related to the auxiliary in obligatory contexts

Results: Alberto was unsuccessful with negative placement, question inversion, supplying grammatical morphemes apart from plural "-s", auxiliaries apart from "can"

Conclusions: 'In general Alberto can be characterised as using a reduced and simplified form of English' (Schumann, 1978a, p. 65), resembling pidgins

---

Other Work with Pidginisation

Related work was carried out by Andersen (1984), who argues for 'a principle that accounts for not only the characteristics of "pidginisation" but of interlanguage construction in general' (Andersen, 1984, p. 78). This is the *One-to-One Principle* that 'an IL [interlanguage] system should be constructed in such a way that an intended underlying meaning is expressed with one clear invariant surface form (or construction)' (Andersen, 1984, p. 79). Andersen adduces several types of evidence: one is that the "No V" stage found both in Alberto and in pidgins is an attempt to standardise the grammar so that there is only one possible position for negation rather than several; a second is that the preference for SVO order among L2 learners and pidgins shows consistency in keeping to a single order, even though a language such as German has several. Hence the simplification in L2 learners' speech and pidgins reflects the speakers' desire for uniformity of realisation in a language. Andersen has developed the single principle mentioned here into a 'Cognitive–Interactionist' theory (Andersen, 1989) related to Slobin's operating principles of language acquisition (Slobin, 1973).

Pidgin studies look at the dynamic behaviour of groups – how a group invents a pidgin for day-to-day communication. Hence they are motivated by the social relationships between the groups – domination, enclosure, and the rest. They make predictions about groups, not about individuals. How successfully can they be applied to the behaviour of individuals? Hari Seldon's fictional theory of psychohistory worked admirably at forecasting the demise of galactic empires but was unable to predict the lives of individuals (Asimov, 1952). The same with creole theories: it is hard to extrapolate from the relationships of groups to the development of individual learners. A single learner's progress into a language is different from the invention or adoption of a language by a social group. The jump from pidginisation of groups to the L2 learning of individuals such as Alberto is extreme, and needs to be massively supplemented by insights into the individual's psychology, such as the concept of psychological distance in the Acculturation Model; Schumann (1990) in fact tries to reconcile acculturation with contemporary 'cognitive' theories, but finds 'little basis for adopting any of the models presented in this paper except as useful frameworks or depictions that allow us to think about cognition in SLA in different ways' (Schumann, 1990, p. 682). In the same way pidginisation should perhaps be seen as analogous to L2 learning rather than identical, providing L2 insights that can be tested independently of their original source.

Other criticisms have been made of pidgin-based work. McLaughlin (1987) points to its lack of falsifiability and to its reliance on analogy; he claims that an evaluation of the pidginisation models cannot take place because 'presently, there simply is not enough information' (McLaughlin, 1987, p. 132). Ellis (1985a) emphasises the limitation implied in the pidginisation analogy and in basing research on contact situations, rather than on school situations where there is no actual social relationship between the learners and the target group; 'what is missing from these models is an account of the role of the interaction between situation and learner' (Ellis, 1985a, p. 255). The hard core of these theories is not the acquisition of knowledge of language by the individual – the acquisition question; instead they are concerned with how pidgin languages that didn't previously exist come into being.

4.2 CREOLES AND SECOND LANGUAGE ACQUISITION

Unlike a pidgin, a creole language such as Jamaican Creole is learnt by children as their first language. The characteristics of creoles given in Bickerton (1981) include, using his examples of Hawaiian Creole English:

- putting focused constituents at the beginning of the sentence: "O, dat wan ai si" (Oh, that one I saw);
- a uniform article system with three possibilities (specific, non-specific, zero): "Dag smart" (the dog is smart);
- use of preverbal markers such as "stei" to indicate tense, mood, and aspect: "Wail wi stei paedl, jaen stei put wata insai da kanu" (while we were paddling, John was letting water into the canoe); and so on.

A characteristic of pidgins in the Bickerton framework is their expression of tense and aspect via preverbal markers such as "bin" and "stei". Andersen (1981) for instance interprets Alberto's frequent use of "need" as the pidgin-like use of a preverbal marker.

'Creolisation' is the process through which children exposed to a pidgin acquire a creole as a first language; at first creoles are spoken as a native language by children but not by their parents; they are in effect inventing a new language in a single generation. Creolisation increases the complexity of pidgins so that they have the sophistication of full languages and take on their full range of functions. Again, creoles are created diachronically as language systems, not invented anew every day by individuals. Some 80 creole and pidgin languages are listed in Romaine (1988), ranging from Australian Pidgin English to Creole Portuguese of Sri Lanka. The above represents one interpretation of an area that is full of debate and in which the terminology varies from author to author. Mufwene (1991) points out, for instance, that Chinese would be a creole if these syntactic criteria were applied blindly. He also stresses the alternative explanation favoured by some linguists that creoles are based on 'substrate' languages; instead of adopting universal features, most creoles seem to have made a selection from their two base languages. A clear account of this area can be found in Adamson (1988).

Bickerton and the Bioprogram

Bickerton (1981) suggested that crucial aspects of language can be established by studying how a language comes into being. People create a creole language from scratch out of a pidgin; seeing what they invent tells us about the biological basis for language in their minds. The features that creoles share reveal the properties of the human mind which created language; 'if all creoles could be shown to exhibit an identity far beyond the scope of chance, this would constitute strong evidence that some genetic program common to all members of the species was decisively shaping the results' (Bickerton, 1981, p. 42). The human mind contains a 'bioprogram' for language, which acts as the default that the individual child learner starts off with. One element in this built-in program is the article system; creoles have a three-way division between 'a definite article for presupposed-specific NP, an indefinite article for asserted-specific NP and zero for non-specific NP' (Bickerton, 1981, p. 56). Another is the use of preverbal markers to convey distinctions of Tense, Modality and Aspect.

' "Learning" consists of adapting this program, revising it, adjusting it to fit the realities of the cultural language he happens to encounter' (Bickerton, 1981, p. 297). Bickerton sees the bioprogram as the core of language, only detectable when a language is being used for the first time; the more a language departs from a creole the more it forsakes the simplicity of the bioprogram, and the more problems a learner has to learn it. The crucial process is not pidginisation, which creates a pidgin without native speakers of its own, but creolisation, which produces a systematic new language with native speakers out of a pidgin. In pidginisation the learner is coping with the deficient language input represented by a pidgin, largely by relexifying the L1 with new vocabulary. In a much-cited quotation, Bickerton (1977, p. 49) remarks 'Pidginisation is second language learning with restricted input and creolisation is first language acquisition with restricted input'.

Children start with the bioprogram and graft on to it the language they are learning. In a sense both first and second language acquisition mean learning another language; 'in both primary and secondary acquisition then, a speaker can be regarded as moving from a known grammar to a novel one: in primary acquisition from the bioprogram to the "native language" grammar, and in secondary acquisition, from that "native" grammar to the second language grammar' (Bickerton, 1984, p. 152). He regards it as an empirical matter whether the bioprogram is involved in second language learning, the evidence for which is at the moment equivocal; Bickerton cites the problem of distinguishing the effects of the bioprogram from those of L1 transfer; for example, in sentences such as "I am liking it" the features of the speaker's L1 Hindi 'overrule' the demands of the bioprogram. He has gone on record that 'no real connection exists between SLA and creolisation: they differ in almost every particular' (Bickerton, 1983, p. 283).

Other Work with Creolisation

A small number of other researchers have looked at the implications of creolisation and the bioprogram.

(a) *Adamson (1988)* tested whether one of the universals of the bioprogram was involved in L2 learning, namely Bickerton's specific/non-specific distinction incorporated in the article system. Korean has no articles; therefore Koreans learning English as an L2 should initially impose the bioprogram two-way specific/non-specific distinction on English, which employs a more complex system. The sentence "Joyce is the man who wrote Ulysses" has a specific "the"; the sentence "The elephant is a wondrous beast" has a non-specific "the"; "Man is mortal" indeed has a non-specific zero article, but "Today I ate cookies" has a specific zero article. The crucial test is whether the learners make the pidgin distinction between presence of articles before specific NPs and absence of articles before non-specific NPs.

Adamson interviewed 14 adult Korean learners, who were divided into high-proficiency and low proficiency groups by a cloze test; he scored all NPs as specific or non-specific, except for set expressions, proper names and those marked with other quantifiers. One result was that, when the learners actually used an article, they did so correctly. The difference between the frequency of articles before specific and before non-specific NPs did not reach statistical significance for either high proficiency or low proficiency learners. However, analysis of variance revealed that the low proficiency group used articles significantly more often in front of specific NPs than the high-proficiency group. This was taken by Adamson to show that the specific/non-specific distinction was still available to L2 learners, and so to support the presence of the bioprogram in L2 learning.

(b) *Andersen (1983)* has developed the related concepts of *nativisation* and *denativisation*. Nativisation is any process whereby the learner creates a grammar of his or her own from input; it adapts the language that is being acquired to built-in universal tendencies; it progresses towards an 'internal norm' set by the learner's mind. Nativisation thus includes both pidginisation and creolisation. Denativisation on the other hand is any process which adapts the grammar to fit the input, going away from the universal built-in forms towards the language-specific; it progresses towards an 'external norm' set by the target language. Together nativisation and denativisation represent 'the different directions the learner takes in building his interlanguage' (Andersen, 1983, p. 12). They are crucial processes in any language acquisition, whether L1, L2, pidgin, or creole, not dissimilar to Piaget's distinction between assimilation and accommodation in children's learning (Piaget and Inhelder, 1969). In later work, Andersen (1990, p. 48) stresses the links between these two processes: 'nativisation and denativisation are not two separate processes or "forces" but simply represent different extremes in the result of the overall process of second language acquisition'.

The presentation here may give a false impression of unity among the creolists by stressing their similarity of approach, when in fact the field is often acrimoniously split. The type of linguistics utilised in creole and pidgin studies tends to emphasise the semantic meaning of syntax rather than its formal rules, typically citing approaches such as Givon (1979); it is, for example, concerned with the systematic meaning relationships of the articles in the learners' speech rather than with their sheer occurrence. It emphasises a small interconnected set of syntactic features relevant to pidgins and creoles, such as word order, auxiliaries, negation, and tense and modality, at the expense of other aspects. Its description of language knowledge provides a more complex answer to the knowledge question than we have seen so far, overlapping with the use and acquisition questions.

Andersen (1983, p. 43) reminds us that 'all language acquisition and use . . . obey both individual and group constraints . . . and are both psycholinguistic and sociolinguistic phenomena'. The bioprogram indeed looks at the creation of language by individual children. While the bioprogram hypothesis is intriguing and stimulating, it rests on a number of assumptions that are controversial. As outlined in Romaine (1988), the common factors it ascribes to pidgins exclude many languages that other researchers would want to include – Tok Pisin, for example. At the moment many of the aspects of the bioprogram seem to overlap with the proposals for Universal Grammar, to be discussed in Chapter 9; Mufwene (1990), for example, interprets some of the characteristics of creoles within Chomskyan UG.

4.3   SECOND LANGUAGE ACQUISITION AND VARIATION

The third main area in this chapter is variation in language use. Looking at L2 learning from an E-language perspective, it is hard to find the neat regularity that I-language knowledge-based approaches expect; instead there is variation in every aspect – from one learner to another or from one time to another in the same person.

Variation has been studied in linguistics in several ways. One is the Hallidayan strand of stylistics which deals with variation according to *field* (what is going on), *tenor* (who is taking part) and *mode* (what role language is playing) (Halliday, 1985b; Halliday *et al.*, 1964). The child's ability to switch registers has been studied in first language acquisition from Weeks (1971) to E. Andersen (1990). Yet there has been comparatively little investigation of the variation in L2 use, apart perhaps from the notion of codeswitching (Grosjean, 1989). Some SLA work has tackled the variation in register in speech addressed by the L2 learner to different people. Cook (1985a) found that a group of mixed L2 learners of English thanked native speakers differently according to age, and according to whether they were strangers or friends, but not according to sex. Young (1988) had the same Chinese learners of English interviewed by two people who differed in such social factors as ethnicity, sex, and origin. A high degree of 'social convergence' between subject and both native and non-native interviewers in these factors led to better performance with plural "-s" morphemes, while a low convergence led to worse results; ethnicity by itself had no effect. In general such effects are within the bounds of Accommodation theory – how speakers adapt their speech to those they are speaking to (Giles and Smith, 1979), whether in the short term or the long term. It is not surprising that L2 learners vary their speech from one circumstance to another; interlanguage would not be a normal language system if it did not adapt itself to the person addressed or the topic discussed. The factor of variation has to be borne in mind whenever considering examples of L2 learner's language: anything a learner says varies according to the whole context of situation: the speaker's and listener's roles, the structure of the discourse, the functions for which language is being used, and so on.

Labov and Style

The most influential strand of linguistics for the L2 study of variation has, however, been the sociolinguistic work of William Labov. A key piece of research was his investigation of the way in which pronunciation varied according to the speakers' social class and the task that they were performing (Labov, 1966). One example, adapted by many sociolinguists, is whether or not "r" is pronounced when it is present in the spelling of English words. American English is 'rhotic' in that an "r" is pronounced before vowels ("red" /red/), before consonants ("bird" /bə:rd/), and before silence ("centre" /sentər/); British English is 'non-rhotic' in pronouncing /r/ before vowels ("red" /red/) but not before consonants ("bird" /bə:d/) or silence ("centre" /sentə/). Labov established that the presence of /r/ varied in American speech according to social class; the higher socio-economic groups pronounced "r" more often than the lower groups, with the exception of the 'hypercorrect' lower middle class who exceeded the upper-class scores. The proportion of /r/s also varied according to the task involved; the order of tasks from least to most /r/s supplied for all groups went from casual speech, through careful speech, reading style, and word lists, to minimal pairs. In a given context the presence of /r/ depended on the speaker's class and on the formality of speech required; the more formal the style and the more educated the speaker the more likely an American is to use /r/. This dimension of formality reflects the extent to which the speaker pays attention; 'styles can be ranged along a single dimension, measured by the amount of attention paid to speech' (Labov, 1970b). To establish the speakers' use of language, it is necessary to test them in a range of situations differing in formality, or, at least, for the researcher to be aware of the degree of formality involved in the testing situation employed. Within Labovian theory, the research methodology for establishing variation in an interview has become standardised over the years (Labov, 1984).

A further aspect of Labov's work that has been used by second language acquisition research from time to time is the concept of the variable rule. Labov claimed that conventional rewriting rules of the type seen in Chapter 2 are inadequate because they are all or none; a variable rule captures the possibility that features may or may not occur for a variety of reasons. We have already encountered this concept in the research with Swedish negation by Hyltenstam (1977) in Chapter 2, which expressed the learners' use of negation as a variable rule involving the weighting of the finite auxiliary and verb.

Research by Adamson and Regan (1991) tested whether the speech of L2 learners of English varied according to context of situation. They separated out the factor of acquisition by choosing a phonological feature that gives no problem to L2 learners and also occurs in their L1. This was the "-ing" word ending seen in the progressive morpheme ("is going"), in adjectives ("tempting"), and in other structural contexts. The pronunciation of "-ing" varies in native speakers, chiefly between /iŋ/ and /in/, according to class, sex, formality, and other factors. Adamson and Regan (1991) gave controlled Labovian interviews to 14 Vietnamese or Cambodian learners of English and 31 native speakers, all living in Philadelphia. They looked for the proportion of /in/ variants over /iŋ/. The data were analysed using the VARBRUL 2 computer program, a common tool among sociolinguists for studying variation, which analyses the statistical significance of the various factors in the data; its use is described more fully in Preston (1989). Taking the monitored task as an example, men produced more /in/ variants than women, whether native or non-native, as follows:

	Natives(%)	Non-natives(%)
Men	51	38
Women	8	9

Percentage of /in/ forms in the monitored condition (adapted from Adamson and Regan, 1991, p. 12)

Comparing speakers across tasks yielded a more complex picture. For both native men and women, monitoring produced fewer examples of /in/ compared to /iŋ/ than the unmonitored condition. For non-native speakers, monitoring produced slightly fewer /in/ variants for woman but slightly more for men, as seen in:

		Natives(%)	Non-natives(%)
Men	monitored	51	38
	unmonitored	85	14
Women	monitored	8	9
	unmonitored	42	20

Percentage of /in/ forms in two conditions (adapted from Adamson and Regan, 1991, p. 12)

Other variations correlated with the following phoneme and with the word-class of the word itself. While L2 learners had acquired variation by sex, the men were setting themselves slightly different targets from the women.

This research does not score deviation from a native norm in terms of whether "-ing" is pronounced /iŋ/ but looks at variation between /iŋ/ and /in/ across sexes and across tasks for non-native speakers. It attempts to describe the use of L2 learners' interlanguages without immediate recourse to native targets. At one level this variation in the individual's repertoire simply brings interlanguage in line with other forms of language. As part of the independent grammars assumption, one would expect L2 learners to vary their language performance in ways found in neither L1 nor L2. As Skutnabb-Kangas (1981, pp. 38–39) puts it succinctly, 'A bilingual speaker's choice of variety . . . should be able to be described in the same way as the monolingual speaker's intralingual choice between different varieties.'

Labov's view of stylistic variation by task has been particularly influential on SLA research; a summary can be found in Young (1991), who found 11 tasks named in this type of research. 'Style' in the work of Labov (1966) refers to a continuum of formality from the most formal style, say written reports, to the most casual style or 'vernacular', say conversations with one's family. The most cited research demonstrating stylistic variation in an L2 is by Dickerson (1975), who looked at the speech of ten Japanese learners of English over a period of nine months using three tasks differing in formality: free speech, reading texts aloud, and reading word-lists aloud. Dickerson (1975) reported chiefly on /z/. As Young (1991) points out, the variation is here seen as differences from the target L2 rather than as variation between different forms. Two main factors influenced the learners' success:

(i) The phonetic environment. Only the target /z/ variant was supplied by Japanese learners before vowels; before silence /z/ was often realised as /s/; before dental/alveolar consonants such as /t/ and /ʃ/ it was often omitted; before other consonants /z/ often came out as /s/ or /dʒ/. Improvement occurred in all of the last three environments over the nine months of the study.

(ii) The task. The order of the three tasks from least successful to most successful was: free speech → reading texts → word-list reading. The learners' success varied according to the level of formality: 'in 96 percent of the 227 instances of style stratification, the order was as predicted' (Dickerson, 1975, p. 405). The more formal the task the closer the learners were to the native target. Though the learners improved over time, the difference between environments and tasks still persisted. Other phonological work confirms similar variation: Wenk (1982), for example, found that French-speaking learners of English realised "the sounds" /ð/ and /θ/ differently according to environment.

Some SLA researchers have gone beyond this to see stylistic variation as central to the learning process. Tarone (1983, 1988) postulated a 'capability continuum' of speech styles in interlanguage ranging from 'vernacular' to 'careful':

vernacular style ↔ style 1 ↔ style N ↔ careful style

The vernacular style is used in ordinary conversational contexts; styles 1 to N occur in varieties of tasks such as elicited imitation and sentence-combining; the careful style is found in grammaticality judgement tests. Tarone (1983) describes the vernacular everyday style as more pidgin-like and requiring the least attention by the learner. The careful style is closer to the target-language norm and requires the most attention. The choice between styles is a matter of attention: 'the portion of the continuum which underlies a particular instance of regular learner performance is determined by the degree of attention which the learner pays to language form in that instance' (Tarone, 1983, p. 152). In a sense the careful style is more open to the L2 than is the vernacular. The point of entry for a new form is the careful style, from which it moves along the continuum till it eventually enters the vernacular. Tarone (1985) asked ten Arabic and ten Japanese learners of English to perform three tasks ranging from careful to vernacular styles: a grammaticality judgement test, an interview, and story retelling of a video sequence. The aspects of language that were scored were the occurrence in obligatory contexts of third-person present "-s"; 'the article', plural noun "-s", and object pronouns "him/her/it". Taking the Arabic group, the results were as on p. 87.

This interesting pattern of results showed a consistent variation in the learners' behaviour for the three tasks. But it did not always go in the expected direction. The third person "-s" is indeed best in the careful style and worst in the vernacular; the article and the object pronoun "it" are, however, best in the 'vernacular' story retelling and worst in the 'careful' grammar test. Contrary to expectation, some forms such as the article and

	Vernacular style (non-attended) ←————————→		Careful style (attended)
	Story retelling(%)	Interview(%)	Grammar test(%)
Third person -*s*	39	51	67
Article	91	85	38
Noun plural -*s*	71	83	70
Object pronouns	100	92	77

Results for ten Arabic learners in three tasks (based on Tarone, 1985)

object pronouns are supplied more often in the least attended style than in the most attended. One possible explanation explored by Tarone (1985) is a Krashen-derived distinction between 'acquired' forms such as the article and the direct object "it", and 'learned' forms such as third person "-s"; this is rejected because it provides no clear reason why learners were '*less* accurate in their *grammaticality judgments* of articles and direct object pronouns than they are in their *use* of these structures in vernacular oral discourse' (Tarone, 1985, p. 390).

This experiment provides a useful curb on the more extreme claims of this model. Flanigan (1991) also found the predicted gradient between careful and vernacular styles was lacking in the scores of 20 ESL children given four tasks. Tarone and Parrish (1988) reanalysed the original spoken data for the articles in Tarone (1985) in terms of four subtypes of NP; they found there was variation in the type of NP supplied in the two tasks, but that the story-telling task (closer to the vernacular) still had more accuracy than the interview task; this is ascribed by them 'to the general influence of communicative pressure'. Some of the same problems crop up with Tarone (1985) that were seen earlier: the subjectivity and target-relatedness of obligatory context, the limitations consequent on the scoring of presence of discrete items in observational data, the familiar low-level phrase structure syntax employed, and the collapsing of the article system into one category (see **Research Summary** on p. 88).

Other approaches to second language acquisition research have made use of concepts of variation that differ from Labov in one way or another.

(a) *Ellis* has often claimed that there is variation in the L2 learner's speech that is non-systematic and not explicable in terms of formality of style. Ellis (1985b) cites an 11-year-old boy who, after about one month of learning English, produced two forms of negation: "No look my card" and "Don't look my card". The latter sentence was the first example of "don't" in the boy's speech; by the sixth month there were more forms with "not", such as "don't", than forms with "no". This kind of evidence shows a 'strikingly

---

Research summary: E. Tarone (1985), 'Variability in Interlanguage Use: a Study of Style-shifting in Morphology and Syntax', *Language Learning*, **35** (3), pp. 373–404

Aim: to demonstrate systematic variability going from attended 'careful' to non-attended 'vernacular' 'styles' in L2 learners

Learners: 10 Arabic and 10 Japanese learners of English

Tasks: a fill-in grammar test, interview, and story retelling, reflecting a continuum of attention

Aspects of language: third person present "-s"; 'the article', plural noun "-s", and object pronouns "him/her/it"

Method of analysis: percentage occurrence in obligatory contexts

Results: consistent variation in the learner's behaviour for the three tasks but, contrary to predictions, some forms are supplied more often in the least attended style rather than the most attended

Claims: some tentative support for the continuum of styles

---

high degree of IL variability' (Larsen-Freeman and Long, 1991, p. 82) compared to other varieties of language. Ellis sees this variability as providing the learner with a starting point from which the learner gradually eliminates variation to acquire the target forms; 'non-systematic variability slowly becomes systematic' (Ellis, 1985a, p. 98) under the pressure to simplify form–function relations, that is to say, Andersen's One-to-One Principle, called by Ellis (1990b) the Efficiency Principle: to sum up, 'the resolution of non-systematic variability underlies all language change' (Ellis, 1985b).

(b) *Huebner (1983)* studied the development of Ge, a Hmong learner of English from Laos, over the first year of his life in Hawaii. Variation occurred in several grammatical forms: the article form "da" first occurred in contexts where it had specific reference, it implied speaker knowledge, and it was not the topic; at the next stage "da" could be used with any Noun Phrase; at the third, its use shrank to NPs that did not have specific reference or imply speaker knowledge; and so on, for a further three stages. Ge follows a complex route towards the English article system, namely 'using the form in virtually all environments before gradually eliminating it from the incorrect environments' (Huebner, 1983, p. 147). Among Huebner's overall conclusions are that the learning of some forms may require their over-use in ungrammatical contexts; the learning of others may require 'the reduction of the use of that form in target language obligatory contexts' (Huebner, 1983, p. 207). Huebner's work is then within the tradition of what has now come to be called 'form–function' studies (Ellis, 1990b; Tarone, 1988), seeing how one function is handled by different grammatical forms.

(c) *Young (1991)* investigated the factors responsible for variation in the plural "-s" morpheme in the English of 12 adult speakers of Chinese, a language that does not have inflectional marking of plural. The learners were interviewed twice, once by an English native speaker, once by a Chinese. The aim was to examine a broad range of factors rather than to limit variation to a single dimension such as formality. Fifteen hypotheses were tested, covering a range of factors from the psychosocial and developmental to linguistic environment and communicative redundancy. Analysis by VARBRUL eliminated all but six of the hypotheses. Syntactic factors particularly affected the presence of "-s", partly whether the noun was premodifying another noun, partly the function of the NP in the sentence, as seen in this table:

	Plural **-s supplied(%)**
NP as adverbial	80
NP as complement	71
NP as subject	55
NP as object	57

Variation in plural "-s" supplied by Chinese learners related to function of NP (after Young, 1991, p. 136)

Adverbial NPs attracted most "-s" endings, object NPs least. Other factors that favoured the production of "-s" were: the presence of a preceding vowel or sibilant or a following vowel; and the presence of other plural markers such as "these" in the NP. Thus the importance of syntactic and phonological factors was confirmed; the importance of redundancy was the opposite to what had been predicted in that the presence of other markers encouraged "-s"; the importance of ethnicity of interviewer was not confirmed.

4.4 L2 USE AND L2 LEARNING

The concept of variation has produced a rich new area for SLA research, perhaps showing promise for the future rather than concrete results in the present. It concentrates primarily on the use question, focusing particularly on variation according to context of situation. Some of it, such as Adamson and Regan (1991), starts to take the independent-grammars assumption seriously by looking at the variation within the learner's own system rather than at differences from a native target. The problem is the switch from the use to the acquisition question. However clear it is that L2 users can switch styles in the L2, there is none the less a gap between this and the progress of acquisition. Turning to Tarone's claim that learning amounts to proceeding along the continuum from formal to informal: on the one hand, the evidence is lacking both across styles and from appropriate longitudinal studies; on the other hand, the immense complexities of variation are reduced to a single dimension of formality, dependent on attention. To give evidence of attention, Labov suggests using 'channel cues' such as increase in speed, volume and rate to establish the most relaxed style; other than this, attention seems a vague concept for which there is no independent evidence distinct from the language forms themselves. Dewaele (forthcoming) has suggested that the proportion of nouns, adjectives, and certain other categories, to pronouns and verbs is an indicator of formality, perhaps linked to the differences in the proportion of lexical and grammatical items found by Halliday (1985b) in speech and writing, mentioned in Chapter 2.

As for free variation being an integral element in SLA, Tarone (1988, p. 113) points out 'there are not many studies providing evidence of free variation in second-language acquisition'. The example in Ellis (1985b) of the learner producing "No look my card" and "Don't look my card" is ambiguous. Rather than evidence of grammatical variation, it could show the learner choosing from a limited lexical set that includes "no" and "don't", just as the subject at Milon's stage 1 of negation chose from "not", "no", and "no more"; that is to say, it is simply lexical choice between two items. For, if such free variation in syntax were to be effective, it would have to occur on a large scale, which surely would have manifested itself in many other pieces of research. Calling things free variation may give away our lack of understanding of the principles underlying actual behaviour (Andersen, 1989). Adamson and Kovac (1981) indeed showed that the variation in Alberto's speech between "no" and "don't" was systematic; "no" was used primarily in sentences in which the subject was missing. Even conceding its existence, variation would still need to be shown to be the cause of growth. As Gregg (1990, p. 379) points out, one of the problems with the model is 'that there is no explanation of the acquisition process, even of the comparatively few forms for which there is data available'. The claim that variation is necessary or integral to L2 learning seems unproven, and perhaps unprovable. The change to a form–function analysis is admirable; it is related to the complaint that was made in Chapter 2 against the grammatical morpheme studies: grammar is *not* just the appearance of items in sentences but is the computational system of meaning that underlies these appearances. But this is a matter of what grammar is taken to mean rather than an aspect of variationist theory, and so could be applied to any methodology or theory.

To I-language linguists, the stumbling block is the type of language knowledge implied by variationist work. Chomsky (1965b, pp. 3–4) insisted that 'Linguistic theory is concerned with an ideal speaker-listener, in a completely homogeneous speech-community.' I-language linguistics abstracts a typical speaker out of the throng of diverse humanity; the variation between adult human beings does not matter as they all share a knowledge of human languages – linguistic competence. It is the core element of the speaker's language knowledge that is important: his or her actual physique rather than whether he or she is dressed in a skirt, a suit, or jeans. Variationist theories deny any such claim; rather than variation in use being a sequel to the study of linguistic competence and acquisition, it is located at the centre of linguistic knowledge, seen most overtly in Labov's replacement of the all-or-none rewriting rule with the variable rule; indeed, in a sense, as Halliday and Hasan (1985) point out, from this functionalist point of view, it is not that language *has* uses, as the use question implies, but that language *is* use. This difference of aims seems difficult to bridge; the importance of variation to one's theory depends not on the empirical facts – obviously language use varies in many dimensions – but on the decision whether to eliminate such variation to describe linguistic competence or to insist that variation has to be present at all stages of description. The concept of the idealised speaker is nevertheless an acute problem to SLA research, since the final state of L2 knowledge varies from one learner to another rather than being the single form attributed to linguistic competence in the native speaker; syntactic variation may have to be reconciled with a description of competence in some way; for further discussion see Cook (1991b; forthcoming).

A further way in which variationist research is unsatisfactory comes more within its own terms of reference. As Young (1991) points out, variationist work has mostly adopted the Labovian sense of 'style' as a type of task used in data collecting, rather than looking at the many other dimensions of variation in language use. Much of the L2 research shows that different experimental tasks elicit different behaviour, relevant to second language acquisition methodology but saying little about the L2 learner's actual ability to adapt speech to circumstance let alone acquire an L2. Adamson and Regan (1991) and Young (1991) show how the richness of variation can start to be tapped in L2 work. The opportunity for looking at types of variation in second language acquisition seems open-ended. After all, aspects of variation have been studied in diverse areas and theories, for example the stylistic analysis of Crystal and Davy (1969), the social semiotic theory of Halliday and Hasan (1985), and the education-orientated genre analysis of Swales (1991). But there is no point in multiplying the sheer amount of variational data about L2 learning in this way without looking at an overall theory of acquisition within which these may be accommodated.

This chapter has described a more sociolinguistic perspective on second language acquisition in which use and variation are considered more interesting than knowledge and competence. While originally an offshoot from more general theories, current work is starting to look more specifically at L2 learning in its own right. Both in theory and in methodology, such research has not paid so much attention to issues of acquisition. Its strength is the description of L2 variation in use, whether in its own terms or in terms of pidgins and creoles; its weakness is the lack of testable accounts of how such variation is acquired by the individual. But at least a stab at the use question is being made in sociolinguistic terms, even if its links to the knowledge and acquisition questions are unsure. In my own view such work must bear in mind the multi-competence viewpoint that the L2 learner's mind contains a double system in which two languages are used, rather than concentrating on L2 learners only in terms of their use of the second language.

5 The Multidimensional Model and the Teachability Hypothesis

A further model based on the type of research outlined in Chapter 2 was developed by a group that included Clahsen, Meisel, Pienemann, and Johnston, first in Germany and later in Australia. The most common name for its first version is the Multidimensional Model of Meisel, Clahsen, and Pienemann, (1981); the later version is often called the Teachability Hypothesis, after one of its main claims (Pienemann, 1989). The label 'multidimensional' reflects the central claim of the model that L2 acquisition has two sides: on the one hand there is a rigid *developmental* sequence for certain aspects of language that is unaffected by aspects of the learner or of the environment, on the other a *variational* sequence for other aspects of language which responds to differences in the learner or the situation. The developmental sequence is claimed to depend on general factors of language processing. The variational sequence is based on learner variables such as the extent to which the learners are integrated into the target culture. Thus the Multidimensional Model brings together two of the separate strands seen in Chapters 2 and 4: the common sequences of acquisition found in L2 learners and the variation between learners.

5.1 ORDERS OF ACQUISITION IN GERMAN

The original research was part of the ZISA (Zweisprachenerwerb italienischer und spanischer Arbeiter) project at Wuppertal in the late 1970s. This was concerned with the L2 learning of German word order, using data taken from interviews with 45 foreign workers, 20 from Italy, 19 from Spain, and 6 from Portugal, from longitudinal studies of 12 learners over two years, and from studies of three Italian-speaking children (Meisel, 1991).

The details of German word order are complex. The usual order in declarative main clauses is Subject–Verb–Object (SVO), for example, "Ich liebe dich" (I love you). But non-finite verb forms (that is, not inflected for number and person), such as participles, must occur at the end of main clauses as in "Ich habe dich geliebt", Subject–Auxiliary–Object–Verb (I have you loved); this is called the *Verb Separation rule*. The finite Verb (that is inflected for number and person) and auxiliary also come in the second position in main clauses after certain forms such as adverbs, question words, or topicalised NPs, as in "Immer liebe ich dich", Adverb–Verb–Subject–Object (Always love I you); this is called the *Inversion rule*, which in addition presupposes an *Adverb Preposing rule* that takes the adverb to the beginning. Subordinate clauses have the order SOV rather than SVO as in "Ich sagte dass ich dich liebte" Subject–Verb–[Complementiser–Subject–Object–Verb] (I said that I you loved); this is the *Verb Final rule*.

Meisel *et al.* (1981) claim that 'underlying SVO is an adequate working hypothesis for German'. This SVO order corresponds to the 'canonical order strategy' for German, derived from the concept of canonical forms in L1 acquisition (Slobin and Bever, 1982). Canonical forms are those which are easiest to process because they make least demands on the speaker rather than necessarily being the most frequent in the language; 'In uttering such canonical sentences, the speaker makes minimal assumptions about the background knowledge of the listener' (Slobin and Bever, 1982, p. 230). The canonical order strategy can also be taken as one example of Andersen's general One-to-One Principle discussed in the previous chapter or of Keenan's Principle of Conservation of Logical Structure (Keenan, 1975). Canonical sentence types are related to processing and to the strategies of language performance rather than to linguistic competence. The 'simple active affirmative declarative' sentence is the usual form of the canonical sentence. The word order in such canonical sentence types varies from one language to another; SVO for English, SOV for Turkish, and so on. Other structures are derived from this canonical form; 'a schema formed on the basis of the canonical sentence form is the point of departure for the construction of a series of related schemas for sentence types which are non-canonical' (Slobin and Bever, 1982, p. 232).

The research technique used by Meisel *et al.* (1981) involved scoring the extent to which the 45 L2 learners used various structures in obligatory contexts in the interviews. A learner's success was expressed as a proportion of 1.0; for example, a learner called Benito who has a score of 0.82 for 'Verb Separation' has used the rule in 82 per cent of the obligatory contexts in which it was needed in the transcript. Like the technique of Schumann (1978a) and Cancino *et al.* (1978), putting percentages in sequence yielded a sequence of acquisition. The numbering and details of the stages has varied slightly over the years. The version used here numbers stages from 1 to 6 in a broader sequence that has become well established among this group of researchers (Pienemann, 1987a; Pienemann, Johnston, and Brindley, 1988). Meisel *et al.* (1981) present a fragment of the full set of stages, renumbered here in the later fashion. An alternative numbering system calls the canonical order stage X, numbering the later stages X + 1, and so on (Pienemann, 1987b; 1989).

Stage 1: Formulas and one-word sentences. Initially L2 learners of German start by producing either one word utterances or set formulas, as in "Kinder" (children) or "Madchen" (girl) (Pienemann, 1980).

Stage 2: Canonical order (alias "stage X"). At this stage L2 learners use the SVO canonical order for German, seen in sentences such as "Die Kinder essen Apfel", Subject–Verb–Object (The children eat apple) (Meisel *et al.*, 1981).

Stage 3: Adverb Preposing (stage X + 1). Learners next acquire adverb preposing *without* inversion of subject and verb; "Da Kinder spielen", Adverb–Subject–Verb (There children play) instead of the native Adverb–Verb–Subject, "Da spielen Kinder". This requires a 'movement' rule in which the Adverb is preposed to the beginning of the sentence:

"Ich gehe jetzt nach *Hause*" → *"Jetzt ich gehe nach Hause" (Now I go home).

Though not stated in this form in Meisel *et al.* (1981), we can interpret this as a rule:

Adverb Preposing: Subject–Verb–Adverb → Adverb–Subject–Verb

Stage 4: Verb Separation (stage X + 2). Learners next acquire the rule that the verb is moved to the end of the sentence when it is non-inflected, that is to say preceded by an auxiliary: "Ich habe ein Haus gebaut" (I have a house built) rather than *"Ich habe gebaut ein Haus" (I have built a house). Again we can express this as a rule:

Verb Separation (of non-inflected forms): Subject–Auxiliary–Verb–Object → Subject–Auxiliary–Object–Verb

The non-finite Verb moves to the end of the sentence, thus producing the correct Subject–Auxiliary–Object–Verb.

Stage 5: Inversion (stage X + 3). Learners now discover how to invert Subject and Verb following Adverbs, "Dann hat sie wieder die knoch gebringt", Adverb–Auxiliary–Subject–Adverb–Object–Verb (Then has she again the bone brought), and following question words – "Wann gehst du nach Hause?" (When go you home?) rather than *"Wann du gehst nach Hause?" (When you go home?). This can be expressed as:

Inversion (after certain items): X–Subject–Verb–Object → X–Verb–Subject–Object

Stage 6: Verb Final (stage X + 4). Learners at last move the Verb to Final position in subordinate clauses, "Wenn ich nach House gehe, kaufe ich diese tabac", Complementiser–Subject–Adverb–Verb . . . (When I home go . . .). Hence the rule applies to embedded sentences following subordinating conjunctions such as "dass", to indirect speech clauses, and to relative clauses. It can be expressed as:

> *Verb Final* (in embedded clauses): . . . [complementiser–Subject–Verb–Object] → . . . [complementiser–Subject–Object–Verb]

The pattern of acquisition can be seen in the following table, which adapts some figures for the sample of six learners described in Meisel *et al.* (1981, p. 125). "-" indicates there were no appropriate contexts for the rule to apply in the transcript; "0" shows the rule was not applied in any appropriate contexts or that 'there are less than four possible contexts' (Meisel *et al.*, 1981, p.125).

	Janni	Benito	Maria	Franco	Angelina	Lolita
Stage 4: Verb Separation	1.0	0.82	0.93	0.58	0.71	0.57
Stage 5: Inversion	1.0	0.91	0.85	0.29	0	–
Stage 6: Verb Final	1.0	0.56	0	–	0	–

Stages in L2 acquisition of German (adapted from Meisel *et al.*, 1981, p. 125)

Lolita and Angelina are at stage 4 as they know only the Verb Separation rule; Franco and Maria are at stage 5 as they know both Verb Separation and Inversion; Benito and Janni are at stage 6 as they know Verb Separation, Inversion and Verb Final. This sequence forms an *implicational* series in which knowing a certain rule implies knowing all the earlier rules. Janni therefore knows all three rules, Maria only the first two, Lolita hardly knows the first one, and so on. The learners add one rule at a time in a sequence; 'the structure of a given interlanguage can be described as the sum of all the rules a learner has acquired so far' (Pienemann, 1989, p. 54).

But there is nevertheless variation between learners, seen in the more detailed results for the same learners for some sentence sub-types.

	Janni	Benito	Maria	Franco	Angelina	Lolita
Aux, Verb Particle	1.0	0.71	1.0	0.59	0.7	0.5
Embedded Topicalisation	1.0	0	1.0	–	–	–
Adverb with Inversion	1.0	1.0	0.7	0.18	0	–

Details of L2 acquisition of German (adapted from Meisel *et al.*, 1981, p. 125)

Auxiliary–Verb–Particle is one of the constructions involved in the Verb Separation rule; Embedded Topicalisation ("wenn ich nach Hause gehe, *kaufe ich* diesen Tabac" [. . . buy I . . .]) and Adverb with Inversion are involved in the Inversion rule. Though Lolita and Angelina are both at stage 4 (Verb Separation), Lolita does not use sentence types such as Adverb with Inversion where movement is necessary (that is, this is scored as "-"), while Angelina uses them but gets them wrong (that is, this is scored as "0"). Benito, who is at stage 6, often uses the Verb Final rule properly but has still not acquired Subject Verb inversion in topicalised embedded sentences; yet Maria, who is only at stage 5 and does not use the Verb Final rule, knows both Auxiliary–Verb–Particle and Embedded Topicalisation. Such variation is not encompassed by the sequence of acquisition but forms a separate variational dimension, similar to the pidginisation described in Chapter 4.

The learner's progress on this variational dimension can be affected by several factors; Meisel (1980, pp. 35–6) highlights the difference between those 'who want to go back to their home country as soon as possible' and those 'who want to stay for good, or at least for a longer period of time', dubbed by Meisel *et al.* (1981, p. 129) 'segrative' and 'integrative' orientation. They compare the use of the copula by two Italian girls learning German. One, Concetta, inserted it from the start – "Deutsch is gut" (German is good); the other, Luigina, deleted the copula if an object NP followed – "Ich Madchen" (I girl). As Luigina progressed, she also failed to supply other types of verbs, as in "Meine Mutter Italien, Vater Deutschland. Arbeit" (My mother Italy, father Germany. Work). Insertion of the Verb does not depend on a developmental sequence but varies from one learner to another along a dimension of simplification from most to least pidginised. This is the variational dimension, in which learners simplify their language use to a varying extent. Meisel *et al.* (1981) support this with a factor analysis of 35 types of background data, documented more fully in Clahsen *et al.* (1983), which isolated three main factors that contribute to the learner's success: contacts at the workplace, contacts with family and neighbours, and ties to Germany.

The dimensions of the model are set out in Figure 5.1, adapted from Meisel *et al.* (1981, p. 130). This locates the six learners on the two dimensions of development and variation.

Benito is thus more advanced on the *developmental* dimension than Maria as he knows the Inversion rule, but less advanced on the *variational* dimension because he uses a smaller range of sentence types. All the learners can be located somewhere on these two dimensions. While the model refers to stages, the combination of these two dimensions and the percentage scoring system lead to a continuous picture of development rather than clearly separated stages.

Development

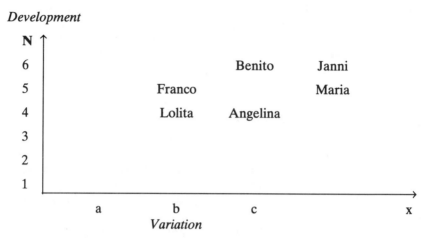

Figure 5.1   The Multidimensional Model (adapted from Meisel *et al.*, 1981, p. 130)

Research summary: J. M. Meisel, H. Clahsen and M. Pienemann (1981), 'On Determining Developmental Stages in Natural Second Language Acquisition', *SSLA*, **3** (2), pp. 109–35.

Aim: to discover the stages in the acquisition of German as L2

Learners: '40 adult learners' taken from the ZISA project concerned with foreign workers in Germany

Data type: interviews

Aspect of language: German word order

Method of analysis: implicational scaling, scoring the proportion out of 1 with which a learner used a rule in obligatory contexts

Results: the discovery of (i) six developmental stages, starting with SVO in main clauses and gradual learning of rules for Adverb Preposing, Verb Separation, Inversion, and Verb Final in subordinate clauses, and (ii) variation between learners along a dimension of simplification

Conclusions: the necessity for a Multidimensional Model to take these factors into account.

5.2   EXTENSIONS TO THE ORIGINAL MULTIDIMENSIONAL MODEL RESEARCH

These developmental stages have been applied to English in an adapted and amplified form by Pienemann and Johnston (1987), based on learners of English in Australia. They also form the basis of a linguistic profiling test

(Pienemann *et al.*, 1988), on the lines of the LARSP (Language Assessment Remediation and Screening Procedure) (Crystal *et al.*, 1976) designed for speech therapists (and now adapted to bilingual children as in Duncan (1989), but using the current categories described in Pienemann *et al.* (1988). This has been turned into a diagnostic kit for the computer called COALA (COmputer Aided Linguistic Analysis) (Pienemann, 1992): the teacher types in sentences produced by the student, and annotates them grammatically; a computer algorithm allocates the student to a particular stage and provides other types of information.

These stages are held to generalise from German to other languages because they result from processes of speech perception (Clahsen, 1980); 'linguistic structures which require a high degree of processing capacity will be acquired late' (Clahsen, 1984, p. 221). Hence canonical forms, which represent the lowest processing demand for a language will be acquired first. The L2 learner relies on simple processing strategies, which will eventually have to be overcome to learn the language adequately. At stage 2 the learner produces SVO sentences; Clahsen (1987) shows that Italian-speaking L2 learners of German assume initially that German is SVO despite the variety of German word orders they are confronted with and despite the fact that Italian identifies the Subject because of its animacy rather than its position (Bates and MacWhinney, 1981), as will be discussed in Chapter 10. Hence learners at this stage are dependent on the *canonical word order strategy* in which 'deep structure relations can be mapped directly onto surface strings' (Clahsen, 1984, p. 221). The canonical order strategy suggests that re-ordering of linguistic material should be avoided: stick to SVO and all will be well. Until the L2 learners overcome this strategy, they will be able to cope only with SVO sentences in German.

Clahsen supports this by citing Slobin and Bever (1982), who showed that L1 children speaking English, Italian, Turkish, and SerboCroatian were happiest with the canonical sentence order of their own language. 'The fact that both L1 and L2 learners use canonical sentence schemas shows that they are sensitive to the underlying (linguistic) structure of the language' (Clahsen, 1987, p. 113). Stage 2, according to Pienemann and Johnston (1987), includes as well the "no" + SVO structure seen in "No me live here" and intonation questions such as "You like me?".

The next group of stages relates to a processing principle called the *initialisation/finalisation strategy* (Clahsen, 1984, p. 222): elements can only be moved to the beginning or the end of the string. Stage 3 (Adverb Preposing in German) depends on 'the learner's ability to identify the beginning and end of the string . . . since no special knowledge of categories within the string is required' (Pienemann and Johnston, 1987, pp. 75–6). Being able to put the adverb at the beginning in "Yesterday I sick" depends on knowing where the sentence actually begins. Other general possibilities for this stage in English are possible such as topicalising the object by putting it at the beginning ("Beer I like"), and putting "do" and Wh-words at the beginning of the sentence (Pienemann, *et al.*, 1988).

Stage 4 (Verb Separation in German) depends on being 'able to characterize some element within a string as being of a particular kind' (Pienemann and Johnston, 1987, p. 77). In German this means moving the verb to the end as in "Alle Kinder muss die Pause machen"; the English equivalent is moving the auxiliary to the beginning as in "Can you tell me?". Both depend on recognising the appropriate category, on the one hand the German Verb "machen", on the other the English Auxiliary "can". Basing the stages on psycholinguistic processing means that word order can be generalised to other features such as the grammatical morphemes. This general ability to single out categories leads in English *inter alia* to the present continuous Auxiliary + Verb + "-ing" (depending on recognising the verb) and to preposition-stranding in questions, as in "Who did you give it *to*?".

Stage 5 (Inversion in German) depends on the more general principle of being able 'to characterise various elements within a string as being of different kinds' (Pienemann and Johnston, 1987, p. 76) so that they may be moved around 'in an ordered way inside the string'. In German, the ability to categorise Adverbs and Auxiliaries results in the Adverb–Auxiliary–Subject construction. In English they claim that the same ability leads to the Wh-word–Auxiliary–Subject construction, as in "What are you studying at Tech?", and to the dative "to" structure, as in "He gave the book to John". Pienemann and Johnston (1987, p. 80) also argue that the third person "-s" depends on movement of the marker "-s" from inside the noun phrase 'to the end of the finite verb following the pronoun or noun phrase'; hence third person "-s" also appears at this stage.

Stage 6 (Verb Final in German embedded clauses) involves a third general processing principle – the *subordinate clause strategy* that 'in subordinate clauses permutations are avoided' (Clahsen, 1984, p. 222); if subordinate clauses are processed differently from main clauses, permutations such as the German Verb Final rule will cause great difficulty. The ability to handle subordinate clauses at all rests on 'the learner being able to break down elements within a string into sub-strings' (Pienemann and Johnston, 1987, p. 76). The proper processing of German subordinate clauses depends on overcoming this strategy. The English examples they give are "He asked me to go" with 'the double subject complement', the reflexive pronoun, and dative movement – that is, the difference between "Give the dog a bone" and "Give a bone to the dog".

Table 5.1 sets out the overall characteristics of these six stages, giving both the general principles proposed by Clahsen (1984) and the more specific processes of Pienemann and Johnston (1987), illustrated from English and German.

The distinction between developmental and variational sequences has

Table 5.1   The Developmental Stages in the Multidimensional Model

Stage	general processing principles (Clahsen, 1984)	specific processes (Pienemann and Johnston, 1987)	German examples (Meisel, *et al.* 1981)	English examples (Pienemann and Johnston, 1987)
1			Single words formulas	Single words formulas
2	Canonical order strategy		SVO	SVO *no* + SVO
3	Initialisation finalisation strategy	Distinguishing beginnings and endings of strings	Adverb Preposing (AdvSVO)	Adverb-fronting; topicalisation; initial *do*; initial wh-words; yes/no questions
4		Recognising a category within the string	Verb Separation	Aux *-ing*; preposition stranding
5		Recognising different categories in the string	Inversion (AdvVSO)	Wh Inversion; 3rd person *-s*; dative *to*
6	Subordinate clause strategy	Breaking elements within a string into substrings	Verb Final (SOV)	embedded clauses; reflexives; dative movement

implications for the teaching of second languages. This led to a major feature of the theory known as the *Teachability Hypothesis*; 'an L2 structure can be learnt from instruction only if the learner's interlanguage is close to the point when this structure is acquired in the natural setting' (Pienemann, 1984, p. 201). Pienemann (1984; 1989) conducted an experiment with the teaching of German to ten Italian-speaking children aged 7–9 living in Germany to see 'whether Inversion can be taught before it is acquired naturally'. One child called Teresa was at stage 3 (Adverb Preposing) when she was taught Subject–Verb inversion (stage 5), thus jumping the Verb Separation rule (stage 4); though her success with Inversion leapt up, this was only in formulas or copies of existing sentences. She was incapable of being taught the Inversion rule because she had not yet learnt the Verb Separation rule.

	before teaching	after teaching
Adverb Preposing (stage 3)	Yes	Yes
Verb Separation (stage 4)	0	0
Inversion (stage 5)	0	0.83

Effects of instruction on an Italian child (after Pienemann, 1984, p. 149)

Another child called Giovanni was at stage 5 of the developmental scale as he had acquired the Inversion rule, but did not apply it to many sentence types; teaching him Inversion extended his use to a wider range of types such as question-word questions "Wo bring sie die Sacke?" (Where bring they the sacks?).

Instruction therefore benefited Giovanni but was useless for Teresa. So far as the developmental sequence is concerned, learners have to be 'ready' for the new rule, that is to say at a stage when all the necessary preceding rules are already in place. What about the variational sequence? When the copula was taught to the same ten learners, 'For all of the informants tested, the frequency of copula omission diminished considerably after instructional emphasis' (Pienemann, 1989, p. 61). Teaching may affect the variational dimension or may speed up the learners' progress through developmental stages but does not change the developmental sequence itself.

In general the Multidimensional Model has many of the virtues of the Input Hypothesis without some of its vices. It provides an account of L2 learning whose outline is readily comprehensible; the key factors in the six stages are readily grasped and can be applied to any L2 learning; its implications for teaching seem clear and straightforward. The Model is the outcome of the ZISA project based on the empirical foundation of large-scale observations of L2 learners. Moreover, unlike almost all other models based on the order of acquisition, it advances an explanation for the sequence, namely processing complexity. Quite justifiably, although it has remained essentially the same since around 1981, the model has received more attention within recent years, particularly through the work of Pienemann and his associates in Australia.

5.3 THE LINGUISTIC BASIS FOR THE MULTIDIMENSIONAL MODEL

The foundation for the developmental stages is the concept of canonical word order. Slobin and Bever (1982) defined canonical forms as those which have the least discourse presuppositions; this relates canonical order to language processing in context – to performance rather than to competence (White, 1991). Canonical order is easier to *process* rather than easier to *know*, as it involves the least movement. Slobin and Bever (1982) suggest that learners start with the appropriate canonical order for the language they are learning. But, oddly enough, it is generally accepted that German children start with SOV (Clahsen and Muysken, 1986), apparently going against this principle. This will be pursued in Chapter 9.

Though several L1s have been studied, published research has not yet tackled L2s that have canonical orders other than SVO, say Arabic VSO or Japanese SOV, even if such research is reputedly in progress. Indeed SV0 may be a natural choice for processing reasons because of its clear separation between Verb and Object (Givon, 1979). The evidence for the Multidimensional Model available at present does not distinguish between an SVO strategy and a canonical order strategy as it only deals with English and German, both seen here as having canonical SVO order, rather than a range of languages with SOV, VSO, VOS, and so on. So the evidence here could equally suggest a preference for SVO order rather than for canonical order.

The chief thread in the learner's development is the modification of canonical order by moving elements within the sentence. Let us look for a moment at the concept of movement in syntax. Chapter 1 described phrase structure as a way of dividing the sentence up into smaller parts, easily represented in trees. Chapters 2 and 3 presented the differing approaches of Krashen and Schumann that both draw variously on phrase structure. Chomsky (1957) showed that in principle phrase structure cannot deal with crucial aspects of grammar, such as discontinuous constituents ("*Are* you *leaving*?"). His first solution was to amplify standard rewriting rules with 'transformational' rules that altered the structure of the sentence in various ways, for example by moving elements around in the sentence; the rules we have been using here for describing movement are therefore transformations of this type. Since Chomsky (1965a), another solution has been preferred in various guises, namely to postulate an underlying structure for the sentence which differs from its actual surface form. The current model (Chomsky, 1981; 1986a) claims that the sentence has an underlying form called *d-structure* and a form called *s-structure* which eventually becomes the surface structure; movement is the relationship between the d-structure and s-structure. An English question such as:

"Where did you go?"

is related to the underlying d-structure form seen in:

"You went where?"

It is as if the questioned element "where" had moved from its 'original' position to the beginning of the sentence; movement is the link between the position of "where" in the s-structure and its underlying position in the d-structure, as in:

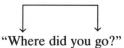

"Where did you go?"

It is usual to see the s-structure of the sentence as preserving an invisible trace (*t*) in the position from which the moved item originated, as in:

"Where did you go *t*?"

Movement also applies to other types of questions. A yes/no question such as:

"Are you going?"

reflects movement of "are" to the beginning, i.e.:

Are you going *t*?

A passive sentence such as:

"The battle was won."

involves movement of "the battle" to the beginning, as seen in the s-structure:

"the battle was won *t*"

And so on for other constructions. Surface structure differs from s-structure in not having the trace of movement.

There are three types of movement: movement of NPs, as in the passive; movement of Wh-phrases, as in questions and relative clauses; and movement of certain heads of phrases. The latter is crucial to the analysis of languages such as German which are regarded by most syntacticians as having one word order at an underlying level (SOV) and another at a surface level in main clauses (SVO), related by the movement of the Verb. More precise details can be found in Cook (1988c); movement will be discussed at greater length in Chapter 9. One of the major variations between human languages is whether indeed they have or do not have syntactic movement, that is to say whether they need the two levels of s-structure and d-structure for describing syntax or require only one. Languages such as Japanese and Chinese, for example, form questions by adding a question word within the sentence without movement. In one sense all languages have movement since it is needed for various semantic operations dealing with the meaning of the sentence. They differ over whether this movement involves syntactic forms.

As the spine of the developmental sequence in the Multidimensional Model is movement, it is hard to see how the main aspects of the model can have anything to say about the L2 learning of languages that have *no* syntactic movement, such as Japanese, and little to say about those with variable movement, such as Turkish. Moreover, important as the relationship between underlying and surface structure is to languages such as English, it is only one element in the complex set of modules that makes up the whole grammar rather than the pivot around which all syntax and language processing revolve. The ways in which movement are described in the Multidimensional Model resemble the older concept of transformations – indeed, they were phrased as such above – rather than more modern concepts; the use of movement to take the agreement marker "-s" from inside the NP to the Verb (Pienemann and Johnston, 1987) is particularly idiosyncratic. Though the Multidimensional Model represents a valiant attempt to go beyond phrase structure syntax, it is hard to assess its claims against current concepts of movement.

The canonical order used in processing is distinct from the underlying word order of the language, which also varies widely across languages. The Multidimensional Model assumes SVO is the canonical order for German and therefore phrases the rules as transformations of the basic SVO canonical order. But many linguists, Clahsen and Muysken (1986) among them, have argued that the underlying word order of German is SOV and consequently different from the canonical order. In this event, there is a tension between the canonical SVO order and the underlying SOV word order; SVO applies to language processing, SOV to language knowledge. The choice between the processing SVO order and the underlying SOV order is crucial to the statement of the movement rules, since these would have to operate in roughly reverse fashion according to whether SVO or SOV is the starting point. With SOV as a starter rather than SVO, the processing rules would move final V to get SVO, move auxiliaries to get SAuxOV, invert XSOV into XVSO, and so on. L2 learners of German usually start from the canonical order SVO, not from the underlying SOV order. This is argued by Clahsen and Muysken (1986) to disprove the availability of UG to L2 learners, as we see in Chapter 9.

Pienemann refers to the rules of the grammar as items to be acquired cumulatively, seeing interlanguage as 'the sum of all the rules a learner has acquired so far' (Pienemann, 1989, p. 54). This again asserts their psychological reality as process. It denies the independent-grammars assumption by assessing how many of the rules of the target language the learners have acquired rather than evaluating their own grammars. Learners do not evolve grammars in the Multidimensional Model; they acquire bits of the target grammar ranged along an implicational scale. Grammar in the Multidimensional Model is a list of things to learn that are largely independent of each other: rules are discrete items. This goes against the nature of grammar as a coherent system where the rules intersect with each other, a fundamental concept of grammar in many linguistic theories.

5.4   THE PROCESSING RATIONALE FOR THE MULTIDIMENSIONAL MODEL

The question is whether the same underlying processing principles occur in other languages. The canonical order strategy that learners are supposed to employ starts them off with the 'typical' sentence order for the language – hardly a unique claim for any model. The initialisation/finalisation strategy has major effects for German in the SVO analysis, but different, and slighter, effects in English. The subordinate clause strategy does not apply to English since main and subordinate clauses have the same SVO order. Hence the actual reflections of these six stages are different in English due to its lack of German SOV constructions.

The defence against such criticisms would be the universal nature of the processing stages, both the overall processes described by Clahsen (1984) and the more detailed versions in Pienemann *et al.* (1988). The canonical word order strategy is only exemplified in the available research from SVO languages as the L2 and seems equivalent to Bever's strategy that a Noun–Verb–Noun sequence is interpreted as Actor–Action–Object (Bever, 1970), to be discussed in a different context in Chapter Seven. The initialisation/finalisation strategy depends on the learner's ability to move things to the beginning or end of 'strings'; in the Pienemann and Johnston (1987) version, stages 4 and 5 depend on the progressive ability to recognise more categories; 'the fourth developmental stage . . . comes when the learner is able to characterise some element within a string as being of a particular kind' (Pienemann and Johnston, 1987, p. 76). Using the argument in Radford (1990), if 'category' is taken in its usual linguistic sense, up to stage 4, L2 learners are incapable of distinguishing nouns from verbs, auxiliaries from articles, and so on. Taking some sentences from their data, stage 1 has "Kinder"; this is the plural form of "Kind" with the "-er" plural ending; if the learner uses this ending correctly only with nouns and not with verbs, he must know that the word "Kind" belongs to the category 'noun'. Stage 2 has "Die Kinder spielen mim ball"; "-en" is the third person plural marker attached to verbs, so the learner must recognise "spiel" as a verb and make it agree in number with the plural subject "Kinder" which in itself has again the correct plural noun ending and is preceded by the article "die" which is only used before nouns. The L2 learners at stages 1 and 2 show every sign of knowing the basic categories; they do not confuse nouns, verbs, and so on. Only if they used, for example, articles with verbs, verb endings with nouns, and so on, could they be said to lack categories. The developmental order based on numbers of categories that can be recognised must therefore be untrue. At best the processing strategy can be phrased more weakly as an ability to know *which* categories are movable rather than as the ability to distinguish the categories themselves.

So far as the subordinate clause strategy is concerned, many learners certainly have problems with subordinate clauses of various types. But almost any model of processing or of linguistic sequencing would predict that processing one clause embedded within another is likely to be more difficult than processing a single non-embedded clause (Miller and Chomsky, 1963), as we see in Chapter 7. The most likely prediction for any model of L2 learning is that subordinate clauses are learnt after main clauses, whether this is based on syntactic or processing grounds.

5.5 METHODOLOGICAL ISSUES

The bedrock of the methodology is observational data – a large database of transcripts for the German learners; unlike other models, there appears to be a solid foundation in actual data. However such observational data have the limitations described in Chapter 2. They are relevant to production rather than to comprehension or to competence (White, 1991). Obligatory contexts deny the independent-grammars assumption by setting up the rules of the target language as the measuring rod. Quantitative corpus-based research entails a statistical duty of demonstrating the reliability of the data (Cook, 1990a). This is particularly crucial for the distinction between "-" (not using the construction) and "0" (using it and getting it wrong), on which the analysis of the variational dimension above largely depends; some learners get a greater number of "0"s, and so are considered more advanced variationally than those who only get "-". Without knowing the actual figures represented by "0" (apart from the fact that they are greater than 4), it is unclear how accidental this phenomenon may be.

Despite the scope of the literature and the data, crucial aspects are not made clear. It is hard, for instance, to find a definition of obligatory context; the usage suggests a strictly linguistic context rather than the fourfold definition of Brown (1973). Some special pleading is made for particular issues. The evidence for Teresa's *lack* of improvement for Inversion after teaching is actually a *gain* from 0 to 0.83; this is dismissed by Pienemann showing that the apparent gain was in fact with formulas and similar sentences rather than spontaneous sentences. But carrying out such reanalysis in one place necessitates applying it everywhere else not just when it suits your convenience; eliminating such sentences might well change many other figures for other learners as well as Teresa's Inversion score. The example that is given to support the claim that stage 2 is canonically SVO is usually Concetta's sentence "Die Kinder spielen mim Ball" (The children play with the ball) which appears to be Subject–Verb–Adverbial-Phrase rather than SVO; the list of SVO sentences in Pienemann (1980, p. 45) is also mostly SV or SVAdvP, for example "Ich gehe in Spielplatz mit meinen Vater" (I go to the playground with my father). Clahsen (1987, p. 110) in fact uses an SVX classification rather than a VO classification and provides only one clear example of a main clause SVO "Meine Schwester kaufen Baum" (My sister buy tree) out of six categories. This is particularly crucial for the position of the Object; the postulation of an SVO order depends on the presence of an Object in the sentence, so that O can be seen to occur after the verb rather than before; SV or SV Adjunct sequences do not count as they include no O. None of these are major design faults but suggest a certain slapdash quality.

The overall evaluation is similar to the Input Hypothesis. The intriguing hypothesis has been put forward that the sequence of acquisition is based on the ways in which L2 learners process sentences. The actual research carried out to support the Multidimensional Model does not suffice to answer this question: not enough languages have been investigated; the linguistic model is too thin and too unconnected to relevant current theories; the psycho-linguistic model is idiosyncratic and unlinked to current ideas; the method-ology does not have sufficient rigour of data analysis. Yet these are potentially rectifiable faults, some of them matters of presentation rather than of substance; a version of the Multidimensional Model might well be possible that would overcome these deficiencies and make firmly based claims rather than programmatic slogans. Chapter 9 will describe how the word order research of the Multidimensional Model has been incorporated into the discussion of Universal Grammar in L2 learning.

5.6   GENERAL IMPLICATIONS OF PSYCHOLOGICAL PROCESSING MODELS

As in the last chapter, one of the main issues raised here is the relationship between SLA research and neighbouring disciplines, in this case psychology. A competence-based model of linguistics is not concerned with psychological processes, which form part of performance, that is, concern the use question. While there must be a relationship between competence and performance – otherwise competence would be redundant – the nature of this remains to be established. A process-based model requires a complex account of how performance data relate to competence and to acquisition.

However, the psychological accounts of processing that SLA research makes use of clearly need to have a reasonable basis in contemporary psychology rather than being isolated exceptions. Studies linking psychological research of the 1980s with SLA research are sparse or non-existent; the next chapter describes work on strategies that takes some steps in this direction. Such studies must be carried out if SLA research is to make proper use of concepts of speech processing. It is not enough to adapt one of the programmatic articles about the diverse aspects of processing, such as Slobin and Bever (1982), without looking at a broader range of the relevant theories and concepts, say, the area of listening surveyed in Rost (1990), the accounts of sentence-processing in Frazier and De Villiers (1990), or the broad accounts of psycholinguistics in Harris and Coltheart (1986) or Garman (1990). In other words, a bridge between the two disciplines needs to be based on sound foundations in both.

The concept of process seems particularly problematic. The Multidimensional Model and the strategies suggested by Clahsen (1984) treat syntactic movement literally as a process rather than as a state. From stage 2 of the sequence onwards, elements seem to move from one place to another. In syntactic theory movement is now thought of as static 'chains' that connect one level of structure with another rather than as dynamic processes; the grammar is a state of knowledge, not a set of processes. So movement is a metaphoric expression for describing a relationship rather than actual movement. In computing, a distinction is made between 'declarative' computer languages that consist of 'facts', such as PROLOG, and 'procedural' languages that consist of 'processes', such as BASIC; this distinction has been adopted in different ways in SLA research and will recur in Chapters 6 and 10 in a specific psychological sense. Competence theories of language are declarative: they describe states of knowledge rather than processes. A famous *faux pas*, called by Botha (1989) the Generative Gaffe, is to use the word 'generative' to refer to the process of speech production rather than in its linguistic sense of explicit description of knowledge; generating sentences is *not* the same as producing sentences. To the linguist, movement is declarative rather than procedural.

Most of the psycholinguistic work on movement has looked at how the mind briefly stores elements in order to relate them to another location in the sentence, rather than on whether actual movement takes place (Wanner and Maratsos, 1978; Marcus, 1980). The Multidimensional Model seems to want movement rules to have a psychological reality as actual processes of production – to be performance processes rather than an abstract relationship between levels of language in competence. In a sense this concept of the processing reality of competence rules was tested and found wanting in the early days of psycholinguistics; as Slobin (1991, p. 634) puts it, 'I know of no convincing evidence for the psychological reality of movement.' Recent discussions of the Teachability Hypothesis (Pienemann, 1992) have started to phrase the rules in terms of Lexical-Functional Grammar (LFG), a model claimed to have more direct correspondence with processes. Pienemann (1992) sees the technical concept of unification (crudely, matching features in different parts of the structure of the sentence) as the key to processing. To my mind, interesting as the applications of LFG are for SLA research, more spadework needs to be done with its basic concepts, such as the uniqueness, completeness, and coherence conditions (Sells, 1985), before adequate SLA implications can be drawn.

Other SLA work, to be described in Chapter 10, has related more closely to psychological theories of L2 learning. Let us take the example of the general phenomenon known as 'cognitive deficit' to give some idea of the complexities of a performance-based model of L2 learning. Cognitive deficit recognises that L2 learners perform below par in their second languages on a great many tasks such as:

- tasks requiring short term storage of information. L2 learners consistently remember fewer items in the L2 than in their L1, whether in digits or in words (Cook, 1979; Lado, 1965; Glicksberg, 1963);
- tasks involving word comprehension. L2 learners have less word associations in the L2 (Lambert, 1955), and increased reaction times for words (Lambert, 1956), for picture-naming and for number-naming (Magiste, 1979);
- tasks involving syntactic comprehension. Decoding abilities do not catch up in an L2 for the first five years of L2 learning (Magiste, 1979);
- simple problem solving. L2 learners find it harder in the L2 to count flashing lights (Dornic, 1969), and to do mental arithmetic (Marsh and Maki, 1978).
- understanding and storage of information in texts. L2 learners read their L2 more slowly (Favreau and Segalowitz, 1982), find more difficulties in recalling information (Carrell, 1984), and remember information from texts less efficiently (Long and Harding-Esch, 1977).

To sum up, L2 learners are deficient on virtually every cognitive process that has been tested in the L2; they have reduced 'channel capacity' in the

L2 (Cook, 1985b; 1988b). Indeed such results have often been explicitly used to define a learner's dominant language as the one in which reaction times are faster (Lambert, 1956), word associations more extensive (Lambert, 1955), and so on.

Cognitive deficit illustrates the complexity researchers are forced to investigate once they step outside the language-based view of SLA. Invoking psychological processes is one way of circumventing the acquisition problem by advancing psychological processing explanations rather than linguistic ones; this does not absolve one from putting forward solutions that are soundly based processing alternatives rather than *ad hoc* explanations. This will be pursued in Chapter 10. An argument in favour of linguistics-based approaches to second language acquisition is simply that linguistics has provided detailed descriptions and explanations of language acquisition and use, while psychology has skimmed the surface.

The concept of L2 cognitive deficit itself has an importance for SLA research in that it undoubtedly affects all the sources of evidence it can employ: L2 learners perform less well in the L2 than equivalent native speakers across the board. Anything involving processes of speech production, comprehension, memory, information storage, and so on, shows a deficit compared to natives. This affects sources of L2 data ranging from spontaneous speech to written examination papers, from elicited imitation to grammaticality judgements. Any research that finds L2 users below par in the L2 has to consider whether this shortfall is specific to the issue it is testing or is simply part of the general phenomenon of L2 cognitive deficit.

We shall end this chapter with a final point about the notion of linguistic competence in SLA research, based on my own recent research. The usual linguistics assumption is that *all* adults attain essentially the same L1 grammatical competence. But one of the few things agreed about L2 learning is that learners reach very different levels of L2 knowledge. Some manage a small part of the language, others substantially more, few as much as in the L1. There is no such thing as a standardised idealised SLA linguistic competence; L2 competence varies extremely from one person to another. Much SLA research in fact ignores the independent grammars assumption by insisting that the target that the learner is aiming at is the same as monolingual competence, but in an L2; learning is talked about in terms of 'failure' and 'lack of success' because the L2 learner is different from the native. Second language learners are supposed to be adding another L1 to their repertoire – but they are mostly not very good at it. Grosjean (1989) and Cook (1992) call this monolingual prejudice since the only reality is held to be monolingual grammars rather than multilingual grammars. Cook (1992) reviews the evidence that people who know a language have a distinctive state of mind, multi-competence, that is not the equivalent to two monolingual states. Multi-competence is not a final state of knowledge like the native monolingual's competence but covers all stages of L2 acquisition. The concept of multi-competence changes the target the learner is aiming at in the L2 by refusing to define it in monolingual terms. However clear the concept of final idealised competence may be in linguistics, it needs far more qualification and definition in SLA research, in my view requiring to be replaced by the concept of multi-competence.

6 Learning and Communication Strategies

The research in this chapter treats the production and comprehension of speech as a dynamic choice of strategies within a situation, divided into two broad areas of learning and communication strategies. The original interlanguage concept (Selinker, 1972) saw strategies of L2 learning and communication as two central processes. In a *learning* strategy the learner attempts to bring long-term competence into being, in a *communication* strategy, to solve a momentary communication difficulty; this distinction resembles the codebreaking/decoding division seen in earlier chapters. L2 strategies have largely been studied through schemes of analysis that list strategies at various levels. Hence much of this chapter has to present and annotate the various structured lists that have been devised.

6.1 LEARNING STRATEGIES

A central research project on learning strategies is the comprehensive research programme surveyed in O'Malley and Chamot (1990). Their definition of learning strategy is 'the special thoughts or behaviors that individuals use to help them comprehend, learn, or retain new information' (O'Malley and Chamot, 1990, p. 1). A key piece of research is the paper by O'Malley, Chamot, Stewner-Manzanares, Kupper and Russo contrasting strategies by beginning and intermediate students (O'Malley *et al.*, 1985a). The purpose was to go beyond lists of strategies determined by researchers to discover the strategies L2 learners actually use. The main part of their research investigated what strategies would emerge out of discussions with L2 learners. They interviewed 22 teachers and 70 high-school ESL students, mostly Spanish-speaking, in groups of 3–5 about their L2 activities both inside and outside the classroom; the students were grouped by the educational system into beginners and intermediates.

This data-gathering produced an amplified list of 26 strategies, with 79 per cent agreement amongst the four raters on the strategies used. These were subdivided according to the distinction between *metacognitive* strategies, and *cognitive* strategies derived from A. Brown (1982). They felt it necessary to add a third group of *social mediation* strategies. The full set from O'Malley *et al.* (1985a) is given below; glosses are paraphrased. In later work O'Malley and Chamot (1990) have modified the list slightly, as detailed below. Unfortunately some of the strategies are not explained further or exemplified in O'Malley *et al.* (1985a) or O'Malley and Chamot (1990); examples have been taken where possible from Chamot (1987); cases where the definition is not self-explanatory and no example is given are presented through quotations so that readers can make up their own minds.

Metacognitive Strategies

Metacognitive strategies 'are higher order executive skills that may entail planning for, monitoring, or evaluating the success of a learning activity' (O'Malley and Chamot, 1990, p. 44); in other words they are strategies *about* learning rather than learning strategies themselves. They are divided into nine types:

- advance organisers: planning the learning activity in advance at a general level – "You review before you go into class";
- directed attention: deciding in advance to concentrate on general aspects of a learning task;
- selective attention: deciding to pay attention to specific parts of the language input or the situation that will help learning;
- self-management: trying to arrange the appropriate conditions for learning – "I sit in the front of the class so I can see the teacher";
- advance preparation: 'planning for and rehearsing linguistic components necessary to carry out an upcoming language task' (O'Malley *et al.*, 1985a, p. 33);
- self-monitoring: checking one's performance as one speaks – "Sometimes I cut short a word because I realise I've said it wrong";
- delayed production: deliberately postponing speaking so that one may learn by listening – "I talk when I have to, but I keep it short and hope I'll be understood";
- self-evaluation: checking how well one is doing against one's own standards;
- self-reinforcement: giving oneself rewards for success.

Cognitive Strategies

Cognitive strategies 'operate directly on incoming information, manipulating it in ways that enhance learning' (O'Malley and Chamot, 1990, p. 44). They recognise 16 cognitive strategies:

- repetition: imitating other people's speech, silently or aloud;
- resourcing: making use of language materials such as dictionaries;
- directed physical response; 'relating new information to physical actions, as with directives' (O'Malley *et al.*, 1985a, p. 33);

- translation: 'using the first language as a basis for understanding and/or producing the L2' (O'Malley *et al.*, 1985a, p. 33);
- grouping: organising learning on the basis of 'common attributes';
- note-taking: writing down the gist of texts;
- deduction: conscious application of L2 rules;
- recombination: putting together smaller meaningful elements into new wholes;
- imagery: turning information into a visual form to aid remembering it – "Pretend you are doing something indicated in the sentences to make up about the new word";
- auditory representation: keeping a sound or sound sequence in the mind – "When you are trying to learn how to say something, speak it in your mind first";
- key word: using key-word memory techniques, such as identifying an L2 word with an L1 word that sounds similar;
- contextualisation: 'placing a word or phrase in a meaningful language sequence' (O'Malley *et al.*, 1985a, p. 34).
- elaboration: 'relating new information to other concepts in memory' (O'Malley *et al.*, 1985a, p. 34)
- transfer: helping language learning through previous knowledge – "If they're talking about something I have already learnt (in Spanish), all I have to do is remember the information and try to put it into English";
- inferencing: guessing meanings by using available information – "I think of the whole meaning of the sentence, and then I can get the meaning of the new word";
- question for clarification: getting a teacher to explain, help, and so on.

Social Mediation Strategies

Social mediation strategies, or social/affective strategies, 'represent a broad grouping that involves either interaction with another person or ideational control over affect' (O'Malley and Chamot, 1990, p. 45). In O'Malley *et al.* (1985a) only one is listed:

- cooperation: working with fellow-students on a language task.

The list in O'Malley and Chamot (1990) differs in that *delayed production*, *self-reinforcement*, and *directed physical response* are dropped; the *advance preparation* strategy is renamed 'functional planning'; the last cognitive strategy, *question for clarification*, is reclassified under social mediation; and the following cognitive strategy is added:

- summarising: making a summary of new information received.

As well as listing the strategies that the students reported, O'Malley *et al.* (1985a) looked at how often they occurred in the interviews. The overall comparison between beginners and intermediates in terms of sheer occurrence is as follows:

	Beginners	Intermediate
Metacognitive	112	80
Cognitive	297	149
Total	409	229

Comparison of learning strategies for ESL beginner and intermediates (adapted from O'Malley *et al.*, 1985a, p. 37)

In itself the sheer number of strategies shows the high level of the students' metalinguistic awareness in a second language. Overall, cognitive strategies are more frequent than metacognitive strategies, 69.9 per cent compared with 30 per cent. Intermediate students had a slightly higher proportion of metacognitive strategies (34.9 per cent) compared to beginners (27.4 per cent), even if their absolute totals are smaller. The most important metacognitive strategies averaged across both groups were: *selective attention* (19.8 per cent), *self-management* (20.8 per cent), and *advance preparation* (22.9 per cent). The important cognitive strategies were *repetition* (14.8 per cent), *note-taking* (14.1 per cent), *question for clarification* (12.8 per cent), imagery (9.4 per cent), and translation (8.5 per cent). Comparing the two levels, beginners scored over intermediates in the amount of strategies reported, 409 compared with 229. Beginners reported more *translation* (9.8 per cent vs. 6.0 per cent), more *imagery* (10.4 per cent vs 7.4 per cent), and more *elaboration* (3 per cent vs 1.3 per cent), but less *contextualisation* (2.4 per cent vs 7.4 per cent). A division by learning task showed that strategies were mentioned most often in connection with vocabulary work, pronunciation, and oral drills, least often with listening comprehension.

Later research, summarised in O'Malley and Chamot (1990), has been extensive. The same interview approach was tried with 111 American learners of Spanish and Russian (O'Malley and Chamot, 1990, pp. 123–128). Some additional strategies were added to the list, namely the cognitive strategy:

- rehearsal: going over the language needed for a task;

and the social/affective strategy:

- self-talk: boosting one's confidence to do a task more successfully.

Like the ESL students, the foreign language students 'reported using far more cognitive strategies than metacognitive ones' (O'Malley and Chamot, 1990, p. 127). Beginners relied most on *repetition, translation* and *transfer*, while advanced learners used *inferencing* more.

A further experiment reported in O'Malley and Chamot (1990, pp. 133–143) looked at the strategies reported for the same tasks by 19 learners over a period of four 'semesters'. This experiment yielded another metacognitive strategy to add to the list:

- problem identification: identifying important points of learning task.

Actual change in strategy use by the learners over time was hard to find, being related to the type of learning task.

Other studies have tested the extent to which learning strategies can be trained in the student. O'Malley, Chamot, Stewner-Manzanares, Russo, and Kupper (1985b) divided 75 ESL intermediate students into three groups who were given special lessons for 50 minutes a day for eight days: a 'metacognitive' group was explicitly taught the use of all three overall types of strategy; a 'cognitive' group was given cognitive and social/affective strategies; the third 'control' group was given no strategy training. The learners took general language tests. On a speaking task, the metacognitive group who had been taught all three strategy types 'scored higher than the cognitive group, which in turn scored higher than the control group' (O'Malley and Chamot, 1990, p. 174); a listening task was not significant overall, though some of its subtests were; the vocabulary task was not significant.

The research programme carried out by O'Malley and Chamot has been an interesting enterprise. O'Malley and Chamot equate their concept of learning strategy with the stages in Anderson's cognitive model (Anderson, 1983a) in which the initial production rules are converted into knowledge of procedures; this is discussed more fully in Chapter 10. The research thus includes not only theoretical divisions of strategies, but also lists of strategies based on students' actual use, and even actual teaching materials. Its approach is thorough-going and rigorous. As an integrated programme in applied linguistics, it is unique. Nevertheless there are problems over the presentation of the research. It is difficult to cite clear examples from their writings of the strategies they are discussing. The numbers for comparing the two groups are not provided with any test of statistical significance: does the apparent difference between beginners and intermediates actually matter? It could be argued that the research is not of a quantitative type and should not be forced into a numerical square hole. This works admirably if the aim is a cumulative list of all possible learning strategies – a train-spotter's collection. But comparisons of frequency between strategies or between groups require actual figures and these need to be tested by appropriate statistical tests. Sometimes the figures themselves are not reported although clearly available; in the experiment with Russian and Spanish learners (O'Malley and Chamot, 1990, pp. 123–8), for example, the only figures cited are the percentages for cognitive strategies and the average number of strategies per interview.

A problem with the methodology as reported in O'Malley and Chamot (1990, p. 117) is that 'Interviews with beginning level Hispanic students were conducted in Spanish while interviews with intermediate level students were conducted in English', that is, beginners were interviewed in their L1, intermediates in their L2. The group comparisons consequently confuse two factors: stage (beginners versus intermediate) and language (L1 vs L2). The language factor may in itself account for the greater number of strategies reported by the beginners; that is, intermediate learners were not capable of describing the strategies in the L2 and so may have been under-reporting their strategies; indeed the reason for adopting Spanish with the beginners was that it 'would provide more opportunity for students to contribute meaningfully and to describe complicated strategies' (O'Malley *et al.*, 1985a, p. 31). Or indeed, as Ervin-Tripp (1964) showed, people present themselves differently in their L1 and L2; the different strategies reported by beginners and intermediates may be due to their different self-images in the two languages. Without other evidence, we do not know whether the language or the level is responsible for the results. The research with English learners of Russian and Spanish (O'Malley and Chamot, 1990, p. 124) does not state the language of the interview; presumably it was English. The results showed an increase in number of strategies for Spanish from 12.4 for beginner interviews to 16.9 for intermediate/advanced and for Russian from 26.9 to 30.0 – the opposite of the trend in the ESL students, though the exactly equivalent figures are not given. Clearly, language deficiency could be a factor in the low number of strategies reported by intermediate ESL students.

Other approaches to learning strategies have produced lists of strategies based on different criteria. The Good Language Learner research (Naiman *et al.*, 1978) interviewed people who were known to be good at language learning; it reported six main groupings of strategies, chiefly relating to the learner's involvement in L2 learning and awareness of it as a process. Wendon (1987) looked at the views of L2 learning reported in an interview by 25 ESL learners in the US; she extracted three main groups of statement from these, which related to the learner's active use of the L2, the learner's attitude to learning, and personal factors such as self-concept.

> *Research summary*: J. M. O'Malley, A.U. Chamot, G. Stewner-
> Manzanares, L. Kupper, and R. P. Russo, (1985), 'Learning
> Strategies Used by Beginning and Intermediate ESL Students',
> *Language Learning*, **35**, pp. 21–46.
> **Aim**: to discover learning strategies used by L2 learners inside and
> outside the classroom
> **Learners**: 70 Spanish-speaking high school ESL students and 20 ESL
> teachers
> **Data type**: interviews with students and teachers, and classroom
> observation
> **Method of analysis**: interviews scored by four raters for strategies
> **Results**: established a range of 26 learning strategies in three broad
> categories of metacognitive (69.9 per cent), cognitive (30 per cent),
> and social/affective (0.1 per cent)

Fillmore (1976) concentrated on the strategies of young children learning English, dividing these into cognitive strategies such as 'look for recurring parts in the formulas you know' and social strategies such as 'join a group and act as if you understand what is going on, even if you don't'.

6.2 COMMUNICATION AND COMPENSATORY STRATEGIES

Selinker (1972) suggested that, if the fossilised aspects of interlanguage 'are the result of an identifiable approach by the learner to communication with native speakers of the TL, then we are dealing with *strategies of second language communication*'. Most L2 research has limited the term 'communication strategies' to strategies employed when things go wrong rather than applying it to the processes of problem-free communication: a communication strategy is resorted to when the L2 learner has difficulty with communicating rather than when things are going smoothly – a spare tyre for emergencies. Essentially L2 speakers have problems in expressing something because of the smaller resources they possess in the L2 compared to the L1, resembling the ignorance interpretation of transfer (Newmark and Reibel, 1968) mentioned in Chapter 3. To quote Bialystok (1990, p. 35), 'communication strategies overcome obstacles to communication by providing the speaker with an alternative form of expression for the intended meaning'.

L2 researchers into communication strategies tend to divide into two camps: sociolinguistically orientated researchers, such as Tarone (1980), who think of such strategies in terms of social interaction, and psychol-inguistically orientated researchers, such as Faerch and Kasper (1984), who think of them as psychological processes. The aim of both camps is to list the possible strategies available to L2 learners; the methodology is mostly to comb through transcripts of learners' language for specimens of strategies. Clear accounts of the various lists are provided in Poulisse (1989–90) and Bialystok (1990).

Tarone and Social Strategies

In Tarone (1980), the learning strategies seen in the previous section are separated from strategies of use, which are further subdivided into com-munication and production strategies. She defines communication strate-gies as 'mutual attempts of two interlocutors to agree on a meaning in situations where requisite meaning structures do not seem to be shared' (Tarone, 1980, p. 420). A communication strategy is a shared enterprise in which both the speaker and the hearer are involved rather than being only the responsibility of the speaker: when the two participants realise that they are not understanding each other, they fall back on three main groups of strategy: paraphrase, transfer and avoidance. Tarone's overall scheme is described in Tarone (1977) and is summarised in the figure on page 121; examples here are taken partly from Tarone, partly from other sources.

(1) Avoidance. The learner avoids the communication problem by:

- topic avoidance: not saying what he or she originally had in mind;
- message abandonment: giving up speaking in mid-stream.

An example of an L1 avoidance strategy is that in England we now speak of 'hairdressers' rather than 'barbers', to avoid the association with the infamous barber, Sweeney Todd.

(2) Paraphrase. Paraphrase strategies compensate for an L2 word that is not known by:

- approximation: finding a word with as close a meaning as possible, such as "animal" for "horse";
- word coinage: making up a word, say "airball" for "balloon";
- circumlocution: talking round the word – "when you make a container" for "pottery".

Paraphrase strategies rely on the language resources of the second lan-guage to get the meaning across in one way or another without falling back on the first language or on general strategies.

(3) Conscious transfer. Transfer from the L1 helps the participants out by:

- literal translation: a German speaking student says "Make the door shut" rather than "Shut the door";
- language switch: for example "That's a nice tirtil" (caterpillar).

Transfer strategies rely on the knowledge of the first language or the ability to interact effectively, rather than on the learner's limited L2 resources.

(4) Appeal for assistance. For instance, "What is this?"

(5) Mime. Non-verbal activities such as acting out a request for the time by pointing to the wrist.

Avoidance	{ Topic avoidance Message abandonment
Paraphrase	{ Approximation Word coinage Circumlocution
Transfer	{ Literal translation Language switch

Appeal for assistance

Mime

Communication strategies (Tarone, 1977)

Bialystok (1990) reported a later study that produced figures for the use of these strategies. She collected 324 utterances from 18 nine-year-old English-speaking girls learning French, who were playing an information-gap communication game in which one player identifies geometrical shapes described by another. Seventy-eight utterances were chosen 'because they appeared to be representative of the whole set and because their selection allowed all the taxonomic classes (except avoidance) to be illustrated' (Bialystok, 1990, p. 62). The distribution of the strategies was as follows:

		%
Avoidance:	message abandonment	4
Paraphrase:	approximation	12
	word coinage	<1
	circumlocution	80
Transfer	language switch	2
Appeal for assistance		2

Frequency of communication strategies in English-speaking girls learning French (adapted from Bialystok, 1990, p. 77)

Thus the overall category of *paraphrase* accounts for over 92 per cent of the strategies, with *circumlocution* alone taking up 80 per cent; a similar distribution is also found in Bialystok (1983). Bialystok (1990) also scored the success of listeners in choosing the appropriate shape in response to each strategy, with results as follows:

		%
Paraphrase:	approximation	51.05
	word coinage	96.88
	circumlocution	56.38
Transfer:	language switch	60.38

Success of communication strategies for listeners (adapted from Bialystok, 1990, p. 79)

All the strategies seemed surprisingly successful; only *word coinage* (the least frequent) was significantly better than the others.

Faerch and Kasper and Psychological Strategies

The psychological approach of Faerch and Kasper interprets similar data in terms of the individual's mental response to a problem rather than as a joint response by two people. They define communication strategies as 'potentially conscious plans for solving what to an individual presents itself as a problem in reaching a particular communicative goal' (Faerch and Kasper, 1983, p. 81). Their approach is then linked to psychological models of planning such as Miller, Galanter and Pribram (1960), further discussed in Chapter 10. While the difficulty encountered by the learner may seem similar to that described by Tarone, the cause is different: it is the solution of the individual's problems of processing rather than the speaker's and the hearer's mutual problems. Learners have two possible strategies in general for solving a communication problem: avoidance strategies in which they avoid the problem, and achievement strategies through which they find an alternative solution. Faerch and Kasper's overall scheme for communication strategies used in speech production is given in Figure 6.1.

(a) *Achievement Strategies*
Achievement strategies explore alternative ways of executing particular forms or function; the learner attempts to solve the problem he or she confronts. Achievement may be effected by *non-cooperative* strategies, which divide into three sub-groups, and *cooperative* strategies.

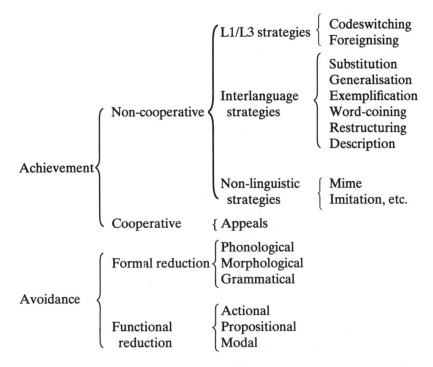

Figure 6.1   Communication strategies in interlanguage production in Faerch and Kasper (1984)

Non-cooperative Strategies. In these the learner tries to solve the problem without resort to other people through:

- *L1/L3 strategies*: that is to say, relying on a language other than the L2 by *codeswitching* ("Do you want to have some ah Zinsen?", the German word for "interest"), or trying out L1 expressions in the L2 with minimal adaptation by *foreignising* ("green things" for "vegetables" as literal translation of the Danish expression "grøntsager").
- *interlanguage strategies*: that is to say, strategies based on the evolving interlanguage such as:
  - putting one item for another – "if" for "whether" if the learner cannot remember if "whether" has an "h" (*substitution*);
  - using a more general word for an unknown word – "animal" for "rabbit" (*generalisation*);
  - describing something – "the thing to cook water in" for "kettle" (description);
  - giving an example of something for which the learner doesn't know the word – "cars" for "transport" (*exemplification*);

- making up a new word to cover a gap – "heurot" for "watch" in French (*word-coining*);
- phrasing the sentence in another way. – "I have two – er – I have one sister and one brother" (*restructuring*).

Finally, there are non-linguistic strategies such as *mime* and *sound imitation*.

Cooperative Strategies. Cooperative strategies involve the help of another person and consist of indirect or direct *appeals* such as "What is Kunst?".

(b) *Avoidance Strategies*
With avoidance strategies the learner either avoids a linguistic form he or she had difficulty with (*formal reduction*) at one of the three linguistic levels of phonology, morphology or grammar, or avoids a language function at the 'actional', 'propositional', or 'modal' level (*functional reduction*) by, for instance, abandoning a topic.

These two classifications by Tarone and by Faerch and Kasper overlap in many ways, though set up with different motivations. Both have general categories for *avoidance* and *cooperative* strategies; both describe *word-coining* and *codeswitching*; Faerch and Kasper have a finer set of non-cooperative strategies. It is not obvious that either of them lives up to their respective goals of seeing strategies as mutual interaction or as individual problem-solving respectively. To study social strategies involving both speaker and hearer in the manner of Tarone, both interlocutors need to be taken into account in the definition of each strategy and in the use of transcripts; how do we know that mutual non-comprehension was occurring simply from the utterance by one speaker of "tirtil", say? Other evidence of mutual incomprehension is needed than the speech of the non-native speaker. Faerch and Kasper claim that the strategies are signs of trying to solve the problems of using an L2. Again no independent evidence of such problem-solving is involved; the types of strategies seem to reflect types of solution rather than types of problem.

The Nijmegen Project and Compensatory Strategies

The most comprehensive project into communicative strategies was conducted at the University of Nijmegen by Kellerman, Bongaerts, and Poulisse in the 1980s. They argue that the schemes of analysis outlined so far have stopped at the level of description: 'the study of communication strategies should reach beyond description to prediction and explanation' (Kellerman *et al.*, 1990, p. 164). They criticise earlier schemes for concentrating on the linguistic form that results from a strategy rather than on the process that leads up to it; 'a taxonomy of CS would be more psychologically plausible if the underlying process were taken as its basis' (Poulisse, 1987, p. 79). Most systems of analysis seen so far for instance treat "hair-cutters" and "ones who, who erm, could cut people's hair" as examples of different strategies rather than as the same process of talking about 'defining attributes' (Poulisse, forthcoming): explanation needs to be based on the processes rather than their linguistic realisations. Bialystok (1990, p. 82) talks of the 'modularity fallacy' 'that linguistically distinct utterances constitute separate strategies'.

Furthermore, though Tarone and Faerch and Kasper include non-lexical strategies, virtually all examples come from vocabulary; communication strategies seem linked to lexis rather than to other levels of language. The Nijmegen project researchers argue that the wide range of strategies seen above does not reflect the actual choice available to the learners so much as the type of word that they are groping for. An alternative way of expressing "moon", such as "it's in the sky", is inherently different from an alternative way of expressing "knife", such as "you use it for cutting" (Kellerman *et al.*, 1990, p. 166); the difference lies in the properties of the words "moon" and "knife", not in the strategies themselves; and so the study of strategies should go beyond the linguistic differences to the underlying processes. They therefore limited the area of investigation in the Nijmegen project to the compensatory strategies through which an individual copes with vocabulary difficulties in expressing himself or herself – the ways in which the L2 user compensates for not knowing a word in the L2; 'communication strategy' is restricted to lexical 'compensatory strategy'.

The Nijmegen project has been written up at several stages of development by different combinations of authors, and the sequence of publication of their articles does not correspond to their place in the historical progression. Poulisse (1989–90) is the most extensive description of the project and will be used here as the main peg for the discussion. She relates her work to Levelt's psycholinguistic model of speech production (Levelt, 1989). This involves a cognitive component called the 'conceptualiser' which produces preverbal messages; these are passed to a linguistic component called the 'formulator' which encodes them grammatically and phonologically, and has access to a lexicon which gives them lexical forms; there is then a clear separation between conceptual and linguistic levels of production. Poulisse believes that, if the L2 production process breaks down for lack of appropriate forms in the mental lexicon, the speaker compensates either by going back to the conceptual stage or by trying out alternative linguistic formulations.

Poulisse (1989–90) therefore uses a process-based analysis consisting of two 'archistrategies': the *conceptual archistrategy* and the *linguistic archi-*

strategy. The conceptual archistrategy reflects a decision by the learner to compensate for a missing word by exploiting conceptual knowledge, the linguistic archistrategy an attempt to compensate through linguistic knowledge. In the conceptual archistrategy 'the speaker analyses the concept semantically, by decomposing it into its defining and characteristic features' (Poulisse, 1990, p. 80). The conceptual archistrategy includes two types of strategy: *analytic* strategies which involve 'a conceptual analysis of the originally intended concept' (Poulisse, 1989–90, p. 61), such as "a talk uh bird" for "parrot" or "he lives in the mountain" for "hermit"; and *holistic* strategies which mainly comprise 'the selection of a different concept which is sufficiently similar to the original one to convey the speaker's intended meaning' (Poulisse, 1989–90, p. 62), as in "table" for "desk".

The linguistic archistrategy relies either on *morphological creativity* through which the speaker creates a new word 'by applying his or her knowledge of L2 morphological rules to an existing L2 word' (Poulisse, 1989–90, p. 62), for instance, "ironize" for "iron", or on *transfer* from the L1, as in "middle" for "waist" based on Dutch "middel". One type of strategy may be embedded within another, thus yielding a distinction between superordinate and subordinate strategies.

Conceptual archistrategy	analytic	*"talk uh bird"* for *"parrot"*
	holistic	*"table"* for *"desk"*
Linguistic archistrategy	morphological creativity	*"ironize"* for *"iron"*
	L1 transfer	*"middle"* for *"waist"*

Compensatory strategies (Poulisse, 1989–90)

In the Nijmegen project 45 Dutch learners of English were tested at three levels of acquisition: advanced (university level), intermediate (higher secondary school), and low (lower secondary). Four tasks were used:

Task I: description of photographs of unusual objects, such as a flyswat;
Task II: description of abstract geometrical drawings in L1 and L2, based on Krauss and Weinheimer (1964);
Task III: retelling four one-minute long scripted stories;
Task IV: a fifteen-minute interview.

Task II then stood out from the others in being concerned with conceptual problem-solving rather than the more linguistic compensatory strategies. The project paid particular care to the identification of strategies, combining judgements by the researcher with recall by the student who was prompted by watching a video of the experiment.

A comparison of the strategies for each group found in tasks I, III, and IV showed that in general the more advanced the student the fewer compensatory strategies they employed; advanced students used 762 strategies compared with the lower secondary students' 1018. The distribution between the types of strategy can be seen below:

| | Conceptual | | Linguistic | | |
	Analytic	Holistic	Morphological	Transfer	Totals
Advanced	466	138	5	53	762
Upper secondary	630	171	9	93	903
Lower secondary	707	182	7	122	1018
Totals	1803	491	19	268	2581
Percentage	69.9	19.2	0.7	10.4	

Superordinate strategies in L2 by group for four tasks (adapted from Poulisse, 1989–90, p.117)

This shows both the disparity between the strategies and the similarity between the groups despite their difference in language proficiency. The more advanced group consistently use fewer superordinate strategies overall, the obvious explanation being that the lower groups necessarily encounter more words that they don't know. In all tasks, the *analytic* strategy is most frequent and the *morphological creativity* strategy is least frequent; the amount of the *holistic* strategy varies according to task, being rare on task I (photo description) and common on tasks III (story retelling) and IV (interview); the *transfer* strategy is rare on task I but frequent on IV. For subordinate strategies, the *holistic* strategy is however more frequent than the *analytic*. The advanced students use more *holistic* strategies on tasks III and IV than the lower students and the lower students use *transfer* more, the explanation again being the smaller vocabulary of the lower learners. Poulisse's conclusions are that strategies vary inversely in number according to proficiency, vary partly in type according to proficiency, vary according to task, and vary according to superordinate versus subordinate level. She sees the variation as linked to the different communicative assumptions reflected in each task; task IV (interview) for example allows actual checking with the listener and so naturally leads to *holistic* and *transfer* strategies.

Poulisse (1989–90) also tested the extent to which the four strategies were successful at communicating information to a native listener. Two tests were conducted with 60 native speakers of English. One used the stories which had been given in task III with learners' responses substituted for various words, using examples of each strategy type; the natives were asked to judge if each response was 'right/possibly right/pure guesswork'. The other test gave a range of learners' responses and asked the natives to guess the word. Some results for the second test were:

Correct(%)		Range(%)	
Holistic	51.2	0 (*tailor*)	to 92.3 (*wig*)
Analytic	69.6	20.6 (*applications*)	to 100 (*hairdressers*)
Holistic			
+ analytic	78.9	34.6 (*hair-restorer*)	to 100 (*lawyer*)
Transfer	59.3	2.9 (*rabbit*)	to 95 (*wig*)

Success of native speakers at guessing words from L2 compensatory strategies (adapted from Poulisse, 1989–90, p.178)

The most effective was the combination of *holistic* and *analytic* strategies, as in "letters to get a job" for "applications"; even *transfer* was reasonably successful, though not with attempts such as "konijnte" for "rabbit" and "to strike" for "to iron". The range of the responses shown above indicates that the crucial factors were the item and the context in which it was placed rather than the strategy itself.

Research summary: N. Poulisse (1989), 'The Use of Compensatory Strategies, by Dutch Learners of English', PhD thesis, University of Nijmegen (published in book form – Berlin: Mouton de Gruijter, 1990)

Aim: to investigate compensatory strategies at different L2 levels, in L1 and L2, and in terms of efficiency

Learners: 45 Dutch learners of English at three levels of acquisition: advanced, intermediate, and low.

Data type: transcripts of four tasks: I photo description, II description of drawings in L1 and L2, III retelling stories, IV interview.

Method of analysis: classification into conceptual (analytic and holistic) and linguistic (morphological and transfer)

Results: strategies vary inversely according to proficiency, vary partly in type according to proficiency, vary according to task, and vary according to superordinate versus subordinate level.

Before we look at Poulisse's task II, it is necessary to look at Kellerman *et al.* (1990), which seems to have been written early in the project, around 1985–6. This employed a three-way classification of referential strategies:

1. Holistic: attempting 'to label the *entire* shape by associating it to a "real world object" or to a conventional geometric figure' (Kellerman *et al.*, 1990, p. 168): "This is a triangle"; "It looks like a letter of the Greek alphabet – omega".
2. Partitive: treating the shape 'as if it were not in fact a single figure but a complex of smaller and therefore simpler shapes' (Kellerman *et al.*, 1990, p. 169): "Two triangles . . . their bases . . . are put together".
3. Linear: breaking 'the shape up into its ultimate one-dimensional components (lines, angles, dimensions, spatial relations)' (Kellerman *et al.*, 1990, p. 169); "Two lines starting in one point . . . one erm goes to the left side and the other goes to the right side erm and erm they're about 3 cm long and er . . .".

Thus their system is similar to that of Poulisse (1989–90) for conceptual archistrategies, except that they divide analytic strategies into partitive and linear.

In their design 17 advanced Dutch university students of English had to describe 11 abstract shapes 'so that the shapes could be redrawn by a native speaker . . . from a recording of the description at a later date' (Kellerman *et al.*, 1990, p. 167). The research yielded 183 usable pairs of descriptions in both languages. The first comparison is between the same person describing the shapes in the L1 and the L2. Dividing the strategies into the three types, 164 (89.6 per cent) were the same for a particular individual across languages.

In 18 of the 19 cases where the same individual used different strategies in the L1 and L2, the L1 description is *holistic*, that is to say, it gives a name for the whole shape, and the L2 strategy is *linear* or *partitive*. This is what would be expected if the communication problem were the speaker's lack of a vocabulary item in the L2; an item such as "omega" for example is available to describe a shape in the L1 but not in the L2. In their L1, Dutch, the learners can call a shape by the single holistic term "diamond" ("ruit", or "Wybertje"); if they don't know the word "diamond" in English, they struggle for alternatives such as "A square which you find on cards" or "It's a figure like two roofs of a house put together". The researchers claim that there is a hierarchy of preference going from the *holistic* strategy to the *partitive* to the *linear*. Only if the learners cannot find a *holistic* term for the shape will they go on to a *partitive* strategy, and only if they cannot describe it as a combination of shapes will they go on to a *linear* strategy. The sample of 19 examples they are drawing on is too small for such an inference to be more than suggestive without more detailed corroboration, or indeed without frequency figures for the common L1/L2 strategies, which are not supplied.

We can now come back to Poulisse's task II (abstract shape description). This was intended to tap the conceptual system rather than the linguistic by using a task that would place equal cognitive demands on reference in the first and the second languages since neither language would have appropriate vocabulary for the unusual geometric shapes. The results for the same 45 learners were as follows:

	English (L2)			Dutch (L1)		
	Holistic	Partitive	Linear	Holistic	Partitive	Linear
Advanced	137	21	22	134	21	25
Upper secondary	119	34	25	124	33	22
Lower secondary	116	32	31	117	43	20
Totals	372	87	78	375	97	67

Comparison of compensatory strategies for shape description in L1 and L2 (adapted from Poulisse, 1989–90, p.160)

As can readily be seen, compensatory strategies are not peculiar to the L2 but are used in the same way in the L1 and the L2; there were, for example, 375 holistic strategies in L1 Dutch, 372 in L2 English. The preference for holistic strategies is also confirmed at around 70 per cent, though this varied slightly according to the actual shape described. Individual learners overwhelmingly used the same strategies in both languages; there were only 32 'real' cases of students switching strategy after second thoughts and some bias in the scoring system had been eliminated. Least-proficient learners shifted most; only eight shifts went against the hierarchy given by Kellerman *et al.* (1990), the preponderance going from *holistic* to *linear* strategies. Again, this sample may be too small to be trusted.

The rationale for seeing communication strategies as a peculiar aspect of L2 learning cannot survive the evidence here and that of Poulisse (1989–90); they must be conceded to be a part of the speaker's speech repertoire available in whatever language he or she wants to use. Bialystok (1990, p. 81) talks of the 'uniqueness fallacy' that 'communication strategies of second-language speakers are a distinctive second-language phenomenon'. The results of both Poulisse (1989–90) and Kellerman *et al.* (1990) suggest that compensatory strategies at least are not specific to second language use. As Kellerman (1991, p. 154) puts it, 'the fundamental difference between a native speaker's and an adult learner's referential behaviour is that the former has a more extensive set of linguistic means available for reaching a particular communicative goal'. Rather than being a difference of quality, it is a difference of quantity: L2 learners use *more* compensatory strategies rather than *different* strategies.

Kellerman, Bongaerts and Poulisse (1987) provide a further variation on the same approach by adopting three archistrategies:

(1) the *approximative* archistrategy. In this the learner substitutes a word whose meaning is as close as possible, thus producing 'approximations' such as "bird" for "robin" or "chicken" for "goose";

(2) the *analytic* archistrategy. In this the learner describes the object for which he lacks a word, producing an 'analytic description'; instead of "knife" a learner might say "the large sharp thing";

(3) the *linguistic* archistrategy. In this the learner fills the gap with a word from the first language; a substitute for "breast" might be the Dutch word "borst".

The linguistic archistrategy is likelier in an L2 as the speaker usually cannot in an L1 duck using a word by substituting one from another language. However, Kellerman (1991) includes mime as an alternative way of filling the gap. Hence he now prefers to call this the 'code' archistrategy since it is not restricted to linguistic means nor to the L2. The research in Kellerman *et al.* (1990) is reanalysed from Kellerman *et al.* (1987) to show a clear preference for the holistic archistrategy over the analytic; the lack of linguistic strategies is seen as due to the comparative advanced level of the learners.

6.3   METHODOLOGICAL ISSUES IN STRATEGIES RESEARCH

The strategy concept presents different problems of research methodology from those encountered so far; a clear account of these is provided in Poulisse (forthcoming). The main reason is the difficulty of obtaining evidence for particular strategies. Much of the research uses something akin to the single sentence evidence of mainstream linguistics; although both Tarone (1977) and Faerch and Kasper (1983) present schemes evidently based on transcripts of learner use, they use single examples rather than presenting a full analysis of their corpora.

One possible form of evidence, used in part by O'Malley and Chamot (1990) and Poulisse (1989–90), is to ask the learners themselves what strategies they employ. This is the first research seen so far in this book to utilise such 'introspective data'. The basic technique is to ask people to report on their own feelings and experiences about L2 learning. Introspective data have had a controversial history. Though the founding father of psychology, Wundt, talked about his own subjective experiences such as listening to metronome beats (Miller, 1964), introspective data were spurned by the behaviourist tradition as mentalistic rather than objective. Single-sentence evidence has been called introspective since it is held to rely on the intuition of the native speaker. The related technique of grammaticality judgements, to be discussed in Chapter 9, differs from most introspective data in that it asks people to describe the knowledge in their mind, not the processes they use. Another type of reporting on mental processes will be seen in Chapter 10.

The danger with introspection is that it limits the data to conscious strategies rather than revealing those of which the learner is unaware; conscious strategies may be the tip of a very large iceberg. Introspective reports may also be distorted in various ways. One is the wish to please the teacher or experimenter; learners say what they expect people to want to hear instead of what they actually believe. Another is that the memory of strategies may in itself be selective because of the time interval between execution and memory or because of systematic distortions induced by the processes of memory. In psychology Ericsson and Simon (1980) argue that verbal reports of mental processes are accurate, provided that the process involved is related to language, that it does not need extra processing to be available for the individual to report, and that it is not transformed in some way before the point at which the report is made. Such research therefore needs to be carried out rigorously and to be supplemented by other data: 'introspection may make the preliminary survey, but it must be followed by the chain and transit of objective measurement' (Lashley, 1923).

The major evidence for strategies consists of deducing them from the learner's visible behaviour. In some sense the presence of a grammatical structure is a sign of itself; the evidence for its existence is the learner's speech, though the differences between surface and underlying structure and between competence and performance must always be borne in mind. So Alberto saying "I no see" is a sign that "no" occurs before the verb at this stage of his development; when Concetta says "Deutsch is gut", this is evidence that she has an SVO copula construction. But a strategy has a less obvious realisation in speech than a grammatical rule. It is true that even grammatical structure is deduced by the researcher from the surface sentence; "I no see" is not audibly marked out into Subject, Verb, Object, and so on. But in a sense deducing linguistic knowledge from linguistic form is not changing the area of discourse. Strategies, however, involve using linguistic forms to deduce psychological processes: 'on the basis of the form of language produced, the claim is that the learner has used a particular strategy' (Bialystok, 1990, p. 47). A strategy has to be inferred by the analyst from some other form of data. Consequently, there is less consensus among researchers over strategies than over grammatical rules; analysts differ widely in the range of strategies that they use, the areas they study, and their actual terminology; Kellerman (1991, p. 146) talks of 'a luxuriant jungle of names and strategies'. To avoid subjectivity, it is necessary to establish rigorous ways of demonstrating how such inferences may be made from data. This means considering the ambiguities in using a set of definitions of strategies such as those above: how do you decide that "sitting in the front of the class" is *self-management* rather than *advance preparation* or *advance organisation*? How do you know that "Make the door shut" is language switch rather than, say, *circumlocution*? If the lists were standardised, at least there would be a agreement about such categories, just as say the Cardinal Vowels diagram in phonetics trains linguists in a common analytical framework even if it distorts the facts of articulation.

One solution is to look for clear markers of strategies in the linguistic data, similar to Labov's use of 'channel cues' to reveal degree of attention. Faerch and Kasper (1984, p. 56) look for 'problem indicators' whether in the form of an 'implicit signal of uncertainty' such as pauses and slips, or an 'explicit (metalingual) signal of uncertainty', such as "I don't know how to say this", or a direct appeal for assistance, such as "I wanted to improve my knowledge of – what is Kunst?". This restricts the number of strategies considerably and biases it towards particular types; in particular such signals work more effectively with communication strategies than learning strategies. Although early research with pauses did argue that some were connected to lexical choice, hesitation phenomena are potentially misleading clues to communication strategies since they have many potential causes (Goldman-Eisler, 1968). To successfully pinpoint strategies from performance evidence, such an approach would have to incorporate a model of speech production of the kind to be discussed in Chapter 10 rather than *ad hoc* allusions to processes for which there is no other evidence. One alternative solution is to get more than one person to assign utterances to strategies; Poulisse (1989–90) checked reliability by asking two judges to score parts of the data. Another alternative is to bring in supporting evidence – what Kellerman (1976) called 'lateralisation' of the data. Poulisse (1989–90) supplemented the strategies scored in the tasks with the strategies recalled by the subjects in a later interview; this doubled the number of strategies and rejected only about 2 per cent. These additional safeguards cut down the subjectivity of the assignment of utterances to strategies, even if they can never eliminate it.

The basic aim of the strategies paradigm is taxonomic description and classification. Taxonomies are age-old systems of description, the most familiar perhaps being the Dewey system for library catalogues, Roget's *Thesaurus*, and the Stanley Gibbons stamp catalogues. Strategy researchers compile an inventory of the possible strategies that L2 learners may use. Hence, with the exception of the work by O'Malley and Chamot and the Nijmegen project, the descriptive work that underpins the research is seldom organised in terms of quantitative measures – *how often* do *how many* people use *which* strategy in *what* circumstance? Instead, it searches for an single sentence example from any source of a learner actually using a strategy: the question is whether a strategy ever occurs anywhere. As Bialystok (1990) points out, the paradigm example of word-coinage that is always cited is the invention of "airball" for "balloon", first given in Varadi (1973), as if there is no need to get fresh sightings of Bigfoot once one person has glimpsed him. Taxonomies of description exist for their own sake; they are collections of found objects, like a beachcomber's collection of pretty stones. The disputes usually concern the nature of the taxonomy – my set of categories is better than yours – and over where a particular example fits into it – that's not a snark, it's a boojum. The original purpose of the research – to find out things we do not know about L2 learning and use – gets lost in the in-fighting.

The concept of taxonomies was disputed for many years in linguistics; were linguists butterfly collectors or armchair speculators? Part of the manifesto of the first Chomskyan revolution was the denial that linguistics was a taxonomic science. Chomsky (1964, p. 23), for example, sees the baleful influence of 'Saussure's conception of language as an inventory of items' on modern linguistics and claims 'the taxonomic model (or any of its variants within modern study of language) is far too oversimplified to be able to account for the facts of linguistic structure' (Chomsky, 1964, p. 27). Perhaps strategies are such a simple domain of investigation that taxonomies are all that is required. Perhaps, however, strategies are as complex linguistic behaviour as any of the formal linguistic levels: taxonomies can never do them justice. Bialystok (1990) calls taxonomies 'a productive first approach to investigating a new domain'; however, none of her examples of taxonomies come from aspects of language other than the mental organisation of the lexicon. Kellerman (1991) puts three conditions on the design of taxonomies: they must be psychologically plausible, that is to say fit in with models of psychological performance; they must be parsimonious and so use a minimal number of strategies; they must be generalisable to different learners, tasks, situations, and so on.

6.4   LINGUISTICS AND STRATEGIES RESEARCH

What aspects of language are covered by strategies research? Learning strategies of the O'Malley and Chamot type depend on metacognitive, cognitive and social strategies, not on anything specifically linguistic. Tarone's communication strategies describe how an idea is expressed through, say, *paraphrase*, or in terms of choice of L1 or L2, say, *word-translation*, rather than in terms of lexical types, relationships, linguistic processes of word-coinage, and so on. Different as the orientation of Faerch and Kasper is claimed to be, the level of language involved is either pragmatic or lexical; other linguistic levels are only mentioned in connection with formal avoidance! The Nijmegen project is avowedly lexical; it is the process through which an idea is expressed that counts, whether conceptually or linguistically. From a linguistics point of view, little contact is made with a range of linguistic phenomena.

Learning strategies research directly answers the acquisition question; communication strategies research answers the use question. The definition of learning strategy given in O'Malley and Chamot (1990) was 'the special thoughts or behaviours that individuals use to help them comprehend, learn, or retain new information'. Language is not mentioned; nothing about these strategies is peculiar to language learning. Indeed O'Malley and Chamot (1990) claim allegiance to the psychological theory of John Anderson, to be discussed in Chapter 10, which does not distinguish language from the other cognitive systems in the mind. All their strategies could be used for studying any school subject. The metacognitive strategy "You review before you go into class" would be as useful for a physics lesson as for a language lesson; the cognitive strategy of organising material for learning on the basis of 'common attributes' would help geography as much as language learning; the social mediation strategy of working with fellow-students is a common principle of education in group work, now, for example, enshrined in the National Curriculum in Great Britain. The metacognitive strategies are not unique to language, apart perhaps from *delayed production* and *self-monitoring*, and even those look as if they are possible with other tasks; all would be useful to *any* learning task. Cognitive strategies could be applied to *anything* one wanted to learn, with the exception of *translation* and *auditory representation*, although the latter resembles standard mnemonic techniques for handling any information. The social mediation strategies were added to Brown's classification but again are not unique to language. 'There is neither a theoretical nor an empirical reason why most of the learning strategies identified in this study should be considered unique to second language learning' (O'Malley *et al.*, 1985b, p. 577). Language learning in this view depends upon mental effort by the learner and on conscious attention to the learning process; 'The principal mechanism by which greater learning efficiency materialises with learning strategies is the active mental processes in which students engage during learning, enabling them to capitalise on available instruction more than less active students unacquainted with the strategies' (O'Malley *et al.*, 1985a, p. 43). There is, however, evidence from Vann and Abraham (1990) that some unsuccessful learners are nevertheless active users of strategies.

But most linguists would deny that natural language acquisition depends on mental effort: instead, it just happens. The learning strategies describe what occurs *if* language is treated as another school subject whether in teaching or in research, not second language acquisition *per se*. To revert to the terms of McLuhan (1964), this confuses message and medium; content school subjects indeed transfer information to the students; in language learning the information in the classroom message is not important in itself; what students are learning is the medium through which they are getting the message – the system of language. Learning the rules of the language has to be distinguished from learning information conveyed through the language; hence there is an unresolved ambiguity in O'Malley and Chamot's definition of strategy in terms of 'new information'. Of course this is denied by the Anderson theory that underpins O'Malley and Chamot's research, in which all learning progresses from acquiring isolated facts to putting them into more economical procedures – to be described in Chapter 10. It is also rejected by those who accept that first language acquisition is learnt by language-specific mechanisms but deny such uniqueness, totally or partially, to second language acquisition; an example is Krashen's distinction between 'learning' and 'acquisition', seen in Chapter 3. This issue will be discussed further in Chapter 9.

The concept of learning strategies therefore goes against the belief that language knowledge differs from other forms of knowledge and that second language acquisition therefore differs from the acquisition of other forms of knowledge; in other words the belief that the mind is modular. One argument for the uniqueness of language knowledge is its special nature. An often-used example is the principle of structure-dependency, to be described in Chapter 9, which entails that "Is Sam the cat that is black?" is grammatical but *"Is Sam is the cat that black?" is not. Principles of language such as structure- dependency are unlike principles operating in other cognitive domains and have not been reduced to more general cognitive principles. Hence there are divisions between the language faculty of the mind and the other mental faculties such as reasoning or mathematics: the mind has distinct modules of which language is one. A further argument is that children with severe cognitive retardation are nevertheless capable of using complex aspects of language (Grant and Karmiloff-Smith, 1991); this could hardly be true if language learning depended on the same mental abilities as general cognition. The same point is true of the 'savant linguist' studied by Smith and Tsimpli (1991), who had an amazing ability to learn second languages despite low cognitive ability.

The chief argument for the uniqueness of language acquisition is that no general learning theory can explain the acquisition of specifically language knowledge. Structure-dependency, for instance, could not be learnt by orthodox means of general learning. Perhaps one day a psychological theory will emerge that can subsume language knowledge and language acquisition; at the moment a separate linguistics account is necessary to describe the nature of linguistic systems and how they are acquired, whether syntax, phonology, or lexis. Thus there is an inherent contradiction between learning strategy research and linguistics. Whatever strategies there might be, they should be *language* learning strategies, not general learning strategies; it may well be that physics, geography, and all other school subjects can be learnt by means of learning strategies; second languages can indeed clearly be learnt in some fashion through Palmer's studial capacity. But this is learning through faculties of the mind other than the language faculty. Research such as that by O'Malley and Chamot can contribute towards our understanding of classroom learning by other routes than the language faculty, but tells us little or nothing about linguistic approaches to SLA itself. It answers the acquisition question by denying the unique nature of language knowledge. Briefly my own feeling is that this should not be seen as a question of all-or-none; SLA takes many forms both inside and outside classrooms. It may indeed be possible for some people in some circumstance to learn some aspects of the second language as if they were not language at all. But SLA research should regard these as spinoffs from other disciplines rather than as its main concern; if SLA is indeed the same as other forms of non-language learning, there is no need for an independent discipline to study it.

The communication strategies research does not in itself attempt to look at acquisition; Poulisse (1989–90, p. 190) emphasises that the Nijmegen project was an investigation of language use and so 'has but few implications for second language acquisition research'. Definitions of communication strategies make no mention of learning, nor indeed do they refer to learners. Much of the research reveals little difference between learners at different stages of L2 development, except in so far as their vocabulary expands. At present the research is SL research rather than SLA research. Obviously, if we accept the equivalence of decoding and codebreaking, communication strategies may also be learning strategies and the use question may contribute to the acquisition question. But, at present, strategies research tells us little directly about either language knowledge or language acquisition. Its full import awaits its integration with the knowledge question: how does knowledge of languages relate to second language use?

In a way, the earlier chapters have treated the L2 learner as having little choice or control over his or her actions. The stages of L2 development were seen as following one another as summer follows spring. The variation between 'styles' reflected chiefly the amount of attention rather than the learners' conscious decision. The concept of strategy, however, starts from the learner's choice. The learner is a human being with the free will to opt for one thing or the other; given that the learner is at a particular moment of time in a particular situation, what can the learner choose to do? This chapter has described some of the possibilities of choice open to the L2 learner in a dynamic situation. The overall message perhaps is the need for SLA research to look at processes of language as well as knowledge of language, to establish the boundaries between language and non-language areas of the mind, and to link the use question more clearly to the knowledge and acquisition questions.

7 Relative Clauses: Beyond Phrase Structure Syntax

This chapter starts to look at views of syntax that go beyond phrase structure through the topic of relative clauses, a complex area surveyed in Keenan (1985). Relative clauses are subordinate clauses that modify nouns within noun phrases in the main clause above them; for example, in "The man who met him was a spy" the relative clause "who met him" modifies the noun "man" in the subject NP "the man". The relative clause often marks the element that is related to the main clause with a relative pronoun such as "who". Relative clauses provide a fruitful area for L2 learning research, being on the one hand linked to 'implicational' universals of language, on the other to constraints of language processing. Implicational universals are common factors to human languages which are established by studying as many languages as possible.

Relative clauses are often handled through the idea of movement, which was introduced earlier: movement links the underlying d-structure of the clause to the s-structure position of the relative pronoun or Wh-phrase in the relative clause construction. The sentence:

"The woman who John saw was his aunt"

is derived from an underlying structure:

"The woman (John saw the woman) was his aunt"

by moving "the woman" to "who" in the initial position in the relative clause:

"The woman who John saw *t* was his aunt"

Different types of relative clauses and different languages vary in the nature of this relationship and in its consequences for the surface of the sentence:

- Which noun phrase in the main clause is involved? It might be the subject NP that has a noun modified by a relative clause, as in:

    "The man who met her was a spy"

or it may be the object NP that is modified, as in:

"She met a man who was a spy".

- Does the relative clause come before or after the noun in the noun phrase it modifies? English always has the relative clause *after* the noun while Chinese has the relative clause *before* the noun. This is dealt with in the next chapter as a general property of subordinate clauses called 'head-direction'.

- Which element in the relative clause is relativised? Various elements in the relative clause can be relativised, such as the subject:

"Keith is the teacher who likes whisky"

or the object:

"Auchentoshan is the whisky he likes best".

The elements in the relative clause that may be relativised vary from one language to another, as we see below.

- Is there a resumptive pronoun in the original position in the relative clause? English does not say:

*"The man who John saw him was Peter"

even if such forms can occasionally be heard in spontaneous speech. But languages such as Chinese and Hebrew consistently keep a copy of the relativised element in the sentence, as in the Hebrew sentence:

"Ha- isha   she- David natan la et   ha- sefer."
the   woman that David gave to her   the book

These 'copies' will here be called 'resumptive pronouns'.

- What relative pronouns are used? Languages such as English have a variety of forms such as "who", "which", and "that" for the speaker to choose from; other languages have a single invariant form, such as "*che*" in Italian. English also has a zero form in object position in relative clauses:

"The doctor I met was an eye specialist"

versus

"The doctor that/who I met was an eye specialist".

The term 'relative pronoun' will be used here to refer to both relative pronouns and "that", though "that" is, not strictly speaking, a relative pronoun but a complementiser also found in sentences such as "I believe that he is crazy".

7.1   RELATIVE CLAUSES AND THE ACCESSIBILITY HIERARCHY

A common theme is how L2 learners deal with the variation over which elements in the relative clause may be relativised. The Accessibility Hierarchy for relative clauses described in Keenan and Comrie (1977) treats this variation systematically. In all languages, it is possible to relativise the subject of the relative clause:

(1) *Subject*: "Emily Bronte was the sister who wrote *Wuthering Heights*".

Most languages, but not Malagasy for example, also permit relativisation of the object:

(2) *Object*: "The place that he visited was called Blenheim Palace".

Many languages, but not Welsh, allow relativisation of indirect objects:

(3) *Indirect object*: "The student he lent the book was Mark".

Some languages allow relativisation of the object following prepositions:

(4) *Object of preposition*: "The hotel she stayed at was in Woburn Place".

Some permit genitive forms to be relativised:

(5) *Genitive*: "The woman whose handbag he stole was furious".

A few also allow the relativisation of objects of comparison:

(6) *Object of comparison*: "The man who Mary is taller than is John".

Or, to take a more convincing, if bizarre, real-life example from Pohl (1987, p. 28): "To Harold's annoyance, the other thing that he was not more of than Sneezy was strong".

Summing up earlier work, Keenan and Comrie (1977) claimed that languages do not select from these types at random; an implicational relationship called the Accessibility Hierarchy runs from type 1 down to type 6. If a language has subject clauses (1), it may have object clauses (2); if it has subject and direct object clauses (1 and 2), it may have indirect object clauses (3), and so on down the hierarchy. But a language never leaves particular types out of the sequence: no language has indirect object clauses (3) that does not also have object and subject clauses (1 and 2); no language has object of comparison clauses (6) without having the preceding five. The Accessibility Hierarchy spells out the possibilities for relativisation that may occur in human languages.

The Accessibility Hierarchy is also connected to performance. A statistical analysis of a large corpus of written English confirms that subject type clauses are three times as frequent as object and object of preposition clauses put together (de Haan and van Hout, 1988). Fox (1987), however, has questioned the weight given to the subject in the Accessibility Hierarchy, partly from an analysis of a spoken English corpus that showed that there are just as many object relative clauses as subject clauses, curious in view of the fact that objects only occur on average in one in three of main clauses in English texts.

Gass (1979) aimed to see how L1 transfer applied to the L2 acquisition of relative clauses. She was particularly concerned with resumptive pronouns, which Keenan and Comrie (1977) claim are likelier to occur further down the Accessibility Hierarchy. She investigated 17 L2 learners of English with nine different L1s; of the languages spoken by the subjects, Chinese, Arabic, and Persian have resumptive pronouns in direct object relative clauses, while French, Italian, Korean, Portuguese, Japanese, and Thai do not. Two tasks were used: an acceptability task and a sentence combining task asking them to combine sentences on the pattern of "The girl ran home" and "The girl was crying" becoming "The girl who was crying ran home". Indirect object and object of preposition types were collapsed into one 'due to their analogous behaviour in English relative clauses' (Gass, 1979, p. 340). The data were scored in terms of mistakes with case marking on the relative pronoun, and retention or omission of resumptive pronouns. Results for the sentence combining task for the different types were as follows:

Subject (1)	Direct object (2)	Indirect object (3)	Genitive (5)	Object of comparison (6)
75%	33%	30%	50%	0%

Correct answers for five relative clause types (derived from a graph in Gass, 1979, p. 340)

This order of difficulty has a clear relationship to the Accessibility Hierarchy: subject clauses are the easiest, object of comparison clauses the most difficult. The only exception is the high score for genitive clauses, which places them second out of five, rather than fourth. This represents an order of difficulty rather than a sequence of acquisition in that it is based on success rates in a single-moment study carried out at one point of time; although the subjects were tested six times over a four-month period, no differences emerged.

The results were also analysed in terms of the various L1s involved. The grammaticality judgement task measured the extent to which the learners accepted resumptive pronouns in the positions possible in their L1s.

	L1s without resumptive pronouns	L1s with resumptive pronouns
Subject (1)	11.85	44.58
Object (2)	30.00	77.50
Indirect object (3)	31.85	80.00
Genitive (5)	32.41	47.29
Object of comparison (6)	37.62	59.00

Judgement of ungrammatical resumptive pronouns in five relative clause types (adapted from Gass, 1979, p. 336)

The differences between the two groups turned out to be significant only for the subject, object, and indirect object types; the presence of resumptive pronouns in the L1 had an effect on the first three types in the Accessibility Hierarchy in the L2, which goes against the claims of Keenan and Comrie (1977) that resumptive pronouns are more likely to occur lower down the hierarchy, and against the evidence by Ioup and Kruse (1977) that L2 learners accept them more easily at lower points on the hierarchy. Gass's overall conclusions are: 'it is apparent from the study that the likelihood of the transferability of linguistic phenomena must take into account both target language facts and rules of universal grammar' (Gass, 1979, p. 343).

Research summary: S. Gass, (1979), 'Language Transfer and Universal Grammatical Relations', *Language Learning*, **29**, pp. 327–44.

Aim: L1 transfer applied to the L2 acquisition of relative clauses

Learners: 17 L2 learners of English with nine different L1s

Aspects of language: the Accessibility Hierarchy as applied to English relative clauses

Method: grammaticality judgements of 29 sentences and combination of sentence pairs

Results: order of difficulty had a clear relationship to the Accessibility Hierarchy, except for genitive clauses

Conclusions: 'the likelihood of the transferability of linguistic phenomena must take into account *both* target language facts and rules of universal grammar' (Gass, 1979, p. 343)

Other work on the Accessibility Hierarchy has used a diversity of approaches:

(a) *Eckman, Bell and Nelson (1988)* argued that, if the Accessibility Hierarchy is somehow built in to the L2 learners' expectations of language, they do not need to learn all the relative types separately; they simply have to discover how far down the hierarchy the language goes. So, once learners identify the maximum point on the hierarchy for the language, they can assume that all the types above it are possible. If they know it has type 5 genitive clauses, they can immediately fill in all the clause types above 5. Eckman et al (1988) tested whether learners could indeed extrapolate the 'missing' relative clause types from knowing the maximum type, extending an experiment by Gass (1982). They tested 36 ESL students, divided into four groups of nine students of equally mixed L1s. Each group was given a pre-test to establish their base-line, one hour's language teaching, and a post-test. The teaching given to the four groups differed according to the type of relative clause they were taught:

- group 1 were taught subject relative clauses (type 1);
- group 2 were taught direct object relative clauses (type 2);
- group 3 were taught object of preposition clauses (type 4);
- group 4 were taught sentence combining techniques unrelated to relative clauses.

The post-test asked them to combine sentences such as "You talked to the teacher" and "The class sent the flowers to the teacher". Students' answers were scored in terms of correctness, whether miscombinations or insertion of resumptive pronouns or retention of the original NP *in situ*. The maximum score for each relative clause type is 63. The results were as follows:

	Subject type (1)	Object type (2)	Object of preposition type (4)
Subject group 1	4	25	38
Object group 2	10	12	38
Object of preposition group 3	0	4	1
Control group 4	23	30	42

Errors in three relative clause types for taught groups (adapted from Eckman *et al.*, 1988, p. 10)

Overall, the learners conform to the Accessibility Hierarchy as an order of difficulty; the subject type (1) is easiest for all groups, the object of preposition type (4) the most difficult for all but one group. But the striking result is the success of the object of preposition group 3, who were better than the other groups not only at this type but also at subject and object clauses – which they had never been taught. As predicted, the learners had extrapolated from the extreme clause type they had been taught to the other types above it in the Accessibility Hierarchy, namely subject and object types. The fascinating implication of this for language teaching is that, where implicational universals are concerned, students should actually be taught the most difficult of a set of structures *first* rather than last, contrary to what most teaching has assumed.

(b) *Hyltenstam (1984)* looked at L2 learners' use of resumptive pronouns in Swedish. He tested 9 Finnish learners, 12 Spanish, 12 Greek, and 12 Persian; Finnish and Spanish have no resumptive pronouns but Greek and Persian have them in some relative clause types. The task was to identify which of two similar pictures a particular sentence referred to by producing relative clauses; the technique is a test of controlled production.

The results were expressed in implicational scales that take up seven pages. Recalculated as the number of subjects who use resumptive pronouns in particular positions, they are as follows:

		Subject	Direct object	Indirect object	Object of preposition	Genitive	Object of comparison
	N	(1)	(2)	(3)	(4)	(5)	(6)
Persian	12	0	7	10	8	12	10
Greek	12	0	5	7	7	11	12
Spanish	12	0	2	6	3	10	7
Finnish	9	0	0	0	0	6	3

L2 learners of Swedish using resumptive pronouns (recalculated from Hyltenstam, 1984)

This shows that 'pronominal copies are used by all language groups in their production of Swedish relative clauses' (Hyltenstam, 1984, p. 47), even by those whose L1s do not have them, that is, the Spanish and Finnish learners. There is nevertheless a difference between the learners according to L1: the Persian and Greek learners, as expected, supply more resumptive pronouns than the Spanish and Finnish. The type on the Accessibility Hierarchy also affects all groups of learners: there are fewest learners who produce resumptive pronouns for the subject type (1) and most for the genitive (5) or the object of comparison (6). However, the correspondence with the Accessibility Hierarchy is not perfect; the genitive type has more resumptive pronouns than does the object of comparison type, rather than the reverse. Hyltenstam concludes that 'learners of a language such as Swedish learn to suppress pronominal copies in the order described by the accessibility hierarchy with the exception of the order GEN – OCOMP' (Hyltenstam, 1984, p. 55).

Hyltenstam's design was replicated by Pavesi (1986) with Italians learning English, 48 children in Italy, and 38 adults working in Edinburgh, the purpose being to compare informal and formal learning. The formal group used resumptive pronouns more often than the informal group; overall order of difficulty went well with the Accessibility Hierarchy, except that the pair genitive/object of comparison were reversed and the pair indirect object/object of preposition could not be distinguished (indeed Gass, 1979, collapsed them into one type).

(c) *Roger Hawkins (1988)* contrasts the Accessibility Hierarchy with a 'configurational' explanation derived from Tarallo and Myhill (1983) that the ease or difficulty of relative clauses depends on 'the proximity of the head of the RRC [restrictive relative clause] to an extraction site in the embedded sentence' (R. Hawkins, 1988, p. 159). He sees knowledge of relative clauses as including at least three of the factors outlined above: the elements that may be relativised, the presence or absence of resumptive pronouns, and the form of the relative pronoun.

His experiment deals with the L2 acquisition of French relative pronouns by English learners. French differs from English not only in the number of relative pronouns that the speaker has to choose from but also in the grounds for choosing them; English distinguishes between "who", "which", and "that" in terms of animacy, while French distinguishes "qui" from "que" in terms of whether it is subject or object of the relative clause; in English the zero relative pronoun may occur when it is not the subject of the relative clause, while French does not allow the zero form at all. Hence English in a sense selects the relative pronoun according to information to its *left* in the sentence while French selects it according to information to its *right*. While the English "whose" only occurs within an NP as in,

"The visitor whose name I had forgotten."

the French equivalent form "dont" must be extracted from the NP:

"Le visiteur dont j'avais oublié le nom."
the visitor whose I have forgotten the name.

Hawkins's analysis of English and French makes the following predictions for a configurational approach:

- L2 learners of French would learn relative pronouns in an order based on how close they are to the original location in the relative clause, that is, "qui""que""dont"; this is, however, the same prediction as the Accessibility Hierarchy;

- learners would misunderstand French relative clauses with stylistic inversion such as "L'homme que connait Pierre". This actually means "the man Peter knows", that is, the same as "L'homme que Pierre connait". But English learners would interpret it as "the man that knows Peter" by incorrectly taking "que" to be the subject of the relative clause, "Pierre" the object. The Accessibility Hierarchy suggests they would not make this mistake;
- learners would develop the different uses of "dont" according to the proximity of the relative clause to the head. The Accessibility Hierarchy on the contrary implies they would learn all contexts of "dont" simultaneously.

Hawkins tested three groups of English learners of French, 25 studying A-levels (the British Advanced Level examination, usually taken at the age of 18), 50 first-year university undergraduates, 44 second year undergraduates. He used a task in which they had to fill in blanks with the appropriate relative pronoun in sentences, such as:

"La personne _____ Marie avait d'abord remarquée dans le jardin public la suivait maintenant"
the person _____ Marie had noticed in the park was now following her.

Hence he was focusing on the learners' choice of correct forms rather than on sheer comprehension.

While the order of difficulty mostly went from subject type to direct object to genitive as predicted, that for the A-level group did not, going instead from direct object to subject to genitive. The scores for the A-level group for "que" and "qui" were as follows:

	Animate head(%)	Inanimate head(%)
qui	61	23
que	30	61.2

Correct relative pronouns for A-level learners of French (adapted from Hawkins, 1988, p. 169)

The learners' problems with subject clauses were based on animacy rather than on position in the relative clause, that is, a leftward strategy rather than a rightward strategy. The results for stylistic inversion, again choosing the A-level group were:

	Animate head(%)	Inanimate head(%)
Direct object	30	61.2
Inversion	14	47

Correct "que" for A-level group (adapted from Hawkins, 1988, p. 171)

All three groups were poor at this, apparently again using a leftward strategy. Finally, the results for "dont" expressed as extraction versus non-extraction were non-significant for all but the first year group. Hawkins concluded that these results provide some support for the configurational approach: '"difficulty" of RRC types for L2 learners is a function of their processing capacity: their ability to parse L2 data' (Hawkins, 1988, p. 178).

7.2 RELATIVE CLAUSES AND PSYCHOLOGICAL PROCESSING

A second line of research has looked at relative clauses from a psychological point of view, in particular exploring the embedding of relative clauses within main clauses. Sheldon (1974) claimed the order of difficulty for first language acquisition is based on 'parallel function'; L1 children find the easiest sentences to understand those in which the NP in the main clause has the same function as the relativised element in the subordinate clause, regardless of whether both are subject or both are object. Thus "The man that saw the cat hated dogs" is maximally easy in that "the man" is the subject of the main clause, and "that" is the subject of the relative clause. "The woman saw the dog that liked bones" is maximally difficult because "the dog" is object of the main clause, "that" is subject of the relative clause. Bever (1970) suggested that the processing problem with some relative clauses is that the same NP plays two syntactic roles: in "The man John liked was Peter" the NP "the man" is at the same time subject of "was" in the main clause and object of "liked" in the relative clause. Clauses with parallel function are easier to process because the element plays the same role in both clauses, whether subject or object.

Gass and Ard (1980) reanalyse the data from the combination task in Gass (1979) to compare with Sheldon. They distinguish four possible sentence types:

(1) Subject in main clause plus Subject relativisation (Subject Subject)
     "The man who came fell down"

(2) Subject in main clause plus Object relativisation (Subject Object)
     "The dog the cat chased ran away".

(3) Object in main clause plus Subject relativisation (Object Subject)
     "John kicked the ball that was rolling down the street".

(4) Object in main clause plus Object relativisation (Object Object)
     "I saw the girl the boy hit"

In the L2, the types 1 and 2 (Subject Subject and Subject Object) were easier than type 4 (Object Object), which was easier than type 3 (Object Subject). It is not parallel function that counts but whether the NP is the subject of the main clause. The L1 and L2 orders of difficulty therefore differ; 'In the second language data the results are compatible in directionality with the Accessibility Hierarchy, whereas the results for first language learners predominantly reflect a principle of cognitive development' (Gass and Ard, 1980, p.450). Ioup and Kruse (1977, p.169) also reported that in an L2 test of the parallel function hypothesis 'the results go significantly in the opposite direction of what is predicted'. Schumann (1980) looked at the transcripts of five of his Spanish-speaking learners and two additional Italian learners; he found that the proportion of the four combination produced were:

Subject Subject	6%
Subject Object	4%
Object Subject	35%
Object Object	53%

The most popular types were then those that related to the Object of the clause; for Subject clauses there was no preference for parallel function, for Object clauses a slight advantage. Position of the modified NP in the main clause was more crucial than either parallel function or type on the Accessibility Hierarchy. Only the results of Flynn (1989), to be discussed in the next chapter, incidentally confirm the parallel function hypothesis.

Since the early days of psycholinguistics, difficulty in understanding relative clauses was believed to vary according to the 'depth' of embedding (Miller and Chomsky, 1963; Blumenthal, 1966). In one sense there is no limit to the number of relative clauses possible in one sentence:

"This is the cat that killed the rat that ate the malt that lay in the house that Jack built"

shows four levels of embedding of subject relative clauses, the nursery rhyme eventually getting up to nine levels. In another sense, actual performance precludes too many of certain types of embeddings as the processing mechanisms cannot cope with them. This is demonstrated by turning the nursery rhyme partly into object relative clauses:

"The house the malt the rat the cat killed ate lay in was built by Jack".

A real, if dated, example of excessive embedding can be found in Trollope (1881): 'We must go again to Merle Park, where the Tringle family was still living – and from which Gertrude had not as yet been violently abducted at the period to which the reader has been brought in the relation which has been given of the affairs at Stalham.'

Cook (1975) took up the basic comprehension strategy from Bever (1970) that English speakers identify any Noun–Verb–Noun sequence as "Actor–Action–Object", already mentioned in Chapter Five. This works perfectly well with subject relative clauses (type 1) such as:

"The man that sees the cat likes the dog."

where the relative clause is in the correct Actor–Action–Object order, but the strategy produces the wrong interpretation with the object type (2) such as:

"The man that the cat likes sees the dog."

where the relative clause is in the Object–Actor–Action order. If difficulties with multiple embeddings are due to an overload on memory processing, Cook (1975) postulated that L2 learners' problems with *single* relative clauses should resemble those of L1 children because both have similar memory deficiencies; L2 learners should also have similar problems to L1 speakers with *double* embeddings since these would tax the natives' memories. The subjects were 52 adult L2 learners of English, 60 native children aged from 4 to 9, and 111 adult native speakers divided into two groups who received either single or double embedded sentences. The materials were sentences that differed in terms of whether the relative clause was a subject or object type:

"The cat that likes the dog bites the horse"

versus:

"The cat that the dog bites likes the horse"

and in terms of whether the relative pronoun was "that", "what", or zero:

"The cat Ø/what/that the cat likes pushes the horse".

"What" was included as a relative pronoun to reflect supposed local usage in East London, where the children lived. Half the sentences tested the main clause, half the relative clause. Two sets of the same sentences were used with single and double embeddings, the latter given only to the native speakers:

"The dog the cat the man sees likes pushes the horse".

The subjects had to show which out of the dog, the cat, or the man had pushed or bitten which of the others, the children demonstrating this individually with dolls, the adults in groups with pencil and paper. Results were scored separately for the subject and object. The results for subject assignment were as follows, expressed as a percentage of correct answers:

		'Subject' type (1)(%)	'Object' type (2)(%)
L2 adults	1 embedding	81	58
L1 children	1 embedding	70	50
L1 adults	1 embedding	99	91
	2 embeddings	90	58

Percentage of correct subject assignment (adapted from Cook, 1975)

All groups therefore found the subject type easier than the object type, even the natives with one embedding; this was argued to fit the Accessibility Hierarchy, even if it tested only the top two types. Increasing the embeddings from one to two indeed reduced the native speakers to the same score on the object type as the L1 children; the same differential patterns of error of subject and object occurred for all three groups once their memory capacities had been equalised.

Cook (1975) concludes that there are two basic strategies that learners use when their memory processes are overloaded, seen in L1 children and L2 learners with one embedding, and in native speakers with two:

- the first NP is interpreted as the Subject;
- the first NP after the verb is interpreted as the Object, sometimes just the last NP in the sentence.

These can be related to Bever's Actor–Action–Object strategy, but are not identical with it.

7.3 THE L2 ACQUISITION OF RELATIVE CLAUSES AND LINGUISTICS

The range of research outlined above indicates some of the links between the acquisition of relative clauses and syntactic issues of concern to linguists. The acquisition question has mostly been merged with the use question by seeing L2 learning as based on performance strategies; acquisition is, for example, linked to the processing difficulty of the Accessibility Hierarchy. Keenan and Comrie (1977, p. 88) suggest 'the AH directly reflects the psychological ease of comprehension'. To provide proper evidence for acquisition, however, too little of the relative clause research has concerned the learner's progress over time, too much is single-moment studies concerned with order of difficulty. Interestingly both Gass (1979) for L2 subjects and Cook (1975) for the L1 group had incorporated longitudinal elements in their research design, which turned out to be of little import.

Part of the attraction of the Accessibility Hierarchy is its link to implicational universals. John Hawkins (1983) proposes a set of implicational universals for word order based on a sample of 336 languages, claiming that if a language has a particular word order in two types of phrase, it 'implies' a particular word order in a third; for instance 'If a language has OV order, then if the adjective precedes the noun, the genitive precedes the noun' (J. Hawkins, 1983, p. 64). Implicational universals define the possibilities for a language by specifying the combinations of construction possible in any one language. Thus the Accessibility Hierarchy describes the possible synchronic states of language; at any moment in time a language must have a range of relative clauses that extend down the hierarchy from the subject type without a break. An interlanguage is subject to the same constraint; an L2 learner couldn't know the object of comparison type without knowing the other five. Other implicational universals have not been much studied in L2 learning, though Cook (1988a) explored the implications of Hawkins's word order universals for L2 learning, but fairly inconclusively. The Accessibility Hierarchy can be interpreted as restrictions on the language knowledge of the individual: the mind permits certain combinations of relative clause and precludes others. In this sense the Accessibility Hierarchy is not just a matter of processing but is in addition a description of linguistic competence. Hence the Accessibility Hierarchy is not dissimilar in its conclusions to the Universal Grammar (UG) theory to be discussed in Chapter 9. Its starting point is nevertheless different: an implicational universal is established by looking for generalisations true of as many languages as possible, while a universal in UG theory is established by looking at the 'logical problem of language acquisition', possibly seen only in a single language, as we see later.

In some ways the research fails to grasp the central linguistic issues, largely because these are now seen as much broader than relative clauses themselves. As with the Multidimensional Model, movement is implicit in much of the discussion; hence relative clauses form part of the general theory of movement to be outlined in Chapter 8. Some steps towards this were made by Adjemian and Liceras (1984); it will partly be covered in the work with subjacency to be described in Chapter 9. The point should also be made that in terms of the level of L2 learning involved, relative clauses are a large jump from the near-beginners mostly discussed in earlier chapters to intermediate or advanced learners.

Much of the research slips into psychological processing, whether the parsing of Hawkins (1988), the strategies of Cook (1975), or the ease of comprehension of Keenan and Comrie (1977). But, to go back to the points made in Chapter 5, appeals to psychological processing need to be based on a proper account of processing itself and should not be made in isolation from the ideas of speech processing being put forward in psycholinguistics. The theory of parsing put forward by Marcus (1980) suggests that there is a 'look-ahead buffer' in the mind – a small capacity memory system – that allows up to three elements to be stored for processing structures such as relative clauses; Wanner and Maratsos (1978) also propose a 'HOLD' memory system in which unidentified elements are stored until they pop out at the right moment in the comprehension of the sentence; both models have been specifically designed to take care of the problems of relative clause interpretation, with Wanner and Maratsos carrying out an experiment with relative clauses to prove their point. If the acquisition of relative clauses is indeed linked to speech processing and memory, it needs to be investigated within adequate performance theories, such as the parsing theory of Hawkins (1990), not by linguists inventing *ad hoc* cognitive processes to explain the results of their relative clause experiments.

7.4 COMPREHENSION AND EXPERIMENTS IN SLA RESEARCH

The research in this chapter demonstrates how L2 research can take on syntax of a more interesting kind and use it to illuminate issues relevant to L2 learning, such as sequence and psychological processing. It illustrates the wealth of types of data that are possible in investigation of SLA syntax, compared to the observational data standardly used in previous chapters: comprehension techniques (Cook, 1975), acceptability (Gass, 1979), sentence combining (Gass, 1979; Eckman *et al.*, 1988), guided production (Hyltenstam, 1984), and filling in the blanks (R. Hawkins, 1988).

In its favour it can be said that this extends the range of perspectives on knowledge of language; rather than solely depending on speech performance, the evidence comes from many sources relating to comprehension and other levels of language. On the other hand it has the disadvantage of creating problems of comparability between research. In Chapter 2 it was possible to compare Wode's 1981 study of negation with that of Cancino *et al.* (1978) as they were drawing on more or less the same source of evidence; but is Gass (1979) really tapping the same knowledge via sentence-combining as the fill-in-the-blanks task of Hawkins (1988) or the comprehension technique of Cook (1975)? Contrary results in different experiments may reflect the different methodologies; similar results may be happy coincidences.

Much of the research concentrates on comprehension. A drawback of comprehension-based studies is that successful comprehension is usually invisible, unlike successful production. It may sometimes be possible to tell from the *non sequiturs* or incorrect responses of L2 speakers that something has gone wrong with their comprehension: I remember the surprise of a stranger who said to me "Quel temps" during a rainstorm in Geneva when I looked at my watch rather than agreed about the weather. But most of the time such clear signs of incomprehension are lacking. L2 comprehension research is forced to ask for visible signs of comprehension from the learners, which already imposes some degree of unnaturalness upon the methodology, whether it is making marks on paper, translating sentences, or answering a string of questions. Hence comprehension methods necessarily involve a degree of unnaturalness that spontaneous observational data do not.

One great advantage is that a comprehension test can compensate for the rarity of certain constructions in natural data. While it might take hours of recording to collect ten relative clauses in speech, comprehension of ten or a hundred clauses can easily be tested in a few minutes. An experiment can produce focused data that would otherwise take a great deal of time to collect and would still often be ambiguous.

There are nevertheless disadvantages to switching to experiment-based comprehension. One is the complement to the disadvantages of natural observational data: while most experiments lend themselves to comprehension rather than production, most spontaneous speech data concern production rather than comprehension; the two data sources are biased towards different aspects of language. Comprehension no more implies production than the other way round. While some would claim that comprehension is more basic and so more generalisable, for example Krashen, this needs establishing from firm evidence comparing the two modes of language. Concluding that production follows the same relative clause hierarchy as comprehension is dangerous without other evidence.

In general, the major charge against experiments is their artificiality. Whatever their demerits as performance, natural observational data can often be authentic speech that people actually produce for reasons of their own. In an experiment the consciousness of being tested affects the learners' behaviour in one way or another; they might show quite different results when they are not deliberately focusing on the test being used. Abstracting language from any context of situation may make its comprehension or production depend on factors not important to the natural language situation; what is left once the real-life context and the discourse structure are removed may be an artificial form of comprehension that is only tenuously connected to natural language use. This is the complaint about all language experiments: by focusing on one aspect of language, they distort the complex nature of the real event. Although the experiment-based paradigm can draw on the extensive tradition of experimental design and statistics in psychology (outlined for instance in such books as Seliger and Shohamy 1989, or Brown, 1988), most Second Language Acquisition researchers are not trained psychologists and so blithely undertake experiments that psychologists can easily find fault with; nor at present is publication in many 'serious' L2 journals or series a guarantee that psychologically valid design and statistical criteria have been met.

In terms of the three questions of linguistics, although research on the knowledge question has typically depended on single-sentence evidence, there is no reason, in principle, why multiple sources of information about linguistic competence cannot be utilised, provided an assessment of their relationship to knowledge is made: data from experiments are all grist to the mill. The use question, when interpreted in psychological rather than sociological terms, has depended on experiments to find out the mental processes of language use, only possible if the link between knowledge and process can be firmly established. Discussion of first language acquisition in the Universal Grammar theory has found data from children unnecessary to answer its main question about the acquisition of knowledge, as argued in Chapter 9. Research into first language acquisition has conventionally used observational data for the early stages, for example Brown (1973) and Radford (1990), but switched to comprehension data for later stages, for example Chomsky (1969). SLA research has not changed its methodology so markedly with the learner's development, presumably because experiments can be carried out with L2 learners at earlier stages as they are older and fewer ethical problems are caused. But the same dilemma arises of how experiment-based data connect to acquisition.

Overall, relative clauses provide an interesting area of SLA research. Indeed, a detailed look at this single area reveals the complexity of the processes and explanations that can be involved in a single syntactic issue. Unlike earlier chapters, the unifying theme has not been an SLA model or approach to data but an area of syntax. In one sense this is a pure linguistic approach to SLA – looking at the linguistic 'facts' in as deep a syntactic fashion as possible, investigating them through a range of techniques, linking them to concepts of first language acquisition, seeing where they lead in terms of second language acquisition and processing, and then feeding them into various linguistic and psychological theories. This approach depends on the validity of isolating relative clauses, or any other area of syntax, as an area of investigation; in the theory to be described in the next two chapters, relative clauses in fact have no existence separate from other forms of movement. Interesting as research into particular syntactic areas can be, its eventual point is what it can contribute to general SLA issues.

8 Principles and Parameters Syntax

The concern of this and the next chapter is the relevance for SLA research of the current Chomskyan model of linguistics. Though theories of syntax and of acquisition go together in this model, this chapter emphasises its syntactic aspects, namely principles and parameters theory, and their relationship to L2 learning, while the next chapter deals principally with the specific model of language acquisition known as Universal Grammar (UG). Principles and parameters theory, also known as Government/ Binding (GB) theory (Chomsky, 1981a; 1986b), has become a mainstay of recent SLA research, partly, as we have seen, because major alternatives such as functionalism (Halliday, 1985a) or Generalised Phrase Structure Grammar (Gazdar *et al.*, 1985) have had little impact as yet.

In principles and parameters theory, the speaker's knowledge of language consists of principles that are common to all languages and of parameters whose values vary from one language to another. The grammar of any one language describes how that language uses the resources available to *all* languages; all grammars are encompassed within the same principles and parameters. This enables second language research to employ a common descriptive framework for L1 and L2, thus making it far easier to compare research done with different L2s or L1s than it was, for instance, with the language-specific descriptions used in the Contrastive Analysis of the 1960s. Hence, at a syntactic level alone, the range of principles and parameters theory has clear attractions for L2 research. This chapter describes three areas: the pro-drop parameter, Binding Theory, and the head-direction parameter.

8.1 SOME CONCEPTS OF PRINCIPLES AND PARAMETERS THEORY: X-BAR SYNTAX

The use of principles and parameters theory in this chapter and the next necessarily involves introducing a more technical apparatus than in earlier chapters. The comparatively brief presentation of the basic concepts possible here inevitably distorts the full picture. More detailed accounts are available in Haegeman (1991) or Cook (1988c). As it is a theory with complex interactions between all its parts, the advice to those unfamiliar with it is to adopt Coleridge's notion of willing suspension of disbelief by not trying to grasp fully each part separately before they can see a broader

156

picture. This section introduces the main concepts of X-bar syntax which underly the SLA research described in these two chapters; to some extent it can be used as a reference section and consulted when the reader wants clarification of the research, rather than digested totally in advance.

Principles and parameters theory embodies the difference between underlying and surface structure as the relationship between three levels, as we have already seen briefly in the discussion of movement in Chapter 5. *D-structure* specifies the underlying structure of the sentence, say:

"John went where"

or, as Chomsky and Lasnik (1991) put it, 'D-structure expresses lexical properties in a form accessible to the computational system'. *S-structure* expresses the relationships in the sentence involving movement, including traces (t) that show the places from which movement takes place:

"Where did John go *t*".

Surface structure is the actual form of the sentence as spoken or written:

"Where did John go?"

As always, the theory represents a declarative state of knowledge, not a procedural model of processing, that is to say, competence rather than performance.

Phrase structure is handled through '*X-bar syntax*', also employed in slightly different ways in other contemporary theories of syntax (Sells, 1985). All phrases have 'heads', such as Nouns or Verbs, around which everything in the phrase revolves. Phrases have three levels, symbolised by 'bars' and usually printed as '''; the three levels of the NP are then N″, N′, and N. The Noun Phrase is a Noun with two bars, abbreviated to N″ or NP, for example "his fear of the dark". This N″ consists of a determiner "his" acting as 'specifier' and a Noun head with one bar (N′) "fear of the dark". This N′ in turn consists of a lexical Noun (N) with no bars, "fear", and a prepositional phrase (PP or P″) "of the dark" acting as complement, as seen in the following tree:

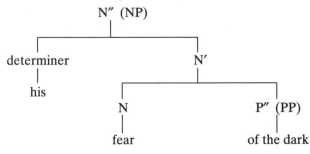

All phrases have the same structure of heads, specifiers and complements: a Verb Phrase is a VP (V″) consisting of a specifier and a single-bar V′; a V′ consists of a V head and a Complement. A Prepositional Phrase (PP) is a double-bar P″, and an Adjective Phrase (AP) is A″, both with the same internal structure. X-bar theory reduces phrase structure to the principles that every phrase (XP) contains one level at which it may have a specifier (specifier X′) and another level at which it has a head and possible complements (X complement). The structure of any phrase is then:

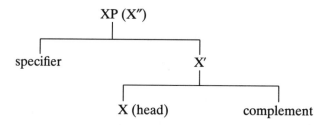

None of the rules that previously spelled out the structure of the separate phrases is now necessary; the X-bar principles subsume virtually all phrase structure rules for all phrases in all languages. They represent a powerful generalisation about the structure of human languages.

In X-bar syntax, the structure of phrases is locked into the lexical items that are in them. Each lexical phrase is built up around a lexical 'head', that is to say a Noun (N), Verb (V), Preposition (P), or Adjective (A); the features of this head dictate what complements, and so on, the phrase may have. Properties of lexical items 'project' on to the sentence the particular structures within which they may appear, known as the *Projection Principle*. D-structure is in a sense a 'pure' representation of what the lexical items project on to the sentence before movement takes place. The verb "sigh" for instance usually has an animate subject in front of it, but no grammatical object after it; "Fred sighed" but not *"The book sighed" or *"Fred sighed Helen"; for stylistic effect, of course, these restrictions can be broken: "The heavens sighed a groan of thunder". The choice of the lexical item "sigh" therefore projects on to the structure of the sentence the necessity for an animate subject and for the lack of an object. The speaker knows the limitations on when this word can occur – and when they can be broken; and so on for all the other words in the language. Much of the complexity of grammar lies in the specification of the idiosyncratic behaviour of lexical items rather than in the syntax itself.

X-bar syntax recognises that there are not only lexical phrases but also functional phrases formed around abstract elements not related to the lexicon. Since its earliest days, Chomskyan grammar has postulated a

constituent that gathers together some of the inflectional aspects of the
sentence, such as Tense and Agreement. Chomsky (1986b) took this to be
an Inflection Phrase (IP or I″) with an Inflection (I or INFL) head consisting of the abstract elements Tense (TNS) and Agreement (AGR). The
subject of the sentence is defined as the NP that acts as specifier of IP.
Thus, setting aside the details of the NP and VP, the IP of the sentence
"Molly prefers Chimay" is:

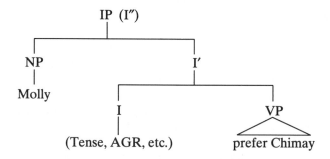

The NP "Molly" is the specifier; I′ consists of a head I and of a VP
"prefer Chimay". The IP (I″) thus behaves like other phrases in having a
specifier, a head, and a complement, except that its head is not lexical. A
further important functional phrase is the Complement Phrase (CP or C″)
which has a similar structure to the IP with specifier, head (C or COMP),
and complement; its nature is described in greater depth in the next
chapter.

So, instead of the grammar of the language containing many rules for
each phrase – rules for NPs, VPs, IPs, and so on – it contains a small
number of X-bar principles that apply to *every* phrase. All phrases in all
languages have the same structure of heads, specifiers, and complements;
all lexical phrases are projected from the lexical specification of the particular lexical item acting as head. X therefore stands for any category – hence
the name X-bar syntax. In some ways X-bar syntax is like describing how
the human cell varies sufficiently to get all the different cells in the human
body but without losing its essential structure.

The aspect of the traditional phrase structure rules that is still not
reflected in the analysis is the variation between languages in word order.
This is captured by parameters that describe the differing orders in which
the specifiers and complements may occur in the phrase – whether the
order is specifier X′ or X′ specifier, and whether it is head complement or
complement head. The *head parameter* (Chomsky, 1988) decides whether
complements come before or after the head of the phrase. English, for
instance, has complements *after* lexical heads in VPs ("likes *coffee*"), in
NPs ("fear *of the dark*"), in PPs ("in *the postroom*"), and in APs ("easy *to
please*"). English therefore has a *head-first* setting for the head parameter

for all phrases. Japanese has complements before heads in the phrase, as in "*Nihonjin* desu" (Japanese am) and "*Nihon* ni" (Japan in). Japanese has a *head-last* setting for the head parameter. Parameters such as the head parameter therefore describe the variation allowed to languages within the general confines of the principles. Parameters are aspects of principles that are left open – the type of category the principle applies to, the area of syntax within which the principle applies, and so on. A parameter is not usually specific to a single construction but has effects in many places in the grammar; thus the head parameter should apply to all phrases in the grammar, not just one type.

However, while it is convenient to refer to a single head parameter specifying the position of the complement in all phrases, it became clear during the 1980s that this is an oversimplification; the word order in the sentence reflects a combination of settings for more than one parameter (Huang, 1982; Travis, 1984). Indeed the caveat should be made that the picture presented here is a snapshot of a theory that is in continuous development. In particular, much syntactic work is being carried out on the functional phrases. On the one hand the Noun Phrase (N″) now forms part of a Determiner Phrase (DP or D″) (Abney, 1987), rather than the determiner being part of the NP (N″). On the other hand the two elements of IP (Tense and AGR) have split into two new phrases, TP (Tense) and AP (Agreement) (Pollock, 1989). Furthermore, the subject is now often introduced within the VP rather than the IP and normally moves to the IP (Chomsky and Lasnik, 1991). Inevitably much of the L2 work to be described here lags behind the current state of the art in syntax.

8.2 THE PRO-DROP PARAMETER AND THE INFLECTION PHRASE

A further principle called the *Extended Projection Principle* claims in part that all sentences have subjects (Chomsky, 1982, p. 10); that is to say, the NP specifier is compulsory in the IP. Languages such as English permit declarative sentences with subjects:

"He speaks"

but not declarative sentences without subjects:

*"Speaks".

However, languages such as Italian allow sentences without apparent subjects in seeming breach of this principle:

"Parla" (He speaks).

Principles and parameters theory maintains that such sentences neverthe-less have a 'null' subject in the underlying d- and s-structure, given the name of *pro*, which does not appear in the surface structure of the sentence. The s-structure of the Italian sentence is therefore:

"*pro* parla" (he speaks)

with the subject specifier position filled by a *pro* that does not appear in the surface structure.

In a group of languages that includes Italian and Arabic, a declarative sentence can have the invisible *pro* as the subject; in a second group of languages that includes English and French, a surface subject must appear. Principles and parameters theory therefore postulates a pro-drop para-meter that has two settings: pro-drop in which *pro* is permitted as subject, and non-pro-drop, in which *pro* is not allowed. In pro-drop languages, the 'empty category' *pro* fills the appropriate part of d- and s-structure but does not appear in the surface of the sentence.

Like other parameters, the pro-drop parameter has a range of effects on different constructions rather than being specific to the presence or ab-sence of subjects. It has been held to account for some or all of the following properties of the sentence in addition to null subjects.

(i) *Subject–Verb inversion*
    In pro-drop languages the subject can also occur after the verb in declarative sentences, for example Italian:

    "Parla lui" (speaks he)

    while it cannot in non-pro-drop languages such as English:

    *"Smoked he a cigar".

(ii) *Presence of that-trace*
    Pro-drop languages such as Spanish permit that-trace; that is to say, the complementiser "que" remains in trace position after Wh-movement from subject position as in:

    "Quien dijiste que vino?" (Who did you say that came?).

    Non-pro-drop languages such as English only have a trace "*t*" in s-structure:

    "Who did you say *t* came?"

rather than:

*"Who did you say that came?";

"*t*" does not appear in the surface form.

(iii) *Expletive "it" and "there"*
Non-pro-drop languages such as English require the dummy subjects "there" or "it" to fill the subject position in certain 'existential' sentences such as:

"There are fairies at the bottom of my garden"

and 'weather' sentences such as:

"It's snowing".

These semantically empty subjects are known in this literature as 'expletive' or 'pleonastic' subjects. Pro-drop languages such as Italian do not require them:

"Piove" (rains).

Christening the variation over the compulsory presence of subjects 'the pro-drop parameter' still does not in itself explain why sentences with *pro* are grammatical in one language but not in another, and why there are other related effects on inversion, that-trace, and expletive subjects: that is, how the pro-drop parameter works. While describing the effects of the pro-drop parameter is comparatively straightforward, its syntactic rationale is harder to describe, on account both of its complexity, and of the differing explanations put forward by linguists. Fortunately, most of the acquisition research on pro-drop can be followed without knowing the entire analysis. The explanations concern different ways in which the subject and Verb of the sentence link to AGR. The following brief account is based on Haegeman (1991). In pro-drop languages, the Verb provides ample clues whether the subject NP is singular or plural (Number) or first, second, or third person; in an Italian sentence such as

"Parliamo" (we speak)

the Verb shows that the null subject *pro* is first person plural. In non-pro-drop languages, the Verb conveys few such clues: the English Verb "go" might have as its subject first person singular "I", first person plural "we", second person "you", or third person plural "they". Non-pro-drop languages seem to compensate for their comparative lack of inflection on the

Verb by having visible subjects; pro-drop languages can have invisible subjects because the necessary information is all displayed on the Verb; they are often referred to as having 'rich' inflectional morphology. The features of Number, Person, and so on, are distributed to the subject and the Verb from the AGR part of IP. The relationship of AGR to the subject then differs in pro-drop and non-pro-drop languages.

As an 'empty category' *pro* is subject to various theoretical restrictions on empty categories, one of which is that they can be 'governed' only by lexical heads. Government is an all-pervasive syntactic relationship involving delicate information about the syntactic configuration of the sentence and the types of item involved; in brief, if two elements have the same maximal phrase (two-bar) above them in the structure of the sentence and no other intervening maximal phrase in between, one may govern the other; more details can be found in Haegeman (1991) or Cook (1988c). In pro-drop languages AGR is able to govern *pro*, in non-pro-drop languages it is not; in pro-drop languages *pro* acts like a lexical head, in non-pro-drop languages it does not. The difference between pro-drop and non-pro-drop languages is then a choice concerning the nature of AGR. This choice affects not just the presence or absence of subjects but also the presence or absence of agreement or tense features on the Verb and of actual auxiliaries or other lexical items within the IP itself.

The Pro-drop Parameter and Second Language Acquisition

The person who has acquired a first language has set the pro-drop parameter appropriately and knows whether AGR may govern the subject or not. Do L2 learners start from scratch, do they transfer the parameter setting from their L1, or do they not use parameters at all? The initial research into pro-drop in L2 learning carried out by White (1986) investigated whether L1 setting of parameters has to be 'deactivated' in L2 learning, that is, learners start by applying L1 settings and gradually switch over. She also tested the hypothesis that all properties of a parameter are mastered simultaneously – lack of subject, inversion, and that-trace. Her method was to see the differences between two groups of intermediate L2 learners of English with different pro-drop settings in their L1s. The learners consisted of 37 French speakers, non-pro-drop like English, and 32 Spanish and 2 Italian speakers, both pro-drop. Their L2 level was equivalent in that they had been put in the same university classes by a placement test. Any difference between these groups of learners would be a sign that their L1 settings had influenced their L2 learning. The learners had to carry out two tasks. One was to give grammaticality judgements on 28 English sentences by saying whether sentences such as

"It is very cold outside"

and

"In winter, snows a lot in Canada"

were 'correct', 'incorrect', or 'not sure'. If they are transferring the L1 setting, Spanish and Italian learners should be more tolerant of Null Subject and Verb Subject sentences in English. The other task was to turn 12 English sentences into questions by questioning a particular constituent such as "Mark" in:

"Peter thinks that *Mark* will be late tonight".

If the L1 setting is being used, Spanish and Italian learners should be more prone to keeping a that-trace, that is:

*"Who does Peter think that will be late tonight?"

Results for the grammaticality judgement test, expressed as a percentage of correct judgements, were as follows:

	Sentences with subjects (%)*	Sentences without subjects (%)	Subject–Verb order (%)	Verb–Subject order (%)
French	97	89	85	96
Spanish/ Italian	90	61	81	91

Correct answers to grammaticality judgements of pro-drop by French and Spanish/Italian L2 learners of English (adapted from White, 1986, pp. 61–3)
* One sentence was not used as its results were anomalous.

The Spanish/Italian pro-drop group were worse on the null subject sentences than the French non-pro-drop learners, that is to say, they wrongly accepted English null subject sentences as grammatical more readily than the French group. But there were no real differences between the groups for the Verb–Subject and Subject–Verb sentences; both groups had a high acceptance rate for Subject–Verb order and even higher rejection rate for Verb–Subject order.

The results for the question-formation test on the three relevant sentences, after subjects who were not capable of carrying out the task were eliminated, were as follows:

	Correct question (%)	that-trace remaining (%)	Other errors (%)
French	20	42	38
Spanish/Italian	17	71	12

Proportions of different mistakes with question formation involving that-trace by French and Spanish/Italian L2 learners of English (White, 1986, p. 66)

Though both groups performed rather poorly, the Spanish and Italian speakers had a higher proportion of incorrect that-trace left in place than the French speakers.

The effects of the L1 setting were apparent. The Spanish/Italians wrongly accepted more Null Subject sentences and made more that-trace mistakes than the French speakers. But this is a matter of percentages rather than an absolute difference; after all, even the French had 42 per cent mistakes with "that". Moreover, there were no differences between the groups on Verb–Subject sentences. The conclusions were that 'L1 parameters influence the adult learner's view of the L2 data, at least for a while, leading to transfer errors' (White, 1986, p. 69). L2 learners tend to start from their L1 setting rather than from scratch. It is harder to decide whether the three aspects of the pro-drop parameter go together; the L1 affects the null subject sentences to a large extent, and that-trace to some extent, but had no appreciable effect on Subject–Verb inversion.

White's research shows the merits of a principles and parameters approach. It deals with phenomena that have effects that are plain to see in the sentence, even if a complex syntactic analysis underlies them. It integrates the notion of transfer with the actual description, providing a well-motivated framework for dealing with English and Spanish – or any other pair of languages. At the same time it raises interesting issues of substance and of methodology for L2 learning, to be discussed further in the next chapter.

Having seen how the L1 parameter setting may in part be carried over to the L2, we need to see where the original L1 setting came from. It might be that one or other of the settings for a parameter is the default from which all L1 children start, or it might be that they effectively start from no setting and can use either. The early work of Hyams (1986) tackled this issue for L1 acquisition of English. She reanalysed various transcripts of children's language to determine which pro-drop setting children use first – whether they start by treating English as a pro-drop or non-pro-drop language. She found that young English children produce many sentences like "Play it" or "No go in" that have null subjects; at the same period they leave the expletive subjects "it" and "there" out of their speech. To them English is indeed a pro-drop language. English

Research summary: L. White (1986), 'Implications of Parametric Variation for Adult Second Language Acquisition: an Investigation of the Pro-drop Parameter', in V. J. Cook (ed.), *Experimental Approaches to Second Language Acquisition* (Oxford: Pergamon Press).

Aim: to test whether L1 parameter settings influence L2 learning and whether all aspects of a parameter hang together in L2 learning

Learners: 37 French speakers, and 32 Spanish and 2 Italian speakers

Aspect of language: the pro-drop parameter that distinguishes non-pro-drop languages like English, from pro-drop languages such as Italian in terms of optional or compulsory presence of subjects, Subject–Verb inversion, and that-trace

Method: grammaticality judgements on 28 English sentences and turning sentences into questions

Results: Spanish/Italians wrongly accepted more null subject sentences and made more that-trace mistakes than the French speakers but there were no differences for Subject–Verb inversion

Conclusions: 'L1 parameters influence the adult learner's view of the L2 data, at least for a while, leading to transfer errors' (White, 1986, p. 69)

children gradually learn that English sentences need lexical subjects and start adding expletive "it" and "there". Spanish children, on the other hand, start by treating Spanish as a pro-drop language and never have to change. The choice between the two settings for the pro-drop parameter is not neutral: L1 children start from the pro-drop setting as a default and so produce sentences without visible subjects in the early stages regardless of language.

Hyams's research has proved the source of much argument; Atkinson (1992) provides a clear account. One alternative explanation has been put forward by Radford (1990), who claims that the entire IP is missing in early speech, giving rise to a variety of phenomena that include lack of subjects. Another explanation has been made by Bloom (1990) based on processing constraints, showing that English children have longer VPs in null subject sentences than in those with full subjects; that is to say, the missing subject is caused simply by the extra length of the sentence being a burden on their memory. The fact that children learning a non-pro-drop language start by mistakenly treating it as a pro-drop language has also been challenged. Hulk (1987), for instance, discovered that children learning French, also a non-pro-drop language, rarely had null subjects in the early stages of acquisition. Valian (1989) found that English children were not the same as

Italian children; although they did indeed leave out some subjects, they nevertheless supplied more subjects than the Italians. Hyams (1987) herself now favours a slightly different, wider, explanation called morphological uniformity, which will be developed below. If we accept the view that L1 learners start with believing that English is pro-drop (Hyams, 1986), the results in White (1986) suggest this is not true of L2 learning, which starts with whatever is the setting in the L1.

L2 researchers have developed the pro-drop parameter research using the two themes of the transfer of the L1 setting and of the relationship between the several aspects of the pro-drop parameter, such as null subjects, inversion, and that-trace.

(a) *Hilles (1986)* looked at longitudinal observational data taken from Cancino *et al.* (1978). She studied Jorge – the 12-year-old Spanish-speaking near-beginner in English already encountered in Chapters 4 and 7. For each of the occasions Jorge was recorded over the 40-week period of the transcripts, Hilles calculated the percentage with which he used null subjects in English sentences that could be subjectless if they were Spanish. Jorge started by having over 80 per cent null subjects; this percentage fell more or less steadily over the first 30 weeks to under 10 per cent, and then remained low. According to the Hyams (1986) analysis, the presence of auxiliaries in the IP should preclude null subjects; Hilles therefore calculated the proportion of negative sentences in which auxiliaries occurred since these would require an auxiliary, that is, 'the emergence of lexical material' in I; this rose gradually from under 10 per cent to over 60 per cent during the 40 weeks, rising as the number of null subject sentences fell. She also found that the first expletive "it" occurred at week 12, just when there was a marked decrease in null subject sentences and the start of the increase in auxiliaries.

	Weeks: 2	10	22	30	38
Proportion of null subject sentences (%)	82	75	15	10	15
Proportion of negative auxiliary (%)	5	18	33	50	68

Percentages of null subject and negative auxiliary supplied by Jorge (adapted from a graph in Hilles, 1986, p. 42)

The number of negative auxiliaries increases as the number of null subjects declines: they form part of the same factor affecting the IP. The production data confirm that the L1 pro-drop setting is transferred and is gradually changed. They support the idea that 'pro-drop is present in early IL, but decreases over time' (Hilles, 1986, p. 48). As Jorge spoke Spanish, a pro-drop language, it is impossible to distinguish whether pro-drop is a default setting for all languages or is a transfer from the L1.

(b) *Liceras (1989)* investigated a range of properties of the pro-drop parameter. The tasks were grammaticality judgements and translations of 17 sentences into the L1. She tested 32 French and 30 English-speaking learners of Spanish, at four levels ranging from beginners to 'high advanced'. Taking the top and bottom French groups as typical, results were:

	Beginners (%)	Advanced(%)
Expletive subjects	6	0
Subject–Verb inversion	18	75
that-trace	50	75

Grammaticality judgements of pro-drop for French learners of Spanish (based on Liceras, 1989)

In other words, the French beginners realised that expletive subjects were ungrammatical in Spanish; beginners did not accept the correct Verb–Subject order, though advanced learners did; even beginners had 50 per cent acceptance of that-trace, while advanced learners had 75 per cent. English learners behaved rather similarly to French learners, although English beginners were slightly worse: they used few expletive subjects, and they came to accept both Verb–Subject inversions and that-trace with time. The conclusions were that 'resetting the pro-drop parameter from English and French to Spanish is not difficult with respect to null subjects' (Liceras, 1989, p. 126), but that 'the three properties attributed to the pro-drop parameter do not have the same status in the interlanguage' (Liceras, 1989, p. 129). Liceras (1988) came to similar conclusions on the ease of Spanish null subject sentences for English and French learners using spontaneous story-telling as well as grammaticality judgements. Phinney (1987) likewise found that, in a comparison of student essays, English learners of Spanish were adept at producing null-subject sentences and leaving out expletive subjects, while Spanish learners of English had particular problems with supplying expletive subjects.

(c) *Lakshmanan (1991) and Hilles (1991)* have explored the implications for L2 acquisition of the later explanation for pro-drop called the *Morphological Uniformity Principle* (Jaeggli and Hyams, 1988). The hypothesis that pro-drop languages have 'rich' inflectional morphology came up against a major stumbling-block: Chinese has no morphology at all despite being a pro-drop language! Jaeggli and Hyams (1988) tackled this issue by dividing languages into two groups; a *morphologically uniform* language either has rich morphology, for example, Spanish has a different ending for each person of the present tense, or has no morphology, for example, Chinese has no verb inflections; a *mixed* language is in between these two possibilities in having some inflectional morphology, but not full morphology; English for example distinguishes the third person singular "-s" ("he sees") but not the other persons of the present tense ("I/you/we/they see"), and so is a mixed language. A pro-drop language is morphologically uniform, a non-pro-drop language is mixed. Hence Italian and Chinese come together as morphologically uniform, English and French as non-uniform. Of course, this analysis too runs into snags; German is morphologically uniform but non-pro-drop, explained by Jaeggli and Hyams (1988) as a side-effect of its Verb-Second nature.

Both Lakshmanan (1991) and Hilles (1991) present similar studies to establish whether null subjects in L2 learners' speech are accompanied by the lack of inflections that morphological uniformity predicts. Lakshmanan (1991) looks at three child L2 learners: four-year-old Spanish-speaking Marta from Cancino *et al.* (1978), four-year-old French-speaking Muriel from Gerbault (1978), and five-year-old Japanese Uguisu from Hakuta (1974). She calculated the percentage of null subjects in sentences with and without forms of "be", and the presence or absence of the inflections, again the familiar morphemes: regular past tense, third person "-s" on regular forms and on "has" and "does".

	Week:	1	5	10	15
Null subjects (%)		63.8	7.1	8.2	2.8
Third person -*s* (%)		–	25.0	9.0	81.0

Results for Marta (based on Lakshmanan, 1991, pp. 399 and 401)

This shows a quick drop in the proportion of null subjects after the first week but no great rise in the numbers of third person "-s" until after week 10. More detailed analysis shows that most of the early null subjects occurred with forms of "be", namely 61.7 per cent of all subjects, ascribed to a matching of "it's/is" with Spanish "es". The percentages for the inflections are based on small numbers (25 per cent for week 5 means 1 out of 4). Lakshmanan (1991, p. 402) claims that 'the sudden drop in null subjects in sample 2 and the continued omission of inflection from sample 4 through sample 10 suggest that omission of inflection and null subjects may not be related, at least not in child L2 development'. The analysis of Muriel's transcripts shows a low amount of null subjects but low frequency of inflections; the data from Uguisu show no null subjects but poor performance on inflections. Children learning an L2 do not therefore behave as the morphological uniformity principle predicts because there are not the expected links between the decline of null subjects and the rise of third person "-s". Hyams and Safir (1991), however, argue that a learner may know that a language is morphologically uniform but simply not know the inflectional forms themselves; to them this research overemphasises production at the expense of knowledge. Confusingly, Gass and

Lakshmanan (1991, p. 188) report that Lakshmanan (1989) also investigated a further subject, Cheo, whose results, not mentioned in Lakshmanan (1991) showed 'that null-subjects and development of verb inflections are related'.

Hilles (1991) looked at the six Spanish speaking subjects from the Cancino *et al.* (1978) study: two children, Marta and Cheo, two adolescents, Juan and Jorge, and two adults, Alberto and Dolores. She presents graphs, but no figures, for each learner showing the percentage of pronoun subjects supplied and the presence of tense inflections, as shown by "be", "do" and "have", and regular past tense. She finds for Marta that 'the acquisition of pronominal subjects and inflections seems to be intertwined' (Hilles, 1991, p. 322) at a statistically significant level – the opposite to the conclusion that Lakshmanan (1991) arrived at for the same data. As for the other learners, Cheo and Jorge both show links between the two factors; but the remaining three do not. This then separates the two child learners and one adolescent, who seem to behave in accordance with the morphological uniformity principle, from one adolescent and two adults. Meisel (1991) similarly presents data from the ZISA project that show great variation between learners in the extent to which null subjects are accompanied by lack of verb inflection. Meisel (1990) investigated from transcripts three very young children simultaneously acquiring German and French; he sums up: 'subjects begin to appear shortly after or simultaneously with the emergence of verb inflection'. He argues that the child's crucial discovery is that verbs can be finite or non-finite; the early null subject sentences are a spinoff from the lack of inflection.

Finally, one must mention briefly the approach of Tsimpli and Roussou (1990), which denies the basic assumption underlying the research cited so far, namely that L2 learners are in fact resetting the pro-drop parameter. Tsimpli and Roussou argue that, while principles are observed in all languages, parameters cannot be reset. The apparent sequence of L2 development is due to the learner exploring other possibilities within the UG principles or to transfer, not to the resetting of parameters. Based on a study of 13 Greek learners of English, they argue that the learners discover that English sentences must have subjects by reanalysing subject pronouns as heads of Agreement Phrases, as can be done in Greek; they, and the other pro-drop learners studied by White (1986) and Liceras (1989), have more acute problems with that-trace because this is indeed a parametric property and so not resettable. The significance of this proposal in fact awaits a fuller discussion of more recent syntax, some of which will be presented in the next chapter.

Linguistics and Methodology of the Pro-drop Research

So far as linguistics is concerned, the research for the first time seems to go hand in glove with current notions of syntax: the pro-drop parameter is applied to second language acquisition (White, 1986) as rapidly as it is to first language acquisition (Hyams, 1986); the change to morphological uniformity (Jaeggli and Hyams, 1988) soon brings its wave of second language papers (Hilles, 1991; Lakshmanan, 1991); the recent distinction between functional and lexical categories almost immediately heralds L2 work (Tsimpli and Roussou, 1990). Doubtless work will soon appear that takes on board the concept that the subject originates in the specifier of VP and moves into the IP (Chomsky and Lasnik, 1991). The pro-drop parameter has been extensively explored in second language acquisition research, showing the usefulness of the questions it poses and of the overall framework that this theory provides. An answer to the knowledge question has been proposed that differs in an interesting way from those seen in earlier chapters, which in turn allows new ways of thinking about the acquisition question.

The use of observational data of L2 learners' speech for pro-drop, as in Phinney (1987), Hilles (1986), Meisel (1990), Lakshmanan (1991), and Hilles (1991), is still problematic. As we saw in Chapter 2, observational data directly reflect performance, not competence, and are limited to speech production. Such data are particularly inappropriate for the pro-drop parameter because it concerns elements that are *missing* from the sentence – subjects, inflections, expletive subjects, and so on – rather than features that are *present* in the sentence, as argued in Cook (1990a). Missing items in performance data, particularly from the beginning of the sentence, invite processing explanations concerned with short term memory and so on, as suggested by Bloom (1990). Many researchers do not provide observational data of their own but analyse other people's transcripts and data, whether it is Hyams (1986), Hilles (1986; 1991), Gass and Lakshmanan (1991), or Lakshmanan (1991). The dangers in interpreting performance data can also be seen in the contradictory conclusions reached by Lakshmanan (1991) and Hilles (1991) about the same question of morphological uniformity using the same data collected from the same subject within the same theory.

In short, if observational data are to be used, they must have a proper basis in terms of an adequate number of learners and languages, size of sample, statistical analysis, methodology of transcription, and so on. As Bloom *et al.* (1975, p. 34) put it, 'if structural features occur often enough and are shared by a large enough number of different multi-word utterances, then it is possible to ascribe the recurrence of such regular features to the productivity of an underlying rule system'. A linguist who uses observational evidence rather than single-sentence evidence has to take such criteria into account; this responsibility is not discharged by most of the observational pro-drop studies with small samples of languages and subjects, lack of statistical analysis, and so on. Grammaticality judgements also have to be fully justified in terms of experimental design, as we see in Chapter 10, needing adequate samples of subjects and sentences, and so on.

8.3 BINDING THEORY

A further area that was central to the principles and parameters theory in the 1980s was the Binding theory. In conventional grammatical terms, binding is concerned with the possible antecedents for anaphors such as "himself" and pronominals such as "her". In the sentence

"Geoff said Steve helps himself"

the reflexive anaphor "himself" must be bound to "Steve"; this is shown conventionally by the subscript "$_i$" appearing after each of the two bound elements, that is:

"Geoff said Steve$_i$ helps himself$_i$."

"Steve$_i$" and "himself$_i$" are bound and refer to the same person. The following interpretation of the sentence is therefore ungrammatical:

*"Geoff$_i$ said Steve helps himself$_i$"

as the anaphor "himself" cannot refer to the same person as "Geoff". However in the sentence:

"Geoff said Steve helps him"

the pronominal "him" must *not* be bound to "Steve" and can*not* refer to the same person as "Steve". Instead "him" may be bound to "Geoff":

"Geoff$_i$ said Steve helps him$_i$."

The interpretation in which "Steve" and "him" are bound is therefore ungrammatical:

*"Geoff said Steve$_i$ helps him$_i$."

"Steve" cannot refer to the same person as "him". The pronominal "him" must instead refer either to "Geoff" or to someone determined by the context of situation but not actually mentioned in the sentence; within the sentence "him" can only be bound to "Geoff".

An important point about binding is that, unlike mistakes in word order, mistakes in binding are, so to speak, invisible, since they rest on the interpretation of the sentence, not on its surface form. Suppose an English speaker says

"Mary said Helen helps herself"

incorrectly intending to mean that Helen helps Mary, that is:

*"Mary$_i$ said Helen helps herself$_i$."

A listener who used the correct form of binding would mistakenly assume that the speaker meant that Helen helped Helen rather than Helen helped Mary; nothing in the sentence itself shows the speaker's error. A sentence with the wrong binding is always interpretable by a listener with the correct binding, whatever the speaker intends. As Berwick and Weinberg (1984, p. 170) put it, 'If an antecedent can be found the sentence will be grammatical, otherwise not; in both cases the sentence will be parsable.' This point is important to language acquisition since it means, on the one hand, that no one will detect that a learner has made a mistake, on the other, that learners will never be able to discover their mistake from sentences they hear as they will put the wrong interpretation on them.

Like the pro-drop parameter above, the basic facts of binding are easy to understand; the SLA research on binding can be grasped to some extent without looking at the extremely complex syntactic theory necessary to explain them. The following gives a sketch of the Binding Theory; fuller accounts in an acquisition context can be found in Goodluck (1991), Atkinson (1992), or Cook (1990b). Binding theory claims there is a 'governing category' in the sentence within which anaphors such as "himself" must be bound but pronominals such as "him" must *not*, that is, they are 'free'; in the sentences used so far, the governing category has been the sentence "Steve helps him/himself". These restrictions on interpretation are captured through three Binding Principles that define the binding possibilities not only for anaphors and pronominals but also for referring expressions (that is, nouns):

Principle A: An anaphor is bound in a governing category.
Principle B: A pronominal is free in a governing category.
Principle C: A referring expression is free.

- *Binding Principle A* states that anaphors such as "himself" must be bound *within* their governing category. "Himself" is bound to "Steve" in:

  "Geoff said Steve$_i$ helps himself$_i$"

  because it is within the same governing category ["Steve helps himself"].

- *Binding Principle B* states that pronominals such as "him" must *not* be bound in their governing category. "Him" is not bound to "Steve" in

  "Geoff$_i$ said Steve helps him$_i$"

  because it is within the same governing category ["Steve helps him"]. "Him" may refer to the person called "Geoff" or to someone not mentioned in the sentence.

- *Binding Principle C* covers the case of referential NPs by stating that "Geoff" and "him" are not bound in

  *"He$_i$ said that Geoff$_i$ had lied"

  that is "Geoff" cannot be linked to pronominals that are higher than it in certain configurations of the sentence (technically a relationship called c-command).

Thus far we have seen what can be called 'classical' Binding Theory consisting of three invariant principles, based on Chomsky (1981a); indeed, much language acquisition assumes this classical model. Yet some subtle differences between languages cannot be explained and have led to a version of binding that uses parameters as well as the three principles. In a Japanese sentence such as:

"John$_i$-wa Bill-ga zibun$_i$-o nikunde iru to omotte iru"
John Bill self hates that thinks
John thinks that Bill hates himself

the anaphor "zibun" may be bound to "John", or to "Bill", even though the English equivalent would *have* to be bound to "Bill", as it is within the governing category "Bill hates himself". Similarly in the Italian sentence:

"Alice$_i$ vide Maria guardare se$_i$ nello specchio"
Alice saw Maria look at herself in the mirror

the anaphor "se" is bound to "Alice"; the English equivalent "herself" would have to be bound to "Maria" as it is within the governing category [Maria look at herself]. Binding Theory therefore needs to incorporate variation between languages.

Wexler and Manzini (1987) parameterised the classical theory by varying the definition of governing category according to the *Governing Category Parameter*. A person who knows English has acquired the English parameter-setting for "himself", specifying one governing category; a person who knows Japanese has acquired the Japanese setting for "zibun", specifying another. The Governing Category Parameter has five settings that define the minimal governing category for anaphors and pronominals:

(a) *A governing category must contain a subject*
The simplest case is that a governing category must include a subject. Languages like English permit

"John heard Peter$_i$'s criticisms of himself$_i$."

but do not allow

*"John$_i$ heard Peter's criticisms of himself$_i$."

The phrase "Peter's criticisms of himself" is a governing category as "Peter" is the subject of "criticisms"; the NP is clearly related to

"Peter criticises himself".

So the anaphor "himself" must be bound within the NP as governing category (Principle A) but the pronominal "him" must *not* (Principle B), as in:

"John$_i$ heard Peter's criticisms of him$_i$."

where "him" refers either to "John" or to someone not mentioned in the sentence, both of which possibilities are outside the governing category.

(b) *A governing category must contain an I*
A phrase that has an I within it may also count as a governing category; there will be a difference in binding between sentences that show I by means of tense markers, say, and those that don't. Taking the reflexive anaphor "se", the Italian sentence:

"Alice$_i$ guardo i retratti di se$_i$ di Maria."
Alice$_i$ looked at Maria's portraits of herself$_i$

allows "Alice" to be bound to "se", while the English version

   *"Alice$_i$ looked at Maria's portraits of herself$_i$."

does not. As Principle A applies,

   "i retratti di se di Maria"
   Maria's portraits of herself

cannot be a governing category for the Italian reflexive "se", even though it contains a subject, "Maria". The difference is the lack of a finite verb form.

(c) *A governing category must contain Tense*
The aspect of I called Tense (TNS) is also involved. In the Icelandic sentence:

   "Jon skipaði mer að raka hann."
   Jon ordered me to shave him

the pronominal "hann" must be free within its governing category. "Hann" comes within an embedded sentence that has an I

   "mer að raka hann"
   me to shave him.

This should therefore qualify as a governing category for "hann", and, according to Principle B, "hann" must be bound outside it, say with the NP "Jon". But in fact it can*not*. That is to say, the following interpretation is ungrammatical:

   *"Jon$_i$ skipaði mer að raka hann$_i$".

The governing category for "hann" must therefore be the main sentence rather than the embedded sentence; the defining property of the governing category is the presence of Tense.

(d) *A governing category must contain an indicative Tense*
It may be not so much the presence of Tense that is important as the *type* of Tense. Take the Icelandic reflexive anaphor "sig":

   "Jon$_i$ segir að maria elski sig$_i$."
   John says that Maria loves (subjunctive) self.

The anaphor "sig" may be bound to "Jon", although the phrase "að Maria elski sig" would prevent it by containing a subject that would qualify it as a governing category for English "himself" under definition (a), an I that would qualify it for Italian "se" under (b), and it has Tense to qualify for (c). Hence, as this phrase forms a governing category for "sig" in Icelandic, there is a further condition that Tense must be indicative rather than subjunctive.

(e) *A governing category must have "root" Tense*
The final possibility concerns the Japanese reflexive anaphor "zibun", to which Principle A should apply:

"John$_i$-wa Bill-ga zibun$_i$-o nikunde iru to omotte iru"
John Bill SELF hates that thinks
John thinks that Bill hates self.

Here "zibun" may be bound to "John" as well as to "Bill", even though it is within a phrase "Bill self hates" that meets all of the requirements (a)–(d) for its governing category by having a subject, I, Tense, and an indicative Tense. "Zibun" is nevertheless bound only within the whole sentence, i.e. wherever the main or "root" Tense of the sentence can be found; it can be bound anywhere in the eh sentence. For Japanese "zibun" and similar items, a governing category must have "root" Tense.

The parameterised Binding Theory therefore accounts for a range of binding relations in different languages – for example the differences between English "himself", Italian "se", Icelandic "sig", and Japanese "zibun".

Binding Theory and First Language Acquisition

The classical Binding Theory led to a generation of research that explored whether L1 children knew the three principles of binding, surveyed in Goodluck (1991). L1 research tended to show that children were more successful at interpreting anaphors than pronominals, that is to say they knew Principle A but not Principle B. Deutsch *et al.* (1986), for example, found that Dutch children aged 6 to 10 were consistently better at comprehending reflexive anaphors than pronominals. Solan (1987) found a similar result with English children aged 4 and 7, which he explained by suggesting that children initially have access only to Binding Principle A. Kapur, Lust, Herbert, and Martahardjono (forthcoming) used evidence from children aged from 3 to 10 in English, Dutch, Spanish, and Chinese to claim that anaphors require a smaller core domain to define than pronominals and so are easier. On similar lines, Jakubowicz (1984) argued that children have a stage during which they treat pronominals as bound within a governing category, that is, as if they were anaphors. However, this view has been challenged by Grimshaw and Rosen (1990) on the grounds that children nevertheless perform above chance with pronominals and that the experimental tasks with pronominals did not take into account whether there were other nouns or objects in the situation to which the pronominal could refer; this leads them to claim children *know* principle B but do not fully *obey* it, a position that will be returned to in the next chapter.

If children get the wrong parameter setting for a particular item in their L1, they would indeed produce mistakes, which would go undetected by those who hear them. As they would never be able to discover their error from the sentences they hear, their misconception could go on forever. To ensure that they do not end up in such a blind alley, children are therefore claimed to proceed cautiously, making the most conservative assumptions from the data, that is to say, always assuming the minimum 'language' (a subset of the whole language that would be possible) rather than the maximum 'language' (a superset including all the possibilities). This limitation is called the *Subset Principle* (Wexler and Manzini, 1987, p. 61). In this context 'language' is a technical term referring to a set of sentences generated by a grammar rather than a general term in the sense of 'English' versus 'French'. The learner always starts with the setting for the parameter that yields the smallest 'language' in this sense. The learner cannot go wrong if he or she gradually expands from this minimal setting; learning would be impossible if learners jumped immediately to the broadest setting because their minds would never encounter appropriate evidence to tell them this was wrong and that the setting had to be more restricted. The Subset Principle is a principle that constrains the possibilities for learning rather than a principle of syntax.

The settings of the Governing Category Parameter can now be expressed in terms of the Subset Principle. Binding Principle A specifies the governing category within which binding can occur for anaphors; each of the settings for the governing category parameter from (a) to (e) generates a larger 'language' for anaphors, that is, the sentences described by (a) (subject requirement) are a subset of those described by (b) (I requirement), the sentences described by (b) a subset of (c) (Tense requirement), and so on. For anaphors, the Subset Principle ensures that the learner chooses only a minimal governing category; it may be that the learner guesses too small, in which case new evidence will put him or her on the right track; but the learner cannot make too large a guess without violating the Subset Principle.

For pronominals such as "him", the Subset Principle makes the opposite prediction. Principle B specifies the *freedom* of pronominals, that is to say, the fact that they may *not* be bound within the governing category. Hence the smallest 'language' is one in which only sentences with free pronominals are permitted, that is to say (e) (root Tense requirement); the next smallest 'language' is one in which all sentences with free pronominals and all those with indicative Tense are permitted, that is (d) (indicative Tense requirement); and so on up to (a). The Subset Principle applies as much to pronominals as to anaphors but makes the *opposite* prediction because of the way in which the 'languages' generated by the settings differ in the subset relationship for pronominals and anaphors: for anaphors, languages get *bigger* from (a) to (e), for pronominals they get *smaller* from (a) to (e); 'the subset hierarchy for pronominals . . . is a mirror image of the subset hierarchy for anaphors' (Saleemi, 1988, p. 113).

Binding Theory and Second Language Acquisition

An experiment that investigated parameterised binding in SLA was reported in Cook (1990b). This tested the interpretation of the reflexive anaphor "himself" and the pronominal "him" in English sentences by 14 adult native speakers and 47 advanced L2 learners from three different language backgrounds – 16 Japanese, 14 Romance, and 17 Norwegian – chosen to exemplify different settings for the governing category parameter. The Romance languages have values for anaphors that incorporate (b), for example Italian "se"; Norwegian has a (c) value for the anaphor "seg" (since according to Hellan (1988) it requires Tense but not indicative Tense); Japanese "zibun" is the classic example of the anaphor that takes (e). A computer-controlled comprehension task gave the subjects 40 sentences (four of each type tested), for each of which they had to decide whether "him" or "himself" referred to "John" or "Peter" by pressing the appropriate key, that is, a multiple choice comprehension test. The response time was also measured for each sentence. Sentence types were:

A. "Peter shot him"	simple	sentence
B. "John$_i$ shot himself$_i$"	"	"
C. "Peter said that John voted for him"	tensed	"
D. "Peter said that John$_i$ voted for himself$_i$"	"	"
E. "John asked Peter to pay for him"	infinitival	"
F. "Peter asked John$_i$ to include himself$_i$"	"	"
G "Peter discovered John's report on him"	noun	phrase
H. "John reported Peter$_i$'s criticisms of himself$_i$"	"	"

One other sentence type was tested but is not reported here, since it was not involved in the major predictions.

Let us take as a base the error rates for anaphors in sentences B, D, F, and H, shown in the following table in terms of percentage of error:

	Natives (%)	Romance (%)	Japanese (%)	Norwegians (%)
B. "John$_i$ shot himself$_i$"	1.8	3.6	1.6	0.0
D. "Peter said that John$_i$ voted for himself$_i$"	9.9	17.7	23.4	3.9
F. "Peter asked John$_i$ to include himself$_i$"	7.1	30.4	40.6	19.1
H. "John reported Peter$_i$'s criticisms of himself$_i$"	16.0	35.7	43.7	33.8

Errors for "himself" in four sentence types (adapted from Cook, 1990b)

Taking the L2 groups together, there is a large difference between the average score for B sentences (such as "John shot himself") with 1.7 per cent errors, D sentences ("Peter said that John voted for himself") with 11.1 per cent, F sentences ("Peter asked John to include him/himself") with 30.0%, and H type sentences ("John reported Peter's criticisms of him/himself") with 37.7 per cent. While the overall error rates between the groups are different, all three L2 groups share the same order of difficulty B<D<F<H.

The time taken for comprehension expressed in seconds and milliseconds shows a similar pattern:

	Natives (secs)	Romance (secs)	Japanese (secs)	Norwegians (secs)
B. "John$_i$ shot himself$_i$"	2.955	3.976	3.592	3.840
D. "Peter said that John$_i$ voted for himself$_i$"	4.219	6.723	6.979	6.558
F. "Peter asked John$_i$ to include himself$_i$"	4.492	7.720	7.180	6.316
H. "John reported Peter$_i$'s criticisms of himself$_i$"	5.922	8.041	8.041	9.591

Average response times in seconds for anaphors in four sentence types (adapted from Cook, 1990b)

Again, there are clear differences between sentence types, ranging for the L2 groups from 3.8 seconds (B) to 8.7 seconds (H). The same difficulty order B<D<F<H is found across the groups, with the exception of F<D for Norwegians. Apart from sentence type B being shorter than the others, this could not be an effect of increasing length since the respective lengths in words of D, F, and H are 7, 6, and 6.

Turning now to pronominals, the order of difficulty for natives is (A/C)<E<G, using 11 per cent as a lower cut off for random errors; for Romance (A/C/E)<G; for Japanese (A/C)<E<G, and for Norwegian

(A/C)<G<E; the overall order for comprehension is A<C<E<G. The order in response times is again A<C<E<G.

The L2 groups behave in the same way on the pronominal sentences but differ on two of the anaphor types, D and F. Consistent orders of difficulty and of response time occurred in all groups regardless of first language, with one minor exception. There are nevertheless some differences between the groups: the Japanese make most mistakes; the Romance are slowest on two sentence types, the Japanese and the Norwegian on one each. The native speakers had similar orders of response time and errors, with one exception (F<D in errors). The relative processing difficulty of binding in different types of sentence in English is the same regardless of the L1 setting for the governing category parameter.

The relative ease of anaphors compared to pronominals found in L1 acquisition is not duplicated; indeed, L2 learners effectively treat both in the same way, as seen in orders of difficulty and response time. This has particular consequences for the Subset Principle which predicts that the order from subset to superset in the five settings of the parameter should be the opposite for anaphors and pronominals. Hence, while it might be argued that the sequence B<D<F<H for anaphors indeed follows the Subset Principle, the sequence A<C<E<G for pronominals is not the opposite to the sequence for anaphors and so has not had the predicted change of direction. If the research had dealt only with anaphors, it could have been interpreted as supporting the Subset Principle; including pronominals shows that some other effect is at work, apparently also in the minds of native speakers.

Research summary: V. J. Cook (1990b), 'Timed Comprehension of Binding in Advanced L2 Learners of English', *Language Learning*, **40** (4), 557–99

Aim: to test the setting of the different values in relation to L1 and to the Subset Principle

Learners: 14 native speakers of English and 16 Japanese, 14 Romance, and 17 Norwegian L2 learners

Aspect of language: the values for the governing category parameter that determines the local governing category within which a pronominal or an anaphor may or may not be bound to its antecedent

Method: comprehension timed by computer

Results: essentially the same difficulty orders in terms of errors and response times for both anaphors and pronominals for all groups

Conclusions: a single phenomenon relates all groups, which does not accord with the Subset Principle or with L1 transfer

Other pieces of research have tackled particular aspects of parameterised binding with L2 learners of English.

(a) *Finer and Broselow (1986)* tested six adult Korean learners of English ranging from level 2 to level 6 of a six level teaching programme. Korean has an L1 (e) setting for the reflexive "caki" equivalent of "himself", meaning that in a sentence such as

"Keith said that Ronnie requires that Bill sacks himself"

"himself" might be bound to *any* of the nouns "Bill", "Ronnie", or "Keith" within the governing category of the 'root' tense, that is, the whole sentence. They tested both pronominal "him" and anaphoric "himself" in two tensed sentences, such as:

"Mr Fat thinks that Mr Thin will paint him/himself"

equivalent to C and D above, and two infinitival sentences such as:

"Mr Fat asks Mr Thin to paint him/himself"

(equivalent to E and F above). The subjects had to choose which of two pictures fitted each sentence. Binding within the governing category was called 'local', correct for reflexive anaphors (Principle A), binding outside the governing category was called 'non-local', correct for pronominals (Principle B). Excluding results for "either", the results were:

	Himself		*Him*	
	correct (local) (%)	incorrect (non-local) (%)	correct (non-local) (%)	incorrect (local) (%)
Tensed clause				
"Mr Fat thinks that Mr Thin will paint himself/ him"	91.7	8.3	54.2	29.2
Infinitive clause				
"Mr Fat asks Mr Thin to paint himself/him"	58.3	37.5	79.2	4.2

Interpretation of "himself" and "him" by six Korean learners (adapted from Finer and Broselow, 1986)

The Koreans had learnt the binding relations for "himself" with an error rate of only 12/48 (25 per cent); they were worse at the infinitive tenseless clauses 14/24 (58.3 per cent). The distinction between these two types is not needed in Korean, nor is it relevant for binding in English. Finer and Broselow conclude that the learners have in a sense 'split the difference' between English and Korean; 'in general it looks as though the subjects show a tendency to follow English principles for tensed complements and Korean principles for infinitival complements'. Finer and Broselow argue that the Koreans do not reactivate the Subset Principle, as this would mean them starting with the conservative (a) setting, nor do they transfer their L1 setting, as this would mean starting from (e).

Finer and Broselow (1986) escape this dilemma by invoking a further parameter called the *Proper Antecedent Parameter*. In both English and Korean it is possible to have

"John$_i$ told Bill about himself$_i$"

where "himself" is bound to a subject. But only in English is it possible to have

"John told Bill$_i$ about himself$_i$"

where "himself" is bound to an *object*; the equivalent Korean sentence would be incorrect. The proper antecedent parameter decides whether an antecedent must be a subject. It has two settings, (a) in which only subjects can be antecedents, and (b) in which anything can be an antecedent. English therefore has a (b) setting, Korean an (a) setting. The Subset Principle is reversed for this parameter compared to the governing category parameter for anaphors; English is the 'larger' language with a (b) setting, Japanese and Korean 'smaller' languages with (a) settings. The anomalous results for the infinitival sentences might indicate that the (a) setting learners were looking for a subject. In this case the learners would be conforming to the Subset Principle by searching for the smallest language compatible with what they see.

In general, Finer and Broselow (1986) feel that 'the developing grammars of these language learners were consistent with the subset of logically possible systems found in actual human languages'. This experiment is small-scale in that it tests four sentences with six subjects. Broselow and Finer (1991) and Finer (1991) extend the approach with 24 sentences about Mr Fat and Mr Thin, two or four pictures to choose from, a range of verbs ("expect", "believe", and so on), and 97 subjects – 30 Korean and 37 Japanese (both (e) setting), and 30 Hindi (c setting); these were tested in both L1 and L2. Broselow and Finer (1991) conclude 'if there is movement along the hierarchy, it is movement toward the target language to a pattern that is consistent with a possible parametric option'. Hirakawa (1990) in a cross-sectional study also found that Japanese children set the proper antecedent parameter to its correct English value, but continued to have problems with the governing category parameter.

(b) *Thomas (1989)* tested 97 learners of English at levels from low intermediate to advanced, plus 4 bilinguals, and 11 native speakers, concentrating particularly on 29 Spanish and 24 Chinese learners. She used a multiple-choice comprehension technique to test whether they allowed binding out of governing categories defined by the (a) setting subject requirement. Type I sentences such as

"David could see that Bill was looking at himself in the mirror"

differed from Type II:

"Mary angrily told me that Sue had spilled a lot of paint on herself"

in that the latter attempted to make the alternative meaning more plausible, for example through the adverb "angrily". She also tested a version of the proper antecedent parameter by seeing if natives and L2 learners were capable of using non-subject antecedents. Type III were single clause sentences, such as

"Susan gave Mary three photographs of herself taken last summer",

and again differed from Type IV

"After the medical tests were completed, the doctor informed Bill about himself"

in pragmatically favouring the alternative interpretation. This research is then dealing only with reflexive anaphors within Principle A.

Results for the four types were as follows:

	Natives (%)	Spanish (%)	Chinese (%)
Type I (NP2 correct)			
"David could see that Bill was looking at himself in the mirror"	99.3	59.5	69.0
Type II (NP2 correct)			
"Mary angrily told me that Sue had spilled a lot of paint on herself"	91.4	49.9	49.0
Type III (NP1 correct)			
"Susan gave Mary three photographs of herself taken last summer"	72.8	59.8	59.7

Type IV (NP2 correct)
 "After the medical tests were   54.2   54.2   45.8
 completed, the doctor informed
 Bill about himself"

Correct results for four sentence types (adapted from Thomas, 1989, p. 301)

L2 learners performed well below native levels on Types I and II, showing that they were less strongly constrained by the type (a) setting. The plausibility of Type II also biased them more than the natives. In the type III sentences L2 learners preferred subject interpretations, though both natives and L2 learners were strongly influenced by the plausibility of type IV. There were no real differences between the two subgroups of Chinese and Spanish, who were matched for level of English. Thomas claims this shows a lack of transfer of L1 settings, on the one hand, through the similarities between the groups, on the other, through the Spanish speakers' bias against the (a) setting in English. Resort to the Subset Principle 'cannot explain why they produce such high levels of long-distance binding of reflexives in English'. Thomas (1991) extends this approach by comparing L2 learners of English and of Japanese through elicited imitation and multiple choice comprehension, concluding that both were attempting to find a setting for the governing category parameter and so 'L2 learners seem able to reset parameters in L2'.

Again, the value of the principles and parameters approach is that it provides a language-independent framework within which different L1s and L2s can be compared and within which L1 acquisition can be compared to L2 acquisition. It specifies in precise terms what the learner has to learn and some of the steps involved in getting there. To sum up, the experiment in Cook (1990b) suggests similarities in processing binding relationships between L2 learners with different L1s and native speakers, not only for anaphors but also for pronominals; the experiments by Finer and Broselow (1986), Broselow and Finer (1991), and Thomas (1989) show that learner languages fall within the compass of parameter theory even when they are not the same as the L1 or the L2; L2 learning is indeed describable in terms of setting values for parameters. A weakness of the current research is that, while the learners have spoken a spread of L1s with different settings for the governing category parameter, the only L2 to be studied is English, with two extreme settings for anaphors and pronominals. Nevertheless, using the distinction between knowing and obeying (Grimshaw and Rosen, 1990), most of the research demonstrates that L2 learners know the Binding principles, even if they do not fully obey them.

The Subset Principle on the other hand is not easily related to the L2 learning of Binding. Cook (1990b) found the same error patterns for anaphors and pronominals, contrary to the predictions of the Subset Principle. Finer and Broselow (1986) found contradictions between the Subset Principle and their results, possibly rescued by the proper antecedent parameter. The other problem with the Subset Principle is the extent to which it can be used with parameters other than Binding. Can it, for instance be reconciled with the pro-drop parameter? It was originally argued that pro-drop languages were 'larger' than non-pro-drop languages; hence the claim by Hyams (1986) that children treat all languages initially as pro-drop is in breach of the Subset Principle as they are starting with the larger rather than the smaller language. One possibility is that, like the head parameter, pro-drop is actually several parameters, as suggested by Saleemi (1990).

Methodological Issues with Binding Research

The overall UG learning model to which Binding and the Subset Principle are related is set aside to the next chapter. The work on binding forces a different type of methodology on the research. Binding is concerned with the invisible relationship of interpretation in the speaker's mind. Hence evidence that L2 learners produce sentences such as "John said Peter helps himself" tells us nothing about whether the learners know the correct binding for "himself"; nor would asking them whether "John said Peter helps himself" is grammatical show whether they interpret it correctly or not. So binding research is more or less compelled to rely on comprehension; only by getting the learner to say which interpretation is involved can we tell what he or she understands. In my view comprehension data score over other types as they are indisputably based on actual use of language, rather than related to it indirectly, as are grammaticality judgements. Nevertheless, the usual caveat has to be made about the artificiality of comprehension experiments, outlined in the last chapter. Cook (1990b) in addition used a measure of response time; this provides another form of measurement which, in this case, corroborates the comprehension scores in that higher error rate goes with greater time. An extensive psycholinguistic literature is in fact now concerned with the on-line processing of reflexives, for example Nagata (1991), which has yet to be utilised in SLA research.

So once again the binding research raises the problem of competence and performance: how can you show that people *know* Binding principles by proving they *use* them in performance? Comprehension measures and response times reflect performance processes, and so require a proper set of links between linguistic competence and a model of speech comprehension. As we see from the arguments of Grimshaw and Rosen (1990) with first language acquisition, on the one hand, results that do not manifest principles can be discounted by claiming that some feature of performance or of the experiment has prevented knowledge from being clearly seen, on the other hand results that show partial knowledge of principles can still be taken to show their existence because they could not be explained in any other way. We shall return to this the next chapter.

In general, principles and parameters potentially have large-scale consequences across the board rather than being rule-specific; hence the L2 pro-drop research quite rightly looked at a range of phenomena in addition to the presence or absence of subjects. But, as the pro-drop research progressed, the other aspects tended to fall away; that-trace constructions for instance did not behave in quite the same fashion as null subject sentences though supposedly part of the same parameter. Perhaps the pro-drop parameter should indeed only be concerned with whether the sentence has to have a subject or not; White (1986) suggests that the L2 evidence could affect syntactic theory by showing the need to separate the null subject construction from Subject–Verb inversion. Even if one accepted this for a particular parameter, in general it would shrink parameters back to construction-specific rules rather than utilising the insight that they apply to all relevant structural relationships of the sentence. Null subjects would be a single construction that differed between languages, little different from the structuralist work of earlier chapters.

8.4 THE HEAD-DIRECTION PARAMETER (PRINCIPAL BRANCHING DIRECTION)

A further L2 research area that has been linked to the principles and parameters framework is *the head-direction parameter*. The terminology in this area is slightly confusing; here the head direction parameter is seen as a distinct parameter from the head parameter mentioned earlier although related to it. Head direction captures a broad division between languages over the location of subordinate clauses within the structure of the sentence. First there is the variation encountered in the last chapter between languages such as English that have relative clauses after the Noun head (postposed), as in

"I liked the meal he cooked"

and languages like Japanese that have relative clauses *before* the Noun head (preposed), as in:

"Gohan-o tabete-iru ko-ga naite-imasu"
Rice-obj. eating is child-subj. crying is
(the child who is eating rice is crying).

Languages that postpose relative clauses also tend to put subordinate clauses to the right of main clauses, as in

"He'll go when I ask him"

where the subordinate "when" clause is postposed. This ordering of subordinate and main clauses is not absolute, as English may also have

"When I ask him he'll go"

with the subordinate "when" clause preposed. Nevertheless, English has a clear preference for postposed clauses. Conversely, languages that prepose relative clauses tend also to prepose subordinate clauses, as in the Japanese sentence:

"Kodomo ga gohan o tabete kara okahsan wa sooji shita"
child rice eating after mother cleared up.
(After the child had eaten the rice, the mother cleared up).

The *head-direction parameter* therefore has two values, according to whether a language tends to postpose or prepose subordinate clauses. In earlier writings the parameter was known as Principal Branching Direction and had two values, right-branching and left-branching (Lust, 1983); preposing creates phrase structure that branches to the left in terms of a tree diagram, postposing creates phrase structure that branches to the right. Later accounts have called it the head-direction parameter or head initial/final parameter (Flynn, 1987a). The parameter affects the 'major recursive devices of a language, e.g. relative clause, adverbial subordinate clause, and sentence complementation' (Lust, 1983). While it is often seen as a more general version of the head parameter, they are distinguished here in that the *head-direction parameter* affects the position of subordinate clauses in general, but the *head parameter* covers only the position of complements within phrases, some of which may indeed be subordinate clauses but which do not include relative clauses since these are not complements.

The research into the head-direction parameter has also relied on a notion of 'anaphora', here meaning either the relationship between an antecedent and its pronoun or that between an antecedent and a missing element in the sentence. Starting with subordinate clauses, English has forward anaphora relating "John" and "he" from left to right in

"*John* locked the door when *he* left"

and backward anaphora relating "Kate" and "she" from right to left in

"When *she* left, *Kate* locked the door".

The choice of head/initial versus head/final also dictates a preference for the direction of anaphora; preposing languages prefer backward anaphora, postposing languages forward anaphora.

The anaphoric analysis is extended to coordination. Coordinate clauses are seen as involving ellipsis of repeated elements; the concept of anaphora is used to refer to the links between the element that is present in the sentence and the element that is missing. These clauses too show a similar head-direction variation. Take

"Jane lost her temper and left!"
Jane lost her temper and ∅ left; i.e. "Jane lost her temper and (Jane) left"

Here there is *forward* anaphora between "Jane" and the gap where the second NP "Jane" could occur, marked by "∅". Compare this with

"Helen and George escaped"
Helen ∅ and George escaped; i.e. "Helen (escaped) and George escaped".

Here there is *backward* anaphora between "escaped" and the gap "∅" where the second Verb "escaped" could occur. Forward anaphora will then be more typical of English, backward anaphora of Japanese.

The head-direction parameter is claimed to affect the preferences of language learners: children learning English as an L1 show an early preference for forward anaphora because it fits their setting for head-direction, children learning Japanese as an L1 have an early preference for backward anaphora because it fits the head-direction of Japanese. Lust (1983) for example found that English children are better at imitating forward anaphora such as

"John ate and read"

in which "John" links with the missing subject of "read":

"John ate and ∅ read"

than backward anaphora such as:

"John and Mary ate lunch"

in which "ate" links with the missing Verb after "John":

"John ∅ and Mary ate lunch".

The reverse is true for Japanese children dealing with the equivalent Japanese sentences.

L2 Work with the Head-direction Parameter

Suzanne Flynn has reported on an investigation of L2 learning within this framework in several linked publications, the most complete of which is Flynn (1987a). Let us take Flynn (1984) as a starting point. Her aim was to see whether adult L2 learners were still sensitive to the head-direction parameter and whether the L1 setting for the head-direction parameter had an effect on the L2. Learning an L2 with the same setting for the head-direction parameter as the L1 should be easier than learning an L2 with a different setting. She took 51 adult L2 learners of English, whose L1 was Spanish, like English a postposed language, and 53 whose L1 was Japanese, a preposed language. They were divided by the University of Michigan English Placement test into three groups of beginners, intermediate, and advanced, and were pre-trained on the vocabulary employed. The test proper consisted of elicited imitation, that is to say, they had to repeat 18 15-syllable sentences aloud after the experimenter. Scoring of the responses was based on counting anything as incorrect that 'altered the syntactic structure or meaning of the original stimulus sentence' (Flynn, 1987a, p. 114). The test anaphora sentences are exemplified by:

Postposed   "The man answered the boss when he installed the television"

in which there is forward anaphora between "the man" and "he".

Preposed   "When he delivered the message, the actor questioned the lawyer"

in which there is backward anaphora between "he" and "the actor".

Equivalent sentences of both types were also used that had no anaphora, for instance:

"The boss informed the owner when the worker entered the office".

In addition there were 'juxtaposed' control sentences with no subordination, such as:

"The man discussed the article; the man studied the notebook."

There were three sentences of each type.

The first results compared the success for the two sets of learners. In all Flynn's experiments the figures are quoted out of 3, since there were three sentences of each type. Here they are converted to percentages of test sentences (that is, not control sentences) from Flynn (1984). Flynn also subjects the figures to a statistical technique to compensate for any peculiarity of the individual sentence by looking at its control equivalent.

	Spanish (%)	Japanese (%)
No anaphora	42.0	15.0
Pronoun anaphors	48.3	24.0

Percentage success on non-anaphora and anaphora "when" sentences (calculated from Flynn, 1984)

Spanish speakers had higher scores than Japanese learners on sentences both with and without anaphora. It was not that the Japanese were worse at English, because this difference held, level for level, across the groups; the advanced Spanish learners for example were 57 per cent correct for sentences without anaphora, the Japanese 24 per cent. The setting for the head-direction parameter of the L1 affected the difficulty of both sentence types for L2 learners, making them comparatively easy for Spanish-speaking learners.

The results for forward versus backward anaphora for intermediate learners were as follows, calculated approximately from a graph in Flynn (1984):

	Spanish (%)	Japanese (%)
Forward anaphora	75	15
Backward anaphora	50	12

Success rate for forward versus backward anaphora for intermediate Spanish learners (from a graph in Flynn, 1984)

Intermediate Spanish-speaking learners were far better at both forward and backward anaphora than the intermediate Japanese; Spanish speakers found forward anaphora easier than backward anaphora while Japanese did not. In terms of error type, 52 per cent of the Japanese errors consisted of failure to repeat the second part of a postposed sentence but only 6 per cent of the Spanish-speaking errors.

Thus Flynn (1984) concludes 'both processing and acquisition of complex sentence structures have been found to be predicted to a significant degree by the PBD [Principal Branching Direction] typology'. She argues that this result cannot be explained by Contrastive Analysis (because it is not part of the surface phrase structure) nor by creative construction (because it shows transfer from the L1); it should perhaps be pointed out that Contrastive Analysis is not necessarily at a surface level, even if this was true of the 1950s work mentioned in Chapter 1. Having ruled out these alternatives, Flynn suggests that the research therefore leads towards the Universal Grammar theory, to be discussed in the next chapter.

Research summary: S. Flynn, (1984), 'A Universal in L2 Acquisition Based on a PBD Typology', in F. R. Eckman, L. N. Bell, and D. Nelson (eds), *Universals of Second Language Acquisition* (Rowley, Mass.: Newbury House)

Aim: to investigate whether adult L2 learners of English are still sensitive to parameter settings and influenced by the L1 setting

Learners: 51 adult learners of English with L1 Spanish, and 53 with L1 Japanese

Aspect of language: the parametric difference in head-direction between postposed languages like Spanish and English and preposed languages like Japanese

Data type: elicited imitation of 18 15-syllable sentences

Results: Spanish speakers had higher scores on sentences both with and without anaphora, were far better at both forward and backward anaphora, and found forward and backward anaphors different in difficulty; while Japanese did not.

Claims: 'both processing and acquisition of complex sentence structures have been found to be predicted to a significant degree' by the head-direction parameter

---

(a) *Flynn* has reported further tasks that were used with these learners in Flynn (1987a) and elsewhere. An elicited imitation task was carried out with postposed and preposed clauses without anaphora; language level made no difference but by the highest level the Japanese had started to find postposed sentences easier than preposed, thus having adopted the English head-direction setting (Flynn, 1987b). Flynn and Espinal (1985) extended the research to 60 adult Chinese learners of English, divided into beginners, intermediate, and advanced by the same test. In both Chinese and Japanese, complements precede heads in NPs and Adjective Phrases, but Chinese has SVO order and prepositions, unlike Japanese SOV and postpositions; indeed the mixed word order of Chinese led to the revisions of the head parameter first seen in Huang (1982) and Travis (1984). Flynn and Espinal (1985) use the same elicited imitation and comprehension tasks as Flynn (1983; 1987a). The results can thus be added to the display for the earlier experiment:

	Chinese (%)	Japanese (%)
No anaphora	25	15.0
Pronoun anaphors	25.3	24.0

Percentage success on non-anaphor and anaphor sentences (calculated from Flynn, 1984; Flynn & Espinal, 1985)

The Chinese behaved like the Japanese in having a low level of success in two-clause sentences; divided into levels, only at the advanced level did they too start to find postposed sentences easier, with 60 per cent accuracy for postposed, and 40 per cent for preposed (from a graph in Flynn and Espinal, 1985). These are similar to the results from the Japanese learners, showing no preference in the head-direction parameter till an advanced level, but overall low performance.

Flynn (1989) turned to relative clauses. Whether the relative clause comes before or after the head of the NP is also taken to be part of the head-direction parameter. Again the experiment refers back to the original groups of 51 Spanish-speaking and 53 Japanese. The same elicited imitation task was employed. Test sentences varied according to the fourfold parallel-function division described in the last chapter (Sheldon, 1974): whether the relative clause modified the subject or object and whether it was a subject or an object clause. A typical example of a Subject–Subject clause was:

"The student who called the gentleman answered the policeman".

Results were:

	Spanish (LB) (%)	Japanese (LB) (%)
Subject main/Subject RC	55	29.7
Subject main/Object RC	39	13.7
Object main/Subject RC	27	22.3
Object main/Object RC	42.3	17

Percentage success on relative clauses (calculated from Flynn, 1989)

The Spanish are better than the Japanese for all sentence types; in other words, the L1 setting for the head-direction parameter makes a difference in L2. Though Flynn does not point it out herself, the results for the

Spanish, but not for the Japanese, unusually confirm the parallel function hypothesis discussed in the last chapter in that the parallel function clauses are easier. The types of error were also different between the groups. The differences between the groups are then held to support the head-direction parameter from another angle: the same setting in the L1 helps, a different setting hinders. Henry (1988) similarly found that English-speaking learners of Chinese who had not heard relative clauses before but had learnt other Chinese word orders assumed that they were preposed although they had not encountered them before.

(b) *Eubank (1989)* replicated Flynn's design with a group of 45 adult speakers of Arabic, which has postposed relative clauses and little backward anaphora. The idea was to test hypotheses 'developed not from Flynn's hypotheses, but directly from her actual findings for ESL learners whose NL [Native Language] is Spanish' (Eubank, 1989, p. 49), drawing particularly on Flynn (1987b). Eubank argues that Flynn's work implies two hypotheses:

(i) there would be 'no significant difference' between postposed and preposed no anaphor subordinate clauses with "when" for the three levels of learner. Flynn (1987a; 1987b) had found differences for advanced Japanese learners but not for Spanish speakers.
(ii) intermediate learners 'will show a significant preference for forward anaphora'. Flynn (1984; 1987b) had found no differences for Japanese learners but a preference for forward anaphors in Intermediate Spanish.

His first results compared the preposed and postposed no anaphor sentences, converted as above into percentages.

Postposed	33.3%
Preposed	47.3%

Percentage success for Arabic learners on left- and right-branching no-anaphor sentences (calculated from Eubank, 1989)

This shows a significant difference between the two sentence types: Arabic learners in fact find preposed sentences easier than postposed, contrary to predictions.

Eubank's second hypothesis requires results organised in terms of forward versus backward anaphors for each level:

	Beginners (%)	Intermediate (%)	Advanced (%)
Forward anaphors	17.7	39.3	56
Backward anaphors	7.7	50	70.7

Success rate for Arabic learners for forward versus backward anaphors (from Eubank, 1989)

Statistical analysis shows that 'neither for the combined scores of these subjects nor for the scores of subjects at particular levels of proficiency is there a significant difference in performance between sentences containing backward anaphora and sentences containing forward anaphora' (Eubank, 1989, p. 55). Thus the oddity Eubank expects for intermediates does not appear. Eubank claims this undermines Flynn's conclusions by showing that Arabic speakers consider English to have a preposed setting for the head-direction parameter. Eubank explains the discrepancy from Flynn in terms of methodological and experimental failings, to be detailed below.

Criticisms of the Head-direction Research

Flynn's work has provoked considerable controversy. The following draws on criticisms made in a review article by Bley-Vroman and Chaudron (1990) and by Eubank (1989), and on a defence by Flynn and Lust (1990). In terms of linguistics, it has already been hinted that the main problem is the relationship between the head-direction parameter and X-bar syntax. The head parameter proper had a precise formulation in X-bar syntax in the early 1980s as a matter of whether the lexical item projected its arguments in the form of complements before or after it – the lexical Verb projecting the object NPs in the VP, and so on. In the later 1980s this became untenable in the light of languages that had different orders for the different phrases, hence the suggestions by Huang (1982) and Koopman (1983) for more complex explanations. But, within the syntactic literature, the position of subordinate clauses was not typically taken to be part of such a parameter; it is not, for instance mentioned in such a comprehensive treatment as Haegeman (1991). Flynn and Lust (1990) argue, on the one hand, that the head-direction parameter relates to the family of word order parameters current in the early 1980s rather than to the specific definition of the head parameter, on the other, that the purpose of research is to contribute to *change* in linguistic theory: postulating a head-direction parameter from acquisitional data can cause the theory of syntax itself to change. The link between the head-direction parameter and the head parameter is in this view a contribution by Lust, Flynn, and their associates to syntactic theory from their work in acquisition.

In terms of principles and parameters theory, this is problematic in several ways. First, a language has only a *preference* for one direction rather than a constant direction; English can after all have both postposed and preposed "when" clauses, even if relative clauses are invariably postposed. The more familiar principles and parameters do not work in this way, as they do not allow for such performance variation. Secondly, there seems no necessary reason why the head-direction parameter should affect both the position of the subordinate clause and the direction of anaphora; these might well be distinct areas, as some of the above results suggest (White, 1989). Thirdly, the idea of 'direction' is hard to relate to the Binding Principles that, after all, also deal with the problems of anaphoric reference but do not refer to left or right direction; White (1989, p. 100), however, feels that 'Flynn's results appear to be perfectly consistent with the operation of the Binding Theory', in so far as it deals with the freedom of pronominals. These criticisms are made at greater length by Bley-Vroman and Chaudron (1990), and by Eubank (1989). My own view is that, like the Accessibility Hierarchy, the head-direction parameter is a concept that has produced interesting research consequences; though it is a parameter of some kind, it is not one that is immediately locatable within current X-bar syntax. This could result in change to the main body of syntactic theory, or it could restrict the generalisations that can be made from Flynn's research to the theory of Universal Grammar to be described in the next chapter.

Methodology of the Head-direction Research

Among the methodological failings listed by Bley-Vroman and Chaudron (1990) and mostly defended by Flynn and Lust (1990) are:

- the Michigan Placement test does not relate sufficiently to spoken language production; the Japanese may therefore not have been equivalent to the Spanish, level for level, in the *spoken* language measured in elicited imitation. Flynn and Lust (1990) point to the standardised nature of the test and to its agreement with other tests. Bley-Vroman and Chaudron (1990) do not, however, support their criticisms with sufficient details of the Michigan Placement test to show its bias. One should perhaps point out how much care Flynn took to obtain independent measurements of the language level of her subjects, far in excess of most studies mentioned in this book.

- the inappropriateness of using elicited imitation to test anaphoric relationships rather than surface form. This is not specifically countered in Flynn and Lust (1990). Elicited imitation simply involves making learners repeat sentence; it is a traditional technique for researching language acquisition, used in L1 by Brown and Fraser (1963), Slobin and Welsh (1973), and others, though not very popular in recent years. The idea behind it is that imitation involves underlying competence since a sentence has to be comprehended before it can be successfully imitated; mistakes in imitation may betray features of the learner's competence; in particular it can be revealing to see what mistakes students make while repeating sentences that are slightly longer than they can imitate with ease. Elicited imitation was used in L2 research by Cook (1973) with relative clauses and has been used occasionally since, but not on a large scale. It is only one form of evidence with its own particular biases; White (1989), for example, points out that elicited imitation cannot show how subjects are resolving the ambiguous reference of pronominals inside or outside the sentence (Binding Principle B). It should therefore be complemented by other methods, such as the comprehension test used by Flynn (1987). As we have constantly seen in this book, interpreting any single form of data as a sign of underlying competence has its own distinctive problems, whether it is observational data or experiments. In my view, the limitation of Flynn's research is the narrow range of data. Or indeed of subjects: like Alberto and his five companions, two of which (Jorge and Marta) have already figured in this chapter, Flynn's 104 subjects have been analysed and reanalysed so many times that a new group is necessary.

- the statistical analysis used by Flynn cannot support the kinds of statement that are made. Naturally Flynn and Lust (1990) claim that it can; this discussion involves technical aspects of statistics and seems best left to the statisticians. Again, we should perhaps point to the sophisticated use of statistics employed in Flynn's research compared with the crude statistics seen in most L2 work, or indeed the absence of statistical treatment from much research, as has been seen from time to time in this book. In my view, while L2 researchers need to check that their figures conform to accepted modern statistical techniques, they should not involve themselves too heavily in arguments about the theory of statistics, unless they want to switch academic disciplines.

- an alternative explanation for the results based on ease of processing is preferable, namely that both postposing and forward anaphora are psychologically easier to process, an argument also put forward by Eubank (1989); this is based on evidence that postposed subordinate clauses are easier to remember in the L1 and claims that forward anaphora is easier to comprehend. Flynn and Lust (1990) point out that this should predict all L2 learners would be the same, while Flynn's results show that they differ; they list other research that shows the opposite from the two claims that Bley-Vroman and Chaudron (1990) advance. Chapter 5 argued that any putative psychological explanation needs justifying through an adequate contemporary psychological framework and through evidence showing the validity of the alternative, not simply an *ad hoc* demolition of other people's work.

To allow Flynn and Lust (1990) the last polemical words, 'It is time for scholars to pursue in a positive manner the real questions that currently challenge the field rather than devise dubious and flawed methodological and theoretical challenges to past foundational work' (Flynn and Lust, 1990, p. 25).

8.5   SYNTAX AND SLA RESEARCH

The three areas dealt with in this chapter show the closest links to linguistics that we have yet seen, hence the necessity for detailing the actual syntactic description here. Since Chomsky (1981a) the pro-drop parameter has been studied in a variety of languages: Binding Theory was crucial to the development of the theory during the 1980s; while the head-direction parameter has less tight links to current syntax, it is within the general mode of thinking. Though the L2 research is also related to contemporary L1 acquisition theories, it does not depend upon them, but makes contributions of its own. Principles and parameters theory has produced a new and fruitful set of ideas about knowledge of language for investigation in SLA research.

Binding theory and the pro-drop parameter also illustrate some dangers in utilising the most current version of linguistics. Principles and parameters theory has an extraordinarily swift rate of change. However much agreement there is on the 'facts' of the pro-drop parameter or of binding, current work is revising both binding (for example, Manzini, 1990) and pro-drop (for example, Saleemi, 1990). Research that is specific to one particular syntactic analysis has a short shelf-life. This book has indeed often made the point that the syntactic framework for one or other piece of research is no longer valid and the research is consequently hard to interpret. This problem is acute in principles and parameters theory; any research carried out by an SLA researcher is out-of-date in terms of syntactic theory more or less by definition, since the theory will have already moved on in the few months or years before the L2 research could take place and will have moved on even further by the time the research is published. To stand on its own feet, SLA research has to decide its level of involvement with syntactic theory; SLA researchers have a difficult task in ensuring that their work is still compatible with the theory by the time it appears in print, if they wish to make valid contributions to linguistics as well as to SLA theory.

There is also the danger that second language researchers may forget that their purpose is to discover how people learn L2s, not see if the latest fashion in linguistics can be applied to L2 research. Haegeman (1991, p. 20) claims 'recently, linguists in the generative tradition have also started to investigate whether the model of first language acquisition that they advocate could be applied to the acquisition of a second language'. The traffic should also go in the other direction: SLA researchers should investigate whether the model of syntax used by linguists is appropriate to the acquisition of second languages: however good the syntactic theory, it has not been devised with SLA in mind or based on SLA types of evidence. For the goal of SL research is to answer the three multi-lingual questions of knowledge, acquisition, and use, rather than to advance syntactic theory itself. It needs to use syntax that is appropriate to its own needs, and to stay with it for long enough to produce properly researched answers. Principles and parameters theory by virtue of its scope and its model of linguistic knowledge has very clear attractions for SLA research. To some extent its practitioners have to decide between being linguists who use the second language field or SLA researchers who use linguistics.

9 The Universal Grammar Model and Second Language Acquisition

The model of language acquisition most associated with SLA research in recent years has been the Universal Grammar (UG) model developed by Chomsky, which uses the principles and parameters syntax described in the previous chapter. This association between linguistics and SLA research reveals some of the potential and some of the dangers involved in the adoption of a complex and specialised learning model. The present chapter introduces the main themes of current UG-related SLA research at the time of writing. The area is, however, vast and rapidly changing. Recent research on UG lines can usually be found in the journals *Second Language Research* and *Studies in Second Language Acquisition*.

9.1 THE UNIVERSAL GRAMMAR MODEL OF LANGUAGE ACQUISITION

Chapter 1 introduced the Language Acquisition Device (LAD) model of language acquisition, which has been implicit in many theories we have discussed, for example in Krashen's Input Hypothesis. The LAD model in Chomsky (1964) is essentially as follows:

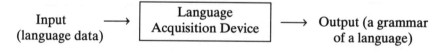

Acquisition is the process through which language data goes into the LAD 'black box' and a grammar comes out; the LAD evaluates alternative grammars to see which best fits the incoming data.

The UG theory fleshes out this model by establishing the crucial features of the input, the contents of the black box, and the properties of the resultant grammar. The major change is a shift to describing grammars in terms of principles and parameters, which are purpose-designed to account for L1 acquisition, rather than rules. The principles are unchanging regardless of the actual language involved. Taking examples from the last chapter, according to the principles of X-bar syntax all phrases have two levels; according to the Projection Principle all lexical items project their syntactic

200

specifications on to the phrases of which they are heads. These principles form part of the language faculty of the mind – Universal Grammar. The claim is that it is impossible for a human mind to know a language without knowing the X-bar and Projection principles, since they are already present inside it. UG allows for variation between languages through parameters; languages can only vary within the pre-set limits for a particular parameter. The parameter itself is universal but the values it may take vary from one language to another. Any language a human being knows must, among other things, be either pro-drop or non-pro-drop, must have a setting for each of the parameters affecting word order, and must have one of the possible settings for the governing category parameter of Binding Theory.

The answer to the knowledge question is that the language knowledge of adult human minds takes the form of universal principles and variable settings for parameters, whatever the language they have learnt. In addition, knowledge of language contains the lexical items of the language, with detailed specifications of how each item may project on to the structure of the sentence. The full schema is a set of principles and parameters arranged into modules such as Binding Theory; it is a 'computational system' that ranges from the component of Phonological Form to the component of Logical Form, that is, from 'sound' to 'meaning', as described at greater length in Cook (1988c). The principles and parameters framework makes no pretence to cover all aspects of language. The whole complex apparatus is concerned with the crucial central area of syntax defined as *core grammar*; much of language is *peripheral*, that is to say, idiosyncratic and linked to UG principles and parameters in a looser way. UG is maximally relevant to the core elements that can be described through its principles and parameters, such as Binding and pro-drop, minimally relevant to other aspects of language, say constructions such as "The more the merrier". As has often been pointed out, for example in Cook (1988c), while this provides a useful delimitation of the areas rightfully considered part of UG, it also provides a convenient way of disposing of elements that do not fit current analyses of UG by pushing them out into an undefined periphery.

How then does someone acquire language? To put the UG theory of acquisition in Chomsky's words, 'what we "know innately" are the principles of the various subsystems of S_0 [the initial state of the child's mind] and the manner of their interaction, and the parameters associated with these principles. What we learn are the values of the parameters and the elements of the periphery (along with the lexicon to which similar considerations apply)' (Chomsky, 1986a, p. 150). First the principles. These are not in a sense 'acquired' from outside since they are already present as part of UG inside the mind; instead, they become attached to the person's knowledge of a particular language together with values for parameters. This is not to say that a child's speech will show immediate signs of, say, the Projection Principle, as he or she may be unable at first to handle the length or type of sentence which would show it in action – you can't project much on to the sentence if you're only able to say one word at a time.

Next, the setting for parameters. Even if you have the pro-drop parameter present in your mind, you still need to detect which setting is right for it – whether your parents are speaking a pro-drop or non-pro-drop language. The parameter has to be 'triggered' by something in the language input the child hears. This is seen predominantly as caused by *positive* evidence – things that are actually present in the input. So the word order parameters for English may be triggered by hearing sentences such as "John ate an apple", the word order parameters for Japanese by hearing "Ojiisan to obaasan ga koya ni sunde imashita" (old man and old woman cottage in lived). The evidence for triggering the setting for the pro-drop parameter is more problematic since pro-drop languages have sentences both with and without overt subjects, and since even non-pro-drop languages have occasional null-subject sentences, "Can't buy me love" in English, for instance. Hyams (1986) originally claimed the crucial evidence to be the presence of stressed subject pronouns and 'expletive' subjects in non-pro-drop languages; once children see that "there" and "it" are necessary as dummy expletive subjects in sentences such as "It's snowing" or "There's a black cloud on the horizon", they can set the English value for the pro-drop parameter to non-pro-drop. As with the principles, there is some dispute over whether all parameters are present in the mind from the outset or whether some come into being at a particular age.

The role of language input is to 'trigger' the appropriate setting for each parameter; though input is necessary to the process of acquisition, its nature does not affect its outcome, provided only that an adequate range of natural sentences is encountered. Instead of language being 'learnt', parameters are 'triggered'. There is no theory of language learning to supplement the principles and parameters contents of the black box apart from the notion of triggering (Saleemi, 1992), with the possible exception of the Subset Principle described in the previous chapter. The model is 'deterministic' in that the input simply triggers a setting (Atkinson, 1992). A problem with the deterministic view is that L1 children may switch parameter-setting, for example from pro-drop to non-pro-drop in the acquisition of English; why does the input not immediately set off the right setting? Ways round this are to suggest that the child may not be able to take in crucial aspects of the input at a particular stage or that the child may at first not have certain aspects of UG available. Atkinson (1992, p. 210), however, discusses whether the concept of triggering actually differs from the concept of learning, concluding that it is difficult to find 'a distinctive role for parameter setting as a developmental mechanism'.

The UG model sees little value for the child in *negative* evidence, consisting either of *direct* correction by parents – "You mustn't say that, Jimmy" – or of *indirect* evidence of what doesn't occur in the language – null-subject sentences do not occur in non-pro-drop languages. Direct correction is rarely found in transcripts of actual conversation with children, and it is not provided by all parents in all cultures; since essentially all human children acquire human language, this rules out direct negative evidence as a main source of language evidence for children, whatever its potential might be. Furthermore, even when correction of children's language does occur, children seem to ignore it. The role of indirect negative evidence in acquisition is also problematic as it is hard to assess how or what the child notices is missing – in a sense very many things are 'missing' from what the child hears; Saleemi (1988) suggests indirect negative evidence is only useful when the child can supplement it with positive evidence.

One of the interesting questions for the UG model concerns the initial setting for parameters. There might be no initial setting, so a child can adopt any setting with equal ease. Or there might be a default setting consisting of one or other of the possible settings. Hyams (1986) showed that the early speech of children learning English has null subjects. Hence, so far as the pro-drop parameter is concerned, the child starts with a particular value, namely pro-drop, rather than having a neutral setting; the setting can remain the same if the child is learning Spanish but must change if the child is to acquire English. There is, however, some controversy whether Hyams's position accurately reflects the facts of acquisition (Hulk, 1987; Radford, 1990; Cook, 1990a) and whether children learning their L1 necessarily start from the pro-drop setting. This distinction between the initial default setting and the learnt setting is sometimes referred to as 'markedness', though this term has many confusing senses: the initial setting is said to be the 'unmarked' setting; the setting that can only be acquired through experience is 'marked'. If the Subset Principle of learning is true, the unmarked default setting should always define a language that is smaller than the marked setting; as we saw in the last chapter, this applies with difficulty to Hyams' first formulation of the pro-drop parameter as pro-drop languages are 'larger' than non-pro-drop languages rather than 'smaller'.

A further controversy surrounds the issue of whether all the principles and parameters are present in the mind to start with, or whether they come into being over time. In other words, are the principles and parameters like the heart, which is structurally complete at birth, or like the teeth, which grow and are replaced over many years? Borer and Wexler (1987) proposed that the UG properties themselves 'grow' in the mind over time. For instance the lack of inflections such as possessive "-s" from children's early speech coupled with the lack of modal auxiliaries like "can", tense forms like "-ed", and other 'functional' parts of the sentence may show that the

IP and CP are not yet present in the child's mind (Radford, 1986; 1990); the reason for the comparatively crude structure of the child's sentences may be that the language faculty in the mind has not yet fully come into being: UG itself develops over time rather than being constant from birth. There is then disagreement between those who accept a 'growth' model of UG which develops over time and those who accept a 'no-growth' model that remains constant over time, except for differences due to other performance factors.

As well as knowledge of syntax, the child also has to have a knowledge of the vocabulary of the language. As we saw in Chapter 8, the Projection Principle makes properties of individual lexical items dictate the syntactic environments in which they can occur. Hence the learner has to acquire a vast number of words, each with its own idiosyncratic syntactic behaviour. Within a different syntactic theory, Gross (1990) analysed 12,000 'simple' verbs in French and found that no two of them could be used in exactly the same way. The learner has to learn the syntactic specification of large numbers of idiosyncratic vocabulary items. In some ways, because of the comparative sparseness of the syntax in this theory, the learning load falls increasingly on vocabulary, a trend that reaches its maximum in Chomsky's startling remark, 'there is only one human language, apart from the lexicon, and language acquisition is in essence a matter of determining lexical idiosyncrasies' (Chomsky, 1989, p. 44).

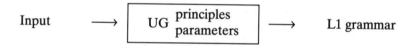

The substance of the change is that the black box now has definite contents; it produces the grammar of the language through instantiating principles, and setting values for parameters; this necessarily depends on acquiring vocabulary items with their specifications. The LAD box is no longer a set of processes along with a way of evaluating alternative grammars but an inventory of principles and parameters. Versions of this redrawn model are often used in the literature, for example Haegeman (1991, p. 15) and White (1989, p. 5). It does nevertheless present certain problems as a metaphorical model, as we shall see later. More detailed critiques of the principles and parameters theory of L1 acquisition can be found in Goodluck (1991) and Atkinson (1992).

Universal Grammar and Second Language Acquisition

In principle the same model could be applied directly to L2 learning, as in the following scheme:

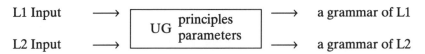

It might be that L2 grammars are not describable in principles and parameters terms. But, if the L2 user's knowledge of language indeed consists of principles and parameters, the principles are no more learnable in an L2 than in an L1. If the UG argument is correct, no grammar should ever exist in the human mind that breaches principles of UG or that has variation in core grammar not covered by the settings for parameters, except for any qualifications that have to be made for a 'growth' model or for performance reasons. If L2 grammars are indeed independent L2 grammars learnt by 'natural' language acquisition, being human grammars, they should manifest the same principles and choose from the same parameter settings as any other language. Rather than having any conceivable grammatical system, they are constrained by principles – the class of model Keil (1981) calls 'structural change governed by constraints'.

Let us first then see whether L2 grammars may in fact be described in principles and parameters terms. The evidence that L2 grammars obey principles is discussed in White (1989) and Cook (1985b). One principle that has been used as a test-case is *structure-dependency*. This has often been employed in an acquisition context as an example of a principle that could not be acquired from positive evidence, for example in the Chomsky/Piaget debate (Chomsky, 1980b); more detailed explanation can be found in Cook (1988c). English allows:

"Is Sam the cat that is black?".

The movement in this question depends upon the position of the "is" in the hierarchical structure of the sentence; it is the "is" within the relative clause that is moved, not the "is" in the main clause. English, however, forbids:

*"Is Sam is the cat that black?"

because the structure of the sentence has been ignored; you can't make a question in English by moving any "is", only the one in the right position in the structure. The principle of structure-dependency claims that all human languages rely on structure in this way; they never move arbitrary words or words in the first, second, or nth position in the linear order of the sentence, but always move an element that plays a particular part in the hierarchical sentence structure. While it is seen here as a limitation on movement, structure-dependency is also needed for Binding Theory and other areas of the grammar. The question is whether L2 learners use structure-dependency in circumstances when they do not need it in their first language; if they do, this ability must be contributed by their own minds rather than transferred from the L1. Japanese, for example, does not have syntactic movement and so does not require structure-dependency for movement; if Japanese learners of English know structure-dependency, it could not come from their L1. White (1989) cites research by Otsu and Naoi (1986) as providing some evidence for use of structure-dependency by L2 learners. Otsu and Naoi (1986) tested 11 teenage Japanese schoolgirls who had just been taught English relative clauses; they were asked to change sentences with relative clauses into questions. All of them bar one succeeded without breaking structure-dependency.

Structure-dependency is perhaps a poor example since it seems in some way a 'macro-principle' of the whole grammar rather than a specific principle of principles and parameters theory; indeed it predates the theory by some years (Chomsky, 1971). Comrie (1990) points out that there are documented languages that occasionally break it, for example Serbo-Croatian, and that it does not apply to phonology, for instance stress-assignment rules. Nor is structure-dependency strictly 'missing' from Japanese, merely not used in movement. Furthermore the need for structure-dependency in the grammar may now be redundant in that such violations would not be permitted by other principles of the theory (Culicover, 1991; Freidin, 1991).

Research that shows that other principles are present in the L2 is cited by Cook (1985b) and White (1989). Felix (1988), for example, tested several UG principles with German learners of English; results indicated that 'adult L2 learners do have consistent intuitions about grammaticality contrasts involving principles of UG' (Felix, 1988, p. 285). On the other hand similar research with classroom learners by Felix and Weigl (1991) showed none of the effects associated with UG; 'whatever the basis for their judgments was, it was almost certainly not UG' (Felix and Weigl, 1991, p. 176). It is then the classroom context that is crucial.

So, though the evidence that interlanguages do not breach UG is sparse, one should point to the lack of evidence for such breaches; no one appears to have produced clear evidence of sentences from L2 learners that breach principles and parameter settings of UG, say, the Projection principle, or Binding principles, frequent as such sentences should be if they were not universal. Hence the knowledge question for L2 learning still seems answerable in terms of principles: L2 learners' grammars indeed conform to the built-in principles of the mind.

But can L2 grammars also be described within the types of variation captured in parameters? Some of the research presented in the last chapter, such as Finer and Broselow (1986) and Broselow and Finer (1991), with the settings for the governing category parameter, has indeed explicitly concerned itself with showing that the L2 learner is working within the bounds of the parameter settings available in UG. The issue that is often debated in this context is how L2 learning relates to the marked and unmarked setting of the parameters. One possibility is that the L2 learner starts with the default unmarked setting regardless of the L1; another is that the L2 learner transfers a particular setting from L1 to L2. As we saw in the previous chapter, White (1986) showed that L2 learners of English who spoke French, a non-pro-drop language, found null subjects less grammatical in English than did learners who spoke Spanish, a pro-drop language. This suggests that the L1 setting for pro-drop is active in the L2. However, Liceras (1989) showed that English learners did not transfer L1 settings to Spanish. Going from the unmarked to the marked setting seems to present more problems for L2 learners than going in the reverse direction.

Second Language Acquisition and the Poverty-of-the-Stimulus Argument

The heart of the UG model of acquisition is the argument that, because people demonstrably know aspects of language that they could not have learnt from the speech they have heard, these must already be built in to the human mind, that is, be innate. This is known as the poverty-of-the-stimulus argument, or 'Plato's problem': 'How do we come to have such rich and specific knowledge, or such intricate systems of belief and understanding, when the evidence available to us is so meagre?' (Chomsky, 1987). The basic form of the argument is that, by comparing what goes in to UG and what comes out, we can establish what is in the middle – the knowledge of language that is necessarily part of the human language faculty. The structure of this argument, as summarised in Cook (1991b), is as follows:

Step A.
A native speaker of a particular language knows a particular aspect of syntax. For example, a speaker of English knows Binding Theory. That is to say, the grammar that comes out of the black box contains the binding principles linking pronominals, anaphors, and lexical NPs with their antecedents.

Step B.
This aspect of syntax could not have been learnt from the language input typically available to children. English children never hear sentences that breach binding principles, nor do they ever produce such sentences so that they could learn by being corrected; indeed, if children actually produced mistakes with binding, adults would not notice them since they would assume correct binding was intended, as we saw in the previous

chapter. In other words, the input to the black box is not sufficient to show the children that the binding principles are necessary.

Step C.
This aspect of syntax is not learnt from outside. Consequently this aspect of linguistic knowledge cannot be a response to any environmental factor outside the learner's mind. If binding principles are present (step A), but are not learnt (step B), they cannot come from outside the child's mind through any form of learning.

Step D.
This aspect of syntax is built-in to the mind. As there is no external source for this aspect of language, it must be an innate part of the human mind. That is to say, binding principles are part of the black box itself.

Once the force of this argument has been accepted, it can be tested on any area of syntax, not just on binding principles. The argument does not depend on any particular syntactic point or type of description; 'if some fact of grammar is unlearnable, then it must be related to UG, independent of whether or not we are able to provide an exact and complete UG-account of that fact' (Felix and Weigl, 1991, p. 168). To test the argument for a particular point, it is not necessary to look at the actual stages that children go through in developing language. Instead, the knowledge of any native speaker, as shown by single sentence evidence of possible sentences in the language, can be used to take step A, from which the other steps logically follow. To repeat the discussion of *single sentence evidence* from Chapter 1, if the single sentence "John loves freesias" is clearly English, and no one would dispute it, then that is all the evidence we need that an English-speaking person knows the structures involved in it. Single-sentence evidence is the basic evidence type used in I-language linguistics.

The strength of the poverty-of-the-stimulus argument partly depends on the types of evidence available to the child under step B. Any aspect of language that the speaker knows must either be learnable from positive evidence, that is to say, through exposure to sentences of the language, or be part of the innate equipment of the human mind. So the syntactic description proposed for it should either be learnable from actual sentences encountered or be built in to the mind. Within this conceptual framework, the theory of syntax is integrated with the theory of acquisition; all aspects of syntax have to be considered from the perspective of acquisition. While actual syntactic descriptions often make no more than a nod in this direction, this is nevertheless the clear premiss of the principles and parameters model. The UG theory of acquisition is not ultimately dependent on evidence from children's speech; its main prop is single sentence evidence of what native speakers know, not the history of how such knowledge came into being. It therefore implicitly makes a distinction between *language acquisition* and *language development* (Cook, 1985a). 'Acquisition' refers to language learning within the poverty-of-the-stimulus argument in its abstract and logical form – how the speaker can in principle acquire a grammar from language data – without looking at actual stages of development or specimens of children's language. 'Development' refers to language learning within a framework of how such knowledge actually develops over time in the learner; its study is based largely on children's performance, whether observational data or experiments. Development is concerned with the chronology of emergence; acquisition pays no attention to time. Development cannot set aside the interaction of language with the psychological and social aspects of the child's development, while acquisition can.

Let us see how the poverty-of-the-stimulus argument works for second language acquisition; while the steps above are fairly conventional, the interpretation for SLA is more idiosyncratic and is described more fully in Cook (1991b). Step A applies in the same way to L2 learning as to L1 acquisition; that is to say, it is necessary to show that the grammar contains some specific aspect of syntax. Showing, say, that L2 learners observe the binding principles, as described in the previous chapter, allows us to take this first step and to describe a part of their grammatical knowledge. A qualification on stage A in SLA, however, is that, while, according to this theory, native speakers all acquire the same L1 competence, few L2 learners reach a level in the L2 that is equivalent to their knowledge of the L1 and their L2 knowledge varies widely. Stage A in first language acquisition describes knowledge common to all speakers, that is, it is a constant from one person to another; Stage A in second language acquisition has to treat this knowledge as varying between L2 learners and not having a single fixed form.

Step B involves seeing whether this aspect of syntax could be learnt from the evidence available to L2 learners. Unlike L1 acquisition, there are sources other than positive evidence from which such knowledge could come. One available source is transfer of parameter settings from the L1, which is not of course possible for the child acquiring the first language. The work with the pro-drop parameter in Chapter 8 provided an example where the learner seems to start with the L1 setting as a basis for the L2, though this is muddied by the controversy over the normal initial setting; arguably in this case and in others, at the initial stage the positive evidence from outside is balanced by the internal evidence of the knowledge of the L1. But some L2 learners, particularly those in classrooms, also encounter types of evidence unavailable to the L1 child. For example, many teachers frequently correct L2 students, unlike parents in the L1. Teachers also often explain particular grammatical points to students, which provides metalinguistic evidence if not negative evidence proper, although few of their explanations are likely to concern those areas of syntax covered by principles and parameters theory. In first language acquisition, variation in language input is irrelevant: all children manage to learn human language irrespective of the input they hear. Hence the poverty-of-the-stimulus argument takes into account only the evidence that is available to *all* L1 children, that is to say, positive evidence, and ignores evidence types occasionally available to some children, for example correction. But L2 learning cannot follow the same route: L2 learners do *not* all achieve the same level of competence. Two causes suggest themselves. One is that the prior knowledge of the L1 inhibits progress. The other is that L2 learning is more sensitive to the type of evidence available than L1 acquisition; successful progress in L2 learning may depend on the nature of the evidence to a greater extent than in L1 acquisition.

Steps A and B of the poverty-of-the-stimulus argument both need qualification in SLA research, as there is variation in both knowledge of language and types of evidence available. Hence the modifications to steps A and B mean that steps C and D are not so inevitable in L2 learning. Indeed, this fact alone may raise some doubts about the relevance of UG to L2 learning. Nevertheless, the basic core of the argument still remains: if some aspect of language that is known by L2 learners could not have been learnt from the types of evidence available to them, its only other source must be the innate properties of the human mind.

Access to UG in Second Language Acquisition

The question that has been most often considered by L2 researchers is whether UG is actually involved in L2 learning. This has been posed as a choice between three possibilities (Cook, 1985a), set out in Figure 9.1.

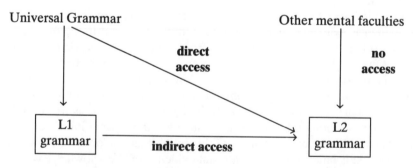

Figure 9.1   Forms of access to UG in L2 learning

In the *no-access* position, L2 learners acquire the L2 grammar without any reference to UG; the grammar is learnt through other faculties of the human mind, and so probably bears little resemblance to usual linguistic competence; it is learnt in the same way as any other aspect of knowledge –

cookery, physics, or whatever. In a *direct-access* position, L2 learners learn in exactly the same way as L1 learners; they set values for parameters according to the L2 evidence they encounter without any other influence. In an *indirect-access* position, L2 learners have access to UG through what they know of the L1, but they start with the L1 parameter settings rather than the initial neutral or default state. Most of the L2 research has treated access to UG as part of a diachronic process of language acquisition rather than as part of the synchronic state of the mind – the sand suspended in the stream rather the sand deposited on the bottom of the lake, to use Weinreich's metaphor (Weinreich, 1953, p. 11).

Let us look at some general arguments that have been made against continued access to UG before taking up two syntactic examples that have been used in this debate.

(i) *Knowledge of L2 is not so complete or so good* (Schachter, 1988; Bley-Vroman, 1989). 'Most proficient ESL speakers do not have fully formed determiner systems, aspectual systems, or tag question systems' (Schachter, 1988, p. 224). L2 learners rarely attain the same level of knowledge in their L2 as in the L1. This is claimed to indicate no access to UG.

(ii) *All languages are not equally easy to learn as second languages*, as they seem to be as L1s. If UG were available, any L2 would be as easy to learn as any other. According to Schachter (1988), this forms 'an insurmountable barrier to the "back to UG" position'.

(iii) *Learners get 'fossilised' at some stage*, rather than progressing inevitably to full native competence (Schachter, 1988). Schachter's example is the overuse of the present indicative tense by English learners of Spanish. As no L1 children get stuck in this way, UG is claimed to be unavailable for learning the L2.

(iv) *L2 learners vary in level of success and in ways of learning*, while L1 children do not (Bley-Vroman, 1989). Again, a fully available UG would help all learners equally; therefore it is claimed to be not available.

These general arguments are taken to support a no-access, or at best restricted access, position in L2 learning. Bley-Vroman (1989) puts forward the *Fundamental Difference Hypothesis* that L2 learning differs from L1 learning because of changes in the language faculty with age. He proposes that, while the child uses UG and language-specific processes to learn the L1, the adult L2 learner uses the L1 and general problem-solving processes; 'the function of the innate domain-specific acquisition system is filled in adults (though indirectly and imperfectly) by this native language knowledge and by a general abstract problem-solving system' (Bley-Vroman, 1989, p. 50). This resembles the division made by Selinker (1972) between the 'latent language structure' (LAD) and the 'latent psychological structure', mentioned in Chapter 1.

To some extent, these general arguments attack a straw man by overstating the claims of the UG model. UG is only concerned with the acquisition of highly abstract and complex principles and parameters of core grammar via the poverty-of-the-stimulus argument; it has no brief to explain language acquisition outside this area by venturing into areas of the periphery, of performance, or of development. It does not stand or fall on areas that are tangentially related to it at best. The lack of completeness (claim i) or of success (claim iv) has nothing to do with the UG model unless L2 knowledge is less complete in the core areas covered by UG; if specific principles or parameter settings are missing, this would indeed be counterevidence. But an overall lack of success and of completeness is a far cry from core grammar. UG does not encompass all, or even most, of L2 learning by any means; claim (ii) for the comparative difficulty of learning Chinese compared to Italian for an English speaker, true as it may well be, is irrelevant unless it is related to the principles and parameters of UG rather than to the many other differences between the two; for example Chinese differs from English in being a tone language rather than an intonation languages, and in having a character-based writing system rather than one based on the alphabet. Even if this claim were conceded, it would refute only the direct access position in which all L2 learners start equal, rather than the indirect access position in which they use their L1 knowledge. The fossilisation of L2 learning (claim iii) and the variation between learners (claim iv) would be telling if it were expressed in principles and parameters terms in the core UG area. If the UG model indeed claimed to be true of all aspects of language learning, these points could be fatal. But it only makes claims for precise syntactic areas, to which much of the evidence for these no-access claims does not relate.

9.2   ACCESS TO UG AND SUBJACENCY IN L2 LEARNERS

There are nevertheless areas where more appropriate research has been carried out to test the no-access position. A key area is *subjacency*, a principle of movement in what is known as *Bounding Theory*. Unfortunately, subjacency is highly technical and exists in several versions both historically and simultaneously; the following tries to give an interpretation that will allow the reader to see the point of the L2 research, without going into the full technical details. Haegeman (1991) provides an up-to-date account in more detail. Essentially subjacency restricts how far elements may move in the sentence – the bounds within which movement can take place, hence the name of Bounding Theory. Elements can move across only one 'bounding node' in the sentence but not more; in English the bounding nodes are IP and NP; the variation between languages over what constitutes a bounding node will be dealt with later. This restriction originates from UG. Some languages do not have syntactic movement, such as Korean. If Koreans who learn English show that they know subjacency, this demonstrates they have access to UG, as it could not be transferred from their L1; conversely, if they do not show signs of subjacency, then they do not have UG available to them.

Let us first expand the concept of movement beyond that used so far. In the principles and parameters theory, as we have seen, movement is the relationship between the d-structure and the s-structure of the sentence. Thus the sentence:

"What did you see?"

has the s-structure:

"What did you see *t*"

This contains a trace (*t*) left in the position from which the item comes. The s-structure is related by movement to the d-structure:

"You PAST see what"

which gives the basic structure projected by the lexical heads in it. The only reason for having distinct d- and s-structures is so that the relationship called movement can be accounted for. As always, this terminology does not mean that an element of the sentence literally 'moves' from one place to another to form an s-structure out of a d-structure; movement is a convenient metaphor for talking about declarative structural relationships between levels of structure, not an actual process.

Where does the moved element go to? The answer is the empty parts in the structure of the Complement Phrase (CP or C″). In X-bar theory, the CP has the same phrase structure of specifiers and complements as other phrases, namely:

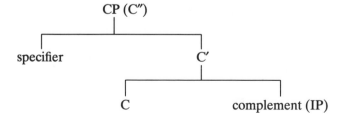

The head of CP, known as C or COMP, may be a complementiser, such as "that", found in subordinate clauses:

"I said that she was here."

But CP need not have a head at all; both the specifier and head positions of the CP can be empty places in the d-structure of the sentence, ready for the elements that are moved to fit into them. In:

"What will he ask?"

"what" therefore has moved to the empty specifier of CP:

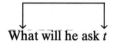

What will he ask t

The auxiliary "will" has also moved from its position as head of the IP so that it precedes the subject "he"; it has landed in the empty head position of C, as shown in:

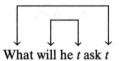

What will he t ask t

This question therefore involves two types of movement into the vacant positions in CP; "what" moves into the specifier position, "will" into the head position, seen in the following simplified diagram of the s-structure:

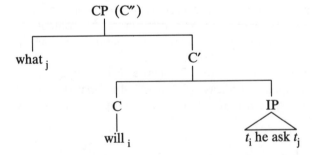

In more complex sentences, movement proceeds in a series of hops, going from an empty space in one CP to one in the next, as in:

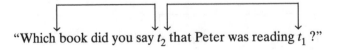

"Which book did you say t_2 that Peter was reading t_1 ?"

"Which book" moves to the front in two steps, using as a staging post the specifier of the embedded CP and leaving behind it a further trace t_2. The reason for this staged movement will become apparent below. Movement from one clause up into another is known as 'long' movement.

The *Subjacency Principle* says in effect that an element that is moved from one position in the sentence to another must not be moved across too many 'bounding nodes'. The bounding nodes for English are IP and NP; they do *not* include CP. In the above sentence, the wh-phrase "which book" moves from its original position t_1 in the sentence to t_2 (the empty specifier of the embedded CP) crossing the bounding node IP_1, then from the new position t_2 to the specifier of the main CP, crossing the bounding node IP_2, as seen in:

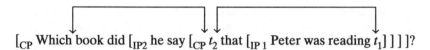

[$_{CP}$ Which book did [$_{IP2}$ he say [$_{CP}$ t_2 that [$_{IP\,1}$ Peter was reading t_1]]]]?

On each hop "which book" crosses over only a single IP, resulting in a grammatical sentence.

Let us switch to the ungrammatical sentence:

*"What did he say Joe told her Bill's guess that Ken liked *t*?"

"What" originates in the most embedded clause on the right. Showing only the relevant IP and NP bounding nodes, the s-structure of this becomes:

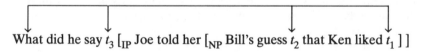

What did he say t_3 [$_{IP}$ Joe told her [$_{NP}$ Bill's guess t_2 that Ken liked t_1]]

"What" moves from the position t_1 to the front of the sentence via the stepping stones t_2 and t_3. The reason for its ungrammaticality is apparent if we count the number of bounding nodes for the hop from t_2 to the next possible resting place in a CP t_3: "what" has to cross not only the NP [Bill's guess . . .] but also the IP [Joe told . . .], that is to say, *two* bounding nodes in one hop. The Subjacency Principle states that 'Movement may not cross more than one bounding node'; an element that is moved can cross only *one* bounding node (IP or NP) in the sentence. This sentence therefore violates subjacency because the movement of "what" crosses an IP and an NP in one step.

This represents the basic analysis of subjacency used in most of the L2 research. Later developments, as we shall see, introduce a parameter over what constitutes a bounding node. Each of the pieces of L2 research uses a slightly different range of structures to which subjacency applies, such as relative clauses, NP complements, embedded questions, and so on; while they will be mentioned briefly, to explore the complexities of these sub-types would go way outside the possibilities of this chapter.

The L2 research again concentrates on comparing L2 learners with L1s that have movement with learners with L1s that do not. A language that does not have syntactic movement, such as Korean, will not require subjacency. So subjacency can provide a test of L2 learners' access to UG. A Korean who knows the Subjacency Principle in English cannot have transferred this knowledge from the L1 since it is no part of Korean, but must have derived it directly from UG; alternatively, a lack of subjacency in Korean learners would be a sign that neither indirect nor direct access was available.

A key experiment was performed by Bley-Vroman, Felix, and Ioup (1988), which tested 92 Korean advanced learners of English and 32 native speakers of English. The learners were selected to be daily users of English and were all advanced, as measured by the TOEFL test (mean score 581), so that they were able to cope with the difficult sentences involved. The technique was a grammaticality judgement task asking the subjects whether each sentence 'sounds possible in English'. Ten sentences violated subjacency, two did not; seven violated the Empty Category Principle (ECP) (not covered here), six did not. A typical sentence which violated subjacency was:

*"What did Sam believe the claim that Mary had bought?"

Its ungrammaticality is due to the long movement of "what" crossing two bounding nodes, NP and IP, without a stopping place:

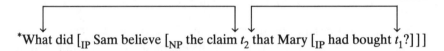

*What did [$_{IP}$ Sam believe [$_{NP}$ the claim t_2 that Mary [$_{IP}$ had bought t_1?]]]

A test sentence that respected subjacency was:

"What did Bill think that the teacher had said?"

Here the movement of "what" crosses only one bounding node at a time (both IPs in this instance):

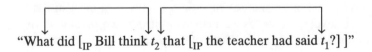

"What did [$_{IP}$ Bill think t_2 that [$_{IP}$ the teacher had said t_1?]]"

The control sentences had other types of movement that do not break subjacency, such as:

"Where is the person that I want you to talk to?"

In terms of all sentences tested, native speakers scored 92.2 per cent correct overall compared to the non-natives' 74.9 per cent. The more detailed results are presented in Bley-Vroman *et al.* (1988) sentence by sentence. A sample of the two grammatical and two ungrammatical complex 'factive' NP sentences is as follows:

	L2 learners (%)	Natives (%)
"What did Bill think that the teacher had said?"	54	94
"What did John realise he could not sell?"	55	97
*"What did Sam believe the claim that Carol had bought?"	79	100
*"What did John hear the news that the mayor would do?"	72	97

Judgements of complex 'factive' NPs (Bley-Vroman *et al.*, 1988, p. 19)

The native scores were way above the non-native scores for all four sentences. The L2 learners found the grammatical sentences more difficult than the ungrammatical sentences to a large extent. The overall results for all sentence types similarly show a deficit for L2 learners and an overall superiority for ungrammatical rather than grammatical sentences.

Bley-Vroman *et al.* (1988) also looked at the learners' consistency of judgement of pairs of grammatical and ungrammatical sentences, such as

"Who does John want to see?"

versus:

*"Where did Bill want to know who put the book?"

Control sentences were paired with different ungrammatical sentences to get six pairs. Again, results are presented sentence by sentence. Turned into percentage of subjects, not done by Bley-Vroman *et al.* (1988), the results for subjacency are:

	Both sentences correct (%)	Both sentences deemed bad (%)	Both sentences deemed good (%)	Backwards (good sentence deemed bad, and vice versa) (%)
Natives	92.3	3.3	3.3	0
Non-native	54.6	26.5	12	6.8

Percentage of subjects correctly judging six sentence pairs differing in grammaticality (adapted from Bley-Vroman *et al.*, 1988, pp. 22–3)

The natives were nearly all consistently right (92.3 per cent); half the non-natives were right (54.6 per cent), though 26.5 per cent consistently marked both sentences as wrong.

Similar tables compare pairs of sentences with the same structure that are both wrong, such as:

*"What did Sam believe the claim that Mary had bought?"

and:

*"What did John hear the news that the mayor would do?"

Calculating the subjacency results for the two resulting pairs yields:

	Both bad (correct) (%)	Both good (%)	1st Bad (%)	2nd Bad (%)
Natives	91	0	1.5	7.5
Non-natives	69	13.5	2.5	14.5

Consistency of subjects at sentence pairs (adapted from Bley-Vroman *et al.*, 1988, pp. 22–3)

Nearly all the natives were correct (91 per cent); two-thirds of the non-natives were correct (69 per cent); the rest were evenly spread between 'Both Good' (13.5 per cent) and '2nd Bad' (14.5 per cent). Both these sets of figures support the claim that the L2 learners have access to the Subjacency Principle, but to a lesser degree than native speakers.

They conclude that 'slightly over half of the non-native speakers typically exhibit the correct UG-based judgements on any given UG effect' (Bley-Vroman *et al.*, 1988, p. 24), which is way above the chance level they claim of 25 per cent but also far below the level of native speakers. So 'adults appear to have some sort of access to knowledge of UG'; their short-fall compared to the natives is due either to UG being 'attenuated' or to the use of 'a general problem-solving system' (Bley-Vroman *et al.*, 1988,

p. 27). Evidence for this attenuation is provided by the non-natives' predilection for rejecting grammatical sentences.

Research summary: R. W. Bley-Vroman, S. Felix, and G. L. Ioup, (1988) 'The Accessibility of Universal Grammar in Adult Language Learning', *Second Language Research*, **4** (1), 1–32.
Aim: to investigate access to UG principles by L2 learners
Learners: 92 Korean advanced learners of English, 32 native controls
Aspect of language: the principle of subjacency concerning how far elements may move in the sentence, not utilised in languages like Korean that have no syntactic movement
Data type: grammaticality judgements
Results: 'slightly over half of the non-native speakers typically exhibit the correct UG-based judgements on any given UG effect' (p. 24)
Conclusions: 'adults appear to have some sort of access to knowledge of UG' (p. 27) but not as complete as natives

---

Other experiments have followed the same logic.

(a) *Schachter (1989)* used a similar research design to test knowledge both of structures with subjacency violations, such as:

*"What party did for Sam to join shock his parents?"

and of equivalent structures without Wh-movement, such as:

"That oil prices will rise again this year is nearly certain."

If subjacency is available to the learners, those who know the unmoved structures will also know that the subjacency violations are incorrect; thus they should *fail* both sentences if they don't know subjacency, *pass* both if they do. The learners she tested were 'highly proficient in English' and consisted of 20 Chinese, 21 Korean, and 20 Indonesian students of linguistics or 'freshman English' in the USA, as well as 19 native speaker controls. She used a grammaticality judgement test in which learners heard 24 grammatical sentences without wh-movement and 24 with equivalent subjacency violations. These divided into four syntactic types: subjects, relative clauses, NP complements, and embedded questions. A footnote mentions nine additional grammatical wh-question controls and nine ungrammatical controls involving rightward movement.

The overall results were as follows, set out here for the relative clause type:

	N	A +Syntax +Subjacency	B −Syntax +Subjacency	C +Syntax −Subjacency	D −Syntax −Subjacency
Natives	19	17	1	0	1
Indonesian	20	6	1	9	4
Chinese	20	10	0	6	4
Korean	21	5	0	8	8

Numbers of subjects adopting particular solutions (adapted from Schachter, 1989, pp. 83–4)

Nearly all the natives (15 out of 19) passed both the declarative sentence sub-test and the relative clause violation sub-test; thus they knew both syntax and subjacency. Only 10 out of 20 of the Chinese passed both sub-tests, 6 out of 20 passing the syntax but not the relative clause sub-test; many of them therefore appeared to know the syntax but *not* the subjacency principle. The highest number of Indonesians (9 out of 20) fell into the category of passing the syntax but not the subjacency. Most Koreans either knew the syntax without subjacency (8 out of 21) or knew neither (8 out of 21). Thus the UG prediction that knowing the syntax means knowing the principle is not correct.

Turning to the overall results for all four sentence types, most natives performed consistently correctly on both syntax and subjacency, namely 56 out of 76 (73.6 per cent); their main problem was with sentences containing noun phrase complements, such as that in

*"Who did the police have evidence that the mayor murdered?"

where only 10 out of 19 (52.6 per cent) were correct. L2 learners were much less successful; those who knew both syntax and subjacency numbered 76 out of 244 (31.1 per cent), the Koreans' total of 13 out of 63 (20.6 per cent) being particularly low; 111 out of 244 (45.5 per cent) knew the syntax but not the principle. Despite some differences between the L1s in terms of subjacency, there were no significant differences between the three groups. Schachter argues that the high proportion of learners who knew the syntax but not the principle provides 'a major difficulty' for 'those who believe that the principles of UG are available and accessible to post-puberty language learners' (Schachter, 1989, p. 85).

(b) *White (1985)* reports a 'pilot' study testing a parameterised version of subjacency. In recent years it has been commonly accepted that the subjacency principle includes a parameter of variation over what constitutes a bounding node. In French one may say:

"Combien as-tu vu de personnes?"

while the English equivalent is ungrammatical:

*"How many did you see of people?"

The reason is that the Inflection Phrase (IP) does not constitute a bounding node in French so that "combien" has to cross only one bounding node to get to the front of the sentence, as in:

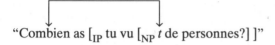

"Combien as [_IP_ tu vu [_NP_ _t_ de personnes?]]"

But IP does constitute a bounding node in English, so "how many" has to cross both an NP and an IP.

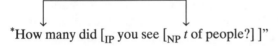

*"How many did [_IP_ you see [_NP_ _t_ of people?]]"

The English bounding nodes are therefore IP and NP, the French are CP and IP. White (1985) tested 73 adult L2 learners of English, divided into groups from beginners to advanced according to a placement test; 19 spoke French, and 54 spoke Spanish, which has the same setting for subjacency as French; there was a control group of 11 native speakers of English. A grammaticality judgement test was given on several constructions inviting 'correct' or 'incorrect' as possible answers and they were asked to rewrite incorrect sentences; the relevant subjacency sentences consisted of six grammatical sentences with movement and seven ungrammatical sentences in which IP was not treated as a bounding node, such as:

*"How many did you buy of the books?"

(In fact some English speakers find such forms grammatical when they include a definite article:

"How many have you got of these old books?")

Overall results summed in terms of percentage correct were:

	Ungrammatical (%)	Grammatical (%)
Natives	89.7	81.8
Non-natives	57.9	81.8

Grammaticality judgements of subjacency (adapted from White, 1985, p. 9)

Native scores were high on both ungrammatical and grammatical sentences, the chief exception being a low of 36 per cent for the apparently grammatical sentence:

"What programme did you say that John watched last night?"

L2 learners were poor at spotting the ungrammaticality of sentences that used IP as a bounding node, being only 57.9 per cent correct. There is improvement with level for the ungrammatical sentences among the L2 learners, showing they gradually acquire IP as a bounding node. So 'the results partially support the claim that the L1 parameter will be carried over' (White, 1985, p. 12), that is, that the learners are affected by the type of bounding node in their L1s. However, this is blurred by the number of 'indecisive' learners who varied their responses. She concludes 'L2 learners cannot approach the L2 as if starting totally from scratch where UG is concerned' (White, 1985, p. 14). White (1988) carried out a similar experiment on French learners of English, concluding again that 'the lower performance of Adults (1) [low intermediate] on these sentences [wh-islands] can be attributed to the L1 parameter'.

(c) *Johnson and Newport (1991)* argued that a sign of access to UG in L2 learning would be that those aspects of language to which UG applies would be easier to learn than those to which it is irrelevant. They asked 23 Chinese learners of English to carry out a grammaticality judgement task. As Chinese has no syntactic movement, it does not require subjacency. Grammaticality judgements tested three types of structure: NP complements, relative clauses, and wh-complements. Each structure was given in four different forms, each form having twelve test sentences. Taking the NP complements as an example, the four types were:

- *declarative sentences*, as in:

    "The teacher knew the fact that Janet liked math."

- *subjacency violations*, as in:

    *"What did the teacher know the fact that Janet liked?"

- *control sentences* consisting of a similar, but grammatical, question:

    "What did the teacher know that Janet liked?"

- *no-inversion sentences* in which the auxiliary and subject remain uninverted:

    *"What the teacher did know that Janet liked?"

In addition 12 'simple' questions were included. The 'universal' ungrammatical sentences with subjacency violations should utilise UG, the language-specific ungrammatical sentences with no-inversion should not. An active UG should make it easier for the learners to detect the ungrammaticality of sentences that break universal principles than of those that have language-specific errors. Results were as follows, here derived from a graph and expressed as the number correct out of a maximum score of 36 (the total number of sentences for each type):

	Simple questions	Declarative sentences	Control questions	No-inversion	Subjacency violations
Natives	36	34	32	35	35
Non-natives	34	31	24	26	22

Native and non-native speakers' judgements of subjacency (adapted from Johnson and Newport, 1991, p. 23)

The L2 learners' success with the parallel declarative sentences and simple questions demonstrates that it was fair to test them on subjacency. They were notably below native levels on the subjacency sentences, even if their scores were above chance and they did reject them more than the control sentences. Crucially their scores on the subjacency sentences were as bad as on the no-inversion sentences, rather than better. UG is little help to the learners.

Johnson and Newport (1991) used the same test in a second experiment with 21 Chinese learners of English who had arrived in the US at different ages between 4 and 16 and had lived there an average of 9.6 years; these were compared with the adults in the first experiment. The results showed a straightforward relationship with age of arrival: the younger the learners had arrived the better they were at subjacency. Furthermore the no-inversion sentences showed a very similar decline in correctness of judgement for age of arrival. Thus access to UG seemed to be progressively cut off for older learners: 'the changes that occur between childhood and adulthood in language learning seem to affect all aspects of grammar acquisition, including access to UG . . .' (Johnson and Newport, 1991, p. 44).

Issues with Subjacency Research

In some ways the subjacency research literature demonstrates the interest of the principles and parameters approach to SLA research and its appropriateness for tackling issues of UG. However, the syntactic theory that underlies it is constantly changing. The first discussion of a predecessor to subjacency called the Right Roof Constraint was in Ritchie (1978); the subjacency principle itself was used in Bley-Vroman *et al.* (1988) and Schachter (1989); parameterised subjacency comes in White (1985) and Johnson and Newport (1991). But the story has not stopped there, bounding nodes being, for example, redefined in Chomsky (1986b); an introduction to such later work can be found in Haegeman (1991). The concept of subjacency is now much less important to the theory, being largely subsumed under the Empty Category Principle, a Pandora's box we shall not open here. As always, the SLA research lags behind the changes in the theory, which, as we saw in the last chapter, inevitably happens when it tries to use the most up-to-date theory available. The advantage of being in touch with current syntactic theory, as exemplified in the subjacency research, is inseparable from the complexity of the syntactic ideas involved and their refusal to stand still.

The methodology of subjacency experiments is entirely based on grammaticality judgements, a general discussion of which is found later in this chapter. Clearly this limits what can be concluded from the research. Other criticisms can be made of the research design of these studies. The following list starts with four points made by Johnson and Newport (1991):

- Bley-Vroman *et al.* (1988) used too small a set of sentences for subjacency in their experiment (Johnson and Newport, 1991), numbering ten if all types of violation are included;
- the design of Schachter (1989) did not test subjects on questions that observed subjacency, only on violations; 'to obtain these results, then, the subjects only needed to respond *yes* to all of the test items, independent of the structure being tested at the time, and similarly independent of any real knowledge of English syntax' (Johnson and Newport, 1991, p. 11). Schachter (1989, p. 81) does, however, mention that nine grammatical controls were given; 'it would not be possible for a subject to infer that all declaratives were grammatical and all questions ungrammatical'; actual results to support this statement are not provided;
- Schachter (1989) categorises results by *subjects* rather than by errors, so there is no indication of how well learners did (Johnson

and Newport, 1991, p. 11). The standard to pass each sub-test seems high at 5 out of 6 (83.3 per cent); the natives in White's experiment, for instance, scored 81.8 per cent on ungrammatical sentences, thus failing this criterion;

- Schachter (1989) compares sentence type X for the syntax task and sentence type X + movement for the subjacency test, in a paradigm going back to Otsu (1981). But movement places an additional memory load on processing, as we have seen earlier. Sentences with movement are intrinsically more difficult to process regardless of violations and should have been compared with equivalent sentences with movement without violation, figures for which are not provided. At the moment it is not clear that the students knew movement itself without the factor of subjacency, in particular 'long' movement from one clause to another; while Johnson and Newport (1991) tested the subjects for long movement, we do not know if the 24/36 subjects who scored such sentences correctly were essentially the same as the 22/36 who spotted subjacency violations – which would imply that 91 per cent of those who knew 'long' movement knew subjacency; in other words the control test should be the control questions, not the simple questions. Crain and Fodor (1984) argue that subjacency violations may be caused by a parsing factor called right attachment (add the item to the structure of the sentence as far down on the right as possible) that conflicts with subjacency, even for native speakers;
- Bley-Vroman *et al.* (1988) compare various sentence pairs. Of the six pairs on subjacency, some have different structures in the two sentences, for example,

    "What did Bill think that the teacher had said?"

has a Verb complement sentence, while:

    *"What did Sam believe the claim that Carol had bought?"

has an NP complement. Furthermore, the six grammatical members of the pair have an average length of 9.1 words, the ungrammatical members 10 words, perhaps inevitable but nevertheless a possible difference between the two;
- a crucial factor in the claims of Johnson and Newport (1991) is the difference between the non-language-specific ungrammatical sentences with subjacency violations and the language-specific ungrammatical sentences with no-inversion, such as

    *"What the teacher did know that Janet liked?"

This sentence is indeed ungrammatical. But *why* is it ungrammatical? It is not without movement since "what" has clearly moved into CP; rather, it is without auxiliary-movement. The 'real' 'uninverted' form of the sentence would be:

*"What the teacher knew that Janet liked?"

Where does the "did" come from in their sentence? "Do" in English is inserted in an auxiliary-less question to carry Tense and Agreement. "Do" has here been given Tense and Agreement as if it were a question, but the final movement into CP has not taken place; in its present position "did" can only be related in some curious fashion to the "did" that carries special emphasis. So the Johnson and Newport sentences are bizarre. Whether such ungrammaticality is language-specific is a moot point; it seems unlikely that any language would insert dummy forms such as "do" unnecessarily into the sentence. I cannot remember encountering such sentences naturally from L2 learners, apart perhaps from double past marking ("I did liked him"). The major difference between the UG-driven and the language-specific forms is not as clear-cut as this experiment requires.

Subjacency had to be included in this chapter because of its importance to the UG-related SLA research. The criticisms above are more niggling than elsewhere because much of the research and methodology is not clearly described, compared to the other areas we have seen. At face value the subjacency research denies that L2 learners have total access to the UG principle of subjacency and supports the no access position. Looked at more closely, the implications are less sure. It is not so much that the principle is unavailable as that it is *less* available; L2 learners show signs of knowing it to some extent. Bley-Vroman *et al.* (1988) have L2 learners who are 82.4 per cent successful, White (1985) 57.9 per cent, Johnson and Newport (1991) 61.1 per cent. Moreover, while natives were better, they were far from perfect, except on the Johnson and Newport test; Bley-Vroman *at al.* (1988) 92.2 per cent, White (1985) 89.7 per cent on ungrammatical sentences, 81.8 per cent on grammatical; on Schachter's test only 73.6 per cent of natives 'passed' overall, down to 52.6 per cent on NP complements.

The poverty-of-the-stimulus argument still applies: as there is no other way the learners could have acquired this knowledge, they must have access to UG, partial as it may be. They possess the principle, even if they show it erratically. The problem is not therefore that access to UG is completely absent but that it is partially blocked. We need to explain why

L2 learners do not show this principle of UG fully rather than why they don't possess it at all. The same problem is encountered in first language acquisition: to get round L1 children's apparent lack of Binding principle B for pronominals, Grimshaw and Rosen (1990) distinguish *knowledge* of a principle from *obedience* to a principle. Most of the L2 research shows knowledge of subjacency but partial obedience to subjacency. What is needed is not so much explanations for lack of access as explanations for lack of obedience. The most likely relate to the performance nature of grammaticality judgements; though not relying primarily on the speech or comprehension processes of actual conversation, grammaticality judgements are none the less aspects of performance. Whatever account of mental parsing one assumes, the comprehension of subjacency involves storing an element in the mind to link to something later in the sentence: it puts a load on memory. The way that subjacency is couched in Berwick and Weinberg (1984), for example, is in terms of counting; knowing that crossing more than one barrier is not permitted means counting how many barriers are involved, hence a storage problem. Presumably the storage system involved also has some effect on the processing of movement in grammaticality judgements. Another performance factor is the sheer length of sentence overloading the memory system; Bley-Vroman *et al.* (1988, p. 20) point out 'Non-native speakers do seem to reject at a high rate grammatical examples which are long, especially with more than one embedding.' If it is worthwhile persevering with subjacency research given its problematical syntactic status and its methodological difficulties, future research will need to evaluate the relationship between knowledge and obedience more precisely. In my view, attention should be turned to the many contemporary areas of principles and parameters theory that are simpler to research and yield more clear-cut answers.

9.3 ACCESS TO UG AND GERMAN WORD ORDER

Other syntactic-based arguments for the no-access position are based on the type of movement used in German. In Chapter 5 we saw that German has a Subject–Object–Verb (SOV) word order in subordinate clauses such as "Ich sage dass ich Englander bin" (I say that I English am), but Verb second order in the main clause resulting in SVO, Adverb–VS, and so on. That is to say, as well as SVO "Ich bin Englander" (I am English), it is also possible to have OVS "Englander bin ich" (English am I), and Adverb–VS "Jetzt bin ich Englander" (Now am I English), all with the Verb in *second* position after another constituent. Many syntacticians treat the SOV order as the d-structure and derive the orders found in the main clause by moving the Verb into second position in the s-structure: "Ich bin Englander" has a d-structure "Ich Englander bin". Translating this into the CP and IP framework introduced earlier, the finite Verb moves to the head of CP (called Inversion in Chapter 5), and elements such as the subject or Adverb move to the specifier of CP (called Adverb Preposing in Chapter 5). This fills up both empty places in the structure of the CP, namely the head and specifier, seen in the structure of the CP of the sentence "Morgen gehe ich weg" (Tomorrow go I away):

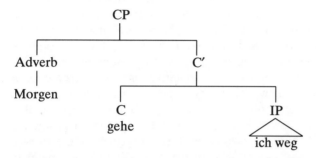

Some elements therefore move twice: an auxiliary such as "muss" first moves to the head of the IP (to get its AGR and TNS), then on to the head of CP as in

"Endlich muss ich gehen."
(at last must I go)

In subordinate clauses the verb cannot move in this way because the head position in CP is already filled by a complementiser such as "dass".

This analysis extends the L2 learning discussion of the last chapter by bringing in the analysis of functional phrases such as IP and CP, a main growth point in principles and parameters theory. Vainikka and Young-Scholten (1991) for instance postulate an order of L2 acquisition of German in which, simplifying slightly, L2 learners start by knowing only a VP, soon acquire the IP (gradually gaining inflections and subjects), and finally acquire the CP (shown by movement in Wh-questions, and so on). A further example is the discussion of null-subject sentences by Meisel (1990) mentioned in Chapter 8; this linked null subjects with the absence of inflected verbs, that is, with the emergence of an IP. Both these follow the type of analysis introduced by Radford (1986; 1990) in which most of the peculiarities of early child speech are ascribed to one simple cause: IP and CP and other functional phrases are missing from early grammars. All the features which are associated with such phrases, such as the subject NPs, past tense "-ed", articles, and so on, cannot be used. A clear discussion of the implications of this approach to first language acquisition can be found in Atkinson (1992). This type of approach is very intriguing for SLA. In one way it seems as if the omission of grammatical morphemes described in Chapter 2 may at last get, if not its missing explanation, at least a more coherent syntactic description. In first language acquisition, missing functional phrases can be ascribed to some type of maturation: some aspect of the children's ageing renders these functional phrases available to them. But, if the same effect is found in adult Second Language Acquisition, maturation cannot be the cause since the L2 learner is well past the age of 20 months at which such features are usually learnt in the L1.

A consequence of the division into lexical and functional phrases is that the load between principles and parameters is now distributed differently. Rather than parameters belonging to principles, they belong to the heads of phrases, whether lexical items or the abstract heads of functional categories; this was foreshadowed in the discussion of parameterised Binding Theory in the last chapter where parameter values were attached to particular anaphors or pronominals, say "himself" or "zibun", rather than to the whole grammar. The approach by Tsimpli and Roussou (1990) treats principles as applying to any acquisition process, whether L1 or L2, while parameters, once set in the L1, cannot be reset. This is the general background to their discussion of pro-drop in Chapter 8, where they claimed that apparent resetting in L2 learning was either L1 transfer or use of UG principles.

However, most work with the CP has been carried out within earlier syntactic frameworks. The key paper bearing on access to UG is Clahsen and Muysken (1986), who compared the learning of German word order by native children and foreign adults using several published studies. Four developmental stages in L1 children learning German were derived from earlier studies:

I   *No fixed order*; verbs occur both in verb second and in sentence final position, but with preference for the verb final position about 60–70 per cent of the time; for example, "Ich Schaufel haben" (I shovel have).

II   *Non-finite verbs occur regularly in final position*, for example, "Deckel drauftun" (cover on-put); finite verbs occur in both verb second and final positions. In other words, the children are starting to restrict the non-finite verb to its correct position, since non-finite verb forms only occur in subordinate clauses.

III *Finite verbs occur only in second position*, for example, "Die Schere hat Julia" (The scissors has Julia), and the finite auxiliary forms and the non-finite main verb are separated in the word order, for example, "Ein Schiff muss du erst jetzt bauen" (A ship *must* you first now *build*). The children have acquired Verb movement; Verb second increases from 40 per cent to 90 per cent over about a month.

IV   *Finite verbs occur in sentence final position in subordinate clauses*, as soon as such clauses first appear, as in "Guck was ich in mein tasche hab" (Look what I in my pocket have). This stage is strikingly error-free and so confirms that children 'make use of learning strategies *specific* to the language acquisition device' (Clahsen and Muysken, 1986, p. 103), that is, UG.

These four stages are taken to be the natural order produced by UG; from the beginning German children have a tendency towards the underlying SOV order rather than SVO or verb second orders even though children are restricted to main clauses.

Clahsen and Muysken's analysis of L2 learning produces very different results. These are based on research with L2 learners of German with SVO L1s, namely Italian and Spanish, and with SOV L1, Turkish, chiefly taken from the ZISA project outlined in Chapter 5. They briefly outline the following six L2 stages, which are basically the same as the Multidimensional Model outlined in Chapter 5; some stages have no examples in their paper, so examples from the Multidimensional Model have been repeated where possible. The stages of the Multidimensional Model will be numbered as in Chapter 5 (pp. 95–6):

I   *Fixed SVO order*, for instance, "Ich studieren in Porto" (I study in Porto). There is no Verb Final influence at this stage. This is the same as stage 2 (Canonical Order) in the Multidimensional Model.

II   *Adverbials come before the Subject*, that is to say, the order is Adverbial–SVO. In other words the learners have acquired Adverb preposing without Inversion, as in "Da Kinder spielen", Adverb–Subject–Verb (There children play), equivalent to stage 3 of the Multidimensional Model.

III   *Non-finite forms move to sentence final position*. Since the learners have verbs in the middle of the sentence, they can separate the non-finite form and move it to the end rather than the reverse; "Ich habe ein Haus gebaut" (I have a house built), the same as stage 4 (Verb Separation) of the Multidimensional Model.

IV   *The Subject occurs after the Verb* in questions and after complementisers. "Dann hat sie wieder die Knoch gebringt", Adverb–Auxiliary–Subject–Adverb–Object–Verb (Then has she again the bone brought). They have now acquired the Inversion rule – stage 5 of the Multidimensional Model.

V   *Adverbial VP*. Adverbials now sometimes occur between finite verbs and the object.

VI   *Finite verbs come at the end in embedded sentences*, where they previously occurred in SVO position. "Wenn ich nach Hause gehe, kaufe ich diese Tabac" (When I to home go . . .). Hence, unlike the L1 learners, the L2 learners at first get the word order in subordinate clauses wrong. This is the same as stage 6 (Verb Final) of the Multidimensional Model.

So, while L1 children start with SOV and gradually learn the verb second position (SVO) of main clauses, adults start with SVO and gradually learn when the verb is final (SOV). The L1 children deduce the underlying order of German and then learn how to modify it by movement; the L2 learners cannot. The L1 children gradually learn *left*ward movement from an *SOV* base, the L2 learners *right*ward movement from an *SVO* base; this poses considerable difficulties for the description of the L2 learners' grammar within a principles and parameters framework, for various technical reasons, for example there is no obvious CP available to the right for the elements to move into. Clahsen and Muysken (1986, p. 116) claim that 'by fixing on an initial assumption of SVO order, and then elaborating a series of complicated rules to patch up this hypothesis when confronted with conflicting data, the L2 learners are not only creating a rule system which is far more complicated than the native system, but also one which is not definable in linguistic theory'. L2 learners clearly have no access to UG as they are producing grammars that do not belong to it. Note that this argument depends on sequence of acquisition, not on a state of knowledge as in the subjacency research, or on the poverty-of-the-stimulus argument.

Research summary: H. Clahsen, and P. Muysken (1986), 'The Availability of Universal Grammar to Adult and Child Learners – a Study of the Acquisition of German Word Order', *Second Language Research*, **2**(2), pp. 93–119.

Aim: to investigate access to UG in L2 learning through word order in German

Learners: chiefly ZISA project learners, mainly 45 migrant workers in Germany

Aspect of language: word order in German

Data type: transcripts of corpora

Method of analysis: construction of stages for L1 and L2 acquisition of German

Results: L1 children start with SOV and gradually learn Verb second and SVO; L2 learners start with SVO and learn SOV

Claims: 'L2 learners are not only creating a rule system which is far more complicated than the native system, but also one which is not definable in linguistic theory' (p. 116); UG is then not involved in L2 learning

A specific refutation of Clahsen and Muysken (1986) was made by DuPlessis, Solin, Travis and White, in the following year (DuPlessis *et al.*, 1987). Their argument has three phases.

(i) the syntactic analysis used by Clahsen and Muysken (1986) is inadequate. A proper analysis of word order in German within the CP/IP framework should involve three parameters: (a) the 'headedness' parameter according to which heads are first or last in the phrase, that is, a version of the head parameter discussed in the last chapter, (b) the Proper Government parameter whether or not COMP (that is, C, the head of CP) may govern I, and (c) the Adjunction parameter whether or not phrases may be adjoined to the IP at the beginning.

(ii) This analysis explains the stages of the L2 learners in terms of setting of the different parameters. Let us lay this out in a table, numbered according to Clahsen and Muysken's L2 stages:

	Headedness parameter	Proper Government parameter	Adjunction parameter
Stage 1	head initial	COMP ≠ Governor	
Stage 2	"	"	yes to fronting
Stage 3	head final	"	"
Stage 4	"	"	?no to fronting
Stage 5	"	"	"
Stage 6	"	COMP as governor	"

Sequence of parameter-setting (according to duPlessis *et al.*, 1987)

At stage 1 the learners use SVO because the parameters are wrongly set. At stage 3 they discover the alternative headedness setting, and so have the verb in the correct final position; they do *not* have the COMP setting right, so the Verb Second analysis applies to both main and embedded clauses. In other words, the learners have switched to an SOV analysis from an SVO one. Around stage 5, their fronting is more limited but still not fully correct; 'our data suggest that they allow both types of fronting and do not reset the Adjunction parameter till later, if at all' (duPlessis *et al.*, 1987, p. 68). Finally, at stage 6 they reset the Proper Government parameter so that COMP may be a governor, thus forcing Verb Final in embedded clauses. The order of acquisition for the L2 learners is claimed to be the product of sequential resetting of three parameters. DuPlessis *et al.* (1987, p. 74) contend 'that the interlanguages of L2 learners fall within the range of grammars permitted by UG, rather than being unnatural'. A later paper by Clahsen and Muysken (1989) accepts that the COMP parameter would explain some of the results but regards it as an *ad hoc* solution; 'the parameter appears to be quite a strange thing' (Clahsen and Muysken, 1989, p. 17). They deny there is evidence for an SVO>SOV switch in stage 3.

(iii) DuPlessis *et al.* (1987) present an additional experiment to support their multiple parameters view, based on evidence from student essays. A group of 28 L2 learners of German made few headedness parameter mistakes with word order but were still having problems with Adjunction and with the nature of COMP; hence duPlessis *at al.* (1987) do not feel that the Clahsen and Muysken sequence of Adjunction before COMP setting is necessarily right. A small group of five advanced L2 learners of Afrikaans similarly had few headedness parameter mistakes but encountered problems with COMP and with Adjunction.

Hulk (1991) also looked at acquisition of grammaticality judgements of word order by Dutch learners of French at four different levels. Dutch is a Verb Second language, like German, while French is SVO. Hulk used a similar multi-parameter analysis, but changed the actual parameters slightly. This produced the interesting result that Dutch learners of French do *not* start with SVO, as Clahsen and Muysken (1986) and the Multidimensional Model insist, but transfer their SOV order to French. A parallel debate can be found over the interpretation of the acquisition of negation in German, for which Clahsen (1988) suggested that 'there was no possible grammatical analysis for the L2 data': Tomaselli and Schwartz (1990) apply an alternative multiple parameter analysis to claim that 'the L2 negative-placement data should be what tip the balance in favour of a UG-based approach'.

To sum up, Clahsen and Muysken's claim for no-access is based upon *one* syntactic interpretation of movement in *one* language. However true it may be, it is scarcely by itself sufficient to disprove access to UG. Even if their stages are correct, there are other differences between L1 children and L2 adults which may explain them. For example, the difference between the two orders is partly that adults get embedded sentences wrong at early stages before getting them right. But children may have been prevented from using subordinate clauses at early stages through perform-ance limitations on sentence complexity that do not apply to adults; if they had used them at the early stages of the adults, they might well have got them wrong. Indeed, children may start by being unable to distinguish subordinate from main clauses, and so use the Verb Final forms interchan-geably with the verb second forms; adults, on the other hand, may start by knowing from their L1 that subordinate clauses exist and have sufficient processing capacity to use them. The adult SVO starting point may be a handicap compared to the children's initial flexibility between Verb Final and Verb Second positions. Or it might be that the input to children and L2 learners is different; even if, say, the sentences directly addressed to children had mostly SVO main clauses, they would still overhear a large range of sentences with other orders; L2 learners, particularly in classrooms, might hear a restricted range of SVO sentences. Interestingly, Issidorides and Hulstijn (1992) report that the speech addressed to both L1 and L2 learners of Dutch, also a Verb Second language, often has Object–Verb order. The final oddness about Clahsen and Muysken's argument is that adults, who actually get the word order of declarative sentences *right* from the beginning, are claimed to have no access to UG, while L1 children, who get the word order *wrong*, do. The adults are said to be using the canonical order strategy suggested by Slobin and Bever (1982), as described in Chapter 5; the children are not. Indeed, a necessary part of the argument in Clahsen and Muysken (1986) consisted of a refutation of the applicability of canonical order to *first* language acquisition because German children do not follow it, regardless of its virtues in second language acquisition, as discussed in Chapter 5.

Alternatives to UG-access

Some of those who believe in the no-access position have put forward psychologically-based alternatives to UG access of the type seen in earlier chapters. The general outline is as follows:

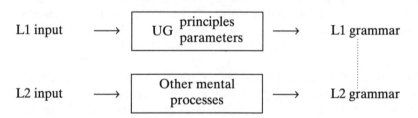

UG is unavailable in the L2, its role being taken by other mental processes. These researchers accept UG for L1 acquisition but believe that it is bypassed or no longer in existence in L2 learning; the L2 grammar is produced by some other means, probably with some contribution from the L1. Three variants on this are:

- Bley-Vroman (1989) suggests that the L2 learner employs a combination of 'native language knowledge' and 'general problem-solving systems'. The L1 acts as 'a kind of surrogate for Universal Grammar'. The problem-solving system involves other capacities of the mind, similar to models of the mind produced in cognitive science such as Anderson's ACT* (Anderson, 1983), to be discussed in the next chapter. No details or evidence are given for either of these proposals.

- Clahsen and Muysken (1989) claim that UG can function as a learning device in two ways: one is by making principles of language directly available to the L1 grammar, indirectly to the L2 grammar via the L1; the other is by having parameters to be available for setting in L1 acquisition but not in L2 learning . The differences in L2 learning are that principles are only available via the L1, parameters are not available at all. L2 learning is 'language acquisition without access to parameter setting' (Clahsen and Muysken, 1989, p. 23). Similar suggestions have been made within the later syntactic theory by Smith and Tsimpli (1991) and Tsimpli and Roussou (1990).

- Felix (1987) developed the idea of two cognitive systems competing in the learner's mind – the language system (equivalent to UG) and 'the Piagetan-type of problem-solving cognitive structures' (Felix, 1987, p. 154). An L2 may also be learnt via this problem-solving system, in Chomskyan terms a general faculty of the mind other than the specific language faculty. While the L1 child has no choice but to use the language system alone, in adult L2 learning there is a competition between these two faculties of the mind, with the problem-solving faculty taking too much responsibility; L2 learning is variable because the problem-solving capacity is subject to individual variation and situational pressure in a way that the language system is not. Schachter similarly invokes 'a set of cognitive systems (or procedures or inference rules) available for second language learning but not specifically designed for second language learning, systems which have access to first language knowledge as well as the ability to abstract out regularities in the linguistic data' (Schachter, 1988). Felix (1991) suggests that the question of access cannot be settled in an all-or-none fashion. Some aspects of syntax such as subjacency may still be accessible in an L2; others, such as X-bar theory, may not. In particular he argues that this is related to age. Johnson and Newport (1991), for example, showed that older learners have less access than younger ones to subjacency. Felix and Weigl (1991) argue that access is also related to the input available in particular situations; classroom language teaching may in effect cut the learners off from UG; 'the sad conclusion may be this: you can't really learn a language successfully in the classroom' (Felix and Weigl, 1991, p. 178).

As the evidence for the no-access position seems murky, it is not clear that it is worth considering in detail the alternatives that have been put forward to explain it. To repeat the general comment made in Chapter 5, there is no point in considering alternatives from within psychology that are simply a means to demolish linguistic work rather than developing alternatives in their own right. Showing that expected differences do not occur is testing the null hypothesis: that is to say, it shows negatively that some explanation does not work, but shows nothing positively about what *does* work. It would be interesting to show that some other pattern of results occurred; it can never be sufficient simply to show that expected differences do not occur. Once some general problem-solving procedure is shown to be capable of accounting for the type of grammatical knowledge that L2 learners have been shown to possess, it may be entertained as an alternative to the UG model. It is not enough to say that Slobin and Bever or Piaget or Anderson can solve the problems of L2 learning without providing concrete evidence how these theories are involved in second language acquisition itself. Indeed, these models are proposed by other people as alternative to UG in *first* language acquisition for similar reasons to those for which these researchers suggest adopting them for *second* language acquisition. It seems strange when a psychologically based theory is rejected for L1 learning, but the very same theory is accepted for L2 learning; why not consider it for L1 acquisition at least? While it may be the case that L2 learning is indeed not based on the same means of learning as L1 acquisition, it seems an odd coincidence that the rejected L1 theory turns out to account for L2 learning, rather than some totally different theory.

UG-related L2 research is interesting in the context of the concerns of this book because it has seen itself more or less as a subfield of linguistics. It has taken pains to explore the most up-to-date syntactic points to which it can gain access, ranging from pro-drop to subjacency. It has often attempted to feed its conclusions back into linguistics, as Flynn and Lust (1990) argue. Sometimes it is unclear whether a paper is a contribution to the theory of syntax itself or to L2 learning theory, or indeed if the author actually accepts this difference. While this close relationship makes for excitement and for constant change, it does not necessarily add to SLA research itself, nor integrate it with other aspects of learning than core UG syntax. Most change seems to come from the development of UG theory rather than from progress in L2 learning research, a criticism that is more true of the execution of the research in practice than of its relationship to UG theory in principle.

Stages of development are less than crucial to the UG model of L1, since it is concerned with acquisition not development; the intervening stages the learner goes through are only one source of evidence. The same point applies to the L2 sequences of development for pro-drop, subjacency, and so on. The logical question is still whether the final knowledge of the L2 learner contains things that could not have been learnt from evidence – the poverty-of-the-stimulus argument. To quote Felix (1988), 'adult L2 learners are able to attain grammatical knowledge which can neither be learnt on positive evidence nor is generally explicitly taught in the foreign language classroom'; without invoking some even more mysterious source for this knowledge, all that remains is UG.

9.4 EVIDENCE IN UG-RELATED RESEARCH AND GRAMMATICALITY JUDGEMENTS

As we have seen, there are considerable methodological problems with empirical L2 research related to UG because of the very nature of this theory. The crux of the UG model is the poverty-of-the-stimulus argument, which starts from 'single sentence' evidence of what the speaker knows; it does not need to be justified by secondary evidence of samples of speech, stages of acquisition, or grammaticality judgement tests, even if these provide helpful confirmation. The poverty-of-the-stimulus argument assumes that the native speaker's knowledge is static and does not vary from one person to another, to all intents and purposes – the idealised speaker in the homogeneous community (Chomsky, 1965b). However, this is far from true of L2 learning. Most L2 learners are in various stages of development, and they differ from each other in many ways; there is no standard, finished, L2 learner in the same sense that there is a monolingual native speaker; the idealisation to competence is different in the case of L2 learning. The access to language knowledge afforded by single sentence evidence is not available to support stage A in the poverty-of-the-stimulus argument – the unquestionable knowledge that native speakers share; any individual's notions about an L2 sentence will be temporary and idiosyncratic.

In Clahsen and Muysken (1986) the evidence is transcripts of learners' speech, in Duplessis *et al.* (1987) student essays; Hilles (1986), Lakshmanan (1991), and Hilles (1991) draw on the same transcripts from the Cancino *et al.* (1978) study: all are samples of natural spoken language. The discussion of observational data in Chapter 2 suggests that samples of L2 learners' speech are pale shadows of their competence. Such evidence needs to be qualified with the usual caveats about performance, and, ideally, related to L2 models of speech processing and memory, as frequently mentioned earlier. In other words, they are directly related, not to acquisition but to development; but development and performance may be significantly different in the L2 because of the differing ages of the learners, L2 cognitive deficit, and so on.

Almost the only other source of evidence used in the experiments outlined in this chapter is the elicitation of grammaticality judgements. In my own view, grammaticality judgement tests are distinct from single-sentence evidence. Grammaticality judgement tests are a controlled experimental measure established from several subjects; single sentence evidence does not necessarily involve a single speaker. So a grammaticality judgement test gives a definite group of speakers a questionnaire or computer display asking them whether a set of sentences, say, on the pattern of:

*"What time will Mary arrive before?"

are grammatical. Single sentence evidence, however, takes *one* sentence such as:

"John ate an apple."

and asserts that its structure is known by speakers of English, without necessarily consulting any speakers; this assumption can always be challenged, and indeed sometimes deteriorates into an argument about whether a particular sentence is English or not. But it does not require a large number of native speakers to justify: it is an obvious fact that any grammar of English must generate "John ate an apple".

The most comprehensive account of grammaticality judgements can be found in Birdsong (1989), who highlights 'the need for L2 acquisition theorists to spell out what it is that they are looking for in learners' metalinguistic data' (Birdsong, 1989, p. 123). Single sentence evidence is used in any linguistics book, usually without any explicit justification; tests of grammaticality judgements, however, have no preferred status within the UG model despite the misleading impression given by much SLA research, summed up, for instance, by Carroll and Meisel (1990, p. 205) as 'Researchers working in the UG paradigm assume that such results are a direct reflection of the learner's underlying competence and therefore evidence in support of UG.' The L1 adult's knowledge is rarely established from a set of grammaticality judgements. Nor has research with first language acquisition used them to any extent, for the obvious reason that it is unclear what young children's answers would mean, although McDaniel and Cairns (1990) argue that judgements can be elicited from young children if the task is well designed. While grammaticality judgement tests produce interesting data, their status is far from clear; 'deeper understanding will enable us to identify in just what respects informal judgements are useful or unreliable and why' (Chomsky, 1986a, p. 37).

Grammaticality judgement tests are a form of performance, no closer to or farther from competence than other forms of evidence. Whether in L1 or L2, there is a tricky relationship between the act of judgement and the knowledge on which it is based; 'in general, informant judgements do not reflect the structure of the language directly' (Chomsky, 1986a, p. 36). One necessary safeguard for L2 research therefore is to check the knowledge of native speakers through grammaticality judgement tests as well as from single-sentence evidence. Any comparison between natives and non-natives must use similar sources of evidence for both. The subjacency research established that even native speakers' access to competence is between 10 per cent and 27 per cent inaccurate in grammaticality judgement tasks. In a sense, grammaticality judgements are inevitably biased towards what Bley-Vroman (1983) calls the Comparative Fallacy of treating the native as the target; a grammaticality judgement test is designed with regard to native competence; it is easier for it to show differences from natives than idiosyncratic interlanguage systems. This requirement for native controls is not to insist that native speakers are to be accepted as the yardstick against which L2 learners are measured; the nature of the interlanguage system is important, not its deficiencies *vis-a-vis* natives. But the actual scores for grammaticality judgements at least indicate how well native speakers who supposedly know the grammar do on the specific task involved, whatever their competence may seem to be on the basis of single sentence evidence.

The demands of the task are also crucial: to what extent do judgements of grammaticality test people's competence? How can competence factors be disentangled from factors of performance? Discussions of this in the context of L1 competence can be found in Quirk and Svartvik (1966) and Greenbaum and Quirk (1970). One such factor is level of self-awareness; Carroll *et al.* (1981) demonstrated that judgements were affected by whether the subjects had to look at themselves in a mirror, that is to say, self-consciousness. Other factors that influence judgement are context or familiarity, as shown by Nagata (1988); Birdsong (1989, p. 64) and Ellis (1991) both found that L2 learners did not score the same sentence in the same way when it was repeated. Individual differences between learners may also affect judgements; Elliot (1981) points to the link between grammaticality judgements and level of literacy, supported by L2 research described in Birdsong (1989, p. 100). Quirk and Svartvik (1966) showed that native speakers' judgements on relative clauses did not correspond to their use in actual writing. Judgements also involve social factors of what forms are socially acceptable and of what reactions people feel the experimenter is looking for. They hark back to the question of introspective data discussed in Chapter 6 – the relationship between metalinguistic awareness and knowledge of language – an issue that extends way beyond the L2 area. So grammaticality judgements seem to be neither stable nor reliable.

The use of grammaticality judgements in SLA research brings unique problems. Much SLA research has shown that L2 users are either better at metalinguistic judgements than monolinguals or more advanced developmentally: bilingual children develop semantic awareness of words ahead of monolinguals (Ianco-Worrall, 1972), and are superior at evaluating semantically anomalous sentences (Bialystok, 1987; 1990); bilinguals have enhanced metalinguistic awareness (Galambos and Hakuta, 1988). On the one hand, such evidence has been used to show that bilingualism is advantageous for the individual; on the other hand, it has been used in support of the place of foreign languages in the school curriculum. L2 learners also tend to have a response bias, seen in some of the above studies, towards judging ungrammatical sentences right, but grammatical sentences wrong (Birdsong, 1989, pp. 101–107). Using grammaticality judgements as a research methodology with L2 users is therefore problematic in that the very act of judgement has been affected by L2 learning. Furthermore L2 learners are also subject to the well-known 'cognitive deficit' on performance described in Chapter 5: L2 learners are less efficient than monolinguals on tasks involving short-term (Cook, 1979) or long term (Long and Harding-Esch, 1977) memory for information. It is hardly surprising that they are less efficient than natives on grammaticality judgement tests of principles such as subjacency, for reasons to do more with general processes of performance than with linguistic competence.

Above all, unlike single sentence evidence, grammaticality judgements are a form of experiment. They need to be handled in a proper experimental way in terms of design, presentation, and analysis, as argued in Chapter 7. A full discussion of these design features is provided in Birdsong (1989), Ellis (1991), and Chaudron (1983). The elements of the actual task may be crucial to the result – whether the learners have a binary choice between 'correct' and 'incorrect', a three-way choice adding 'not sure', and so on. A choice between terms such as 'correct', 'acceptable', 'grammatical', 'possible', and so on, may affect their understanding of the task and weight different aspects of social use or grammatical knowledge. There has to be an adequate number of test sentences and controls, presented in a standardised way that is explicitly described and analysed statistically. The sentences have to be checked carefully to ensure that they are actually testing the grammatical point in question rather than some semantic oddity or some social shibboleth. Not all of the above experiments meet these criteria, as Johnson and Newport (1991) point out. The use of written sentences is also debatable, since these may not only involve the syntax typical of the written language, that is, a different 'standard' from the spoken, but may also utilise different performance processes from speaking; for instance the length of sentence may be more sensitive in a spoken than in a written test. Some of my own work has used computers to administer written grammaticality judgements, in a similar fashion to Cook (1990b) described in Chapter 8. The program controls and standardises presentation and also provides additional information on the time that a learner takes to make a response, providing an additional measure of performance.

Using the UG model in L2 learning involves a research paradox that is almost unresolvable. There is no access to the speaker's intuitions via proper single-sentence evidence, except in rare instances, since there are so few 'perfect' L2 learners. Other sources involve performance, whether the natural performance of transcribed speech, or the controlled perform-ance of the grammaticality judgement. The UG model is peculiarly untes-table in L2 learning, as it is cut off from its major source of evidence.

Other possible sources of evidence are relatively unexplored. The poverty-of-the-stimulus argument may be exploited; if an individual L2 learner can be shown to know something for which he or she has never had evidence, this argument works as well for L2 learning as for L1 learning, provided some adequate way of demonstrating the speaker's knowledge can be found. Another possibility is to test UG through Micro-Artificial Languages (MALs); Cook (1988a), for example, taught children MALs that varied in word order – SOV vs. VSO, prepositions vs. postpositions, and Adjective–Noun vs. Noun–Adjective order, and so on – and tested the extent to which they extended the parameter setting from the phrase types they had learnt to one they had not. Or it is possible to use comprehension techniques, such as those used with Binding in the last chapter. Perhaps multiple sources of evidence should be devised in line with the approach to science of Feyerabend (1975). Even if one form of measurement is inad-equate in itself, several forms of evidence showing the same point may cumulatively be more convincing – say, observational data plus grammati-cality judgements plus comprehension. As Chomsky (1986a, pp. 36–37) puts it in a wider context, 'In principle, evidence . . . could come from many different sources apart from judgements concerning the form and meaning of expressions: perceptual experiments, the study of acquisition and deficit or of partially invented languages such as creoles, or of literary usage or language change, neurology, biochemistry, and so on.'

My own chief worry with the UG model in Second Language Acquisition research has been that too much is expected of it; as we have seen, the UG theory is only concerned with core grammar and has no brief to make claims outside this area. Within a broad framework of SLA research, it has a part to play but that part should not be exaggerated; much, or even most, of the totality of L2 learning lies outside the core. Even within the UG area, it is unfortunate that so much research has concentrated on aspects that are fairly idiosyncratic to one language, such as Verb Second in German; few of the actual principles and parameters used in UG theory have been investigated apart from those mentioned in these two chapters. To take a handful of elements missing from the research, virtually nothing is known in L2 learning about the Projection Principle, Theta-theory, or Case theory. Whatever its potential, 'at present the research has achieved rather little, either by its own lights in terms of current syntactic theories, or by the standards of those approaching it from a broad perspective of L2 learning' (Cook, 1991c).

The criticisms of UG from those working outside this area seem fairly mild. Its advantages, as seen by Ellis (1985a) are that it 'focuses attention on the nature of the target language itself' and 'it provides a subtle and persuasive reconsideration of transfer'; both Ellis (1985a) and McLaughlin (1987) see its main weakness as the vagueness of the concept of markedness separating core from periphery and default from acquired parameter settings. Indeed, markedness has not been employed here as a major concept for this reason: it is perhaps 'a classic instance where someone invents a poorly-defined concept and then research is carried out to investigate its usefulness, not unexpectedly yielding confusing results' (Cook, 1991c). McLaughlin (1987, pp. 105–6) attacks the poverty-of-the-stimulus argument, claiming that 'parents and caregivers tailor their speech to young children', and that negative evidence is provided by listener signals of non-comprehension; the usual linguist's answer is that these factors have never been been shown to be true of the type of core syntax that UG is about, however valid for other areas. Ellis (1985a) and McLaughlin (1987) both draw attention to the problem of evidence within a UG model because of the levels of abstraction involved, an issue raised throughout this chapter. Ellis (1985a, p. 213) in a related comment points out that UG 'tends to discount pragmatic explanations and ignores variability in interlanguage', the areas discussed in Chapter 4; it can hardly be denied that UG is a model of knowledge rather than a model of performance.

9.5   UG AND MULTI-COMPETENCE

While it may have been plain that I find the UG model and the principles and parameters syntax the most plausible linguistics-based approach to Second Language Acquisition, not only am I worried by its methodological problems with L2 data but also I am not convinced that it is being used in the most appropriate fashion. This section briefly describes some ideas of my own that develop and react to the ideas seen above. They are reported more fully in Cook (1991b; 1992). Let us start with the 'metaphoric' LAD model of acquisition that underlies much of the discussion. As depicted in UG terms in the figure on p. 205, input goes into a box labelled UG that contains principles and parameters and out comes a grammar, with parameter settings triggered by the input. But this is not quite the metaphor used within the access debate; here people talk of the learning process having 'access' to UG, as if it were a separate module inside the box. The black box apparently contains not only UG but also something else that has 'access' to UG. We could redraw it as follows:

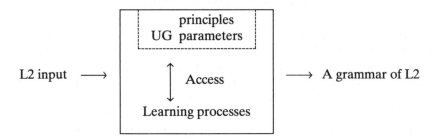

The access debate thus conceptualises UG as distinct both from the processes of language learning and from the grammar itself. A learning component has wormed its way into the discussion distinct from the triggering concept that is the 'learning' module allowed by UG theory. The grammar is a product and so separate from the box out of which it comes. The SLA debate has not then been fair to the original UG model because it asks 'Is there access by some learning process to UG in SLA?' not 'Does L2 learning take place through UG?'

But is the LAD metaphor helpful in either form? Alongside it in the literature runs another conceptualisation in which UG is the initial state of the human language faculty (S_0); 'a study of English is a study of the realisation of the initial state S_0 under particular conditions' (Chomsky, 1986a, p. 37). In first language acquisition, S_0 is changed into a final steady state S_s by having parameter settings triggered, and so on. In this case, nothing comes out of the box: the box itself changes. The language faculty is transformed into a final state representing one of the possible human languages. Let us call this the *'states'* metaphor. For SLA it needs the qualification that there is no single final steady state, as assumed in the poverty-of-the-stimulus argument, hence I have termed the 'terminal' state of the L2 learner S_t to distinguish it from S_s (Cook, 1985b). The box metaphor no longer works since there is no product from the box, only changed contents within the box. There is no process separate from UG through which the grammar is created, simply changes in UG itself. The question of access to UG does not arise since UG is not separate from the grammar. The question 'Is there access to UG in L2 learning?' reifies UG by granting it existence as a distinct object separate from the L1 grammar and from the processes of learning. But, if UG *is* the L1 grammar S_s, the question of access has no meaning. A computer occasionally warns one 'A file cannot be copied on to itself'; it is just as meaningless to speak of UG having access to itself. The question of 'access' may be an artefact of the LAD metaphor; looked at from the vantage point of the states metaphor, it vanishes. Perhaps there is indeed a real question concealed here. But it would seem better first to tackle the three straightforward questions of knowledge of languages, acquisition of languages, and use of languages before dealing with questions that may be artefacts of our metaphoric models.

There is also for me a problem about the actual perspective from which UG research starts. Virtually the whole UG literature assumes that it is normal to know one language, unusual to know two. L2 users do not acquire the same knowledge in an L2 as monolinguals in an L1; they are seen as failing or inefficient in some way compared to L1 children. The L2 users' lack of success formed a strong plank in the arguments for no access, as we have seen. But suppose the L2 user's knowledge is not the same as that of a monolingual. As Meara (1983, p. iv) points out, 'There is no reason why a person who speaks both English and Spanish should behave in the same way as a monolingual speaker of either language'. Why should L2 users be treated as failed monolinguals? Their competence is whatever it is, not to be compared in derogatory fashion with monolingual competence: it is a different kind of thing. Grosjean (1989) talks of this attitude as a monolingual view of bilingualism since it treats both languages as if they were the first language. Indeed, the basis of the interlanguage concept was that such comparisons should not be made, at least initially, but that interlanguage grammars should be studied in their own right. A proper account of L2 learning would treat multi-competence in its own terms, not in L1-related terms. Linguists learnt many years ago not to discriminate against speakers of 'primitive languages', class dialects, regional dialects, sex dialects, and so on, but to accept them as equals; the parallel to the L2 situation is that any measure that evaluates L2 learners against L1 natives in terms of success or failure neglects their existence as L2 users. Their target is multi-competence at some level, not ersatz monolingualism in another language. The starting point of SLA research should not be that its subjects are deficient compared to a group of which they can never be members by definition. In a sense bilinguals are obviously superior to monolinguals in transcending the limitations of one language system, to whatever extent. Of course it is easier to say that multi-competence should be the standard than to assess it; how do we set a standard of multi-competence against which L2 users can be measured when it contains so much variation?

This line of thinking also feeds back into mainstream linguistics and first language acquisition. Chapter 1 suggested that the normal state of mankind is to know and speak one or more languages, not simply one language. Chomsky defines the basis of linguistics in monolingual terms: 'We exclude, for example, a speech community of uniform speakers, each of whom speaks a mixture of Russian and French (say, an idealized version of the nineteenth-century Russian aristocracy). The language of such a speech community would not be "pure" in the relevant sense, because it would not represent a single set of choices among the options permitted by UG but rather would include "contradictory" choices for certain of these options' (Chomsky, 1986a, p. 17). The monolingual presents a 'pure' case for study, according to this argument. (Notice by the way the use of the metaphoric term 'pure' in this context.) But, if most human beings arguably use more than one language, basing linguistics on monolinguals is not so much a convenient idealisation as a misleading representation of the human species. The system of mental representation of language has to be flexible enough to deal with knowledge of more than one language by the same mind, not just one. Suppose you have a desk with six drawers. You may decide to put all your clothes in one drawer and have the others empty. But, to describe the desk, you still need to talk about all six drawers because they are potentially available even if you yourself do not happen to use them. Illitch and Sanders (1988, p. 52) point out that 'One obstacle most modern readers face when they want to study the history of "language" is their belief in monolingual man. From Saussure to Chomsky "homo monolinguis" is posited as the man who uses languages.' The multilingual questions thus should take precedence over the monolingual questions; second language acquisition becomes a core area of linguistics rather than something tacked on as an afterthought.

While this argument is hardly likely to be accepted by many linguists, it should nevertheless remind them that linguistic theories and descriptions have ultimately to account for the multilingual nature of most people's knowledge of language; principles and parameters cannot be expressed in such a form that it is impossible for one mind to hold more than one grammar at a time. As Stenson (1990, p. 194) puts it, 'Any grammatical theory that purports to account for human linguistic competence must also be able to account for bilingual competence and the associated performance.' Taking the monolingual's knowledge of language as the basis of linguistics may be as useful as investigating cycling by looking at a man on a monocycle.

This approach feeds back on to the description of principles and parameters. If an L2 learner can be shown to know some aspect of language that is not present in the input or the L1, everything else being equal, this shows it must be part of the UG in the person's mind, regardless of whether it has ever been found in L1 acquisition; it is the description of UG that is at fault, not the L2 learner. If there are specific peculiarities to the instantiation of UG in an L2, this does not mean they are 'wrong' because they are not found in L1 acquisition, but that a model of UG based solely on L1 acquisition is inadequate. The notion that the mind may simultaneously have two settings for a parameter rather than one means that the actual forms of description have to allow for one mind to switch from one setting to another over short periods of time in codeswitching or long periods of time in L2 learning. The model of parameter setting must then be considerably more flexible than is normally taken to be the case in principles and parameters theory in allowing one mind to have two settings for any parameter at once.

10 Cognitive Approaches to Second Language Acquisition Research

Most of this book has assumed that language is represented and acquired by the human mind in ways that are different from any other knowledge. This chapter examines research that has mostly made the opposite assumption: namely, that language can be accommodated in a broader framework of how people store and acquire knowledge in general rather than being seen as something unique and peculiar of its own. It denies any special importance to the knowledge question 'What constitutes knowledge of language?' by rejecting any special status for language. The chapter spells out some alternatives to the linguistics-based approach to second language acquisition research that have been alluded to from time to time in this book, for example by Clahsen in Chapter 5, O'Malley and Chamot in Chapter 6, and Bley-Vroman and Schachter in Chapter 9.

10.1 ANDERSON'S ACT* MODEL

A major alternative approach to linguistic theories of acquisition is that of John Anderson, who insists that 'the adult human mind is a unitary construction'. Apart from a few minor adaptations, 'the language faculty is really the whole cognitive system', evidence for this being 'the remarkable communalities between language and other skills' (Anderson, 1983a, p. 3). This chapter takes Anderson's work as a reference point for psychological work and looks at how some of its themes relate to L2 research.

The fullest statement of Anderson's model is presented in the ACT* model (Anderson, 1983a); ACT stands for Adaptive Control of Thought, '*' for the ultimate version in the development of a sequence of models on which Anderson has been working – although it has, in fact, been slightly revised in MacWhinney and Anderson (1986). Anderson (1983a) is a highly technical psychological work, to which the following can only give a brief guide. The core concept in the model is the production system, made up of production rules, sometimes known simply as productions. A production rule consists of an IF THEN statement in the form IF x is true THEN do y, such as:

"IF it's too dark to read THEN turn on the light."

Such productions are the basis for language production, ranging from plurals (Anderson, 1980, p. 239) (note that in this context 'generate' is not used in its usual sense in linguistics but means 'produce'):

IF the goal is to generate a plural of a Noun
  and the Noun ends in a hard consonant
THEN generate the Noun + s

to SVO order (Anderson, 1983a, p. 262) (LV stands for Local Variable):

IF the goal is to communicate a meaning structure of the form (LV relation LV agent LV object)
THEN set as subgoals
  1. to describe LV agent
  2. to describe LV relation
  3. to describe LV object

Paraphrasing this production rule, IF you want to say something about an agent being related to an object, THEN you have to first describe the agent, secondly, describe the relationship; thirdly, describe the object. This rule creates three new sub-goals, which will be achieved in turn by other production rules, leading to further subgoals and eventually to the actual sentence. Rather than a description of static linguistic knowledge, this reflects a dynamic view of language as production. Furthermore, production rules are not specifically linguistic but true of all aspects of the mind.

Anderson's theory distinguishes three forms of memory: working memory, procedural memory, and declarative memory. *Working memory* is used for the actual performance of the production rule and draws on the other two. *Declarative memory* is for storing actual information in the form of cognitive units such as propositions or images. *Procedural memory* consists of processes for checking the parts of the rule against declarative memory. Unlike some otherwise similar theories to be encountered later, ACT* insists on the separation between declarative and procedural memories. This goes back to the distinction made by philosophers such as Ryle (1949) between 'knowing how' to do something and 'knowing that' something is true; some knowledge is about how to do things, other knowledge describes facts about things. An example of declarative knowledge might be knowing *that* 'Margaret Thatcher was the first woman Prime Minister of England'; an example of procedural knowledge could be knowing *how* to ride a bicycle. Anderson claims that procedural knowledge of language is not available to consciousness. It consists of ways of constructing sentences; grammatical morphemes such as "the", for example, are part of procedural knowledge and so not available to conscious attention while production is taking place. Declarative knowledge of language, however, consists of lexical morphemes such as "tree", whose meanings are specific and consciously available to the speaker. Use of a production rule in working memory requires an interaction between declarative and procedural memory.

When learning anything new, the mind moves from declarative to procedural knowledge in three stages:

(i) *the declarative stage* (sometimes called the 'cognitive' stage). New information is perceived as declarative 'facts'. When the mind starts to learn a new production rule or system, it has no pre-set procedures, so it relies purely on declarative knowledge. When we start learning how to drive a car, we begin by learning the rules for changing gear by heart; we learn *that* you must depress the clutch, turn the ignition key, let off the handbrake, and so on. Such new declarative information can be handled by following general problem solving procedures, or by inference or analogy from already known behaviours, that is to say by making use of productions already available to the mind;

(ii) *the knowledge compilation stage* (sometimes called the 'associative' stage). As it is cumbersome to use declarative knowledge in this way, the mind tries to 'compile' the information into more specific procedures. Gradually the learner-driver puts together the different elements involved in starting the car and begins to coordinate accelerator, handbrake, clutch, and gear-lever; the learner discovers *how* to drive the car. One form of knowledge compilation is through 'composition', in which several productions are collapsed into one. A rule for producing Agent–Object SVO relations might be collapsed with one for producing the present continuous to get a single rule for present continuous transitive sentences (MacWhinney and Anderson, 1986, p. 21). Another process of compilation is 'proceduralisation' which 'takes a general rule and makes it specific to a particular circumstance of application' (MacWhinney and Anderson, 1986, p. 21); a general procedure for choosing lexical items evolves into a specific procedure for uttering the word "dad";

(iii) *the tuning productions stage* (sometimes called the 'autonomous' stage). Even when a working solution is arrived at, the mind may still fine-tune the production by generalising productions to other conditions, for example, by discovering that "good" in "good girl" and "good" in "good girls" is the same word (MacWhinney and Anderson, 1986, p. 20), and by finer discrimination of the occasions when productions may be used, say, by distinguishing when a particular verb needs past or present forms (MacWhinney and Anderson, 1986, p. 21). The procedural ability to do something is no longer available to consciousness; an experienced driver may find it impossible to describe the actual components involved for moving off, or a speaker the stages in producing a sentence.

Anderson often uses classroom L2 learning as an illustration of his model. The L2 learner starts with declarative knowledge of a rule supplied by the teacher; 'we seek to learn the language by using general rule-following procedures applied to the rules we have learned, rather than speaking directly as we do in our native language' (Anderson, 1980, p. 224). This gradually turns into the ability to use the foreign language without thinking; 'it is as if the class-taught declarative knowledge had been transformed into a procedural form'.

The L2 research carried out by O'Malley and Chamot (1990), described in Chapter 6, is explicitly related to Anderson's theory. O'Malley and Chamot (1990, p. 43) see learning strategies as 'a set of productions that are compiled and fine-tuned until they become procedural knowledge'. They claim that L2 learning follows Anderson's three stages in broad outline; first, a declarative stage in which the learning process is 'intensive attention to the new language and deliberate efforts to make sense of it' (O'Malley and Chamot, 1990, p. 78); secondly, a compilation stage that develops procedural knowledge so that less conscious attention is needed; thirdly, a fine-tuning stage during which native-like automatic processing gradually improves.

Anderson's ACT* Model (Adaptive Control of Thought) based chiefly on Anderson (1983a)

A **production system** consists of **production rules** such as:
IF the goal is to generate a plural of a Noun and the Noun ends in a hard consonant
THEN generate the Noun + s
Working memory is used for actual performance of the rule
Declarative memory stores factual information
Procedural memory checks the rules against declarative memory

Stages in learning new production rules:
(i) *declarative* (or 'cognitive')
(ii) *knowledge compilation* (or 'associative'); composition, procedural-isation
(iii) *tuning productions* (or 'autonomous' stage); generalisation, finer discrimination

Their research with learning strategies showed students tapping into declarative knowledge of the topic. Procedural knowledge is involved, they claim, because of the goal-directed nature of the students' strategies. 'To the extent that these [goal directedness, adaptability and contingent planning] are evident in learning strategies and in language use, we believe that production systems can be a useful device for describing underlying processes' (O'Malley and Chamot, 1990, pp. 145–6).

10.2   TEMPORAL VARIABLES

A group of researchers working at Kassel, consisting chiefly of Hans Dechert, Manfred Raupach, and Dorothea Mohle, has explicitly linked L2 learning to Anderson's stages of learning and to his distinction between declarative and procedural memory; a useful article putting this approach in context is Mohle and Raupach (1987). In broad terms one might expect that speech produced from procedural knowledge would be more fluent than speech originating from declarative knowledge, though of course many other factors are involved. Dechert (1986) for instance claimed that the smooth production of a German translation "zum Beispiel" (for example) by a student shows 'totally proceduralised retrieval'. Raupach (1987) applied a number of psycholinguistic measurements, known as 'temporal variables', to the speech of two adult German learners of French recorded in interviews. One temporal variable is pauses, both in terms of duration and of distribution. Smooth production of "Quelques français que j'ai rencontré" (Some French people that I have met) he attributes to procedural learning, hesitant sections with long pauses to declarative knowledge, such as "une opinion (1.06) euh quelquefois (0.50) a" (an opinion er sometimes); figures in brackets refer to the length of pause in seconds. Such a progression is supported by the improved fluency of six German students after a term in France: again a precise measurement of fluency is involved, namely the 'run' of speech uninterrupted by pauses. The average number of syllables per run goes up from 5.90 to 8.43 (compared to a control native speaker's 14.43). He finds several indications in one learner of the L1 being used as the starting point, such as hesitations before lexical items that need to be supplied by the interlocutor. This use of the L1 plus translation rules is equivalent to Anderson's declarative stage in which the mind tries to cope with new declarative information through existing procedures such as inferencing. The combination of the L1 with translation is ineffective, and will not be improved greatly by the process of tuning.

Raupach compares the speech of the second student before and after *her* term in France. The main changes are:

- total speaking time was up from 132.30 secs to 283.28 secs;

- pause/time ratio (the percentage of time spent pausing) was down from 37.56 per cent to 30.39 per cent, that is to say on the second occasion the student paused for around 7 per cent less than on the first;
- length of runs was up from 6.56 to 7.61 syllables; that is to say, the average length of an uninterrupted stretch of speech went up by about one syllable;
- the number of hesitations was reduced; for example the student no longer paused for so long to think of the gender of a noun. Before going to France, she produced "une opinion . . . a assez mauvais (0.32) mauvaise" (an (fem.) opinion (fem.) . . . has enough bad (masc.) (0.32) bad (fem.)), hesitating *before* the choice of gender on the adjective; after going, she produced "une (0.98) opinion" (an (fem.) opinion (fem.)), pausing *after* the choice of gender of the article. Hesitations now tend to occur in a native-like fashion after conjunctions, relative pronouns or prepositions, as in "Ils m'ont toujours dit *que* (0.86)" (They have always told me), and "Oui ils pensent *que* (0.30)" (Yes they think that (0.30));
- before going to France, sentences were based on transfer of L1 procedural knowledge, such as "J'ai déja (1.26) euh: parlé la-dessus avec (.) quelques français" (I have already er talked about it with some French people); after going, they are based more on L2 procedures as in "J'en ai parlé a quelques français" (I have talked about it to some French people).

	Total speaking time	Pause/time ratio	Run length
Before	132.30	37.56%	6.56
After	283.28	30.39%	7.61

Temporal variables for a student before and after visiting France (adapted from Raupach, 1987)

But Raupach also finds direct transfer of L1 procedural knowledge without new declarative information; a student who uses "je suis été" (lit. I am been) rather than "j'ai été" (lit. I have been) is transferring a German procedure to French.

Raupach's conclusions are:

- Anderson's learning progression from the declarative to the tuning stage does not apply in a straightforward fashion to L2 learning, which involves other mechanisms and varies from one individual to another.

- in particular L2 learning often involves direct transfer of L1 procedures and translation from the L1.

Clearly, the weight to put on these conclusions depends on whether Raupach's chain of argument is in fact correct: does fluency of speech as measured by runs, speed, proportion of pauses, and so on, correspond to procedural memory? Or are these signs too indirectly linked to this type of memory?

Research summary: M. Raupach (1987), 'Procedural Learning in Advanced Learners of a Foreign Language', in J J. Coleman and R. Towell (eds), *The Advanced Language Learner* (London: CILTR) pp. 123–56.

Aim: application of temporal variables to L2 speech

Learners: adult German learners of French

Aspect of language: temporal variables of pauses, run-length, speaking time, etc.

Data type: interviews transcribed with pauses, etc.

Results: improvement on measures of fluency after visiting France

Conclusions: Anderson's view of learning as shift from declarative to procedural memory is complicated in L2 learning by the possibility of L1 transfer and translation

---

Several articles come to similar conclusions based on slightly different data. Mohle and Raupach (1989) look at a monologue by a German learner of French about the reorganisation of German education; they conclude that Anderson has overestimated the importance of learning from teachers' instruction and L2 learning therefore differs from the paradigm L1 case. Mohle (1984) compares the speech of three French speakers of German and three German speakers of French in both L1 and L2, showing that speakers have the same patterns in both languages and improve when they stay in the target country. Towell (1987a, 1987b) presents similar data concerning the improvement of English learners of French. Towell (1987a) reports a learner who improved over a period of four years from a speaking rate of 122.46 syllables per minute to 177.45, from a pause ratio of 52.59 per cent to 78.5 per cent, and from 75 per cent of runs being 1 to 4 syllables long to only 50 per cent being 1 to 4 syllables. Towell (1987b) describes another L2 learner of French who improved between year 1 and year 3 of an undergraduate course from a speaking rate of 118.20 to 195.20, from a pause ratio of 64.03 to one of 88.02, and from a run length of 4.30 to 8.40.

		Syllables per minute	Pause/time ratio(%)	Run length
	Natives	264.00	84.45	12.00
Towell (1987a)	Year 1	122.46	52.59	*75.75%
	Year 4	177.45	78.5	*50%
Towell (1987b)	Year 1	118.20	64.03	4.30
	Year 3	195.20	88.02	8.40

Improvement in L2 temporal variables over time in two English learners of French (adapted from Towell, 1987a, p. 168; 1987b, p. 124)
* % of runs from 1–4 syllables

Towell argues that L2 learners use 'chunks', such as the introductory formula "c'est" (that's), as declarative knowledge which gradually becomes part of their procedural knowledge. That is to say, in general this line of research sees increase in fluency as dependent on reorganising declarative 'facts' into more efficient procedures.

Research by Olynk *et al.* (1990) has shown that it is not so easy to equate fluency with advanced knowledge as might be thought. Instead, different types of 'speech markers' have to be distinguished. Olynk *et al.* (1990) looked at conversations involving 10 French learners of English in Quebec. They found that the fluent L2 users had more 'repeats' "comme un, comme un pas bon" (like a, like a not good) and more 'transition' markers where a change of speaker could take place ("You've got to try to meet her *uh*, well, down where you are") while the less-fluent had more 'repair conversions' in which something that has been produced is modified, as in "It's like, it was kind of a preparatory year". In general, the less fluent speakers had more 'regressive' markers, that is to say linking backwards, the more fluent speakers more 'progressive' markers linking forwards.

10.3   INFORMATION PROCESSING

Though using a different terminology and source material, the information-processing model of L2 learning put forward by Barry McLaughlin also emphasises a progression through learning stages. This model sees human beings as processors of information limited both by how much attention they can give to a task and by how well they can process the information. Different tasks require different amounts of attention and capacity. In particular, following Shiffrin and Schnieder (1977), McLaughlin distinguishes 'automatic' processes from 'controlled' processes. An automatic process is quick and requires little attention; it has been built up by practice and it needs little capacity to perform. A controlled process is slow because it is temporary and under the control of attention; it is therefore limited in capacity. Learning starts with a controlled process, in which the learner makes a one-off attempt to handle new information by giving it maximum attention; this is gradually transformed into an automatic process as the learner gets more used to handling the process. 'Thus controlled processing can be said to lay down the "stepping stones" for automatic processing as the learner moves to more and more difficult levels' (McLaughlin *et al.*, 1983, p. 141). Hence this bears a strong resemblance to Anderson's three stages of learning: new information is stored by the mind uneconomically as masses of undigested bits; learning consists of finding more economical and efficient ways of storing this information.

The usual support for this model is psychological experiments that show that the speed of L2 learners on various cognitive tasks is below that of L1 learners or that it increases with experience of the L2, that is to say, the type of evidence associated with the concept of L2 cognitive deficit outlined in Chapter 5. Reaction times to words such as "left" and "blue" are longer in an L2 (Lambert, 1956); picture and number naming take longer in an L2 and improve slowly over at least five years (Magiste, 1979); proficient bilinguals read more slowly in their L2 (Favreau and Segalowitz, 1982); Finnish L2 learners of English are on average 0.81 second slower at orally presented grammaticality judgements than natives (Lehtonen and Sajavaara, 1983). Cook (1988b) linked these L2 shortfalls to the Andersonian stages of learning, claiming they reflect the knowledge compilation and fine-tuning stages. Overall it is the additional strength of the L1 gained via experience that counts.

The experiment of Hulstijn and Hulstijn (1983) demonstrates the usefulness of an information-processing approach. They postulate that learners differ both on a dimension of executive control between controlled and automatic processing and on a metacognitive dimension between implicit and explicit knowledge of language. That is to say, they distinguish 'intuitive' control over a particular structure from conscious knowledge of a structure when 'the learner is able to verbalise the rule in sophisticated metalinguistic terms' (Hulstijn and Hulstijn, 1983, p. 25). Exercising control should take time; making learners with a limited L2 channel capacity speak fast should increase their errors. Focusing on the content rather than the form of the message should also increase errors because of the overload on the processing channel.

Dutch is similar to German in word order in that it has Verb Second order in main clauses, here called Inversion, and SOV in subordinate clauses, here called Verb Final. Hulstijn and Hulstijn (1983) pre-tested 157 L2 learners of Dutch to find those who scored between 10 per cent and 90 per cent for Verb Second and Inversion. The purpose was to select 32 L2 learners, half with English L1, half with varied L1s, who were neither totally ignorant of the rules nor so good at them that they would make no errors. The test proper consisted of 68 short passages of Dutch; after listening to each text, they were given a prompt phrase to start them retelling the story – an adverbial to force Inversion and a reported speech phrase such as "This man says that . . ." to force Verb Final. They were tested under four conditions, which varied the two factors 'attention to information' or 'attention to grammar' (Information versus Grammar), and 'presence of time pressure' or 'absence of time pressure' (that is, Fast versus Slow); learners were asked to pay attention to the four possible combinations, Information/Fast, Information/Slow, Grammar/Fast, Grammar/Slow. Their answers were analysed in terms of response length in seconds, an information score according to whether they included the four pieces of information in the text, and correctness. The learners were also given an interview in which they looked at their own answers and discussed their mistakes: their responses were scored in terms of whether they could formulate the rules explicitly or not.

Some of their results are displayed in the following table:

	response length (secs)	information score (max=8)
(1) Information/Fast	21.2	6.14
(2) Information/Slow	30.9	6.22
(3) Grammar/Fast	25.4	5.29
(4) Grammar/Slow	42.2	5.32

Response length and information for L2 learners of Dutch (adapted from Hulstijn and Hulstijn, 1983, p. 32)

As can be readily seen, time pressure had an effect on the overall length of response timed in seconds, cutting 9.7 seconds in the Information conditions, and 16.8 in the Grammar conditions, but it had hardly any effect on the information score, lowering it by 0.08 for Information and 0.03 for Grammar. Thus there were indeed overall effects from the two factors of Time and Attention. The results for the two sentence types were:

	Inversion score (%)	Verb Final score (%)
(1) Information/Fast	81.0	36.12
(2) Information/Slow	77.6	37.6
(3) Grammar/Fast	85.7	55.7
(4) Grammar/Slow	87.9	59.1

Scores for Inversion and Verb Final in L2 learners of Dutch (adapted from Hulstijn and Hulstijn, 1983, p. 33)

The crucial test was the effect that the two factors of time pressure and attention had on the Inversion and Verb Final scores. Time pressure cut the score marginally in the Information and Grammar conditions (between 1.48 per cent and 3.4 per cent). Attention to information rather than grammar reduced the scores for Inversion and for Verb Final to a greater extent (between 4.7 per cent and 21.5 per cent). Thus 'Focus of Attention on grammar increased the percentage of correct realizations of INV [Inversion] and VF [Verb Final], but Time Pressure had no effect' (Hulstijn and Hulstijn, 1983, p. 39). Although learners who were aware of the rules, as indicated by the interviews, showed overall better scores, the differences between the Grammar/Slow condition and the Information/Fast condition were no different for them than for the others; that is, the explicitness of their knowledge was no particular help. The results are taken to demonstrate the independence of the control and metacognitive dimensions. The experiment also had the clear implication for the Input Hypothesis Model that time was not relevant to Monitoring, as was discussed in Chapter Three.

Research summary: J. H. Hulstijn and W. Hulstijn (1983), 'Grammatical Errors as a Function of Processing Constraints and Explicit Knowledge', *Language Learning*, **34** (1): pp. 23–43

Aim: to investigate control and metacognitive dimensions via factors of time pressure and attention to form

Learners: 32 learners of Dutch (from a larger sample of 157)

Aspect of language: Dutch syntax involving 'Inversion' (Verb Second) and 'Verb Final' (SOV in subordinate clauses)

Design: variation of Time Pressure (Fast/Slow) and Focus on Form (Information/Grammar)

Data type: retelling 68 stories following prompts to elicit Inversion or Verb Final, plus follow-up interviews

Method of analysis: response length and information content scores

Results: Attention had an effect, Time Pressure did not; extra time helped both those who knew the rules explicitly and those who did not

Conclusions: this demonstrates the independence of the control and metacognitive dimensions

---

10.4 MACWHINNEY'S COMPETITION MODEL

A further general approach that sees information-processing as the key to language is the Competition Model put forward by Brian MacWhinney and his associates. This has been explicitly seen as complementing Anderson's ACT* model (MacWhinney and Anderson, 1986), though more recently it has been linked to connectionism theory (MacWhinney, 1989). The Competition Model concentrates on aspects of the channel capacity for using language; it is functionalist in that it starts from language as serving the function of communication; 'proponents of the functionalist approach regard communicative need as the most fundamental force in language use' (Cooreman and Kilborn, 1991, p. 198). A human language can utilise four types of signals to convey its meanings: *word order, vocabulary, morphology*, and *intonation*. The human information-processing system can use only a limited number of things at a time, so human languages have arrived at different ways of fitting these four types of signal into the same channel. English relies heavily on word order and makes comparatively little use of morphology; Latin relies on morphology and makes little use of word order; Chinese uses intonation and ignores morphology; and so on. The different aspects of language compete for the same limited processing space. The child learning the L1 is acquiring the appropriate weightings for each of these four factors – deciding which factors are crucial to processing. Learning an L2 is in part overcoming the biases of the first language by reweighting the factors as necessary.

The area always used to demonstrate the Competition Model is the subject of the sentence. There seem to be at least four ways in which speakers can identify subjects in speech:

(i) *word order*. The subject may come in a definite location in the sentence with respect to the Verb and Object. Thus, in SVO languages such as English, it comes first; in VSO languages it comes second; in VOS languages it comes last;

(ii) *agreement*. The subject may agree in number with the Verb. Thus in English singular subjects go with singular verbs, plural subjects with plural verbs, as in "He likes whisky" versus "They like whisky";

(iii) *case*. The subject may have to be in the Nominative Case, which may be distinguished by a particular morphological ending. In English this only applies to the pronoun system – "He likes whisky" rather than *"Him likes whisky";

(iv) *animacy*. In some languages the subject must be animate rather than inanimate. In Japanese, for instance, it is impossible to say "The typhoon broke the window" because "typhoon" is inanimate.

The usual experimental design to test the Competition Model asks speakers of different languages to identify the subject in sentences that differ in the weightings of these factors (Bates and MacWhinney, 1981). Speakers are asked to distinguish the subject in sentences that vary in word order, animacy, and so on, such as the various permutations:

"The horse hits the cow."

"Sniffs the cube a monkey."

"The lamb a dog pats."

The results are calculated in terms of the percentage with which the speakers choose the *first* noun in the sentence as subject. It is necessary first to look at the processing of different languages by native speakers. In the original experiment by Bates and MacWhinney (1981) the speakers were English, German, and Italian. The following table shows results for sentences in the three languages that kept animacy and agreement constant but differed in word order between NVN, VNN and NNV. Strictly speaking, N here stands for a whole Noun Phrase rather than a single Noun.

	NVN (%)	VNN (%)	NNV (%)
English	95	10	15
German	85	65	55
Italian	80	45	70

Assignment of subject by word order by native speakers of three languages (adapted from a graph in Bates and MacWhinney, 1981, p. 204)

The English results show a dramatic effect of word order. For NVN the choice is entirely in terms of the *first* Noun, for VNN and NNV almost entirely in terms of the *second* NP. While the preference for the second noun with VNN and NNV is surprising and seems to have no clear explanation, it still indicates that order is the relevant factor for English speaker; it is found in all the experiments to be discussed. The Italians and the Germans also chiefly rely on word order for NVN, though to a slightly lesser extent, but are hardly influenced by the position of the noun in VNN and NNV.

Let us now look at the results of sentences that keep word order constant but differ in terms of Animate (An) versus Inanimate (Inan), again calculated in terms of choice of the first noun rather than the second.

	An/An (%)	An/Inan (%)	Inan/An (%)
English	35	50	30
German	70	80	10
Italian	65	95	20

Assignment of subject by animacy by native speakers of three languages (adapted from a graph in Bates and MacWhinney, 1981, p. 204)

The English choose the first noun the least when it is animate in both

An/An and An/Inan conditions, compared to the other two groups, and choose it the most when it is inanimate (Inan/An). While animacy is crucial to Italians and Germans, it plays a smaller role for the English.

Finally the results for sentences that differed in terms of agreement; the Verb agreed either with both Nouns or with the first or the second; the results are again scored as a percentage of *first* Noun chosen:

	Both Nouns agree (%)	First Noun agrees (%)	Second Noun agrees (%)
English	50	65	30
German	65	85	15
Italian	70	95	5

Assignment of subject by agreement by native speakers of three languages (adapted from a graph in Bates and MacWhinney, 1981, p. 205)

Again, there are clear differences between speakers of the languages; English speakers are the least affected by agreement of the first Noun and the most affected by the agreement of the second Noun. Hence Bates and MacWhinney (1981, pp. 203–5) conclude that 'the order of importance of cues in English is word order first, followed by agreement and animacy. The order of importance of cues in both German and Italian is agreement first, followed by animacy and order'.

Bates and MacWhinney (1981) provide some tentative results for bilinguals; 'of four German bilinguals tested, three very clearly are using German processing strategies to interpret English sentences'. They argue that this demonstrates transfer of L1 to L2 at a deeper level of processing than is usually studied.

The same experimental paradigm has been applied to L2 learning by several researchers. Let us take Harrington (1987) as an example. This looks at Japanese learners of English. English has rigid SVO order and is non-pro-drop. Japanese has SOV order and is a pro-drop language; furthermore, it requires subjects of transitive verbs to be animate. The question is whether Japanese learners will carry over this preference for animacy to English and will neglect word order. Harrington used the standard Competition Model experiment with 12 Japanese in Japanese, 12 Japanese studying English at university, and 12 English-speaking native controls. The results for different word order combinations were expressed in the usual way as a percentage of choice of first N:

	NVN (%)	VNN (%)	NNV (%)
English L1	81	33	35
Japanese L1	59	54	56
Japanese L2	68	56	59

Assignment of subject by word order by Japanese and English (adapted from Harrington, 1987, pp. 364 and 368)

There is a difference between the speakers' performance in their respective L1s; the English were dominated by the word order strategy, taking the first Noun as subject in NVN sentences (corresponding to the correct SVO order in English), and the second Noun in VNN and NNV sentences – the English preference for the second Noun found previously; the Japanese show little reliance on word order, even for the NNV order that corresponds to the correct SOV order in Japanese. The Japanese have carried over their L1 lack of reliance on word order to L2 English: for NVN they show some small influence of the order strategy (68 per cent), but for VNN and NNV they show no signs of the English second Noun strategy with 56 per cent and 59 per cent respectively.

Turning to animacy, again presenting the results in terms of choice of the first rather than the second noun:

	An/An (%)	An/Inan (%)	Inan/An (%)
English	50	75	23
Japanese L1	69	98	3
Japanese L2	67	93	23

Assignment of subject by animacy by speakers of English and Japanese (adapted from Harrington, 1987, pp. 364 and 368)

In the L1 the Animacy or Inanimacy of the first Noun had a substantial effect on the Japanese, less effect on the English. The Japanese results for L2 English were 'indistinguishable' from their L1 Japanese for the An/An and An/Inan conditions, but were the same as the English L1 for Inan/An.

Harrington (1987) concludes that this demonstrates, on the one hand, the transfer of the L1 weighting in favour of Animacy, on the other the acquisition of the English word order preference for initial Subjects, though not the Subject Second phenomenon. This has to be qualified by the discovery of two groups within the native English, one tending to Animacy strategies, the other to word order strategies.

Research summary: M. Harrington (1987), 'Processing Transfer: Language Specific Processing Strategies as a Source of Interlanguage Variation', *Applied Psycholinguistics*, **8**, pp. 351–77

Aim: to apply the Competition Model to L2 learning

Learners: 12 Japanese in Japanese, 12 Japanese studying English at university, and 12 English-speaking native controls

Aspect of language: assignment of the subject according to factors of word order and animacy

Data type: choice of subject in experimental sentences, calculated as percentage of first noun chosen in various conditions

Results: English dominated by word order, whether SVO or Second Noun, Japanese by animacy in L1 and L2

Conclusions: transfer of L1 weightings to L2 and gradual acquisition of SVO, though not English Second Noun preference

---

This conclusion is supported by several other experiments using the same design. Kilborn and Cooreman (1987) looked at 20 Dutch learners of English; Dutch pays more attention to morphology than to word order and is an SOV language with SVO main clauses, as we saw earlier. They added to the standard test a set of sentences testing morphology; these varied according to whether both nouns agreed with the verb, the first noun agreed, or the second noun agreed. Results are expressed as usual in percentages of first noun, using the Bates and MacWhinney (1981) figures as the basis for the native English speakers:

	NVN (%)	VNN (%)	NNV (%)
English (B&MacW)	95	10	15
Dutch L1	61	59	58
L2 English	68	62	44

Assignment of subject by word order by Dutch speakers (Kilborn and Cooreman, 1987, p. 423)

The Dutch were less dominated by word order in English than the natives, particularly by the Second Noun strategy, though they had moved slightly from their Dutch weightings. Results for agreement were:

	Both Nouns agree (%)	First Noun agrees (%)	Second Noun agrees (%)
English (B&MacW)	50	65	30
Dutch: L1	70	91	19
L2 (English)	66	83	29

Assignment of subject by agreement by speakers of Dutch (Kilborn and Cooreman, 1987, p. 424)

Again, the Dutch relied more on agreement in English than the English themselves, although they had moved slightly towards the English weightings. Kilborn and Cooreman conclude that Dutch speakers transfer weightings to English but that there is a large amount of individual variation. McDonald (1987) also compared Dutch/English bilinguals with English/ Dutch bilinguals on sentences with three order constructions – datives, NVN order, and relative clauses; Dutch relies on morphological Case for interpreting these constructions while English relies on order. In all cases the L2 learners were found to be carrying over the L1 weighting and gradually losing it with experience of the L2. Issidorides and Hulstijn (1992) used the Competition Model to test out the intelligibility of grammatical Dutch AdverbVSO sentences versus ungrammatical AdverbSVO sentences for English and Turkish learners; this showed, that, provided animacy was clear, comprehension was no more difficult for the grammatical sentences, suggesting that word order transfer is not so dominant and that animacy may be an over-riding factor.

10.5   PLANS AND GOALS

A further characteristic of this psychological tradition is its emphasis on plans and goals. Anderson's production rule is set in motion by a goal – "IF you want to bake a cake"; the consequence may set a new series of subgoals – "THEN get the appropriate ingredients". The production system moves from the topmost goal to the bottom-most, starting with the overall decision to bake a cake and ending with putting on the icing.

The planning model is present within the model of speech production used in the strategies framework discussed in Chapter 6 (Faerch and Kasper, 1983) and in schema theory as applied to L2 reading (Carrell, 1984). A particular application occurs in the Competing Plans Hypothesis advanced by Dechert (1983; 1984a) and derived from Baars (1980). This sees the speaker progressively losing control as production moves from top to bottom of the sentence; lower level plans may compete with higher, leading to pauses, false starts, blends, and so on. The research paradigm used by Dechert and his colleagues to investigate the Competing Plans Hypothesis is to ask students to retell a short L2 written story in their own words (Dechert, 1980; 1984a). Folk stories such as 'The Lonely Opossum' and 'The War of the Ghosts' are chosen because of their differences from the story expectations of European readers. Dechert (1984a) argued that the speaker would have to activate various processing strategies to understand the story. Dechert (1987) described how one student, Dorothy, gave the story a coherent European structure as she retold it. Dechert (1984b) looked at two students handling the same story. One, Eva, took 138.2 seconds to read the passage. She used the concept of 'islands of reliability' – areas that the speaker has confidence in at the preplanning stage, here, key words or phrases from the original that allow the learner to reproduce the structure of the story. Only about one-third of her sentences resemble the original. Competitive planning is shown for example in her use of 'blends' in which two plans are combined into one, as when she said "borrow" when she meant "bow and arrow". A second student, Adam, on the other hand took 2155 seconds to read the story. About 72 per cent of the words and expressions of the original are found in his version; 87 per cent of his sentences rely heavily on the original.

	Oral production time (secs)	Speaking time (%)	Reading time(secs)	Similarity to original (%)
Eva	138.2	59.7	327.00	35.17
Adam	194.80	37	2155	87

Temporal variables in story-retelling by two students (Dechert, 1984b)

Dechert claims that Adam is in general behaving analytically, Eva synthetically. Dechert also tested Adam and Eva with an equivalent story in L1 German; the same differences between them are found. He concludes that the strategies adopted by each learner for carrying out this task were the same in both languages, similar to the conclusions the Nijmegen project reached on compensatory strategies (Poulisse, 1989–90).

Dechert (1984a) asked a student called Christa to describe a cartoon and found similar 'islands of reliability'; these are the more practised items of language on which the speaker needs to spend less time. Clearly, this is related to the continuous runs of speech emanating from procedures used by Raupach and Towell. Christa also produced blends; while she referred to the dog in the story as "it" and the birds as "he", she produced "And the bird eats his um it – hit – its food" in which "hit" is a blend caused by the competing plans for "its" and "his".

10.6 OTHER FEATURES OF COGNITIVE THEORIES

Two other points are common to Anderson's and similar theories. One is the actual model of learning presented in Anderson (1983a), chiefly through a computer simulation. Learning language means discovering the relationships between the semantic structure the speaker already knows and the unknown linguistic structure. Learners start by wanting to express an idea – a semantic base. They transform this into a sentence by using the production rules they already possess. Feedback on the appropriateness of their sentences to their intentions is provided. They modify their production rules to take account of this feedback. So, when they want to express something again from a semantic base, they can use this new improved set of production rules to turn the semantic base into a sentence; feedback again leads them to modify the rules; and so on in the constant cycle given below.

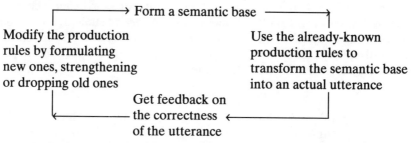

The language learning cycle (derived from Anderson, 1983a)

The vital elements in this, as in many psychological models, are the priority of the semantic base and the necessity for feedback, both questionable to many linguists. In the principles and parameters framework for example, there is no priority between the modules of semantics or syntax. Since at least Chomsky (1959), feedback has been seen both as irrelevant to language acquisition and as not occurring in actual language development.

The second shared concept is the idea of activation; 'if two structures might be matched to the same pattern, ACT* will prefer the more active one' (Anderson, 1983a, p. 26). Aspects of the mind that are frequently used will be 'active' and so can be accessed more easily; aspects of the mind that are not used will be accessed with much greater difficulty. For example, in producing "The robber took the money from the bank", the speaker chooses the sense of "bank" as "monetary institution" rather than the sense of "side of a river" because it would be more active in the context of "robber". The strength of such activation is at many levels, reflecting the frequency with which a rule is used. The mind is conceived as a network in which everything is connected to everything else. Activation spreads through this network, always choosing the most active path; hence it is known as a 'spreading activation' theory. 'At any point in time certain working memory elements are sources of activation . . . Activation can spread from these elements to associated elements in the network of elements and units' (Anderson, 1983b).

The concept of spreading activation is common to the main rival to ACT* in cognitive science, namely the powerful theory of connectionism (McLelland *et al.*, 1986; Bechtel and Abrahamson, 1990). This, like ACT*, sees the mind as a single highly complex network through which activation spreads; this too builds up complex processes that mimic the effects normally seen in rules; activation similarly depends on strength, built up through frequency. Two differences between ACT* and connectionism are that connectionism denies the need for separate declarative and procedural memory systems and it does not use the production system convention. ACT* and connectionism share the general view of the mind as a network and of learning as a matter of building up strengths through practice. Connectionism, however, sees learning as weighting the strength of the connections rather than the points where they meet in the network – the nodes. Its application to language has so far been limited, chiefly relying on the simulation of past tense learning in Rumelhart and McLelland (1986); its adequacy to deal with linguistic structure has been severely questioned by Pinker and Prince (1988). As yet connectionism has only been applied to second language acquisition in programmatic articles that do not distinguish L1 from L2 acquisition (Gasser, 1990; Sokolik and Smith, 1992), though it clearly has potential for actual L2 research.

To sum up, some common factors in these 'cognitive' approaches are:

(i) the mind is seen as a single overall 'network' in which everything is connected; 'language universals derive from universal properties of the human mind' (MacWhinney and Bates, 1989, p. 6);
(ii) speech production is information-processing – a process of activating the network in all its complexity, driven top-down to achieve particular goals;
(iii) learning is a progress from declarative, 'controlled', well-attended, data to procedural, 'automatic', non-attended, processes;
(iv) learning is acquiring strengths for parts of this network based on frequency of occurrence; 'language acquisition is cue-driven distributional analysis' (MacWhinney and Bates, 1989, p. 26).

The L2 work discussed here has developed different aspects of this general framework, ranging from the controlled-to-automatic processing of McLaughlin to the weightings of the Competition Model to the use of declarative and procedural memories by Raupach.

10.7   METHODOLOGY

In many ways the research methods used by the cognitive approaches described in this chapter are closer to the mainstream psychological tradition than to the linguistic tradition of earlier chapters. They rely on the measurement of pauses, mistakes, syllables spoken per minute, response times, and so on – almost any physical aspect of speech that can be quantified. Griffiths (1991) provides a critique of the use of such 'temporal variables' in some L2 research, though not the papers described here, arguing that the L2 work should show more awareness of the ways in which temporal variables have been used in L1 processing research. To a linguist these almost accidental features of speech performance are interesting in so far as they reveal aspects of language such as syntax, phonology, or vocabulary. While insights into the mechanics of speech production can provide one way into these, they are not language itself. Above all they are performance, not competence.

The bias of this research towards psychology rather than linguistics might be thought to entail other aspects of the mainstream psychological method – adequate size of speech samples, sufficient number of subjects, statistical rigour, and so on. Yet much of the L2 research is based on short transcripts from single individuals; Crookes (1991) emphasises the methodological problems this creates because of the wide variation between learners in temporal variables. For example the Kassel group typically deal with one or two learners: Raupach (1987) interviews with two learners, Mohle and Raupach (1989) a monologue by a single learner, Dechert (1987) one student retelling a story. Methodologically this blends a case-study tradition in which one example is exhaustively explored with an experiment-based method in which precise measurements are made. It avowedly belongs to a philosophical tradition known as 'objective hermeneutics'; this strives to balance the analysis of psychological data from *without* with the study of the mind from *within* (Rommetveit, 1991); it claims both to respect the individuality of human beings through the use of case studies and to meet standards of evidence by looking at measurable data. My own feeling is that these single or double-person studies need to be replicated on a larger scale to fit the more standard psychological paradigm. The figures in these papers are for the most part not couched in such a way that appropriate tests of significance can be applied to them. They provide revealing insights into individual L2 learners but they are aperçues on which further experimentation can build rather than fully supported by evidence in their own right. Obviously, this complaint cannot be levelled at the experimental designs of Hulstijn and Hulstijn (1983), Harrington (1987), and others.

10.8　THE LINGUISTIC BACKGROUND

The standard complaint by linguists is that this research ignores the distinctive features that make up the core of language knowledge. The notion of grammatical structure is almost completely absent from such processing accounts as Raupach, Towell, McLaughlin, and Dechert – not that they would necessarily interpret this as a criticism. Indeed MacWhinney's Competition Model uses the concept of subject as a central issue; but it is not subject in a configurational sense as defined, say, in principles and parameters theory. Nor is it clear how this approach can be extended to the other aspects of grammatical knowledge – binding, negation, grammatical morphemes, to take a quick selection. As MacWhinney and Bates (1989, p. xv) point out, 'our crosslinguistic database currently reflects the application of only two or three basic techniques applied to only a subset of the structures and functions that characterise all natural languages'. It is above all a grammar of processing rather than of knowledge, of performance rather than competence. Consequently it answers the use question rather than the acquisition question.

　　Anderson's ACT* at first sight appears to bear more resemblance to a grammatical description. A production rule such as:

> IF the goal is to generate a plural of a Noun
> 　　and the Noun ends in a hard consonant
> THEN generate the Noun + s

looks rather like a linguistic rewrite rule such as:

> S → NP VP

The most obvious difference is that Anderson is describing generation in the non-linguistic sense of 'production', that is to say performance, while a rewrite rule is describing generation in the linguistic sense of giving a correct structural description – that is to say, competence. As Anderson provides a mere sketch of what such a production system would look like for language, it is hard to see how it can be extended and what its full implications are. To start with, it is semantically driven; the speaker has a semantic base which is transformed into syntax by 'graph deformation'; questions about how the original structure is derived are put back one stage into semantics, and then back another stage into cognition, since there is no separation of these in a unitary model. To a linguist, this raises three issues. First, moving the structure back into the semantics is insufficient if a full theory of semantic structure is not supplied. Secondly, it implies that all language structure is semantically driven. Thirdly, it implies language as process rather than language as knowledge. Linguists claim that language has unique properties of its own which are not related to cognition – the concept of modularity; principles such as binding, or subjacency to them are properties of language that do not have counterparts in the rest of the mind (though Anderson, (1983a, p. 268, himself gives a general cognitive status to structure-dependency, which has an odd status in current principles and parameters theory, as we saw in Chapter 9). Cromer argued over the years, (for example, Cromer, 1991) that, while there are indeed some areas in which cognitive development leads to language development, there are many in which the two are unrelated to each other.

At best such rules constitute a Phrase Structure Grammar which yields regular branching trees of the familiar type. The adequacy of such rules has been debated throughout this book. Principles and parameters theory gets round the deficiencies it sees in phrase structure by relating the two levels of syntax, d-structure and s-structure, through movement. Some version of these objections is maintained by most linguists; those who advocate phrase structure grammar do so in an augmented form with a particular emphasis on vocabulary (Gazdar *et al.*, 1985). While this alternative could lend itself to some form of production system, this would undoubtedly end up looking rather different from the production rules of ACT*.

The view of language acquisition seen in these cognitive theories is also disputed by linguists on several counts. One is the necessity for feedback, seen fairly typically in the ACT* version above. The child's grammar changes because kindly people correct the child's sentence when it differs from what was clearly intended. But correction of this kind simply does not occur; parents do not explicitly correct their children's grammar on the points for which it is necessary, nor do children make the kind of mistake involving subjacency or structure-dependency that would provoke correction. Although implicit correction by repetition and so on has been argued for as more important than explicit correction (Hirsh-Pasek *et al.*, 1984), this too depends on children making appropriate mistakes and parents spotting them, neither of which has been observed. Second language acquisition is arguably different, in that the variety of learning situation means that some L2 learners indeed encounter correction and profit from it. But again L2 learners do not seem to make the relevant types of mistake or to get the relevant correction for central grammatical principles such as binding. While it may indeed be possible to learn an L2 through feedback, this is only one route to the L2 out of many and does not seem to apply to its most central aspects.

Another important aspect of this approach is the notion of frequency – how often the learner hears or says something. The weightings or strengths given to various aspects of the network in the mind are built up by encountering something time and again. How often something is used leads to its strength in the mind. Again, linguists have disputed the validity of this account of first language acquisition. McNeill (1966) showed that the value of practice was belied by the fact that L1 English children learn irregular past tenses such as "came" first, then regular endings such as "played", then start incorrectly generalising irregular forms such as "comed": despite the large amounts of practice children have devoted to "came", children abandon it for "comed" which they have never actually heard. Strength is irrelevant. Similarly there are accounts of children learning aspects of language such as "eager/easy" after hearing a few examples (Cromer, 1987). Nor can frequency of occurrence explain the argument from negative evidence: how does the child acquire aspects of language for which there is no positive evidence in the input?

Within its own limits, the work in this chapter has provided an alternative to the linguistics approach to second language acquisition research. Its strength is its integration with other approaches to the human mind, compared with the isolation of, say, principles and parameters theory from much of contemporary psychology or cognitive science, that is to say autonomous linguistics. But clearly at the moment it has a small coverage of language and language acquisition, examining surface phenomena and simple learning constructs rather than the complexity of linguistic approaches. If these approaches to research are to provide a valid alternative, they will have to encompass a wider range of language phenomena. But it is through detailed experimental work of the type carried out by Hulstijn and Hulstijn (1983), Harrington (1987), and Raupach (1987) that such an approach will be vindicated, not by the habit, illustrated chiefly in Chapters 5 and 9, of invoking cognitive processes as alternatives to UG without giving them any empirical substance.

10.9   LINGUISTICS AND SECOND LANGUAGE ACQUISITION

Let us bring together briefly some of the issues about the relationship of SLA and linguistics that have pervaded this book. Linguistics clearly provides a useful perspective on L2 learning and has led to stimulating ideas and research. SLA research takes part in the same endeavour as first language acquisition, sociolinguistics, phonology, and so on; it is one of the sciences of language. Yet it must be remembered that linguistics is only one of the disciplines that SLA research can draw on; the full richness of the discipline rests on the variety of ways that second languages impinge on the minds and lives of L2 users. If one is going to give linguistics a role in SLA research, on the one hand, one has the obligation to use a coherent and currently acceptable form of linguistics rather than approaches that have been discarded; on the other hand, one has to remember that the relevance of linguistics for SLA research is primarily to questions of L2 learning, only secondarily to questions of linguistic theory. There is a balance between making good use of linguistics and being taken over by linguistics. In particular the type of linguistics employed has to have a connection with issues of acquisition – hence the interest inherent in the UG theory.

A main issue that has occurred in every chapter is what SLA is about. The competence/performance problem is a methodological issue for any area of linguistics that bases itself on evidence other than single sentences. Multiple sources of information are needed to build up a picture of the language knowledge in the mind; assumptions about performance processes have to be clearly stated. In L2 research this is complicated by the intertwining, not just of L1 and L2 competence, but also of L1 and L2 performance, as we saw with the Competition Model's illuminating insights into the practical issues of identifying subjects in sentences, as well as the existence of cognitive deficit in processes using the L2.

It is clear what the linguistic competence of a native speaker may be, for all intents and purposes, since native speakers effectively share the same knowledge of language – the steady-state S_s. This competence can be studied through single sentence evidence. But there is no such clear-cut target in SLA; L2 learners are all different, few achieving the same level in the L2 as in the L1; other sources of evidence have to be consulted to make their competence clear. It has been implied here that L2 learners should not be treated as two native speakers in the same mind but seen as having the unique compound system called multi-competence: they are successful bilinguals, not failed monolinguals. SLA research has to clarify whether to continue taking the balanced bilingual as its model with the implied assumption that the only true L2 knowledge is that which is equivalent to a monolingual's, or to look at the 99 per cent of L2 learners who are not balanced and where knowledge does not duplicate a monolingual's. As Sridhar and Sridhar (1986) point out, 'Paradoxical as it may seem, Second Language Acquisition researchers seem to have neglected the fact that the goal of SLA is bilingualism.' L2 users are not imitation monolinguals in a second language but possessors of a unique form of competence in their own right.

Activities

The purpose of these activities is to bring the reader closer to the points made in the text by looking at data or questions that illuminate the discussion in each chapter. While they may be done individually, they also lend themselves to group or pair-work in classes and seminar groups.

CHAPTER 1

Activity 1

As we have seen the field of second language acquisition research has drawn in people from other disciplines, with different motivations such as:

(i)   investigating L2 learning for its own sake;
(ii) improving language teaching;
(iii) contributing to linguistics and the linguistic theory of language acquisition;
(iv) contributing to general issues in psychology.

How would you classify each of the following researchers from their own words?

- 'The ultimate goal of Second Language Acquisition research is the development of a theory of Second Language Acquisition' (Kevin Gregg, 1990).
- 'The acquisition of a second language, be it by everyday communication or by instruction, follows certain principles . . . The objective of second language acquisition studies is to uncover these principles' (Wolfgang Klein, 1986).
- 'I have been interested for a long time in how an understanding of Second Language Acquisition can contribute to language pedagogy' (Rod Ellis, 1990).
- 'In this book, the potential relationship between linguistic universals and second language acquisition will be explored. In particular we shall be concerned with a principles and parameters approach to Universal Grammar (UG) as realised in Government and Binding (GB) (Chomsky, 1981a)' (Lydia White, 1989).
- 'We hope that in the course of this book, we shall be able to present arguments and illustrate procedures which will make sense in terms of

language teachers' intuitions and which will not only provide guidance to the novice, but will in effect provide experienced teachers with ways to become more articulate about their experience in the classroom so that they can say why they believe their approach worked' (Elaine Tarone and George Yule, 1989).
- 'The goal of this book then is certainly not to propose a new method but rather to explore the requirements for a general theory of second language learning by examining the conditions under which languages are learnt, and to consider the relevance of such a theory for language teaching' (Bernard Spolsky, 1989).
- 'This book is about theory and the role of theory in research on adult second language learning. My principal goal is to examine what position theory plays in this growing subfield of applied linguistics and to evaluate present theories' (Barry McLaughlin, 1987).
- 'The book represents applied linguistics in its truest sense – the application of research findings to language teaching' (Andrew Cohen, 1990).
- 'The purpose of this book is to elucidate these issues from a linguistic point of view, focussing in particular on the potential relationship between second language acquisition and linguistic theory' (Susan Gass and Jacquelyn Schachter, 1989).

Activity 2

Here are some sentences from essays written by Moroccan learners of English who speak both Arabic and French, collected by Maria Saadi. French adds "-s" to a noun ("femme"/"femmes" – woman/women) or to an adjective to make it plural, while Moroccan Arabic shows plural by changing the position of the vowel (/ra:ʒl/ vs plural /rʒa:l/ – man/men). French expresses negation with "ne" before the verb, "pas" after it "je *ne* suis *pas* français" (I'm not French), Arabic has negation before the verb.

(a) What rules do you think the interlanguages of these learners have for English?
(b) Which language has influenced them most? Why?
(c) Do you think there are 'covert' errors in Corder's sense where the learner actually means something different from what he or she writes?

The bigs boxes
They are kinds
Her hairs are black
The mans in the corner are my teachers
All my teeths need to be controlled
Their wifes are all crazy

I caught many fishes
These revisions will bring my end
Saw he his father?
She managed to do a pizza
They not like me
I not eat apples
I not like this
Nobody is not here
These are shoes's mum
The house's father
Newspapers daddy

CHAPTER 2

Activity 3: Grammatical Morphemes

Here are two near-beginner adult learners of English trying to write a description of a still from *The Boyfriend* showing two people in 1920s clothes dancing on a giant record. Try to score them for absence of grammatical morphemes in obligatory contexts as described in the discussion of Dulay and Burt.

1. there are in this picture two persons, woman and man, and they are dancing with them selvies. one of classical dancing. The man wears a white trousers, and a white shirt, and he wears a small hat on his head, so the woman wears a light and white adress, both they wear in their foots a small shoes. Dancers are dancing on the deck of ~~theatre theatre~~ the theatre, finaly that picture is too nice.
2. In this picture taw puopal maks dancing (clasic dancing). His clothis are wait. The boy wear trouser and shirt The girl wear a waid clothis. The boy pant a hat in his haned. They dancing on a ~~deask~~ a dck The are very interesting when the dancing The dck in the ~~that theatre~~ and they have a butiful clothis all of it is wait until the shos.

In the light of your experiences with this:

- Are the learners typical of those studied in the morpheme studies?
- What do you make of the over-supply of some morphemes?
- How significant a component of the learner's interlanguage system is the omission of grammatical morphemes?
- Can you tell which learner speaks Spanish as L1, which Arabic?

Activity 4: Negation

Here are 20 sentences taken from Wode (1981). First classify each sentence into one of Wode's five stages; then put them in order.

1. you not dummy
2. no cold
3. I see nothing
4. no, Tiff
5. me no close the window
6. that's no right
7. no catch it
8. hit it not over the fence
9. no bread
10. I can't get him out
11. I catch that not
12. you no can have it
13. don't broke
14. you have a not fish
15. I got nothing shoe
16. no steep
17. everybody catch no the fish
18. shut not your mouth
19. John go not to the school
20. you not shut up

If Wode's analysis of the stages is correct, your order should correspond with the chronological order in which his children used them. What problems of analysis did you find with Wode's system?

The actual order was: 2 7 16 9 6 13 14 1 8 19 20 3 4 17 18 11 10 5 15 12. Does your order correspond to this? Does this order, based on only 20 sentences, support Wode's overall five stages or not?

CHAPTER 3

Activity 5

Three representative quotes from Krashen's critics are:

> each of Krashen's hypotheses is marked by serious flaws: undefinable or ill-defined terms, unmotivated constructs, lack of empirical content and thus of falsifiability, lack of explanatory power. (Gregg, 1984, p. 94).

> Krashen's theory fails at every juncture . . . Krashen has not defined his terms with enough precision, the empirical basis of the theory is weak, and the theory is not clear in its predictions. (McLaughlin, 1987, p. 56)

> the Monitor Model 'poses serious theoretical problems regarding the validity of the "acquisition-learning" distinction, the operation of Monitoring, and the explanation of variability in language-learner language'. (Ellis, 1985a, p. 266)

What evidence do you find in the account of Krashen's work in Chapter 3 that makes you agree or disagree with these criticisms?

Activity 6

According to the Input Hypothesis, teaching activities will succeed to the extent that they involve comprehensible input. Here is a list of teaching activities; first try to think how each would be carried out in a teaching context that you are familiar with, and then rate each of them on a scale of 1–10 for amount of comprehensible input.

- repetition of sentences containing a pronunciation point such as "Red leather, yellow leather";
- the teacher reading a story aloud and asking the students questions about it;
- students exchanging their views about their favourite music;
- students translating individual sentences into their first language;
- students listening to a grammatical explanation of a particular point;
- students listening to an explanation of an activity and then carrying it out;
- students learning lists of vocabulary with their L2 translations;
- students studying a poem in the target language.

CHAPTER 4

Activity 7

Here are some of the sentences spoken by Schumann's subject Alberto that contain negatives, interrogatives and declaratives. Looking at the criteria for pidgins on pp. 69–70, to what extent do you think that these support Schumann's contention that Alberto is a pidginised speaker?

Negatives

I don't understand that.	That "learn" no understand.
I don't have much time.	No remember.
I don't have the car.	No have pronunciation.
I don't understand.	No understand all.
You don't understand me.	No is mine.
No like walk.	I no may explain to you.
I no understand.	No pass.

Interrogatives	*Declaratives*
What is surance?	This picture is 'On the Point'.
This is apple?	It's problem for me.
You may change the day,	Picture is very dark.
the lesson the day?	In my country is six years in primaria.
You will come back?	Is necessary.
Will you come here next	Is very bad, no?
Monday?	This man is wrong.

Activity 8

One of Labov's famous techniques for discovering if people used "r" before consonants was to visit large stores in New York and ask for directions to a department he knew to be on the 'third' floor. What naturalistic tasks could you devise to learn if, in a given situation, L2 learners of English used /in/ or /iŋ/, clear or dark "l" (clear "l" occurs in native English at the beginning of words as in "loot", dark "l" at the end as in "tool"), left out or inserted the copula "be" in sentences, pronounced "t" as /t/ or as a glottal stop /ʔ/?

CHAPTER 5

Activity 9

Here are two essays written by teenage children learning English in England; names have been changed. Try scoring them according to the Multidimensional Model. Which stage is each one of them at?

A. Birthday Robbery
one day there was party a Birthday Party.
It was Mr and Mrs Smiths Sons Birthday he was twelve They invited all the friends fo their son and their parnets. By the way the boy who's Birthday was his name was Keith.
Two of his best friend were there too named peter and jhon.
They were really not his Bestfriends they were sons of big whealthy Robbers they were planing to Robb Mrs Smiths richness.
As Peter asked Keith for a drink. While John went upstairs to Mrs Smith's room and got the necholes out of the sofe and came downstairs and sat by Keith as he sat some ~~nose~~ noise came out of his cloths and Keith said that in you pocket.
John said oh nothing.

Keith said I want to see the object in your pocket and when he got the necholes out and both started to run John and Peter.
And some other boys court them.

B. *My self*
I am a ~~gril~~ girl and my name is Joan and I am 11 yea old and I go to Camford School. and I live on 224 Camford Road and I have one Brother and one brother and Brother name is Fred an brother [teacher's interpretation: sister] is name is Jane and ~~my Brothe and I hope two two~~ I like ta da vaeg to redy and raetga. [teacher's interpretation: to do washing, to reading and writing]

How useful do you feel that the Multidimensional Model was with these essays?

CHAPTER 6

Activity 10

Extract from a Dutch student retelling a story
Here is an example taken from Nanda Poulisse (1989–90) of a Dutch student retelling a story in English. Take one of the schemes of analysis from Faerch and Kasper or from the Nijmegen project and see what strategies you discover. To what extent do you feel this shows that the bulk of communication strategies are in fact due to lack of lexical knowledge?

> it's a story which call, the representer <laughs> it's a man uh, uh, uh who has uh, discovered, uh 1, uh 1 ja, a thing you can put on your head and then your hair will grow, when you're bald, that's very nice and uh, he tries to sell it, to uh, /so/ uh, to a lot of, erm, 1 haircutters <laughs>, erm 1 he does it uh, very, uh xxx clever, he's uh, bald, self, his himself, and uh, then, he puts on uh, uh <laughs> 3 'n pruik (= a wig) <whispers> 2 erm 6 erm, a thing which is made of uh, other man's hair or static hair, and you can put it on your head and then uh, it seems if you're not bald, and uh, then he, uh beweren (= claims), uh <whispers> 4 he says to the, to to the hair-cutter that uh 2 that uh has come because he has use his own uh 2 own, wat is uitviubdig nou weer (now what is invention?) <whispers> 2 own uh thing which he /ha/ had d discovered, uh. he, uh 2 he 2, he uh, earned a lot of money, uh, until the day of uh, the 2 meeting which is hold every year, in 1 outside of uh the houses, in the air, and the wind had uh, blew off, that thing 1 which he had on his hairs, and so 1 uh they discovered that he was a liar <laughs>.   (Poulisse, 1989–90, p. 128)

CHAPTER 7

Activity 11

Relative clauses
Find a person who does not know linguistics and try them with the
following sentences, taken from Cook (1975), choosing either sentences
1–6 if they are L2 learners or children, or sentences 7–12 if they are adult
native speakers. They have to indicate who is biting or pushing by saying
"cat bites dog" etc. for each sentence. Read them in a jumbled order.

1. The cat that likes the dog bites the horse.
2. The dog that pushes the cat likes the horse.
3. The dog that the cat likes pushes the horse.
4. The cat that the dog bites likes the horse.
5. The dog the cat likes pushes the horse.
6. The cat the dog bites likes the horse.
7. The cat that likes the dog that sees the man bites the horse.
8. The dog that pushes the cat that sees the man likes the horse.
9. The dog that the cat that the mans sees likes pushes the horse.
10. The cat that the dog that the man sees bites likes the horse.
11. The cat the dog the man sees likes pushes the horse.
12. The cat the dog the man sees bites likes the horse.

Which sentences did they make mistakes on? What were the causes? Does
this support the Accessibility Hierarchy explanation or one based on
processing, or some other explanation? To what extent do you feel such an
experiment is too artificial to really measure language comprehension?

CHAPTER 8

Activity 12

These are the detailed results for the experiment with Binding reported in
Cook (1990b) and described on pp. 179–81.

Table 1 Error rates for comprehension (% errors per sentence type)

	Native	Romance	Japanese	Norwegian
N:	14	14	16	17
A Peter shot him	10.8	5.3	10.9	5.9
B John shot himself	1.8	3.6	1.6	0

C Peter said that John voted for him	7.1	1.8	7.8	8.8
D Peter said that John voted for himself	8.9	7.1	23.4	2.9
E John asked Peter to pay for him	12.5	5.4	23.4	17.6
F Peter asked John to include himself	7.1	30.4	40.6	19.1
G Peter discovered John's report on him	14.3	16	28.7	13.2
H John reported Peter's criticisms of himself	16.0	35.7	43.7	33.8

Table 2 Timing results (average seconds and milliseconds to respond per sentence type)

	Native	Romance	Japanese	Norwegian
N:	14	14	16	17
A Peter shot him	3.303	4.992	4.282	4.220
B John shot himself	2.955	3.976	3.592	3.840
C Peter said that John voted for him	4.591	6.628	7.614	6.238
D Peter said that John voted for himself	4.219	6.723	6.979	6.558
E John asked Peter to pay for him	4.708	7.381	7.627	6.215
F Peter asked John to include himself	4.492	7.720	7.180	6.316
G Peter discovered John's report on him	5.190	8.690	8.724	7.703
H John reported Peter's criticisms of himself	5.922	8.041	8.530	9.591

Here are the questions and the answers that this paper attempted to give; to what extent do you think each answer is justified by the data above?

(i) *Are pronominals more difficult than anaphors?*
   'the anticipated difficulty for pronominals is found only with error rates for simple and tensed sentences, with certain exceptions.'
(ii) *Are pronominals treated as anaphors?*
   'such complementarity is never the case. . . . arguments based on the

misinterpretation of pronominals as anaphors are clearly otiose at this stage.'

(iii) *Are there differences across a range of sentence types?*
'the difficulty order between the sentence types is the same for both comprehension and response times for all three groups, with the exception of the Norwegian group's performance on DF for response time.'

(iv) *Does the L1 of the learner affect the results and in what way?*
'It does not seem on the basis of the results here that large quantitative differences exist between the groups.'

(v) *How is the Subset Principle involved in L2 learning and using?*
'If the Subset Principle were involved in any way, it would make opposite predictions for anaphors and pronominals, which are not found.'

Activity 13: The Head Direction Parameter

The main criticisms of the head direction parameter research are given below. Check back to the presentation of the research on pp. 190–2 and see whether you think they are justified:

- the placement test used was not appropriate for spoken language production;
- elicited imitation does not test underlying interpretations sufficiently;
- the statistical analysis is inadequate;
- alternative explanations can readily be found based on ease of processing;
- the syntactic description is inadequate.

CHAPTER 9

Activity 14

Here are some of the sentences used in the experiment by Bley-Vroman *et al.* (1988) with subjacency. First, satisfy yourself you can tell which ones are grammatical and which ungrammatical. Then try them on another 'naive' native speaker or a non-native speaker, asking them if each sentence is grammatical or not.

1. *"What does Mary want to know whether John has already sold?
2. "What did Bill think that the teacher had said?"
3. *"What did Sam believe the claim that Carol had bought?"

4. "What did John realise that he could not sell?"
5. *"What did John hear the news that the mayor would do?"
6. *"Who did John buy the house that had recommended to him?"
7. *"What did the police arrest the men who were carrying?"
8. *"What did John find the ball and?"
9. *"What does John like to eat tomatoes and?"
10. "Who does John want to see?"
11. "What did John think Carol wanted her mother to give to the postman?"
12. "Where is the person that I want you to talk to?"

Do you think this confirms the partial access to UG principle claimed for it? Do you think such grammaticality judgments reflect what the speaker might do in 'real life'?

CHAPTER 10

Activity 15

Here is an extract from a student retelling a story taken from Dechert (1987). The following conventions are used in the transcript: pauses are marked in hundredths of a second; finished speech is in capitals; "/" means a rise–fall or fall–rise intonation with a pause; "//" means a falling intonation with a 'long' pause.

(a) Where are the pauses located? The smooth runs? The less fluent sections?
(b) To what extent does this extract support Anderson's declarative/ procedural distinction used by Raupach?

THE OPOSSUM CAME TO A HOUSE (16) WHERE SHE ASKED THE PEOPLE IF THEY HAD SEEN (56) HER BABY (50)/
THE PEOPLE ANSWERED YES (10)/
AND the w THE OPOSSUM WALKED IN (84) TO THE (50) DIRECTION THE PEOPLE POINTED TO (143)//
uhm (149) THEN SHE HAD (39) MET (122) TWO PEOPLE (11)/
AND EVERY TIME (70) SHE SANG HER LONESOME SONG (266) //
AFTER A WHILE SHE CAME TO A FEW HOUSES (24)/
SOME WERE EMPTY AND (66) SOME WERE OCCUPIED (90)/
AND: SOMEONE POINTED (28) S uhm (132) TO THE HOUSE WHERE HER BABY WAS (140)//

she found (410) SHE FOUND HER BABY IN ONE HOUSE (46)/
SOMEONE HAD (108) KILLED A RATTLESNAKE (18) AND (68)
GIVEN (30) COOKED IT AND GIVEN IT to HER BABY (58)/
THE OPOSSUM WAS ang (10) VERY ANGRY ABOUT IT (10)
TOOK HER BABY AND WENT AWAY (28) (coughing) (210)//
ON HER WAY (176) SHE (46) KILLED A FAWN (104) HAD SOME
OF THE MEAT AND GAVE SOME TO HER BABY (104)/

Activity 16

The last part of this chapter makes explicit a theme that has run through this book: L2 users are not failed monolinguals in an L2 but a particular type of their own, *de sui generis*. Look at the following quotations and decide the extent to which, given that they are out of context, the writers seem to assume that L2 users are deficient monolinguals and the extent to which they see them as people in their own right:

- 'Condition 2. Native speaker target condition (typical graded): second learner language approximates native speaker language' (Spolsky, 1989, p. 35).
- 'children generally achieve full competence (in any language they are exposed to) whereas adults usually fail to become native speakers' (Felix, 1987, p. 140).
- 'learners' errors need not be seen as signs of failure' (Littlewood, 1984, p. 22).
- 'In L2 acquisition, on the other hand, it is common for the learner to fail to acquire the target language fully; there are often clear differences between the output of the L2 learner and that of native speakers, and learners differ as to how successful they are' (White, 1989, p. 41).
- 'The lack of general guaranteed success is the most striking characteristic of adult foreign language learning. Normal children inevitably achieve perfect mastery of the language; adult foreign language learners do not' (Bley-Vroman, 1989, p. 42).
- 'a bilingual will develop his or her languages to the level of fluency that is needed for communication. For some this is near perfect and equal fluency in both languages; others do not need to be as fluent in one language as in the other' (Grosjean, 1982, p. 307).
- '. . . those adults who seem to achieve native speaker "competence", i.e those who learn a second language so that their "performance" is indistinguishable from that of native speakers (perhaps a mere 5% of all learners)' (Selinker, 1972).
- 'Unfortunately, language mastery is not often the outcome of SLA' (Larsen Freeman and Long, 1991, p. 153).

References

Ableman, P. (1969), *The Twilight of the Vilp* (London: Gollancz).

Abney, S. (1987), 'The English Noun Phrase in its Sentential Aspects', PhD thesis, unpublished.

Abraham, R. (1984), 'Patterns in the Use of the Present Tense Third Person Singular "-s" by University Level ESL Speakers', *TESOL Quarterly*, **18** (1), pp. 55–69.

Adams, M. A. (1978), 'Methodology for Examining Second Language Acquisition', in Hatch, E. (ed.) *Second Language Acquisition: A Book of Readings* (Rowley, Mass.: Newbury House) pp. 278–96.

Adamson, H. D. (1988), *Variation Theory and Second Language Acquisition* (Washington: Georgetown University Press).

Adamson, H. D. and Kovac, C. (1981), 'Variation Theory and Second Language Acquisition: an Analysis of Schumann's Data', in Sankoff, D. and Cedergren, H. (eds), *Variation Omnibus* (Edmonton, Alberta: Linguistic Research Inc.) pp. 285–92.

Adamson, H. D. and Regan, V. (1991), 'The Acquisition of Community Speech Norms by Asian Immigrants Learning English as a Second Language: a Preliminary Study', *Studies in Second Language Acquisition*, **13** (1), pp. 1–22.

Adjemian, C. and Liceras, J. (1984), 'Accounting for Adult Acquisition of Relative Clauses', in F. Eckman *et al.* (eds), *Universals of Second Language Acquisition* (Rowley, Mass.: Newbury House).

Andersen, E. (1990), 'Acquiring Communicative Competence: Knowledge of Register Variation', in R. C. Scarcella, E. S. Andersen and S. D. Krashen (eds), *Developing Communicative Competence in a Second Language* (Rowley, Mass.: Newbury House), pp. 5–25.

Andersen, R. W. (1981), 'Two Perspectives on Pidginisation as Second Language Acquisition', in Andersen (ed.) (1981).

Andersen, R. W. (ed.) (1981), *New Dimensions in Second Language Acquisition Research* (Rowley, Mass.: Newbury House).

Andersen, R. W. (1983), 'Introduction', in Andersen (ed.) (1983), pp. 1–58.

Andersen, R. W. (ed.) (1983), *Pidginisation and Creolisation as Language Construction* (Rowley, Mass.: Newbury House).

Andersen, R. W. (1984), 'The One to One Principles of Interlanguage Construction', *Language Learning*, **34** (4), pp. 77–95.

Andersen, R. W. (ed.) (1984), *Second Languages: A Crosslinguistic Perspective* (Rowley, Mass.: Newbury House).

Andersen, R. W. (1989), 'The Theoretical Status of Variation in Interlanguage', in S. Gass, C. Madden, D. Preston and L. Selinker (eds), *Variation in Second Language Acquisition: Psycholinguistic Issues* (Clevedon: Multilingual Matters) pp. 46–64.

Andersen, R. W. (1990), 'Models, Processes, Principles and Strategies: Second Language Acquisition Inside and Outside the Classroom', in B. VanPatten and J. F. Lee (eds), *Second Language Acquisition/Foreign Language Learning*

(Clevedon: Multilingual Matters), pp. 45–68.

Anderson, J. R. (1980), *Cognitive Psychology and Its Implications* (San Francisco: Freeman).

Anderson, J. R. (1983a), *The Architecture of Cognition* (Cambridge, Mass: Harvard University Press).

Anderson, J. R. (1983b), 'A Spreading Activation Theory of Memory', *JVLVB*, **22**, pp. 261–95.

Arabski, J. (1979), *Errors as Indicators of the Development of Interlanguage* (Katowice: Uniwersiteit Slaski).

Asher, J. (1986), *Learning Another Language Through Actions: The Complete Teacher's Guidebook* (Los Gatos, Cal.: Sky Oaks Productions).

Asimov, I. (1952), *Foundation and Empire* (Gnome Press).

Atkinson, M. (1992), *Children's Syntax: An Introduction to Principles and Parameters Theory* (Oxford: Basil Blackwell).

Baars, B. J. (1980), 'The Competing Plans Hypothesis: an Heuristic Viewpoint on the Causes of Errors in Speech', in H. W. Dechert and M. Raupach (eds), *Temporal Variables in Speech: Studies in Honour of Frieda Goldman-Eisler* (The Hague: Mouton) pp. 39–49.

Baddeley, A. D. (1986), *Working Memory* (Oxford: Clarendon Press).

Bates, E., Bretherton, I. and Snyder, L. (1988), *From First Words to Grammar* (Cambridge: Cambridge University Press).

Bates, E. and MacWhinney, B. (1981), 'Second Language Acquisition from a Functionalist Perspective', in H. Winitz (ed.), *Native Language and Foreign Language Acquisition*, *Annals of the New York Academy of Sciences*, **379**, pp. 190–214.

Bauer, L. (1988), *Introducing Linguistic Morphology* (Edinburgh: Edinburgh University Press).

Bechtel, W. and Abrahamson, A. (1990), *Connectionism and the Mind: An Introduction to Parallel Processing in Networks* (Oxford: Basil Blackwell).

Belasco, S. (1971), 'The Feasibility of Learning a Second Language in an Artificially Unicultural Situation', in P. Pimsleur and T. Quinn (eds), *The Psychology of Second Language Learning* (Cambridge: Cambridge University Press) pp. 1–10.

Berko, J. (1958), 'The Child's Learning of English Morphology', *Word*, **14**, pp. 150–77.

Berwick, R. C. and Weinberg, A. S. (1984), *The Grammatical Basis of Linguistic Performance* (Cambridge, Mass.: MIT Press).

Bever, T. G. (1970), 'The Cognitive Basis for Linguistic Structure', in J. R. Hayes (ed.), *Cognition and the Development of Language* (New York: John Wiley) pp. 279–352.

Bialystok, E. (1983), 'Some Factors in the Selection and Implementation of Communication Strategies', in C. Faerch and G. Kasper (eds), *Strategies in Interlanguage Communication* (London: Longman).

Bialystok, E. (1987), 'Influences of Bilingualism on Metalinguistic Development', *Second Language Research*, **3**(2), pp. 154–66.

Bialystok, E. (1990), *Communication Strategies* (Oxford: Basil Blackwell).

Bickerton, D. (1977), *Change and Variation in Hawaiian English*, vol. II (University of Hawaii at Manoa).

Bickerton, D. (1981), *Roots of Language* (Ann Arbor, Mich.: Karoma).

Bickerton, D. (1983), 'Comments on Valdmann's "Creolisation and Language Acquisition" ', in Andersen (ed.) (1983), pp. 235–40.

Bickerton, D. (1984), 'The Language Bioprogram Hypothesis and Second Language Acquisition', in W. E. Rutherford (ed.), *Language Universals and Second Language Acquisition* (Amsterdam: John Benjamins).

Bickerton, D. and Odo, C. (1976), *Change and Variation in Hawaiian English*, vol. I (University of Hawaii at Manoa).

Birdsong, D. (1989), *Metalinguistic Performance and Interlinguistic Competence* (New York: Springer).

Bley-Vroman, R. W. (1983), 'The Comparative Fallacy in Interlanguage Studies: the Case of Systematicity', *Language Learning*, **33**, pp. 1–17.

Bley-Vroman, R. W. (1989), 'The Logical Problem of Second Language Learning', in S. Gass and J. Schachter (eds), *Linguistic Perspectives on Second Language Acquisition* (Cambridge: Cambridge University Press) pp. 41–68.

Bley-Vroman, R. and C. Chaudron (1990), 'Second Language Processing of Subordinate Clauses and Anaphora – First Language and Universal Influences: a Review of Flynn's Research', *Language Learning*, **40**, pp. 245–85.

Bley-Vroman, R. W., S. Felix and G. L. Ioup (1988), 'The Accessibility of Universal Grammar in Adult Language Learning', *Second Language Research*, **4**(1), pp. 1–32.

Bloom, L. (1970), *Language Development: Form and Function in Developing Grammars* (Cambridge, Mass.: MIT Press).

Bloom, L., P. Lightbown and Hood, L. (1975), *Structure and Variation in Child Language*, Monographs of the Society for Research in Child Development, serial no. 160, vol. 40, no 2.

Bloom, P. (1990), 'Subjectless Sentences in Child Language', *Linguistic Inquiry*, **21**(4), pp. 491–504.

Bloomfield, L. (1933), *Language* (New York: Holt).

Blumenthal, A. L. (1966), 'Observations with Self-embedded Sentences', *Psychonomic Science*, **6**, 453.

Borer, H. and Wexler, K. (1987), 'The Maturation of Syntax', in T. Roeper and E. Williams (eds), *Parameter Setting* (Dordrecht: Reidel) pp. 123–87.

Botha, R. P. (1989), *Challenging Chomsky: The Generative Garden Game* (Oxford: Basil Blackwell).

Braine, M. (1963), 'The Ontogeny of English Phrase Structure: the First Phase', *Language*, **39**, pp. 1–13.

Brooks, N. (1960), *Language and Language Learning* (New York: Harcourt Brace).

Broselow, E. and Finer, D. (1991), 'Parameter Setting in Second Language Phonology and Syntax', *Second Language Research*, **7**(1), pp. 35–60.

Brown, A. (1982), 'Inducing Strategic Learning from Texts by Means of Informed, Self-control Training', *Topics in Learning and Learning Disability*, **2**, pp. 1–17.

Brown, J. D. (1988), *Understanding Research in Second Language Learning* (New York: Cambridge University Press).

Brown, R. (1973), *A First Language: The Early Stages* (London: Allen and Unwin).

Brown, R. and Fraser, C. (1963), 'The Acquisition of Syntax', in C. Cofer and B.

Musgrave (eds), *Verbal Behaviour and Learning: Problems and Processes* (New York: McGraw-Hill) pp. 158–201.

Brown, R. and Hanlon, C. (1970), 'Derivational Complexity and the Order of Acquisition in Child Speech', in J. R. Hayes (ed.), *Cognition and the Development of Language* (New York: John Wiley) pp. 155–207.

Bruner, J. (1983), *Child's Talk* (London: Oxford University Press).

Cancino, H., Rosansky, E. and Schumann, J. (1978), 'The Acquisition of English Negatives and Interrogatives by Native Spanish Speakers', in E. Hatch (ed.), *Second Language Acquisition* (Rowley, Mass.: Newbury House) pp. 207–30.

Carden, G. and Stewart, W. A. (1988), 'Binding Theory, Bioprogram, and Creolisation: Evidence from Haitian Creole', *Journal of Pidgin and Creole Languages*, **3**(1), pp. 1–67.

Carrell, P. L. (1984), 'Evidence of a Formal Schema in Second Language Comprehension', *Language Learning*, **34**, pp. 87–111.

Carroll, J. B. (1967), 'Foreign Language Proficiency Levels Attained by Language Majors near Graduation from College', *Foreign Language Annals*, **1**, pp. 131–51.

Carroll, J. M., Bever, T. G. and Pollack, C. R. (1981), 'The Non-uniqueness of Linguistic Intuitions', *Language*, **57**(2), pp. 368–83.

Carroll, S. and Meisel, J. M. (1990), 'Universals and Second Language Acquisition: Some Comments on the State of Current Theory', *Studies in Second Language Acquisition*, **12**(2), pp. 201–8.

Chamot, A. (1987), 'The Learning Strategies of ESL Students', in A. Wendon and J. Rubin (eds), *Learner Strategies in Language Learning* (Englewood Cliffs, N. J.: Prentice-Hall).

Chaudron, C. (1983), 'Research on Metalinguistic Judgements: a Review of Theory, Methods, and Results', *Language Learning*, **33**(3), pp. 343–77.

Chomsky, C. (1969), *The Acquisition of Syntax in Children from 5 to 10* (Cambridge, Mass.: MIT Press).

Chomsky, N. (1957), *Syntactic Structures* (The Hague: Mouton).

Chomsky, N. (1959), 'Review of B. F. Skinner *Verbal Behavior*', *Language*, **35**, pp. 26–58.

Chomsky, N. (1964), *Current Issues in Linguistic Theory* (The Hague: Mouton).

Chomsky, N. (1965a), 'Formal Discussion: the Development of Grammar in Child Language', in U. Bellugi and R. Brown (eds), *The Acquisition of Language* (Lafayette, Ind.: Purdue University Press).

Chomsky, N. (1965b), *Aspects of the Theory of Syntax* (Cambridge, Mass.: MIT Press).

Chomsky, N. (1971), *Problems of Knowledge and Freedom* (New York: Pantheon Books).

Chomsky, N. (1972), *Language and Mind*, enlarged edn (New York: Harcourt Brace Jovanovich).

Chomsky, N. (1980a), *Rules and Representations* (Oxford: Basil Blackwell).

Chomsky, N. (1980b), 'On Cognitive Structures and their Development', in M. Piattelli-Palmarini (1980) (ed.), *Language and Learning: The Debate between Jean Piaget and Noam Chomsky* (London: Routledge & Kegan Paul).

Chomsky, N. (1981a), *Lectures on Government and Binding* (Dordrecht: Foris).

Chomsky, N. (1981b), 'Principles and Parameters in Syntactic Theory', in N. Hornstein and D. Lightfoot (eds), *Explanations in Linguistics* (London:

Longman).

Chomsky, N. (1982), *Some Concepts and Consequences of the Theory of Government and Binding* (Cambridge, Mass.: MIT Press).

Chomsky, N. (1986a), *Knowledge of Language: Its Nature, Origin, and Use* (New York: Praeger).

Chomsky, N. (1986b), *Barriers* (Cambridge, Mass.: MIT Press).

Chomsky, N. (1987), Kyoto Lectures, unpublished MS.

Chomsky, N. (1988), *Language and Problems of Knowledge: The Managua Lectures* (Cambridge, Mass.: MIT Press).

Chomsky, N. (1989), 'Some Notes on Economy of Derivation and Representation', *MIT Working Papers in Linguistics*, **10**, pp. 43–74.

Chomsky, N. and Lasnik, H. (1991), 'Principles and Parameters Theory', in J. Jacobs, A. von Stechow, W. Sternefeld and T. Vennemann (eds), *Syntax: An International Handbook of Contemporary Research* (Berlin: de Gruyter).

Clahsen, H. (1980), 'Psycholinguistic Aspects of L2 Acquisition', in S. W. Felix (ed.), *Second Language Development* (Tubingen: Gunter Narr) pp. 57–92.

Clahsen, H. (1984), 'The Acquisition of German Word Order: a Test Case for Cognitive Approaches to L2 Development', in Andersen (ed.) (1984) pp. 219–42.

Clahsen, H. (1987), 'Connecting Theories of Language Processing and Second Language Acquisition', in C. W. Pfaff (ed.), *First and Second Language Acquisition Processes* (Rowley, Mass.: Newbury House) pp. 103–16.

Clahsen, H. (1988), 'Critical Phases of Grammar Development: A Study of the Acquisition of Negation in Children and Adults', in P. Jordens and J. Lalleman (eds), *Language Development* (Dordrecht: Foris) pp. 123–48.

Clahsen, H. and Muysken, P. (1986), 'The Availability of Universal Grammar to Adult and Child Learners – a Study of the Acquisition of German Word Order', *Second Language Research*, **2**(2), pp. 93–119.

Clahsen, H. and Muysken, P. (1989), 'The UG Paradox in L2 Acquisition', *Second Language Research*, **5**, pp. 1–29.

Clahsen, H., Meisel, J. M. and Pienemann, M. (1983), *Deutsch als Zweitsprache: Der Sprachenerwerb auslandischer Arbeiter* (Tubingen: Gunter Narr).

Clark, E. V. and Hecht, B. F. (1983), 'Comprehension, Production and Language Acquisition', *Ann. Rev. Psychol.*, **34**, pp. 325–49.

Cohen, A. (1990), *Language Learning: Insights for Learners, Teachers, and Researchers* (Rowley, Mass.: Newbury House).

Comrie, B. (1990), 'Second Language Acquisition and Language Universals Research', *Studies in Second Language Acquisition*, **12**(2), pp. 209–18.

Cook, V. J. (1969), 'The Analogy between First and Second Language Learning', *IRAL*, **7**(3), pp. 207–16; reprinted in R. Lugton (ed.), *Towards a Cognitive Approach to Second Language Acquisition* (Philadelphia, Pa: Center for Curriculum Development, 1971).

Cook, V. J. (1973), 'The Comparison of Language Development in Native Children and Foreign Adults', *IRAL*, **11**(1), pp. 13–28.

Cook, V. J. (1975), 'Strategies in the Comprehension of Relative Clauses', *Language and Speech*, **18**, pp. 202–12.

Cook, V. J. (1979), 'Aspects of Memory in Secondary School Language Learners', *Interlanguage Studies Bulletin – Utrecht*, **4**(2), pp. 161–72.

Cook, V. J. (1985a), 'Language Functions, Social Factors, and Second Language Teaching', *IRAL*, **13**(3), pp. 177–96.

Cook, V. J. (1985b), 'Chomsky's Universal Grammar and Second Language Learning', *Applied Linguistics*, **6**, pp. 1–18.

Cook, V. J. (1986), 'Experimental Approaches Applied to Two Areas of Second Language Learning Research: Age and Listening-based Teaching Methods', in V. J. Cook (ed.), *Experimental Approaches to Second Language Learning* (Oxford: Pergamon Press).

Cook, V. J. (1988a), 'Language Learners' Extrapolation of Word Order in Phrases of Micro-Artificial Languages', *Language Learning*, **38**(4), pp. 497–529.

Cook, V. J. (1988b), 'Cognitive Processing and Second Language Learning', *Polyglot*, **9**, microfiche 2.

Cook, V. J. (1988c), *Chomsky's Universal Grammar: An Introduction* (Oxford: Basil Blackwell).

Cook, V. J. (1990a), 'Observational Evidence and the UG Theory of Language Acquisition', in I. Roca (ed.), *Logical Issues in Language Acquisition* (Dordrecht: Foris) pp. 33–46.

Cook, V. J. (1990b), 'Timed Comprehension of Binding in Advanced L2 Learners of English', *Language Learning*, **40**(4), pp. 557–99.

Cook, V. J. (1991a), *Second Language Learning and Language Teaching* (London: Edward Arnold).

Cook, V. J. (1991b), 'The Poverty-of-the-Stimulus Argument and Multi-competence', *Second Language Research*, **7**(2), pp. 103–17.

Cook, V. J. (1991c), 'Review of Lydia White, *Universal Grammar and Second Language Acquisition*', *System*.

Cook, V. J. (1992), 'Evidence for Multi-competence', *Language Learning*, **42**(4), 557–91.

Cook, V. J. (forthcoming), 'The Metaphor of Access to Universal Grammar', in N. Ellis (ed.), *Implicit Learning of Language*.

Cooreman, A. and Kilborn, K. (1991), 'Functionalist Linguistics: Discourse Structure and Language Processing in Second Language Acquisition', in T. Huebner and C. A. Ferguson (eds), *Crosscurrents in Second Language Acquisition and Linguistic Theories* (Amsterdam: John Benjamins) pp. 195–224.

Corder, S. P. (1967), 'The Significance of Learner's Errors', *IRAL*, **5**, pp. 161–70; reprinted in Richards (ed.) (1974).

Corder, S. P. (1971), 'Idiosyncratic Errors and Error Analysis', *IRAL*, **9**(2), pp. 147–59; reprinted in Richards (ed.) (1974).

Corder, S. P. (1973), *Introducing Applied Linguistics* (Harmondsworth, Middx: Penguin Books).

Corder, S. P. (1974), 'Error Analysis', in J. P. B. Allen and S. P. Corder (eds), *The Edinburgh Course in Applied Linguistics:* vol. 3: *Techniques in Applied Linguistics* (London: Oxford University Press) pp. 122–54.

Corder, S. P. (1978), 'Language-learner Language', in J. C. Richards (ed.), *Understanding Second and Foreign Language Learning: Issues and Approaches* (Rowley, Mass.: Newbury House) pp. 71–93.

Corder, S. P. (1981), *Error Analysis and Interlanguage* (London: Oxford University Press).

Crain, S. and Fodor, J. D. (1984), 'On the innateness of subjacency', in G. Alvarez, R. Brodie and P. McCoy (eds), *Proceedings of the East Coast Conference on Linguistics* (Columbus, Ohio: Ohio State University) pp. 191–204.

Cromer, R. (1970), ' "Children are Nice to Understand": Surface Structure Clues to the Recovery of a Deep Structure', *British Journal of Psychology*, **61**, pp. 397–408.

Cromer, R. F. (1974), 'The Development of Language and Cognition: the Cognition Hypothesis', in B. Foss (ed.), *New Perspectives in Child Language* (Harmondsworth, Middx: Penguin Books).

Cromer, R. F. (1987), 'Language Growth with Experience without Feedback', *Journal of Psycholinguistic Research*, **16**(3), pp. 223–31.

Cromer, R. F., (1991), *Language and Thought in Normal and Handicapped Children* (Oxford: Basil Blackwell).

Crookes, G. (1991), 'Second Language Production Research: a Methodologically Oriented Review', *Studies in Second Language Acquisition*, **13**(2), pp. 113–32.

Cross, T. (1977), 'Mothers' Speech Adjustments', in C. Snow and C. Ferguson (eds), *Talking to Children* (Cambridge: Cambridge University Press) pp. 151–88.

Crystal, D. and Davy, D. (1969), *Investigating English Style* (London: Longman).

Crystal, D., Fletcher, P. and Garman, M. (1976), *The Grammatical Analysis of Language Disability* (London: Edward Arnold).

Culicover, P. W. (1991), 'Innate Knowledge and Linguistic Principles', *Behavioral and Brain Sciences*, **14**(4), pp. 615–16.

Dakin, J. (1973), *The Language Laboratory and Language Learning* (London: Longman).

Danchev, A. (ed.) (1988), *Error Analysis of Bulgarian Learners of English* (Sofia: Narodna Prosveta).

Davies, A., Criper, C. and Howatt, A. (eds) (1984), *Interlanguage* (Edinburgh: Edinburgh University Press).

Dechert, H. (1980), 'Pauses and Intonation as Indicators of Verbal Planning in Second Language Speech Production', in H. Dechert and M. Raupach (eds), *Temporal Variables in Speech* (Amsterdam: Mouton) pp. 271–86.

Dechert, H. (1983), 'The Competing-plans Hypothesis Extended to Second-Language Speech Production', in R. J. Di Pietro, W. Frawley and A. Wedel (eds), *The First Delaware Symposium on Language Studies: Selected Papers* (Newark, Del.: University of Delaware Press) pp. 269–82.

Dechert, H. (1984a), 'Second Language Production: Six Hypotheses', in H. Dechert, D. Mohle and M. Raupach (eds), *Second Language Productions* (Tubingen: Narr) pp. 211–30.

Dechert, H. (1984b), 'How a Story is Done in a Second Language', in C. Faerch and G. Kasper (eds), *Strategies in Interlanguage Communication* (London: Longman) pp. 174–96.

Dechert, H. (1986), 'Thinking-aloud Protocols: the Decomposition of Language Processing', in V. Cook (ed.), *Experimental Approaches to Second Language Learning* (Oxford: Pergamon Press) pp. 111–26.

Dechert, H. (1987), 'Understanding Producing', in H. Dechert and M. Raupach (eds), *Psycholinguistic Models of Production* (Norwood, N.J.: Ablex) pp. 229–38.

Dechert, H. (1989), 'On the Natural Order of Events', in H. Dechert and M.

Raupach (eds), *Transfer in Language Production* (Norwood, N.J.: Ablex) pp. 237–70.

de Haan, P. and van Hout, R. (1988), 'Syntactic Features of Relative Clauses in Text Corpora', *Dutch Working Papers in English Language and Linguistics*, 2, pp. 1–28.

Deutsch, W., Koster, C. and Koster, J. (1986), 'What can we Learn from Children's Errors in Understanding Anaphora?', *Linguistics*, 24, pp. 203–25.

de Villiers, J. and de Villiers, P. (1973), 'A Cross-sectional Study of the Acquisition of Grammatical Morphemes in Child Speech', *J. Psycholing. Res.*, 2(3), pp. 235–52.

Dewaele, J. M. (forthcoming), 'La Composition Lexicale des Styles Orales et écrits', *Language and Style*.

Dickerson, L. J. (1975), 'The Learner's Interlanguage as a System of Variable Rules', *TESOL Quarterly*, 9(4), pp. 401–7.

Dornic, S. (1969), 'Verbal Factor in Number Perception', *Acta Psychologica*, 29, pp. 393–9.

Dulay, H. C. and Burt, M. K. (1973), 'Should we Teach Children Syntax?', *Language Learning*, 23(2), pp. 245–58.

Dulay, H. C. and Burt, M. K. (1974a), 'Natural Sequences in Child Second Language Strategies', *Language Learning*, 24, pp. 37–53.

Dulay, H. C. and Burt, M. K. (1974b), 'Errors and Strategies in Child Second Language Acquisition', *TESOL Quarterly*, 8(2), pp. 129–36.

Dulay, H. C. and Burt, M. K. (1978), 'Some Remarks on Creativity in Language Acquisition', in W. C. Ritchie (ed.), *Second Language Acquisition Research* (New York: Academic Press) pp. 65–86.

Dulay, H. C. and Burt, M. K. (1980), 'On Acquisition Orders', in S. Felix (ed.), *Second Language Development: Trends and Issues* (Tubingen: Gunter Narr) pp. 265–328.

Dulay, H. C., Burt, M. and Krashen, S. (1982), *Language Two* (Rowley, Mass.: Newbury House).

Duncan, D. (ed.) (1989), *Working with Bilingual Language Disability* (London: Chapman & Hall).

duPlessis, J., Solin, D., Travis, L. and White, L. (1987), 'UG or Not UG, That is the Question: a Reply to Clahsen and Muysken', *Second Language Research*, 3(1), pp. 56–75.

Eckman, F. R., Bell, L. and Nelson, D. (1988), 'On the Generalisation of Relative Clause Instruction in the Acquisition of English as a Second Language', *Applied Linguistics*, 9(1), pp. 1–20.

Elkind, D. (1970), *Children and Adolescents: Interpretive Essays on Jean Piaget* (New York: Oxford University Press).

Elliot, A. J. (1981), *Child Language* (Cambridge: Cambridge University Press).

Ellis, R. (1982), 'The Origins of Interlanguage', *Applied Linguistics*, 3, pp. 207–23.

Ellis, R. (1985a), *Understanding Second Language Acquisition* (London: Oxford University Press).

Ellis, R. (1985b), 'Sources of Variability in Interlanguage', *Applied Linguistics*, 6(2), pp. 118–31.

Ellis, R. (1988), 'The Effects of Linguistic Environment on the Second Language Acquisition of Grammatical Rules', *Applied Linguistics*, 9(3), pp. 257–73.

Ellis, R. (1990a), *Instructed Second Language Acquisition* (Oxford: Basil Blackwell).

Ellis, R. (1990b), 'A Response to Gregg', *Applied Linguistics*, **11**(4), pp. 384–91.

Ellis, R. (1991), 'Grammaticality Judgments and Second Language Acquisition', *Studies in Second Language Acquisition*, **13**, pp. 161–86.

Ericsson, K. A. and Simon, H. A. (1980), 'Verbal Reports as Data', *Psychological Review*, **87**(3), pp. 215–51. Reprinted in Faerch and Kasper (eds) (1983).

Ervin, S. and Osgood, C. (1954), 'Second Language Learning and Bilingualism', *Journal of Abnormal and Social Psychology*, **49**, pp. 139–46.

Ervin-Tripp, S. (1964), 'Language and TAT Content in Bilinguals', *Journal of Abnormal and Social Psychology*, **68**, pp. 500–7.

Ervin-Tripp, S. (1972), 'Is Second Language Learning Like the First?', *TESOL Quarterly*, **8**(2), pp. 111–19.

Eubank, L. (1987), 'The Acquisition of German Negation by Formal Language Learners', in B. VanPatten, T. Dvorak and J. Lee (eds), *Foreign Language Learning: A Research Perspective* (Rowley, Mass.: Newbury House) pp. 33–51.

Eubank, L. (1989), 'Parameters in L2 Learning: Flynn Revisited', *Second Language Research*, **5**(1), pp. 43–73.

Eubank, L. (ed.) (1991), *Point Counterpoint: Universal Grammar in the Second Language* (Amsterdam: Benjamins).

Faerch, C. and Kasper, G. (1980), 'Processes in Foreign Language Learning and Communication', *Interlanguage Studies Bulletin: Utrecht*, **5**, pp. 47–118.

Faerch, C. and Kasper, G. (1983), 'Plans and Strategies in Foreign Language Communication', in C. Faerch and G. Kasper (eds), *Strategies in Interlanguage Communication* (London: Longman) pp. 20–60.

Faerch, C. and Kasper, G. (1984), 'Two Ways of Defining Communication Strategies', *Language Learning*, **34**, pp. 45–63.

Favreau, M. and Segalowitz, N. S. (1982), 'Second Language Reading in Fluent Bilinguals', *Applied Psycholinguistics*, **3**, pp. 329–41.

Felix, S. (1984), 'Maturational Aspects of Universal Grammar', in Davies *et al.* (eds), 1984.

Felix, S. (1987), *Cognition and Language Growth* (Dordrecht: Foris).

Felix, S. (1988), 'UG-generated Knowledge in Adult Second Language Acquisition', in Flynn and O'Neil (eds) (1988).

Felix, S. (1991), 'The Accessibility of Universal Grammar in Second Language Acquisition', in L. Eubank (ed.), pp. 89–104.

Felix, S. and Weigl, W. (1991), 'Universal Grammar in the Classroom: the Effects of Positive and Negative Evidence in the Classroom', *Second Language Research*, **7**(2), pp. 162–80.

Feyerabend, P. (1975), *Against Method* (London: Verso).

Fillmore, L. W. (1976), *The Second Time Around: Cognitive and Social Strategies in Second Language Acquisition*, PhD thesis, Stanford University.

Finer, D. (1991), 'Binding Principles in Second Language Acquisition', in L. Eubank (ed.), *Point Counterpoint* (Amsterdam: J. Benjamins).

Finer, D. and Broselow, E. (1986), 'Second Language Acquisition of Reflexive Binding', *NELS*, **16**.

Flanigan, B. (1991), 'Variable Competence and Performance in Child Second Language Acquisition', *Second Language Research*, **7**(3), pp. 220–32.

Fletcher, P. (1985), *A Child's Learning of English* (Oxford: Basil Blackwell).

Flynn, S. (1983), 'Similarities and Differences between First and Second Language Learning', in D. R. Rogers and J. A. Sloboda (eds), *Acquisition of Symbolic Skills* (New York: Plenum) pp. 485–500.

Flynn, S. (1984), 'A Universal in L2 Acquisition Based on a PBD Typology', in F. R. Eckman, L. N. Bell and D. Nelson (eds), *Universals of Second Language Acquisition* (Rowley, Mass.: Newbury House) pp. 75–87.

Flynn, S. (1987a), *A Parameter-setting Model of L2 Acquisition* (Dordrecht: Reidel).

Flynn, S. (1987b), 'Contrast and Construction in a Parameter-setting Model of L2 Acquisition', *Language Learning*, **37**(1), pp. 19–62.

Flynn, S. (1989), 'The Role of the Head-Initial/Head-Final Parameter in the Acquisition of English Relative Clauses by Adult Spanish and Japanese Speakers', in S. M. Gass and J. Schachter (eds), *Linguistic Perspectives on Second Language Acquisition* (Cambridge: Cambridge University Press) pp. 89–108.

Flynn, S. and Espinal, I. (1985), 'Head Initial/Head Final Parameter in Adult L2 Acquisition of English', *Second Language Research*, **1**, pp. 93–117.

Flynn, S. and Lust, B. (1990), 'In Defense of Parameter-Setting in L2 Acquisition: a Reply to Bley-Vroman and Chaudron '90', *Language Learning*, **40**(3), pp. 1–31.

Flynn, S. and O'Neil, W. (eds) (1988), *Linguistic Theory in Second Language Acquisition* (Dordrecht: Kluwer).

Fox, B. A. (1987), 'The Noun Phrase Accessibility Hierarchy Reinterpreted: Subject Primacy or the Absolutive Hypothesis', *Language*, **43**(4), pp. 856–69.

Fraser, C., Bellugi, U. and Brown, R. (1963), 'Control of Grammar in Imitation, Comprehension, and Production', *JVLVB*, **2**, pp. 121–35.

Frazier, L. and de Villiers, J. (eds) (1990), *Language Processing and Language Acquisition* (Dordrecht: Kluwer).

Freed, B. (1980), 'Talking to Foreigners Versus talking to Children: Similarities and Differences', in R. Scarcella and S. Krashen (eds), *Research in Second Language Acquisition* (Rowley, Mass.: Newbury House) pp. 19–27.

Freidin, R. (1991), 'Linguistic Theory and Language Acquisition: a Note on Structure-Dependence', *Behavioral and Brain Sciences*, **14**(4), pp. 618–19.

Gaies, S. (1977), 'The Nature of Linguistic Input in Formal Language Learning: Linguistic and Communicative Strategies in ESL Teachers' Classroom Language', in H. D. Brown, C. Yorio and R. Crymes (eds), *Teaching and Learning English as a Second Language: Trends in Research and Practice* (Washington, D.C.: TESOL) pp. 74–80.

Galambos, S. J. and Hakuta, K. (1988), 'Subject-Specific and Task-Specific Characteristics of Metalinguistic Awareness in Bilingual Children', *Applied Psycholinguistics*, **9**, pp. 141–62.

Gardner, R. (1985), *Social Psychology and Second Language Learning* (London: Edward Arnold).

Gardner, R. C. and Lambert, W. E. (1959), 'Motivational Variables in Second Language Acquisition', *Canadian Journal of Psychology*, **13**, pp. 266–72.

Gardner, R. C. and Lambert, W. E. (1972), *Attitudes and Motivation in Second Language Learning* (Rowley, Mass.: Newbury House).

Garman, M. (1990), *Psycholinguistics* (Cambridge: Cambridge University Press).

Gass, S. (1979), 'Language Transfer and Universal Grammatical Relations', *Language Learning*, **29**, pp. 327–44.

Gass, S. (1982), 'From Theory to Practice', in M. Hines and W. Rutherford (eds), *On TESOL '81* (Washington, D.C.: TESOL) pp. 129–39.

Gass, S. and Ard, J. (1980), 'L2 data: their Relevance for Language Universals', *TESOL Quarterly*, **14**, pp. 443–52.

Gass, S. and Lakshmanan, U. (1991), 'Accounting for Interlanguage Subject Pronouns', *Second Language Research*, **7**(3), pp. 181–203.

Gass, S. and Schachter, J. (eds) (1989), *Linguistic Perspectives on Second Language Acquisition* (Cambridge: Cambridge University Press).

Gasser, M. (1990), 'Connectionism and Universals of Second Language Acquisition', *Studies in Second Language Acquisition*, **12**(2), 179–200.

Gazdar, G., Klein, E., Pullum, G. and Sag, I. (1985), *Generalised Phrase Structure Grammar* (Oxford: Basil Blackwell).

Gerbault, J. (1978), *The Acquisition of English by a Five-Year-old French Speaker*, MA thesis, University of California, Los Angeles; cited in Lakshmanan (1991).

Gibbons, J. (1985), 'The Silent Period: an Examination', *Language Learning*, **35**(1), pp. 255–67.

Gilbert, G. (1981), 'Discussion of "Two Perspectives on Pidginisation as Second Language Acquisition" ', in R. W. Andersen (ed.), *New Dimensions in Second Language Acquisition Research* (Rowley, Mass.: Newbury House) pp. 207–12.

Giles, H. and Smith, P. M. (1979), 'Accommodation Theory: Optimal Levels of Convergence', in H. Giles and R. N. St Clair (eds), *Language and Social Psychology* (Oxford: Basil Blackwell) pp. 45–65.

Givon, T. (1979), *On Understanding Grammar* (New York: Academic Press).

Glicksberg, D. H. (1963), 'A Study of the Span of Immediate Memory among Adult Students of English as a Foreign Language', unpublished PhD thesis, University of Michigan.

Goldman-Eisler, G. (1968), *Psycholinguistics: Experiments in Spontaneous Speech* (London: Academic Press).

Goodluck, H. (1991), *Language Acquisition: A Linguistic Introduction* (Oxford: Basil Blackwell).

Gopnik, I. and Crago, M. (1991), 'Familial Aggregation of a Developmental Language Disorder', *Cognition*, **39**(1).

Grant, J. and Karmiloff-Smith, A. (1991), 'Diagnostics for Domain-Specific Constraints', *Behavioral and Brain Sciences*, **14**(4), pp. 621–2.

Greenbaum, S. and Quirk, R.(1970), *Elicitation Experiments in English* (Ann Arbor, Mich.: University of Michigan).

Gregg, K. W. (1984), 'Krashen's Monitor and Occam's Razor', *Applied Linguistics*, **5**, pp. 79–100.

Gregg, K. W. (1989), 'Second Language Acquisition Theory: the Case for a Generative Perspective', in S. Gass and J. Schachter (eds), *Linguistic Perspectives on Second Language Acquisition* (Cambridge: Cambridge University Press) pp. 15–40.

Gregg, K. W. (1990), 'The Variable Competence Model of Second Language Acquisition, and why it isn't', *Applied Linguistics*, **11**(4), pp. 364–83.

Griffiths, R. (1991), 'Pausological Research in an L2 Context: a Rationale and

Review of Selected Studies', *Applied Linguistics*, **12**(4), pp. 345–64.

Grimshaw, J. and Rosen, S. T. (1990), 'Knowledge and Obedience: the Developmental Status of the Binding Theory', *Linguistic Inquiry*, **21**, pp. 187–222.

Grosjean, F. (1982), *Life with Two Languages* (Cambridge, Mass.: Harvard University Press).

Grosjean, F. (1989), 'Neurolinguists, Beware! The Bilingual is Not Two Monolinguals in One Person', *Brain and Language*, **36**, pp. 3–15.

Gross, M. (1990), 'Lexique – Grammaire LADL', paper given at the AILA Congress, Thessaloniki, April.

Haegeman, L. (1991), *Introduction to Government and Binding Theory* (Oxford: Basil Blackwell).

Hakuta, K. (1974), 'A Preliminary Report on the Development of Grammatical Morphemes in a Japanese Girl Learning English as a Second Language', *Working Papers on Bilingualism*, **3**, pp. 18–38; reprinted in E. Hatch (ed.), *Second Language Acquisition: a Book of Readings* (Rowley, Mass.: Newbury House, 1978) pp. 132–47.

Hakuta, K. (1976), 'A Case Study of a Japanese Child Learning English as a Second Language', *Language Learning*, **26**(2), pp. 321–51.

Halliday, M. A. K. (1975), *Learning How to Mean* (London: Edward Arnold).

Halliday, M. A. K. (1985a), *An Introduction to Functional Grammar* (London: Edward Arnold).

Halliday, M. A. K. (1985b), *Spoken and Written Language* (London: Oxford University Press).

Halliday, M. A. K. and Hasan, R. (1985), *Language Context and Text: Aspects of Language in a Social Semiotic Perspective* (London: Oxford University Press).

Halliday, M. A. K., McIntosh, A. and Strevens, P. (1964), *The Linguistic Sciences and Language Teaching* (London: Longman).

Harrington, M. (1987), 'Processing Transfer: Language Specific Processing Strategies as a Source of Interlanguage Variation', *Applied Psycholinguistics*, **8**, pp. 351–77.

Harris, M. and Coltheart, M. (1986), *Language Processing in Children and Adults* (London: Routledge Kegan Paul).

Hatch, E. (1978), 'Acquisition of Syntax in a Second Language', in J. Richards (ed.), *Understanding Second and Foreign Language Learning: Issues and Approaches* (Rowley, Mass.: Newbury House) pp. 34–70.

Haugen, E. (1953), *The Norwegian Language in America* (Philadelphia, Pa: University of Pennsylvania Press).

Hawkins, J. A. (1983), *Word Order Universals* (New York: Academic Press).

Hawkins, J. A. (1990), 'A Parsing Theory of Word Order Universals', *Linguistic Theory*, **21**(2), pp. 223–61.

Hawkins, R. (1988), 'Do Second Language Learners Acquire Restrictive Relative Clauses on the Basis of Relational or Configurational Information? The Acquisition of French Subject, Direct Object and Genitive Restrictive Relative Clauses by Second Language Learners', *Second Language Research*, **5**(2), pp. 156–88.

Hellan, L. (1988), *Anaphora in Norwegian and the Theory of Grammar* (Dordrecht: Foris).

Henry, A. (1988), 'Linguistic Theory and Second Language Teaching', *Polyglot*, **9**, microfiche 2.

Henzl, V. (1973), 'Linguistic Register of Foreign Language Instruction', *Language Learning*, **23**, pp. 207–22.

Hilles, S. (1986), 'Interlanguage and the Pro-drop Parameter', *Second Language Research*, **2**(1), pp. 33–52.

Hilles, S. (1991), 'Access to Universal Grammar in Second Language Acquisition', in L. Eubank (ed.), *Point Counterpoint: Universal Grammar in the Second Language* (Amsterdam: Benjamins) pp. 305–38.

Hirakawa, M. (1990), 'A Study of the L2 Acquisition of English Reflexives', *Second Language Research*, **6**, pp. 60–85.

Hirsh-Pasek, K., Treiman, R. and Schneiderman, M. (1984), 'Brown and Hanlon Revisited: Mothers' Sensitivity to Ungrammatical Forms', *J. Child. Lang.*, **11**(1), pp. 81–88.

Hoffman, C. (1991), *An Introduction to Bilingualism* (London: Longman).

Howatt, A. (1984), *A History of English Language Teaching* (London: Oxford University Press).

Huang, C.-T. J. (1982), *Logical Relations in Chinese and the Theory of Grammar*, PhD thesis, Massachusetts Institute of Technology.

Huebner, T. (1983), *A Longitudinal Analysis of the Acquisition of English* (Ann Arbor, Mich.: Karoma).

Hulk, A. (1987), 'L'Acquisition du Français et le Parametre Pro-drop', in B. Kampers-Manhe and Co Vet (eds), *Etudes de linguistique française offertes à Robert de Dardel* (Amsterdam: Editions Rodopi).

Hulk, A. (1991), 'Parameter Setting and the Acquisition of Word Order in L2 French', *Second Language Research*, **7**(1), pp. 1–34.

Hulstijn, J. H. and Hulstijn, W. (1983), 'Grammatical Errors as a Function of Processing Constraints and Explicit Knowledge', *Language Learning*, **34**(1), pp. 23–43.

Hyams, N. (1986), *Language Acquisition and the Theory of Parameters* (Dordrecht: Reidel).

Hyams, N. (1987), 'The Setting of the Null Subject Parameter: a Reanalysis', paper presented to the Boston University Conference on Language Development.

Hyams, N. (no date), 'Core and Peripheral Grammar and the Acquisition of Inflection', paper presented to the 11th Boston University Conference on Language Development.

Hyams, N. and Safir, K. (1991), 'Evidence, Analogy and Passive Knowledge: Comments on Lakshmanan', in L. Eubank (ed.), *Point Counterpoint: Universal Grammar in the Second Language* (Amsterdam: Benjamins) pp. 411–18.

Hyltenstam, K. (1977), 'Implicational Patterns in Interlanguage Syntax Variation', *Language Learning*, **27**(2), pp. 383–411.

Hyltenstam, K. (1984), 'The Use of Typological Markedness Conditions as Predictors in Second Language Acquisition: the Case of Pronominal Copies in Relative Clauses', in R. Andersen (ed.), *Second Languages: A Crosslinguistic Perspective* (Rowley, Mass.: Newbury House) pp. 39–58.

Hyltenstam, K. and Pienemann, M. (1985), *Modelling and Assessment of Second Language Acquisition* (Clevedon: Multilingual Matters).

Hymes, D. (1972), 'Competence and Performance in Linguistic Theory', in R.

Huxley and E. Ingram (eds), *Language Acquisition: Models and Methods* (New York: Academic Press) pp. 3–23.

Ianco-Worrall, A. (1972), 'Bilingualism and Cognitive Development', *Child Development*, **43**, pp. 1390–1400.

Illitch, I. and Sanders, B. (1988), *ABC: Alphabetisation of the Popular Mind* (Berkeley, Cal.: North Point Press).

Ingram, D. (1989), *First Language Acquisition* (Cambridge: Cambridge University Press).

Ioup, G. and Kruse, A. (1977), 'Interference Versus Structural Complexity in Second Language Acquisition: Language Universals as a Basis for Natural Sequencing', in H. Brown, C. Yorio and R. Crymes (eds), *Teaching and Learning English as a Second Language* (Washington, D.C.: TESOL) pp. 159–71.

Issidorides, D. C. and Hulstijn, J. H. (1992), 'Comprehension of Grammatically Modified and Nonmodified Sentences by Second-Language Learners', *Applied Psycholinguistics*, **13**(2), pp. 147–72.

Jaeggli, O. A. and Hyams, N. M. (1988), 'Morphological Uniformity and the Setting of the Null Subject Parameter', *NELS*, **18**.

Jakobovits, L. and Lambert, W. (1961), 'Semantic Satiation among Bilinguals', *Journal of Experimental Psychology*, **62**, pp. 576–82.

Jakobson, R. (1953), 'Results of the Conference of Anthropologists and Linguists', *IJAL Supplement*, Memoir 8, pp. 19–22.

Jakubowicz, C. (1984), 'On Markedness and Binding Principles', *NELS*, **14**.

Johnson, J. S. and Newport, E. L. (1991), 'Critical Period Effects on Universal Properties of Languages: the Status of Subjacency in the Acquisition of a Second Language', *Cognition*, **39**, pp. 215–58.

Joos, M. (1964), *The Five Clocks* (New York: Harcourt, Brace, World).

Kapur, S., Lust, B., Herbert, W. and Martahardjono, G. (forthcoming), 'Universal Grammar and Learnability: the Case of Binding Domains and the Subset Principle', in E. Reuland and W. Abraham (eds), *Knowledge and Language: Issues in Representation and Acquisition* (New York: Academic Press).

Keenan, E. L. (1975), 'Logical Experience, Power and Syntactic Variation in Natural Languages', in E. L. Keenan (ed.), *Formal Semantics of Natural Language* (Cambridge: Cambridge University Press) pp. 406–21.

Keenan, E. L. (1985), 'Relative Clauses', in T. Shopen (ed.), *Language Typology and Syntactic Description* (Cambridge: Cambridge University Press).

Keenan, E. L. and Comrie, B. (1977), 'Noun Phrase Accessibility and Universal Grammar,' *Linguistic Inquiry*, **8**, pp. 63–99.

Keil, F. C. (1981), 'Constraints on Knowledge and Linguistic Development', *Psychological Review*, **88**(3).

Kellerman, E. (1976), 'Elicitation, Lateralisation, and Error Analysis', *Interlanguage Studies Bulletin–Utrecht*, **1**(1), pp. 79–114.

Kellerman, E. (1991), 'Compensatory Strategies in Second Language Research: a Critique, a Revision, and Some (non-)Implications for the Classroom', in R. Phillipson, E. Kellerman, L. Selinker, M. Sharwood Smith and M. Swain (eds), *Foreign/Second Language Pedagogy Research* (Clevedon: Multilingual Matters).

Kellerman, E., Ammerlaan, T., Bongaerts, T. and Poulisse, N. (1990), 'System and Hierarchy in L2 Compensatory Strategies', in R. C. Scarcella, E. S.

Andersen and S. D. Krashen (eds), *Developing Communicative Competence in a Second Language* (Rowley, Mass.: Newbury House) pp. 163–78.

Kellerman, E., Bongaerts, T. and Poulisse, N. (1987), 'Strategy and System in L2 Referential Communication', in R. Ellis (ed), *Second Language Acquisition in Context* (London: Prentice-Hall).

Ketteman, B. and Wieden, W. (eds) (1993), *Current Issues in European Second Language Aquisition Research* (Tubingen: Gunter Narr).

Kilborn, K. and Cooreman, A. (1987), 'Sentence Interpretation Strategies in Adult Dutch–English Bilinguals', *Applied Psycholinguistics*, **8**, pp. 415–31.

Kilborn, K. and Ito, T. (1989), 'Sentence Processing Strategies in Adult Bilinguals', in B. MacWhinney and E. Bates (eds) (1989), *The Crosslinguistic Study of Sentence Processing* (Cambridge: Cambridge University Press) pp. 257–91.

Klein, W. (1986), *Second Language Acquisition* (Cambridge: Cambridge University Press).

Klima, E. S. and Bellugi, U. (1966), 'Syntactic Regularities in the Speech of Children', in J. Lyons and R. J. Wales (eds), *Psycholinguistics Papers* (Edinburgh: Edinburgh University Press.

Koenig, E. L., Chia, E. and Povey, J. (1983), *A Sociolinguistic Profile of Urban Centers in Cameroon* (Kinsey Hall, University of California Los Angeles: Crossroads Press).

Koopman, H. (1983), *The Syntax of Verbs* (Dordrecht: Foris).

Krashen, S. (1977), 'Some Issues Relating to the Monitor Model', in H. Brown, C. Yorio and R. Crymes (eds), *On TESOL '77* (Washington, D.C.: TESOL).

Krashen, S. (1979), 'The Monitor Model for Second Language Acquisition', in R. Gingras (ed), *Second Language Acquisition and Foreign Language Teaching* (Washington, D.C.: Center for Applied Linguistics).

Krashen, S. (1981), *Second Language Acquisition and Second Language Learning* (Oxford: Pergamon Press).

Krashen, S. (1982), *Principles and Practice in Second Language Acquisition* (Oxford: Pergamon Press).

Krashen, S. (1985a), *The Input Hypothesis: Issues and Implications* (London: Longman).

Krashen, S. (1985b), *Language Acquisition and Language Education* (Alemany Press; reprinted Englewood Cliffs, N.J.: Prentice-Hall, 1989).

Krashen, S. (1989), 'Comprehensible Input and Some Competing Hypotheses', paper presented at the Conference of Comprehension-based Learning and Teaching of Second Languages, Ottawa, May.

Krashen, S., Butler, J., Birnbaum, R. and Robertson, J. (1978), 'Two Studies in Language Acquisition and Language Learning', *ITL: Review of Applied Linguistics*, **39–40**, pp. 73–92.

Krashen, S., Scarcella, R. and Long, M. (eds) (1982), *Child–Adult Differences in Second Language Acquisition* (Rowley, Mass.: Newbury House).

Krashen, S., Sferlazza, V., Feldman, L. and Fathman, A. (1976), 'Adult Performance on the SLOPE Test: More Evidence for a Natural Sequence in Adult Second Language Acquisition', *Language Learning*, **26**(1), pp. 145–51.

Krashen, S. and Terrell, T. D. (1983), *The Natural Approach* (Oxford: Pergamon Press).

Krauss, R. and Weinheimer, S. (1964), 'Changes in Reference Phrases as a Function of Frequency of Usage in Social Interaction: a Preliminary Study', *Psychonomic Science*, **1**, pp. 113–14.

Labov, W. (1966), *The Social Stratification of English in New York City* (Washington, D.C.: Centre for Applied Linguistics).

Labov, W. (1970a), *The Study of Non-Standard English* (Champaign, Ill.: National Council of Teachers of English).

Labov, W. (1970b), 'The Study of Language in its Social Context', *Studium General*, **23**, pp. 30–87.

Labov, W. (1984), 'Field Methods of the Project on Linguistic Change and Variation', in J. Baugh and J. Sherzer (eds), *Language in Use: Readings in Sociolinguistics* (Englewood Cliffs, N.J.: Prentice Hall) pp. 28–53.

Lado, R. (1957), *Linguistics Across Cultures* (Ann Arbor, Mich.: University of Michigan Press).

Lado, R. (1964), *Language Teaching: A Scientific Approach* (New York: McGraw-Hill).

Lado, R. (1965), 'Memory Span as a Factor in Second Language Learning', *IRAL*, **3**, pp. 123–9.

Lakoff, G. and Johnson, M. (1981), 'The Metaphorical Structure of the Human Conceptual System', in D. A. Norman (ed.), *Perspectives on Cognitive Science*, (Norwood, N.J.: Ablex) pp. 193–206.

Lakshmanan, U. (1989), *Accessibility to Universal Grammar in Child Second Language Acquisition*, PhD thesis, University of Michigan.

Lakshmanan, U. (1991), 'Morphological Uniformity and Null Subjects in Child Second Language Acquisition', in L. Eubank (ed), *Point Counterpoint: Universal Grammar in the Second Language* (Amsterdam: Benjamins) pp. 389–410.

Lambert, W. E. (1955), 'Measurement of the Linguistic Dominance of Bilinguals', *J. Ab. Soc. Psych.*, **50**, pp. 197–200.

Lambert, W. E. (1956), 'Developmental Aspects of Second Language Acquisition,' *Journal of Social Psychology*, **43**, pp. 83–102.

Larsen-Freeman, D. (1975), 'The Acquisition of Grammatical Morphemes by Adult ESL Learners', *TESOL Quarterly*, **9**, pp. 409–19.

Larsen-Freeman, D. (1976), 'An Explanation for the Morpheme Acquisition Order of Second Language Learners', *Language Learning*, **26**(1), pp. 125–34.

Larsen-Freeman, D. and Long, M. H. (1991), *An Introduction to Second Language Acquisition Research* (Harlow, Essex: Longman).

Lashley, K. (1923), 'The Behavioristic Interpretation of Consciousness', *Psychological Review*, **30**, pp. 329–53.

Leather, J. and James, A. (eds) (1990), *New Sounds 90* (Amsterdam: University of Amsterdam Press).

Lee, D. J. (1981), 'Interpretation of Morpheme Rank Ordering in L2 Research', in P. Dale and D. Ingram (eds), *Child Language: An International Perspective* (Baltimore, Md: University Park Press).

Lehtonen, J. and Sajavaara, K. (1983), 'Acceptability and Ambiguity in Native and Second Language Message Processing', in H. Ringbom (ed.), *Psycholinguistics and Foreign Language Teaching* (Abo Akademi, Finland).

Levelt, W. (1989), *Speaking: from Intention to Articulation* (Cambridge, Mass.:

Bradford Books).

Liceras, J. M. (1988), 'Syntax and Stylistics: More on the Pro-drop Parameter', in J. Pankhurst and M. Sharwood-Smith (eds), *Learnability and Second Languages* (Dordrecht: Foris).

Liceras, J. M. (1989), 'On Some Properties of the "pro-drop" Parameter: Looking for Missing Subjects in Non-native Spanish', in S. M. Gass and J. Schachter (eds), *Linguistic Perspectives on Second Language Acquisition* (Cambridge: Cambridge University Press) pp. 109–33.

Lightbown, P. M. (1984), 'The Relationship between Theory and Method in Second Language Acquisition Research', in A. Davies, C. Criper and A. Howatt (eds) (1984), *Interlanguage* (Edinburgh: Edinburgh University Press) pp. 241–53.

Lightbown, P. M. (1987), 'Classroom Language as Input to Second Language Acquisition', in C. W. Pfaff (ed.), *First and Second Language Acquisition Processes* (Rowley, Mass.: Newbury House).

Lightbown, P. M., Spada, N. and Wallace, R. (1980), 'Some Effects of Instruction on Child and Adolescent ESL Learners', in R. C. Scarcella and S. Krashen (eds), *Research in Second Language Acquisition* (Rowley, Mass.: Newbury House) pp. 162–72.

Linguistic Minorities Project (1983), *Linguistic Minorities in England* (London: University of London Institute of Education, distributed by Tinga Tonga).

Littlewood, W. (1984), *Foreign and Second Language Learning* (Cambridge: Cambridge University Press).

Long, J. and Harding-Esch, E. (1977), 'Summary and Recall of Text in First and Second Languages: Some Factors Contributing to Performance Difficulties', in H. Sinmaiko and D. Gerver (eds), *Proceedings of the NATO Symposium on Language Interpretation and Communication* (New York: Plenum Press).

Long, M. (1983), 'Native Speaker/Non-native Speaker Conversation in the Second Language Classroom', in *ON TESOL* (Washington, D.C.: TESOL) pp. 207–25.

Long, M. and Sato, C. (1984), 'Methodological Issues in Interlanguage Studies: an Interactionist Perspective', in A. Davies, C. Criper and A. Howatt (eds) (1984), *Interlanguage* (Edinburgh: Edinburgh University Press) pp. 253–79.

Lust, B. (1983), 'On the Notion "Principal Branching Direction": a Parameter in Universal Grammar', in Y. Otsu, H. van Riemsdijk, K. Inoue, A. Kasimo and N. Kawasaki (eds), *Studies in Generative Grammar and Language Acquisition* (Tokyo: International Christian University) pp. 137–51.

MacWhinney, B. (1989), 'Competition and Connectionism', in B. MacWhinney and E. Bates (eds), *The Crosslinguistic Study of Sentence Processing* (Cambridge: Cambridge University Press).

MacWhinney, B. (1991), *The CHILDES Project* (Hillsdale, N.J.: Lawrence Erlbaum).

MacWhinney, B. and Anderson, J. (1986), 'The Acquisition of Grammar', in I. Gopnik and M. Gopnik (eds), *From Models to Modules* (Norwood, N.J.: Ablex) pp. 3–23.

MacWhinney, B. and Bates, E. (eds) (1989), *The Crosslinguistic Study of Sentence Processing* (Cambridge: Cambridge University Press).

Magiste, E. (1979), 'The Competing Linguistic Systems of the Multilingual: a Developmental Study of Decoding and Encoding Processes', *JVLVB*, **18**, pp.

79–89.

Makino, T. (1980), 'Acquisition Order of English Morphemes by Japanese Secondary School Students', *Journal of Hokkaido University of Education*, **30**(2), pp. 101–48.

Manzini, R. (1990), 'Locality and Parameters Again', in I. Roca (ed.), *Logical Issues in Language Acquisition* (Dordrecht: Foris) pp. 235–58.

Maple, R. F. (1982), *Social Distance and the Acquisition of English as a Second Language*, PhD. thesis, University of Texas at Austin; cited in Schumann (1986).

Maratsos, M. (1983), 'Some Current Issues in the Study of the Acquisition of Grammar', in J. Flavell and E. Markman (eds), *Handbook of Child Psychology* vol. III (New York: John Wiley) pp. 189, 226–8.

Marcus, M. P. (1980), *Theory of Syntactic Recognition for Natural Languages* (Cambridge, Mass.: MIT Press).

Marsh, L. G. and Maki, R. H. (1978), 'Efficiency of Arithmetic Operations in Bilinguals as a Function of Language', *Memory and Cognition*, **4**(4), pp. 459–64.

McDaniel, D. and Cairns, H. S. (1990), 'The Child as Informant: Eliciting Linguistic Intuitions from Young Children', *J. Psycholing. Res.*, **19**(5), pp. 331–44.

McDonald, J. (1987), 'Sentence Interpretation in Bilingual Speakers of English and Dutch', *Applied Psycholinguistics*, **8**, pp. 379–413.

McLaughlin, B. (1978), *Second Language Acquisition in Childhood* (Hillsdale, N.J.: Lawrence Erlbaum Associates).

McLaughlin, B. (1987), *Theories of Second-Language Learning* (London: Edward Arnold).

McLaughlin, B., Rossman, R. and McLeod, B. (1983), 'Second Language Learning: an Information-processing Perspective', *Language Learning*, **33**, pp. 135–58.

McLelland, J. L., Rumelhart, D. E. and the PDP Research Group (1986), *Parallel Distributed Processing*, vol. 2: *Psychological and Biological Models* (Cambridge, Mass.: MIT Press).

McLuhan, M. (1964), *Understanding Media: The Extensions of Man* (London).

McNeill, D. (1966), 'Developmental Psycholinguistics', in F. Smith and G. A. Miller (eds), *The Genesis of Language: A Psycholinguistic Approach* (Cambridge, Mass.: MIT Press).

Meara, P. (1983), 'Introduction', in P. Meara (ed.), *Vocabulary in a Second Language* (London: CILTR) pp. i–iv.

Meisel, J. M. (1980), 'Linguistic Simplification', in S. W. Felix (ed.), *Second Language Development* (Tubingen: Gunter Narr) pp. 9–40.

Meisel, J. M. (1990), 'INFL-ection: Subjects and Subject-Verb Agreement', in J. M. Meisel (ed.), *Two First Languages: Early Grammatical Development in Bilingual Children* (Dordrecht: Foris) pp. 237–300.

Meisel, J. M. (1991), 'Principles of Universal Grammar and Strategies of Language Learning: Some Similarities and Differences between First and Second Language Acquisition', in L. Eubank (ed), *Point Counterpoint: Universal Grammar in the Second Language* (Amsterdam: Benjamins) pp. 231–76.

Meisel, J. M., Clahsen, H. and Pienemann, M. (1981), 'On Determining Developmental Stages in Natural Second Language Acquisition', *Studies in Second Language Acquisition*, **3**(2), pp. 109–35.

Miller, G. A. (1964), *Psychology: The Science of Mental Life* (London: Hutchinson).

Miller, G. A. and Chomsky, N. (1963), 'Finitary Models of Language Users', in R. D. Luce, R. Bush and E. Galanter (eds), *Handbook of Mathematical Psychology* vol. II (New York: John Wiley).

Miller, G. A., Galanter, E. and Pribram, K. H. (1960), *Plans and the Structure of Human Behavior* (New York: Holt, Rinehart and Winston).

Milon, J. P. (1974), 'The Development of Negation in English by a Second Language Learner', *TESOL Quarterly*, **8**(2), pp. 137–43.

Mohle, D. (1984), 'A Comparison of the Second Language Production of Different Native Speakers', in H. W. Dechert, D. Mohle and M. Raupach (eds), *Second Language Productions* (Tubingen: Gunter Narr) pp. 26–49.

Mohle, D. and Raupach, M. (1987), 'The Representation Problem in Interlanguage Theory', in W. Lorscher (ed.), *Perspectives on Language in Performance* (Tubingen: Gunter Narr) pp. 1158–73.

Mohle, D. and Raupach, M. (1989), 'Language Transfer of Procedural Knowledge', in H. W. Dechert and M. Raupach (eds), *Transfer in Language Productions* (Norwood, N.J.: Ablex) pp. 195–216.

Moulton, W. G. (1966), *A Linguistic Guide to Language Learning* (New York: MLA).

Mufwene, S. S. (1990), 'Creoles and Universal Grammar', *Linguistics*, **28**, pp. 783–807.

Mufwene, S. S. (1991), 'Transfer and the Substrate Hypothesis in Creolistics', *Studies in Second Language Acquisition*, **12**(1), pp. 1–24.

Murakmi, M. (1980), 'Behavioral and Attitudinal Correlates of Progress in ESL by Native Speakers of Japanese', in J. Oller and K. Perkins (eds), *Research in Language Testing* (Rowley, Mass.: Newbury House).

Nagata, H. (1988), 'The Relativity of Linguistic Intuition: the Effects of Repetition on Grammaticality Judgements', *J. Psycholing. Res.*, **17**(1), pp. 1–17.

Nagata, H. (1991), 'Temporal Course of Activation of the Antecedent by the Reflexive in Syntactically Ambiguous Sentences in Japanese', *J. Psycholing. Res.*, **20**(6), pp. 501–20.

Naiman, N., Frohlich, M., Stern, H. H. and Todesco, A. (1978), *The Good Language Learner* (Toronto: OISE).

Nelson, K. E. (1982), 'Toward a Rare-event Cognitive Comparison Theory of Syntax Acquisition', in P. Dale and D. Ingram (eds), *Child Language: An International Perspective* (Baltimore, Md: University Park Press).

Nemser, W. (1971), 'Approximative Systems of Foreign Language Learners', *International Review of Applied Linguistics*, **9**, pp. 115–23; reprinted in Richards (1974).

Newmark, L. and Reibel, D. A. (1968), 'Necessity and Sufficiency in Language Learning', *IRAL*, **6**(3), pp. 145–64.

Newport, E. L. (1976), 'Motherese: the Speech of Mothers to Young Children', in N. Castellan, D. Pisoni and G. Potts (eds), *Cognitive Theory*, vol. 2 (Hillsdale, N.J.: Erlbaum).

Nicholas, N. (1985), 'Learner Variation and the Teachability Hypothesis', in Hyltenstam and Pienemann (1985).

Odlin, T. (1989), *Language Transfer* (Cambridge: Cambridge University Press).

Oller, J., Perkins, K. and Murakmi, M. (1980), 'Seven Types of Learner Variables in Relation to ESL Learning', in J. Oller and K. Perkins (eds), *Research in Language Testing* (Rowley, Mass.: Newbury House).

Olton, R. (1960), *Semantic Generalisations Between Languages*, MA thesis, McGill University, Montreal; cited in Romaine (1989).

Olynk, M., d'Anglejan, A. and Sankoff, D. (1990), 'A Quantitative and Qualitative Analysis of Speech-markers in the Native and Second Language Speech of Bilinguals', in R. C. Scarcella, E. S. Andersen and S. D. Krashen (eds), *Developing Communicative Competence in a Second Language* (Rowley, Mass.: Newbury House) pp. 139–62.

O'Malley, J. M. and Chamot, A. U. (1990), *Learning Strategies in Second Language Acquisition* (Cambridge: Cambridge University Press).

O'Malley, J. M., Chamot, A. U., Stewner-Manzares, G., Kupper, L. and Russo, R. P. (1985a), 'Learning Strategies Used by Beginning and Intermediate ESL Students', *Language Learning*, **35**, pp. 21–46.

O'Malley, J. M., Chamot, A. U., Stewner-Manzares, G., Russo, R. P. and Kupper, L. (1985b), 'Learning Strategy Applications with Students of English as a Second Language', *TESOL Quarterly*, **19**(3), pp. 557–84.

Otsu, Y. (1981), *Universal Grammar and Syntactic Development in Children*, PhD thesis, Massachusetts Institute of Technology.

Otsu, Y. and Naoi, K. (1986), 'Structure-dependence in L2 Acquisition', paper presented at JACET, Keio University, Tokyo, September; cited in White (1989).

Palmer, H. E. (1926), *The Principles of Language Study* (London: Harrap).

Pateman, T. (1987), *Language in Mind and Language in Society* (London: Oxford University Press).

Pavesi, M. (1986), 'Markedness, Discoursal Modes, and Relative Clause Formation in a Formal and Informal Context', *Studies in Second Language Acquisition*, **8**, pp. 38–55.

Perkins, K. and Larsen-Freeman, D. (1975), 'The Effect of Formal Language Instruction on the Order of Morpheme Acquisition', *Language Learning*, **25**, pp. 237–43.

Phinney, M. (1987), 'The Pro-drop Parameter in Second Language Acquisition', in T. Roeper and E. Williams (eds), *Parameter Setting* (Dordrecht: Reidel).

Piaget, J. and Inhelder, B. (1969), *The Psychology of the Child* (New York: Basic Books).

Pica, T. (1984), 'Methods of Morpheme Quantification: Their Effects on the Interpretation of Second Language Data', *Studies in Second Language Acquisition*, **6**(1), pp. 69–78.

Pica, T. (1985), 'Linguistic Simplicity and Learnability: Implications for Language Syllabus Design', in K. Hyltenstam and M. Pienemann (eds), *Modelling and Assessing Language Acquisition* (San Diego, Cal.: College Hill Press).

Pienemann, M. (1980), 'The Second Language Acquisition of Immigrant Children', in S. W. Felix (ed), *Second Language Development* (Tubingen: Gunter Narr) pp. 41–56.

Pienemann, M. (1984), 'Psychological Constraints on the Teachability of Languages', *Studies in Second Language Acquisition*, **6**(2), pp. 186–214.

Pienemann, M. (1987a), 'Learnability and Syllabus Construction', in K. Hyltenstam and M. Pienemann (eds), *Modelling and Assessing Second Language*

Development (Clevedon: Multilingual Matters).

Pienemann, M. (1987b), 'Determining the Influence of Instruction on L2 Speech Processing', *Australian Journal of Applied Linguistics*, **10**(2), pp. 83–113.

Pienemann, M. (1989), 'Is Language Teachable?', *Applied Linguistics*, **10**(1), pp. 52–79.

Pienemann, M. (1992), 'COALA: a Computational System for Interlanguage Analysis', *Second Language Research*, **8**(1), pp. 59–92.

Pienemann, M. (forthcoming), 'The Teachability Hypothesis', MS, Language Acquisition Research Centre.

Pienemann, M. and Johnston, M., (1987), 'Factors Influencing the Development of Language Proficiency', in D. Nunan (ed), *Applying Second Language Research* (Adelaide, Australia: NCRC) pp. 45–141.

Pienemann, M., Johnston, M. and Brindley, G. (1988), 'Constructing an Acquisition-based Procedure for Second Language Assessment', *Studies in Second Language Acquisition*, pp. 217–43.

Pinker, S. and Prince, A. (1988), 'On Language and Connectionism: Analysis of a Parallel Distributed Processing Model of Language Acquisition', *Cognition*, **28**, pp. 73–193.

Pohl, F. (1987), *The Annals of the Heechee* (London: Gollancz).

Pollock, J.-Y. (1989), 'Verb Movement, Universal Grammar, and the Structure of IP', *Linguistic Inquiry*, **20**, pp. 365–424.

Porter, J. H. (1977), 'A Cross-sectional Study of Morpheme Acquisition in First Language Acquisition', *Language Learning*, **27**(1), pp. 47–61.

Poulisse, N. (1987), 'Classification of Compensatory Strategies', *Second Language Research*, **3**(2), pp. 141–53.

Poulisse, N. (1989–1990), *The Use of Compensatory Strategies by Dutch Learners of English*, PhD thesis, University of Nijmegen (published in book form, Berlin; Mouton de Gruijter, 1990).

Poulisse, N. (1990), 'Variation in Learner's Use of Communication Strategies', in R. Duda and P. Riley (eds), *Learning Styles* (Nancy: PU) pp. 77–87.

Poulisse, N. (forthcoming), 'Strategies', in P. Jordens and J. Lalleman (eds).

Preston, D. R. (1989), *Sociolinguistics and Second Language Acquisition* (Oxford: Basil Blackwell).

Pujol, M. and Véronique, D. (1991), *L'Acquisition d'une langue étrangère: recherches et perspectives*, Université de Genève, Faculté de Psychologie, *Cahiers de la Section des Sciences de l'Education, Cahier* 63.

Quirk, R. and Greenbaum, S. (1973) *A University Grammar of English* (London: Longman).

Quirk, R. and Svartvik, J. (1966), *Investigating Linguistic Acceptability* (The Hague: Mouton).

Radford, A. (1986), 'Small Children's Small Clauses', *Bangor Research Papers in Linguistics*, **1**, pp. 1–38.

Radford, A. (1988), *Transformational Syntax* (Cambridge: Cambridge University Press).

Radford, A. (1990), *Syntactic Theory and the Acquisition of English Syntax: The Nature of Early Grammars in English* (Oxford: Basil Blackwell).

Raupach, M. (1987), 'Procedural Learning in Advanced Learners of a Foreign Language', in J. Coleman and R. Towell (eds), *The Advanced Language Learner*

(London: CILTR) pp. 123–56.

Ravem, R. (1968), 'Language Acquisition in a Second Language Environment', *IRAL*, **6**(2), pp. 165–85; reprinted in Richards (ed.) (1974).

Richards, J. C. (ed.) (1974), *Error Analysis* (London: Longman).

Ritchie, W. (1978), 'The Right Roof Constraint in an Adult Acquired Language', in W. Ritchie (ed.), *Second Language Acquisition: Issues and Implications* (New York: Academic Press) pp. 33–63.

Rizzi, L. (1990), *Relativised Minimality* (Cambridge, Mass.: MIT Press).

Romaine, S. (1988), *Pidgin and Creole Languages* (Oxford: Basil Blackwell).

Romaine, S. (1989), *Bilingualism* (Oxford: Basil Blackwell).

Rommetveit, R. (1991), 'Psycholinguistics, Hermeneutics, and Cognitive Science', in G. Appel and H. W. Dechert (eds), *A Case for Psycholinguistic Cases* (Amsterdam: Benjamins) pp. 1–15.

Rost, M. (1990), *Listening in Language Learning* (London: Longman).

Rumelhart, D. E. and McLelland, J. L. (1986), 'On Learning the Past Tenses of English Verbs', in J. L. McLelland, D. E. Rumelhart and the PDP Research Group, *Parallel Distributed Processing*, vol. 2: *Psychological and Biological Models* (Cambridge, Mass.: MIT Press) pp. 216–71.

Ryle, G. (1949), *The Concept of Mind* (London: Hutchinson).

Sajavaara, K. (1981), 'Contrastive Linguistics Past and Present and a Communicative Approach', in J. Fisiak (ed.), *Contrastive Linguistics and the Language Teacher* (Oxford: Pergamon Press) pp. 33–56.

Sajavaara, K. (forthcoming), *Proceedings of the Second EUROSLA Conference 1992*.

Saleemi, A. (1988), 'Learnability and Parameter Fixation', PhD thesis, University of Essex.

Saleemi, A. (1990), 'Null Subjects, Markedness, and Implicit Negative Evidence', in I. Roca (ed.), *Logical Issues in Language Acquisition* (Dordrecht: Foris) pp. 235–58.

Saleemi, A. (1992), *Universal Grammar and Language Learnability* (Cambridge: Cambridge University Press).

Schachter, J. (1974), 'An Error in Error Analysis', *Language Learning*, **24**, pp. 205–14.

Schachter, J. (1988), 'Second Language Acquisition and its Relationship to Universal Grammar', *Applied Linguistics*, **9**(3), pp. 219–35.

Schachter, J. (1989), 'Testing a Proposed Universal', in S. Gass and J. Schachter (eds), *Linguistic Perspectives on Second Language Acquisition* (Cambridge: Cambridge University Press) pp. 73–88.

Schank, R. and Abelson, R. (1977), *Scripts, Plans, Goals, and Understanding* (Norwood, N.J.: Lawrence Erlbaum).

Schermerhorn, R. A. (1970), *Comparative Ethnic Relations* (New York: Random House).

Schmid, S. (1993), 'Learning Strategies for Closely Related Languages: on the Italian Spoken by Spanish Immigrants in Switzerland', in B. Ketteman and W. Wieden (eds) (1993).

Schmidt, R. W. (1983), 'Interaction, Acculturation, and the Acquisition of Communicative Competence: a Case Study of an Adult', in N. Wolfson and E. Judd (eds), *Sociolinguistics and Language Acquisition* (Rowley, Mass.: Newbury

House) pp. 137–74.

Schumann, J. (1975), 'Affective Factors and the Problem of Age in Second Language Acquisition', *Language Learning*, **25**(2), pp. 209–35.

Schumann, J. (1976), 'Social Distance as a Factor in Second Language Acquisition', *Language Learning*, **26**(1), pp. 135–43.

Schumann, J. (1978a), *The Pidginisation Process: A Model for Second Language Acquisition* (Rowley, Mass.: Newbury House).

Schumann, J. (1978b), 'The Acculturation Model of Second Language Acquisition', in R. C. Gingras (ed.), *Second Language Acquisition and Foreign Language Teaching* (Washington, D.C.: Center for Applied Linguistics) pp. 27–50.

Schumann, J. (1980), 'The Acquisition of English Relative Clauses by Second Language Learners', in S. Krashen and R. Scarcella (eds), *Issues in Second Language Acquisition Research* (Rowley, Mass.: Newbury House) pp. 118–31.

Schumann, J. (1986), 'Research on the Acculturation Model for Second Language Acquisition', *Journal of Multilingual and Multicultural Education*, **7**, pp. 379–92.

Schumann, J. (1990), 'Extending the Scope of the Acculturation/Pidginization Model to Include Cognition', *TESOL Quarterly*, **24**(4), pp. 667–84.

Seliger, H. W. and Shohamy, E. (1989), *Second Language Research Methods* (London: Oxford University Press).

Seliger, H. W. and Vago, R. M. (eds) (1991), *First Language Attrition* (Cambridge: Cambridge University Press).

Selinker, L. (1972), 'Interlanguage', *IRAL*, **10**(3); reprinted in Richards (ed.) (1974).

Selinker, L. (1992), *Rediscovering Interlanguage* (London: Longman).

Sells, P. (1985), *Lectures on Contemporary Syntactic Theories* (Stanford, Cal.: CSLI).

Sheldon, A. (1974), 'On the Role of Parallel Function in the Acquisition of Relative Clauses in English', *JVLVB*, **13**, pp. 272–81.

Shiffrin, R. and Schneider, W. (1977), 'Controlled and Automatic Human Information-processing', *Psychological Review*, **84**, pp. 127–90.

Sinclair, B. and Ellis, N. (1992), 'The Silent Period and Working Memory', in Sajavaara (forthcoming).

Singleton, D. (1989), *Language Acquisition: The Age Factor* (Clevedon: Multilingual Matters).

Skinner, B. F. (1957), *Verbal Behavior* (New York: Appleton-Century-Crofts).

Skutnabb-Kangas, T. (1981), *Bilingualism or Not: The Education of Minorities* (Cleveland: Multilingual Matters).

Slobin, D. I. (1973), 'Cognitive Prerequisites for the Development of Grammar', in C. A. Ferguson and D. I. Slobin (eds), *Studies of Child Language Development* (New York: Holt Rinehart Winston) pp. 175–208.

Slobin, D. I. (1991), 'Can Crain Constrain the Constraints?', *Behavioral and Brain Sciences*, **14**, pp. 633–34.

Slobin, D. I. and Bever, T. G. (1982), 'Children Use Canonical Sentence Schemas: a Crosslinguistic Study of Word Order and Inflection', *Cognition*, **12**, pp. 229–65.

Slobin, D. I. and Welsh, C. (1973), 'Elicited Imitation as a Research Tool in Developmental Psycholinguistics', in C. Ferguson and D. Slobin (eds), *Studies of Child Language* (New York: Holt Rinehart Winston).

Smith, N. (1973), *The Acquisition of Phonology: A Case Study* (Cambridge:

Cambridge University Press).

Smith, N. and Tsimpli, I. (1991), 'Linguistic Modularity? A Case Study of a Savant Linguist', *Lingua*, **84**, pp. 315–51.

Sokolik, M. E. and Smith, M. E. (1992), 'Assignment of Gender to French Nouns in Primary and Secondary Language: a Connectionist Model', *Second Language Research*, **8**(1), pp. 39–58.

Solan, L. (1987), 'Parameter Setting and the Development of Pronouns and Reflexives', in T. Roeper and E. Williams (eds), *Parameters and Linguistic Theory* (Dordrecht: Reidel).

Spolsky, B. (1989), *Conditions for Second Language Learning* (London: Oxford University Press).

Sridhar, K. K. and Sridhar, S. N. (1986), 'Bridging the Paradigm Gap: Second Language Acquisition Theory and Indigenised Varieties of English', *World Englishes*, **5**(1), pp. 3–14.

Stauble, A.-M. (1984), 'A Comparison of a Spanish–English and Japanese–English Second Language Continuum: Negation and Verb Morphology', in R. Andersen (1984), *Second Languages: A Cross-linguistic Perspective* (Rowley, Mass.: Newbury House) pp. 323–54.

Stenson, N. (1990), 'Phrase Structure Congruence, Government, and Irish–English Code-switching', in R. Hendrick (ed.), *Syntax and Semantics,* vol. 23: *The Syntax of the Modern Celtic Languages* (San Diego, Cal.: Academic Press) pp. 169–99.

Stockwell, R., Bowen, J. D. and Martin, J. (1965), *The Grammatical Structures of English and Spanish* (Chicago, Ill.: University of Chicago Press).

Svartvik, J. (ed.) (1973), *Errata: Papers in Error Analysis* (Lund: University of Lund).

Swain, M. (1985), 'Communicative Competence: Some Roles of Comprehensible Input and Comprehensible Output in its Development', in S. Gass and C. Madden (eds), *Input in Second Language Acquisition* (Rowley, Mass.: Newbury House) pp. 235–45.

Swales, J. (1991), *Genre Analysis* (Cambridge: Cambridge University Press).

Tarallo, F. and Myhill, J. (1983), 'Interference and Natural Language Processing in Second Language Acquisition', *Language Learning*, **33**, pp. 55–76.

Tarone, E. (1977), 'Conscious Communication Strategies in Interlanguage: a Progress Report', in *On TESOL 1977* (Washington, D.C.: TESOL).

Tarone, E. (1980), 'Communication Strategies, Foreigner Talk, and Repair in Interlanguage', *Language Learning*, **30**(2), pp. 417–31.

Tarone, E. (1983), 'On the Variability of Interlanguage Systems', *Applied Linguistics*, **4**, pp. 142–63.

Tarone, E. (1985), 'Variability in Interlanguage Use: a Study of Style-shifting in Morphology and Syntax', *Language Learning*, **35**(3), pp. 373–404.

Tarone, E. (1988), *Variation in Interlanguage* (London: Edward Arnold).

Tarone, E. and Parrish, B. (1988), 'Task-related Variation in Interlanguage: the Case of Articles', *Language Learning*, **38**(1), pp. 21–44.

Tarone, E. and Yule, G. (1989), *Focus on the Language Learner* (London: Oxford University Press).

Thomas, M. (1989), 'The Interpretation of English Reflexive Pronouns by Non-native Speakers', *Studies in Second Language Acquisition*, **11**, p. 3.

Thomas, M. (1991), 'Universal Grammar and the Interpretation of Reflexives in a

Second Language', *Language*, **67**(2), pp. 211–39.

Tomaselli, A. and Schwartz, B. (1990), 'Analysing the Acquisition Stages of Negation in L2 German: Support for UG in Adult SLA', *Second Language Research*, **6**(1), pp. 1–38.

Tomlin, R. S. (1990), 'Functionalism in Second Language Acquisition Research', *Studies in Second Language Acquisition*, **12**(2), pp. 155–78.

Towell, R. (1987a), 'Approaches to the Analysis of the Oral Language Development of the Advanced Language Learner', in J. Coleman and R. Towell (eds), *The Advanced Language Learner* (London: CILTR) pp. 157–82.

Towell, R. (1987b), 'Variability and Progress in the Language Development of Advanced Learners of a Foreign Language', in R. Ellis (ed.), *Second Language Acquisition in Context* (Oxford: Pergamon Press) pp. 113–28.

Travis, L. (1984), *Parameters and Effects of Word Order Variation*, PhD thesis, Massachusetts Institute of Technology.

Trollope, A. (1881), *Ayala's Angel* (London: Chapman and Hall).

Tsimpli, I.-M. and Roussou, A. (1990), 'Parameter-resetting in L2', *UCL Working Papers in Linguistics*, pp. 149–89.

Vainikka, A. and Young-Scholten, M. (1991), 'Verb Raising in Second Language Acquisition: the Early Stages', Dusseldorf University *Théories des lexikons*, **4**.

Valian, V. (1989), 'Children's Production of Subjects: Competence, Performance, and the Null Subject Parameter', *Papers and Reports on Child Language Development*, **28**, pp. 156–63.

van Els, T., Bongaerts, T., Extra, G., van Os, C. and Jansson-van-Dieten, A.-M. (1984), *Applied Linguistics and the Learning and Teaching of Foreign Languages* (London: Edward Arnold).

Vann, R. J. and Abraham, R. G. (1990), 'Strategies of Unsuccessful Language Learners', *TESOL Quarterly*, **24**(2), pp. 177–98.

VanPatten, B. (1984), 'Processing Strategies and Morpheme Acquisition', in F. R. Eckman, L. H. Bell and D. Nelson (eds), *Universals of Language Acquisition* (Rowley, Mass.: Newbury House) pp. 88–98.

Varadi, T. (1973), 'Strategies of Target Language Learner Communication: Message Adjustment', paper presented at the sixth conference of the Romanian–English Linguistics project in Timisoara; reprinted in Faerch and Kasper (eds) (1983).

Wagner-Gough, J. (1978), 'Comparative Studies in Second Language Learning', in E. Hatch (ed.), *Second Language Acquisition: A Book of Readings* (Rowley, Mass.: Newbury House) pp. 155–74.

Wanner, E. and Maratsos, M. (1978), 'An ATN Approach to Comprehension', in M. Halle, J. Bresnan and G. A. Miller (eds), *Linguistic Theory and Psychological Reality* (Cambridge, Mass.: MIT Press).

Wardhaugh, R. (1987), *Languages in Competition* (Oxford: Basil Blackwell).

Weeks, T. (1971), 'Speech Registers in Children', *Child Development*, **42**, pp. 1119–31.

Weinreich, U. (1953), *Languages in Contact* (The Hague: Mouton).

Wells, C. G. (1985), *Language Development in the Preschool Years* (Cambridge: Cambridge University Press).

Wendon, A. (1987), 'How to Be a Successful Language Learner: Insights and Prescriptions from L2 Learners', in A. Wendon and J. Rubin (eds), *Learner*

Strategies in Language Learning (Englewood Cliffs, N.J.: Prentice Hall) pp. 103–18.

Wenk, B. (1982), 'Articulatory Setting and the Acquisition of Second Language Phonology', *Revue de Phonetique Appliquée*, **65**, pp. 51–65.

Wexler, K. and Manzini, M. R. (1987), 'Parameters and Learnability', in T. Roeper and E. Williams (eds), *Parameters and Linguistic Theory* (Dordrecht: Reidel).

White, L. (1985), 'The Acquisition of Parameterized Grammar: Subjacency in Second Language Acquisition', *Second Language Research*, **1**(1), pp. 1–17.

White, L. (1986), 'Implications of Parametric Variation for Adult Second Language Acquisition: an Investigation of the Pro-drop Parameter', in V. J. Cook (ed.) (1986), *Experimental Approaches to Second Language Acquisition* (Oxford: Pergamon Press).

White, L. (1987), 'Against Comprehensible Input: the Input Hypothesis and the Development of L2 Competence', *Applied Linguistics*, **8**, pp. 95–110.

White, L. (1988), 'Island Effects in Second Language Acquisition', in Flynn and O'Neil (eds) (1988).

White, L. (1989), *Universal Grammar and Second Language Acquisition* (Amsterdam: John Benjamins).

White, L. (1991), 'Second Language Competence Versus Second Language Performance: UG or Processing Strategies?', in L. Eubank (ed.), *Point Counterpoint* (Amsterdam: John Benjamins).

Wieden, W. and Nemser, W. (1991), *The Pronunciation of English in Austria* (Tubingen: Gunter Narr).

Winitz, H. (1981) (ed.), *The Comprehension Approach to Foreign Language Instruction* (Rowley, Mass.: Newbury House).

Wode, H. (1977), 'Four Early Stages in the Development of L1 Negation', *Journal of Child Language*, 4, pp. 87–102.

Wode, H. (1980), 'Phonology in L2 Acquisition', in S. Felix (ed.), *Second Language Development* (Tubingen: Gunter Narr).

Wode, H. (1981), *Learning a Second Language* (Tubingen: Gunter Narr).

Wode, H. (1984), 'Some Theoretical Implications of L2 Acquisition Research and the Grammar of Interlanguage', in A. Davies, C. Criper and A. P. R. Howatt (eds), *Interlanguage* (Edinburgh: Edinburgh University Press).

Young, R. (1988), 'Variation and the Interlanguage Hypothesis', *Studies in Second Language Acquisition*, **10**, pp. 281–302.

Young, R. (1991), *Variation in Interlanguage Morphology* (New York: Peter Lang).

Zwicky, A. M. (1975), 'Settling an Underlying Form: the English Inflectional Endings', in D. Cohen and J. R. Wirth (eds), *Testing Linguistic Hypotheses* (New York: Wiley) pp. 129–86.

Index